THE OTHER SIDE OF EDEN

THE OTHER SIDE OF EDEN

LIFE WITH JOHN STEINBECK

JOHN STEINBECK IV & NANCY STEINBECK

Prometheus Books

59 John Glenn Drive
Amherst, New York 14228-2197

Published 2001 by Prometheus Books

Unless indicated otherwise, all photographs in the photo inserts
have been provided by Nancy Steinbeck.

Inquiries should be addressed to
Prometheus Books
59 John Glenn Drive
Amherst, New York 14228-2197
VOICE: 716-691-0133, ext. 207
FAX: 716-564-2711
WWW.PROMETHEUSBOOKS.COM

05 04 03 02 01   5 4 3 2 1

Library of Congress Cataloging-in-Publication Data

Steinbeck, John, 1946-1991
        The other side of Eden : life with John Steinbeck / John Steinbeck IV and
Nancy Steinbeck.
                p. cm.
        Includes bibliographical references and index.
        ISBN 1-57392-858-5 (cloth : alk. paper)
        1. Steinbeck, John, 1902-1968. 2. Novelists, American—20th century—
Family relationships. 3. Novelists, American—20th century—Biography.
4. Steinbeck, John, 1902-1968—Family. 5. Steinbeck, John, 1946-1991.
I. Steinbeck, Nancy, 1945- II. Title.

PS3537.T3234 Z86685 2000
813'.52—dc21
[B]   00-045840

Printed in the United States of America on acid-free paper

This book is dedicated to our children,

Megan and Michael Steinbeck.

What a long, strange trip it's been . . .

CONTENTS

ACKNOWLEDGMENTS

I would like to thank my agent, Laurie Harper, for her unwavering enthusiasm, and my editor, Steven L. Mitchell, for believing the two voices could work together.

I am grateful to Paulette Mariano for her humor and encouragement, to Cynthia Lester for her insight, and to Brad Paulson for his love, wisdom, and inspiration.

Special appreciation to those who sustained and maintained me during the writing of this book: Pete Beevers, Beth Robinson, Andrew Harvey, Eryk Hanut, Jay Rosenthal, Mimi Gladstein, Ted Hayashi, Louis Owens, Mary A. Read, Carol Hammond and the Wichita girlz, Kim Wann, Irma Preston, Shannon Smith, Lisa Buchanan, Missy Wyatt, Pat Lawler, Nan de Grove, Luigi Tindini, Marie and Sean Warder, Carol and Jim Heidebrecht, and Duncan Campbell.

FOREWORD
BY ANDREW HARVEY

I am honored to write a foreword to this lacerating, profound, and exquisitely written book. *The Other Side of Eden* has harrowed and elated me, shattered my heart, and made me laugh raucously out loud. In John and Nancy Steinbeck's sophisticated and naked company, few extremes of human emotion go unexplored, often with a brutal brilliance that is as purifying as it is terrifying. This is one of the most original memoirs of the twentieth century. Anyone who finds the courage to read it as it deserves to be read—slowly, rigorously, bringing to it the whole of their feeling and intelligence—will find themselves changed.

All great memoirs are a clutch of different books marvelously conjured into one. *The Other Side of Eden* is no exception. It is at once an exorcism of family wounds and secrets, an exposé of the projections of religious seekers and of the baroque and lethal world of New Age cults and gurus. This poignant unfolding of a great love affair between two wounded, difficult, but dogged lovers is also the account of a journey into awakening through the massacre of illusion after illusion, to the awakening that lies on the other side of Eden. Few books risk, or achieve, so much under such blisteringly candid authority. Reading it is as much a rite of passage as a literary experience.

First, the exorcism. Many readers will undoubtedly be attracted to the most "sensational" aspects of the book—John Steinbeck IV's terrible alcohol-and-drug-ravaged struggle with the shadow of his famous father. Anyone hungering for cheap dirt or the easy satisfaction of the destruction of a celebrity idol will go away disappointed. The younger Steinbeck shirks nothing of his father's violence, inner desolation, addictions, occasionally pathetic and outrageous phoniness, and is honest about the lifelong, life-sabotaging wounds these caused him. He is far too intelligent, however, not to know and celebrate also how generous and tender his father could sometimes be. John is also far too wise not to understand that the very terror of his father's legacy was itself a kind of appalling grace—one that would nearly kill him again and again, yes, but which would also constantly goad and harass him, against great odds, to discover his essential self and the supreme values of spiritual clarity and unconditional love. Those who admire the elder Steinbeck's writing, as I do, will find nothing here that sours their admiration. If anything their respect for both the work and the man will only grow sadder and more mature as they acknowledge the struggles both had to endure. Dreadful though his father's legacy partly was, the younger Steinbeck did not allow it to annihilate him. He fought it, and himself, with agonizing courage to finish his life at peace with those he loved, with his past, and with the world. His father left two or three real masterpieces as signs of his truth. The younger John's masterpiece was the scale, reach, and passion of his life, a life that could only be written by a combination of Thurber, Dostoevsky, and Milarepa. The marvelous writing he achieved in this memoir is also in itself a victory, all the more rare because of the atmosphere of forgiveness and awareness that bathes it with a final, and healing, light.

This light of rare, bald awareness also bathes Nancy and John Steinbeck's exposé of their disillusion with Tibetan Buddhism and its guru system. Searching for a spiritual truth that could spring them free of their inherited agonies and also for a "good parent," they both became in the seventies, like so many other seekers, enamored of the "crazy wisdom" teacher, Trungpa Rinpoche. As Nancy Steinbeck writes, "A magnetic aura surrounded Rinpoche. . . . Infamously wild, in his mid-thirties, wearing Saville Row suits, he smoked Raleighs, drank whiskey, ate red meat, and sampled the entire panoply of hippie pharmaceuticals." Initially intoxicated by Trungpa's extravagance and brilliance, the Steinbecks came gradually to see how abusively and absurdly, dangerously grandiose he could be. They began to understand how sick with denial of his alcoholism and sexual cruelty the community that surrounded him was. This shocked them both into awakening from "the guru dream." Inspired by their own struggle with abuse and codependency, they were compelled to speak out, especially when Trungpa's successor, Tom Rich, ran the risk of spreading AIDS with a complete lack of conscience and with the corrupt connivance of his "henchmen." Just as the Steinbecks had both lived through the exposure of their own family myths, they now lived together through the equally anguishing process (one that I know too well) of recovering from the delusion of projecting their own power onto a so-called enlightened master and from the savage, intricate cruelties of a community rotten with denial. Their account of this devastating time is one of the triumphs of their book. Both admit they learned a great deal from Trungpa and praise his sometimes astounding acumen. It is this fairness that makes all the more unarguable their analysis of his hypocrisies and ruthlessness, along with those of his community. All those who continue, despite a mountain of damning evidence, to believe that Trungpa and his obscene Regent were "enlightened masters" and who, in the name of "crazy wisdom" continue to threaten and deride their critics, need to suffer and read *The Other Side of Eden*. So, in fact, do all serious seekers, especially those still in the thrall of the various contemporary manifestations of the guru system. The New Age at large is still horribly vulnerable to the fantasies of brilliant maniacs and the all-explaining, all-absolving circular rhetoric of a guru system that is now, to any unbiased eye, wholly discredited. The Steinbecks make clear that the alternative to the worship of false gods is not despair; it is freedom and self-responsibility, the dissolving of a brilliant illusion into a far more empowering if less glamorous truth.

The most moving of all the different facets of *The Other Side of Eden* is that it is a great love story, all the more greater and challenging because it shows how the jewel of unconditional love is only revealed when all the fantasies about love are incinerated. In the course of their extreme and extraordinary marriage, the Steinbecks explored and exploded all love's ravishing but lesser myths. In the end, they were left not with disillusion, but with a mystery, the mystery of a love that transcends all known categories to exist simply in the boundless and eternal. As Nancy Steinbeck writes, "I rode astride the razor's edge with John and although we place our bets on victory, the odds were on insanity or death, or both. As a result, I learned about unconditional love. There is a bond so profound that it can surpass the ravages of child abuse, a garbage pail of addictions, and finally even death." The road to such a love cannot be smooth or dragon-free. Because it gives everything, it costs everything. One of the permanent contributions this book makes to the exploration of the nature of love lies in its blistering honesty about the price of authentic commitment and about the continual leaping-off into darkness and mystery beyond all dictates of sense or even, sometimes, self-preservation. At stake in the alchemy of such a love is nothing less than the forging of the whole human and divine self of both partners. The final, amazing grace of the Steinbecks' marriage reveals that this, in fact, took place. Their long, often tormented struggle yielded the golden peace that passes understanding and the divinity of human passion lived out to its end in acceptance.

If *The Other Side of Eden* were simply an exorcism, exposé, and account of a transfiguring marriage, it would still be a most haunting and remarkable book. It is, however, something more than the sum of its parts. After many readings and rereadings, I have come to experience it as an account of the cost and joy of real awakening in a modern world largely controlled by competing lethal myths.

Those who want true and unshakable self-knowledge have to be prepared to sacrifice every inner and outer comfort, every consoling fantasy or dogma, every subtle hiding place, everything that prevents them from taking full, stark, scary responsibility for themselves and their actions in and under the Divine. There is no other way to full human dignity and no other way to the radical self-empowerment beyond the betrayal of dogma, religion, and system of any kind. The human race now needs to reach for this degree of honesty if it is going to meet, embrace, and survive the challenges of our time.

All systems, religious or political, have clearly failed us. We stand, naked and afraid, before doors that are opening into the apocalypse of nature and the massive degradation of the entire human race and Creation. If we go on letting the lies or half-truths of the past haunt and mold us, we will die out. If we risk the terrible and dangerous journey into naked truth beyond illusion, we have a chance of discovering what John and Nancy Steinbeck both discovered at the exhausting but exalted end of this book— an unshakable belief in the sacred power of true love to overcome and transform extreme disaster. The Steinbecks' eventual ferocious spiritual strength allowed them to witness truth and justice in all circumstances against all possible opposing powers. From this marriage of what Jesus called the "innocence of the dove" and "the wisdom of the serpent" outrageous possibilities of freedom and creativity can still—even at this late hour—be born.

The questions that this wonderful book leaves us all with are these: Are we willing to pay the price for this marriage of unillusioned hope and illusionless wisdom to be born in us? Will we risk, as John and Nancy have done, the stark and glorious alchemy of honesty and embrace the spiritual Darwinism of the survival of the most candid? Are we ready to travel through the incineration of every false truth to arrive in the Real, empowered with its hilarity and mystery? One of the most moving legacies of this book is that for all its exploration of horror, agony, betrayal, tragedy, corruption, and sheer brutal psychic suffering, it leaves us with the conviction that the truth is worth everything it costs because it sets us free. Free to love and weep and laugh and rejoice, free to witness, with steely and beady eyes, the rigors of justice. Free to become as Nancy and John Steinbeck became, electric nuisances to all myth-making systems—personal, political, and religious—that in any way diminish or imprison the secret of our splendor.

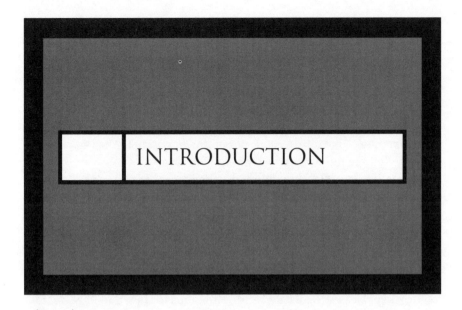

INTRODUCTION

My husband, John Steinbeck IV, started to write his autobiography, with some mixed feelings and much trepidation, in the spring of 1990, after two years of sobriety. He was excited about finally receiving recognition for his talents, and felt a renewed sense of direction based upon the positive reaction of his agent and editor. By that winter, he had traced the serrated edge of his life up to 1979, the year we fell in love.

John had lived with Promethean intensity. Surrounded by celebrities of the forties and fifties, he was raised in an atmosphere of shameless, alcoholic abuse and neglect. At the age of twenty, he was drafted into the Vietnam War. After a year of service, he remained there for five more, as a civilian and Emmy award-winning journalist, as a Buddhist monk, and as a father and a junkie. Back in the States, he became a voice in the antiwar movement. In 1969 he published *In Touch,** a highly acclaimed book about his experiences in Vietnam. He also studied Tibetan Buddhism with the notorious Crazy Wisdom guru, Chogyam Trungpa Rinpoche, in Boulder, Colorado, where we met in 1975.

John's mother, Gwyn, had launched his massive addiction to various chemical substances when she medicated him with codeine at the tender age of four. In the last decade of his life, battling with those demons brought him to death's door and a miraculous recovery in Alcoholics Anonymous.

---

*Please refer to the bibliography for a complete list of all books mentioned.

The gentle magic of his writing profoundly touched everyone who read the first draft of his autobiography. As he mailed it off to his editor, Linda Cunningham, he threw a handful of mylar confetti in the envelope. He knew how hard it is to vacuum up the vivid stars and hearts. "I want her to see those sprinkles on her office floor till they publish the book, so she'll remember me." Linda was ecstatic about the manuscript. After he died, she called to tell me the confetti was still in her carpet.

Since he had quit drinking and using drugs, John replaced alcohol sugars with pints of ice cream, tranquilizing the pain of unearthed memories with fat-filled food. His health had been precarious during the 1980s. He was hoping that along with his recovery, his metabolism would eventually stabilize and he would lose the excess pounds he had gained. We joined an exercise class together; it was so touching to see his painstaking concentration on the workouts, and he was enthusiastic about the endorphines they released. Sadly, it was too strenuous for him and in November of 1990 he ruptured a disc. He worked with a chiropractor for three months in the hope of avoiding radical procedures. When he grew impatient with the intense pain, he decided to undergo surgery in February of 1991.

Unfortunately, we were not made aware that the tests taken to clear John for the operation had come back with abnormal results, though we had cautioned the doctor of that possibility. Ignoring the red flags, he mindlessly misjudged my husband's candidacy for surgery. We had no idea that some surgeons are addicted to cutting. The knife wields power and, for them, the slash is the answer to everything. Mirroring John's needle jones, the orthopedist lusted to use his scalpel.

John died immediately following the operation. He suffered cardiac arrest, though they tried for an hour to revive him. When I left the hospital with our children, after saying a final good-bye, my first thought was to finish John's manuscript. Through the shock and pain, I felt an enormous responsibility to complete his work. I spent the next six months writing about his last years and the story of our love affair.

Being married to John was like having Scheherezade on call. He enjoyed telling tales and he recounted them dozens of times. His stories, and his life, were like music to me, leitmotifs as familiar as Beethoven; though there were times, especially when he was drinking, when I was convinced he would never shut up.

John was the only person who could write the chronicle of his family, a story that is much more than the voyeuristic and lurid exposé of Steinbeck family secrets that readers have come to expect these days. His working title for the autobiography was *Legacy*, which speaks of the many qualities handed down from his ancestors, often simultaneously virtuous and twisted, sacred and wounding. He did not intend his book to be a scholarly evaluation of the immense talents of his father or mother, and it was not to be an entertaining journal of his wayward youth. Nor did he want to glorify his emotional pain. His story of the Steinbeck family was to be a process through which he could heal his own very deep and personal wounds.

John's story is not unique. Statistics claim that 98 percent of families are dysfunctional. Where it becomes exceptional is the way it speaks so eloquently of such archetypal themes as power struggles between father and son, psychological suicide, abusive mothers, calculating stepmothers, and so much more. He wrote about the three rules that render families psychologically sick: Don't talk. Don't trust. Don't feel.

For years, John kept the secrets of his family, a conspiracy that eventually killed him. As a wounded warrior, he lived his life partly as the dutiful son, trying hard to win his father's love and approval, even long after Steinbeck's death. The loyal part of him kept his mouth shut to protect his parents, all the while committing emotional suicide. In the process he became an alcoholic and an addict, just like his mother and father.

In family photographs, John is always impeccably groomed, with a stiff posture that displays an anguished attempt to appear dutiful. He reminded me of one of those pictures when, on the day he died, he asked me: "Have I been a good boy through this?" Of course, he meant the debilitating agony that eventually forced him to take the very painkillers to which he had previously been addicted. I told him he'd been wonderful. At the height of his addiction, John was accustomed to taking quadruple doses of his medication. Concerned that the children and I might be distressed by his mood swings, he had been very conscientious during the past several months about letting us know when he took the prescribed amount.

For John, writing his autobiography was about balancing the ledger. Until he got sober, John had few choices in life because his addiction drove him. His healing produced a physical and emotional calm that brought him a measure of confidence in his ability to overcome his past. John's successful effort to recovery from alcoholism was probably the single greatest Steinbeck family achievement since *The Grapes of Wrath*. While this achievement would not win him a Nobel Prize like the one bestowed upon his father, it is far more pertinent to the human condition in America today. He refused to be victimized by his alcoholic genes or the suicidal dynamic between many famous fathers and their sons, in which the father's presence overshadows the son's sense of himself. From the sons of Cronos, whose jealous father swallowed them whole as they were born, to those of Bing Crosby, we know the archetypal tragedy and waste that occur when a father's persona devours his offspring.

John made a profound impression on everyone he met, no matter how casually. People sensed a depth of compassion, humor, and dignity in him, which they wanted viscerally to bottle, later to uncork and relive the impact. As one whom he intimately affected on a daily basis, I wanted to preserve the memory of his uncanny instinct for waking people up.

I needed to finish his manuscript for our family. As a survivor of severe childhood abuse, I, too, am balancing a ledger by lending completion to the process John started. Nobel Prizes and international acclaim do not sustain a family, or even the person getting the awards for more than the time it takes to receive them. By the time John Steinbeck accepted the 1962 Nobel Prize for literature, John IV and his brother, Thom, were already alcoholics and addicts. Their mother was in the late stage of her own alcoholism and Steinbeck himself was burned out on life, alcohol, and drugs. These awards did not help him or his family get better. They merely provided more varnish to cover up the pain, their collective illness, and their profound vulnerability.

John Steinbeck Sr. knew life at a readily observable, but illusory and transitory level. John IV, however, discovered what his father and much of his adoring public missed. That *The Grapes of Wrath* kind of poverty was Steinbeck's own. Not the poverty of corporeal substance that the great author immortalized, but a deeper, more insidious and lethal poverty of the soul and the spirit.

By slowly working through his recovery, John emerged victorious over anger, resentment, rejection, and humiliation. He could take his seat as a person in his own right, removed from the shadow of his father's haunting presence and his mother's violent temper. Writing his autobiography allowed him to heal the emotional wounds buried deep in his heart. He was finally looking ahead to a life he himself defined, a life that included loving friends and family instead of heaps of abuse and both physical and emotional toxicity.

In the years before his death, John was joyously playing with the different hats of a contented midlife man, a father, a husband, and a sober friend. Johnny would proclaim, "No drug is as potent as sobriety. Accepting life on life's terms is the strongest dope on earth. I wish I had known that twenty years ago." He found it amazing that creativity and joy were the extraordinary fruits that freedom from addiction offered.

The clarity and serenity that John had achieved in his last years were a great solace to those of us who were close to him. His difficulties with finances, setting boundaries, and trying to please people stopped being so unmanageable. He was proud of his maturity. The old feelings had not completely disappeared. Instead, they merely lost their crippling power to cramp his self-image.

Johnny used to tell me how lucky I was that he was even alive because of the short-lived track record of sons of famous fathers, such as John F. Kennedy, Paul Newman, and William Burroughs. I am grateful for every day we spent together, in spite of the pain and confusion of the early years. The success of our journey to heal childhood wounds eventually left us breathless and secretly believing we had discovered an enlightened kingdom in the heart of our relationship.

Unfortunately, the wounds were too deep for John's body to recover enough to grant him longevity. For some, the diseases of child abuse and addiction are fatal. Left untreated, they end in death or insanity. Johnny worked diligently to achieve his emotional recovery. He regained his sanity, but the abuse heaped upon his body proved too much for his system. His loyal heart gave out. Perhaps abuse and sorrow were the lessons he had to master, even if it cost him his life. The joyous rewards ahead were not the harvest he was destined to reap. In his life and his death there are messages John would have wanted to transmit, to ease the suffering caused by poisonous family dynamics.

The night before John's operation, I had a dream that Sable, our German Shepherd puppy, had died. A voice said, *I am taking my angel back today. I want you to have acceptance about the death, and never doubt that it was not meant to be. You must not feel sorry for yourself. This sacrifice is evidence of a greater plan.*

Johnny and I lay in bed the next morning, drinking coffee, sharing dreams, as we did every morning of our lives together. We never tired of that ritual. Born in the Chinese year of the Fire Dog, he groaned, "I hope that dog in your dream isn't me." I had never thought about his dying in surgery until then. I looked at him in horror.

"Johnny, if something happens, will you promise to come back as our guardian angel?"

He didn't miss a beat. "If I die today, I will always be with you and Megan and Michael. I will never leave you."

I didn't miss a beat either. "What about the book? Do you want me to finish it . . . you know, like *The Ghost and Mrs. Muir*?" That was our favorite movie, about a woman who writes best-selling adventure stories dictated by an adoring, phantom sea captain.

"Absolutely," he said, before I could finish the sentence. "It'll be easy. I'll be there to finish it with you."

And then we laughed. We thought it was banter. We thought we were cute. We never thought either of us would die young. We finished our coffee and drove to the hospital. A few hours later, John was dead.

Our daughter, Megan, went on a personal photographic expedition the summer after Johnny's death. She stopped at the Steinbeck Library in Salinas, California, to find photographs of him for the book. She called to tell me about one picture in particular that had a powerful effect on her. It was taken a few days before John and I met and fell in love, at the commemoration ceremony of the Steinbeck postage stamp in Salinas. When Megan came home, we looked at it together and I experienced a similarly intense reaction.

There was the Johnny I'd fallen in love with. Gorgeous. To-die-for gorgeous; hair tousled by the wind and his wise, bemused smile. I finally shed the tears that I never unleashed when the grief first started, when his drinking was relentless, when the diseases such as cirrhosis, diabetes, and hemochromatosis started coming like locusts during a summer plague. I cried for the beauty lost and for when it was regained in his sobriety. Johnny called them "Tara Tears," after the Tibetan goddess who wept when she saw the relentless suffering that is the fabric of human existence.

I wept for the pain that engulfed Johnny and for the nobility and integrity that dwelled in his heart. For the humor, the generosity, and the wisdom that spilled out onto everyone he met, in spite of his ailments and depression. The complexity of his life, his mysticism and depth, is a Gordian knot that still challenges me. Just as our marriage provided emotional and spiritual growth, I became stronger as I emerged from my grief. Johnny relied heavily on humor just to get through a day. When I see him in that picture—young and vital and the charisma glowing from every pore—the paradox slices clean through me. My only solace is to remember how much he loved paradox.

After his death, I thought of all the resolutions and convergences that allowed John to regain his dignity and to step out of his father's shadow, events that eased his transition and allowed him to establish his sense of self. One of the most significant was Johnny's delivery of an acclaimed keynote speech at the 1990 Salinas Steinbeck Festival, a memory of which we were enormously grateful.

For years, John had avoided appearing at any Steinbeck celebration because he dreaded having to answer questions about his name. He had little patience for sycophants, and he was not interested in playing the "I knew your father" game with Monterey Peninsula locals. He couldn't even make dinner reservations without someone saying sarcastically, "Any relation?" People would ask, "If it's that bad, why don't you change your name?" The dead sons of Errol Flynn and Bill Cosby were not named after their fathers. The curse is not in the name. Those modern sons of Cronos, swallowed alive by their father's fame, cannot change their fate with their name.

Robert De Mott, one of the foremost Steinbeck scholars, wrote his impressions of John's speech for the John Steinbeck IV memorial issue of the *Steinbeck Quarterly*. "All I can say I knew of John IV in his various selves is that he seemed to have had a roller-coaster life, which he approached with the nervous abandon of a man looking for his own name. Lately, he seemed to have found his name, for that evening in Salinas I felt again both a shock of recognition and a frontal assault on my half-baked, conflicting store of rumors and hearsay. I sensed an unanticipated calm, a Buddha-like repose, as John IV read from his movingly written, calmly measured prose memoir, *Legacy*, a personal study of the inheritance of addiction handed on from fathers to sons. This once-turbulent and clearly talented man stepped out of the long shadow his father threw. He wasn't shining, he wasn't reveling in self-pity or victimization, but he was settling the score with his inherited and self-created demons by enacting his own healing process, in which the gift of language became an act of homage and a celebration of an enduring link. John IV's words may have been too little, but now in the wake of his untimely death, I prefer to think that they were not too late."

After the speech, Johnny and I took the kids to the merry-go-round on Cannery Row, Monterey's historical fish-packing district which Steinbeck memorialized with his unforgettable characters. We observed a family ritual we had started years ago. After riding the ancient carousel, we matched wits with the caged chicken who faithfully plays Tic Tac Toe and wins every game. Then we posed for the last family portrait we'd ever have taken. Finally, we patted the bust of John Sr. as we paid him homage. And then we drove back to our hotel in Carmel Valley. As Johnny was hanging up his suit jacket, a piece of paper fell out of the pocket. It was a note someone had slipped him unnoticed, after his speech. Written in the quivering hand of an elderly woman, this is what it said:

How cruel it seems to me to be that John Steinbeck's own flesh and blood have to play the game I call Who Knew John Steinbeck Best. Any boy suf-

fers when there is a divorce and his father leaves the family home. I found
it very sad that someone in the audience would question just how well
you knew your father. You handled it extremely well. He lives in you. God-
speed. A friend.

This was about a question about how well John had known his father,
since his parents were divorced when he was two.

As we read the note, we were moved to tears, because someone had
been sensitive to the immensity of John's burden. This woman's sympathy
for his peculiar fate touched him and us as his family. The audience had
appreciated him for his own unique and brilliant self, for the magic of his
words and the gentleness of his presence. It was a homecoming, a reunion,
rich in its outpouring of genuine mutual recognition. After years of being
treated as the black sheep of the family, the event gave him great pleasure.
We were looking forward to future appearances, and often spoke of moving
to the Monterey Peninsula after John published his memoirs. We dreamed
of building a house in Carmel Valley, with room for our animals and
grandchildren. Long before Fate brought us together, it was mutually our
favorite spot on earth, and we decided it was time to surround ourselves
with its beauty.

Many of my dreams died with Johnny, but one will always live on
within me and the friends who loved him. We hope that the impact he had
upon the people he touched will always be remembered. Later, we may
make some sense of his death. Much later, there may even be certainty. For
now, there exists only the rawness and the sadness that such great gifts were
silenced much too soon. And gratitude for the arc of his white-hot clarity,
which lives on like a perpetual shooting star.

When my publisher suggested the book be titled *The Other Side of Eden*,
I was quite intrigued. It intimated the shadow side of fame, an underbelly
of which few are truly aware. I was, however, a bit taken aback by the subtitle, *Life with John Steinbeck*. It seemed to be a stretch, considering that I
had never met John's father, and anyway, the book contains the epic sweep
of our lives, much of which happened long after Steinbeck's death. However, as time went by, I began to understand the levels on which my life
with John Steinbeck operated.

It has often felt strange, being married to and now the widow of a man
named John Steinbeck. The name summons up two mental and emotional
images which I have to sort through whenever I hear it. The image for Steinbeck Sr. is an almost Jehovah-like figure, formidable, brooding, melancholy. When I think of it as Johnny's name, I feel a sense of warmth and res-

olution which overshadows my memories of darker times. I am, after all, Mrs. John Steinbeck. In the past twenty-five years, I have come to terms with the effect John's father had on him. Those negative aspects had a profound developmental impact on our children. Ten years after John's death, the three of us continue to heal from the gothic Steinbeck legacy.

In that sense, there has been a running conversation between Steinbeck and me that resembles Abra's pleas in *East of Eden*, as she begs Adam to bless his son so that Cal may individuate and mature. And so, I came to accept that it was fitting for my memoirs to contain the subtitle *Life with John Steinbeck*.

This phrase also refers to John's life with his father, mother, stepmother, and brother and how he came to terms with his immediate family. John's memoirs are also a personal account of his attempt to come to grips with his own life and what it meant within and independent of the Steinbeck myth. *The Other Side of Eden* blends these three psychological portraits, sometimes like well-mixed paint and other times like the clash of fire and water, but always in the spirit of genuine, unadulterated realism. They intermingle and interact as John, in the present, reflects about his life as a boy, a Vietnam vet, a journalist, and a struggling addict. Toward the end of the book, John reflects on the process by which he came to terms with his father, his addictions, and our marriage, which was often torn apart by his substance abuse.

This book is uniquely neither biography nor autobiography, but rather a conversation with two people that provides discrete insights into our enigmatic family. Because my husband's manuscript was unfinished when he died, there were various gaps in the chronology which I have filled in order to give the reader a greater sense of continuity and understanding. John's writing sheds light on his father's character in a way that Steinbeck would never have explained himself. The inclusion of my memories about our life together lends an additional perspective that neither writer might have ever revealed. In order to weave our voices together, John's memories are interspersed among mine throughout the book in a way that requires the reader to dwell in the present moment of each vignette. This format seems particularly fitting; drunk or sober, the *Now* was always John's favorite state of mind. A time line is available at the end of the book for readers who prefer a more linear approach.

At a bookstore reading last year, I was put on the spot by one of those colorful Steinbeck Country old-timers who think because they've lived in Monterey for eighty years, they can claim a peculiar proprietariness about their town's favorite son, a man they never met. "Your husband speaks of Steinbeck in such a negative way," he said belligerently. "As one of our greatest authors, don't you owe him more respect?"

It was a fair question and I had to think for a moment before replying. "If Steinbeck were to portray himself as a fictional character, he would not have hesitated to show the reader the full sweep of his spirit, his darkness, his shadow side, as well as his exalted, enlightened qualities. Steinbeck dove into the deepest recesses of his complex psyche and surfaced with an uncanny insight into the human condition that few authors have ever accomplished, before or since. In that sense, this book both explains and honors his amazing ability to create unforgettable characters."

Three days before his death, John asked his brother to create a logo for my psychotherapy workshops, which he had christened "Plan B" in reference to the escape hatch every codependent needs when relating to insanity and abuse. John had in mind an image of a briar intertwined around a rose, taken from the old English folk ballad *Barbry Allen*, which I used to sing in San Francisco's North Beach coffeehouses as a teenager.

> *Barbry Allen was buried in the old churchyard*
> *Sweet William was buried beside her*
> *And from her grave sprung a red, red rose*
> *And from Sweet William's a briar*
>
> *They grew and grew up the old churchyard*
> *Till they could grow no higher*
> *At the end they formed a true love's knot*
> *And the rose grew 'round the briar.*

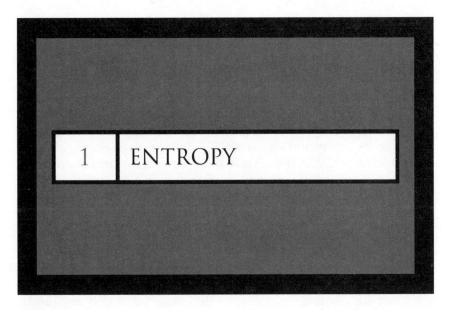

JOHN

I n 1949, New York City in spring was as beautiful as any vaulted redwood forest might have been to a country child of three. Sunlight
splashed on iridescent pigeon wings turning them into birds of paradise,
and when the rain came to our brownstone glade, it made the pavement
smell sweet and cool as it dripped from the elms that lined my block.

What I think of as solid facts are nearly impossible to isolate even in the
present, and then the distant past echoes with such an enormous range of
dream bytes that interlock so faithfully to themselves with tongues in grooves
that they speak to me almost past meaning. A flavor happens, but my childhood impressions are so thoroughly mixed in with things that I remember,
things I have heard and things that my nerves prefer, that I have no need for
conscious fabrication. I do know that I remember big. My red wagon was the
size of a stagecoach in the little garden that was Sherwood Forest. Feelings
follow suit as they get lacquered back and forth from the present to the past,
building up in layers until they glow alluringly like a black pearl.

I am told that I was a very sick infant with a convulsive stomach that
brought me little agonies. Still my brother, Thom, who is twenty-two
months older, tells me I was a mild child. He says he determined this in
part as a result of an early art experiment that he performed when I was age

1

two. Inclined from birth toward graphics and costume design, he used me as his constant subject. His medium in this particular case was a pint of liquid ox-blood shoe polish. This day, he had decided to paint me red, "like an Indian." He remembers standing me in the tub where he started out with just the war paint thing in mind. However, going off in the other direction from the sort of amateur barber who continues to shorten sideburns into nonexistence, in Thommy's search for perfect symmetry the effect here started to grow into total coverage.

After he had gotten through with my face and chest and then on to my back, the liquid polish started to drip down my butt and legs splashing luridly into the tub. Suddenly startled by the sight of his creation, he thought he had finally crossed the line and begun to kill me. Perhaps somewhere in his unconsciousness was imprinted the specter of human sacrifice, we don't know. It is true that he gestated in Mexico, but notwithstanding the possibility of some remembered Aztec codex, aghast and horrified he ran downstairs screaming of murder. He shrieked to my mother and her gaggle of afternoon guests that I was bleeding to death up in the bathroom. The assorted friends, who in all likelihood were gassed on afternoon screwdrivers, flew up the three flights of stairs to find me waiting passively for more detail work. But then, surprised as well and seeing the expressions on this horde, I must have realized that something untoward and probably dangerous was afoot. I immediately went square-mouthed into tears, stamping and looking wildly around for what the peril might be. I think I actually remember this part, as soon something started to sting.

My mother's friends, the *New Yorker* crowd, continued to have their cocktail hour at our home, and my brother maintained his talent for art. With fondness and a kind of pride, Thom tells me that at this age anyway, I somehow remained a stalwart and trusting sort, and that I accepted further experimentation at his hand without much blame or suspicion.

By four, I was accosting most everyone on the street with what I thought was my extraordinary ability to count to ten and spell my name . . . "You wanna hear me?" Then, to amuse his friends, my father had carefully taught me to respond by rote to the question "What is the second law of thermal dynamics?" In what I am told was a deep froglike croak, I would answer, "Entropy always increases." Indeed it does, but precocious as I must have been, outside of breaking some of my toys, a real grasp of systems and the notion of an integral disintegration from order to chaos was difficult for a four-year-old to really cotton to. Nonetheless, I was well warmed and surely nuzzled in the glow of after-dinner conviviality and the adult enjoyment of this feat.

My father, with too much time on his hands, was given to developing a lot of theories about child rearing. He could be a very kind and wonderfully funny man, but he was also *his* father's son, and I think a too-casual admirer of ancient Greece. When his mind was idle, I'm afraid it sometimes turned toward Sparta. He had a feeling that training a small child to jump off a high chair into the arms of a parent taught one thing, but allowing the child to fall to the floor at random was the better and deeper lesson. With this grave instruction, a child might learn something about physics, but more importantly he would also learn about life: that the parent would not always be there for him and then he would be better "prepared" for any eventuality. This approach did not entertain the possibility of causing paranoia or bodily injury, so father was quite sure that this was useful and right. Taking everything into account it probably *was* good to be classically prepared when it came to surviving such a creative family as mine, though the invitation to jump into *anyone's* open arms remains a sticky business for me and I'm almost never to be found standing on a high chair.

We lived in a four-story brownstone on East Seventy-eighth Street in Manhattan. Though it was surrounded by large apartment buildings, our house sat alone and even had a little wrought-iron fence right on the sidewalk in front and a large pebbled yard in back. All spring and summer, morning glories mixed in with ropes of ivy covering the entire front of the house.

The subway was still elevated on that part of Third Avenue and the sound of the "El" had a comforting quality that made me feel connected to all sorts of strange and exotic things and also to the characters who came walking off the train and up the street. Though some of these folks muttered angrily to themselves and jousted at invisible enemies, New York was a safe place. You could sleep in Central Park without fear.

Organ grinders with monkeys and photographers leading ponies came past my house like a circus train, along with ice cream vendors, hoboes, and tinkers who could fix anything. I watched and saw that the hoboes would make secret signs on your front steps or near the door to signal to other floaters that the family within was good for a cup of coffee or maybe even a sandwich. Since I was often unsupervised and it was the only thing I could make, I was a master of a Blue Plate Half-Pounder baloney special. We got a lot of hoboes.

In summer, everyone talked about the beach and something called Coney Island. The name told me that it was probably the home of ice cream. There was also some kind of a field apparently owned by a Mister Ebbetts where the Brooklyn Dodgers played baseball. This was really *very* important to know about if you wanted to get a smile of benediction south of a place called the Bronx. There were mean and bad people called the Yankees way up there in the Bronx.

Though we lived right in the heart of the city, hummingbirds drank nectar from the flowers by the balcony outside my third-floor window. Once I woke up to discover a praying mantis on my pillow case. It turned its wonderful head to look at me, I swear it smiled a hello, and I saw it was enchanted.

There was real magic everywhere I looked. Most of it I didn't understand. I became quite busy trying to, but the fact of the matter was that it was impossible to get the world to stay the same long enough for me to figure some of it out. There were a lot of mysteries.

Eager to get a handle on the big stuff, I snuck into the local church on a weekday. After going as high as I could by the stairs, I found a dusty ladder and searched around for God way up in the rafters. I had seen the priest often point and say He was "up there." I was disappointed at not finding Him or much of anything but some old light bulbs and newspapers. I really sensed that the priest was earnest though, and I knew that only big important people read the newspapers, so I figured that God had probably just gone out somewhere. Shopping? Getting groceries maybe?

I was fairly convinced that there was a landlocked crew of desperate Em-pirates on top of what they called their "State Building," and when people complained that they had to *make* money, I couldn't see in my mind's eye what was so bad about standing by a machine that probably stamped out all those shiny bright coins that could buy candy. But no matter, I could count to ten and spell "Johnny," my mother was pretty, I had a brother named Thommy and a cat named Doctor Lao from Siam.

I don't remember winter as much. I expect this is just an attempt to block out the agony of galoshes and snowsuits and vaporizers, as well as the bizarre emotional calamities that percolated all through the holidays with the spiced cider. Any four adults obviously had at least twelve personalities. It was deeply confusing. In spite of all the nice smells, the atmosphere sometimes just hung dangerously. Thanksgiving, Christmas, and New Year's were for me an immediate source of primal apprehension. They were always festooned, but with a weird mélange of turkey dressing, hurt feelings, pine needles, scotch and soda, anger, gifts, violence, and tears, and all of this was called a celebration. Now that was especially hard to figure out. The God thing was much easier. The presents helped a lot though, and anyway, I know my parents tried. I felt sure that they were very smart and presumably knew best. After all, they were very big, and all grown up.

My parents were divorced in 1949. After a while Dad fell in love with Aunt Elaine and moved to his own brownstone six blocks away on Seventy-second Street. Mother had been a singer, and my father wrote about the dusty song of eternal hope that common people share with their dogs. She never forgot a tune, and he could repeat to perfection the tones of the stories that he heard. He heard them so often that eventually he could just make them up and they remained true. She had perfect pitch, but without any sin, she was just compelled to lie. He wrote skewered parables, while she was a paradox. For the most part hers were haunting lies, intended to make the listener wonder and shiver with her hints of magic. Both he and she were rich with wide-eyed fantasy and inspiration despite their own deep and hidden despair and a glimpse of impermanence. Either way, it was the song and the stories, and the karma of words that drew them to each other; and then, it was the wine with its sorry bite that severed the eloquence and the charm and pulled them apart.

By the time I was five years old, under some East Side Knickerbocker's stewardship, I, too, drank a lot of champagne to ring in the New Year. So it was, that on the first day of 1951 I woke up from my first blackout in a little ring of vomit, but by then I could count much higher than ten and entropy *was definitely* increasing.

2 | MOM AND POP

JOHN

Salinas, California, today looks like many towns, almost any town in the area. Though he wrote about it, and the valley that shares its name had almost mystical significance for him, Salinas was not my father's favorite place on earth. And even though today we have the Steinbeck Library, and a Luncheon Club signals the institutionalization of the house where he was born, when he was alive, John Steinbeck was never his town's favorite son.

My father's grave site is in an old, run-down cemetery, near the Shillings Spice Company's truck yards. It's by the highway past a small airport, in the shade of a spreading Denny's and various warehousing concerns. His ashes are under a cracked slab with those of his mother, Olive; his father, John Ernst Steinbeck; and his little sister, Mary Decker. The scene in this tiny Hamilton family plot is more apt than the monumental hypocrisy of the people who swear they knew and revered him.

My father was by many accounts a bad boy, and the only boy in a brood of four. His three sisters spoiled and idolized him and though two of them were older, he was the family's hero. The family was Welsh-Irish-German. My paternal grandmother, Olive, was the Irish daughter of Samuel Hamilton of *East of Eden* fame, and almost as humorless as her mother,

Liza, though she was more refined and loved books. By all accounts, Samuel was a strong and extremely decent man. My father's interest seems to have dwelt on Samuel and his aunts and uncles far more than on his own parents or siblings. Precious few people can recall my dad ever talking much about his parents or growing up with the girls. The exception was his beloved sister, Mary.

My father's Aunt Dessie, Olive's sister, appears in some detail with her brother Tom in the Hamilton sections of *East of Eden*. Tom was Dad's favorite uncle. Since Olive was made of sterner stuff, Dessie was the *sweet* Hamilton girl. Sadly, she died of appendicitis while staying out in the country alone with Tom, a tragedy for which he blamed himself unto suicide. Apparently, thinking it only a tummy ache, he gave her a bromide and before morning came, both their lives were fatally ruptured.

Tom was in his early thirties when he died, but he was a lost child in his generation. He was a lovely man caught up in a time that was becoming mechanical in a way that he did not choose to understand. The industrial haughtiness of the day had a withering effect on his being and he retired away from town until his soul finally winked out in grief. And in truth, my older brother, Thom, who bears his name, is another man with his heart in a more graceful past.

There were a lot of stillbirths and fatal childhood accidents in the world of the Steinbecks and the Hamiltons. This was true in the Old World that they had left as immigrants a generation earlier, and carried right through into California where three generations of John Steinbecks lost lots of sons to disease or misadventure. My father, too, almost died of pleurisy shortly after his birth in 1902, but a drunken country surgeon tunneled into his chest by way of his armpit, and drained his lungs in time.

In the Salinas Valley, life could be very raw, even for what passed as the middle class. That term simply meant that you knew where tomorrow's meal was coming from, a condition that more and more resembles today. Nonetheless, long before the Great Depression, times could be hard, and small accidents could prove lethal.

Most people couldn't wait for John Steinbeck the writer to leave Salinas. His books, which used his hometown as background, reminded them of their foolishness. He made delicious mention of their whorehouses and the people's ambient racism, too. His deceptively folksy attitude also spooked them with the possibility of just plain spontaneity coming from . . . why anywhere! It somehow frightened them. His personality had a prankster's twist to it that would last a lifetime in one form or another. His mad, merry eyes exuded it. When drunk, he sometimes spoke mischief under his breath in a mumbled darkness.

Though in person Dad was considered a shy man, today he would be described as distinctly passive aggressive. In any case, the town didn't trust him and they didn't like him much. People aren't stupid; they knew this man had real resentments, and could explode on them, possibly with reason. Indeed, eventually he did; and he did it memorably, with his fine craft, even cunning. My father *always* had a taste for the grapes of wrath and he knew a revenge of good vintage with just one whiff.

Beyond all of that, he is now remembered with a kind of reverence by many. In a lot of ways, my father convinced people that it was all right to read. When he was a boy, among the people he grew up with, if you had time to read it meant you were probably lazy. Most people needed that time to do their chores. Abstract thinking, or thinking too much was the Devil's work. The Bible was the only book that really required reading, and that was reserved for just before you went to sleep and a little bit on Sundays. If you weren't lazy, then you were probably an "egghead" and that was just a little bit better than being a queer. Reading was something done by city people or the schoolmarm, and anyway, books were probably difficult to begin with and the ideas that they contained were for great men, or dangerous men. But underneath this there was the fear that one wouldn't be able to understand a real book.

My father wrote simply; not in the way that Hemingway is thought to be "simple," but rather he wrote about common things, things that everybody knew to be true, and if they weren't offended by the truth, they were glad to see these things written in books by this man. It sort of legitimized them, and John Steinbeck became *their* voice . . . *in books*!

By the time my generation started exploring their truth in the post-Hiroshima environment of the day, another reactionary loop had developed. For a while, history was not kind to John Steinbeck, especially during the sixties, when he lost favor for supporting the war in Vietnam. Hurt, reacting to this rebuff, he at times seemed to begin to take on some of the values of those narrow-minded folks that he wrote about; the ones who actually hated his books and had given him hell when he was young, for wasting his time by indulging in the demonic enterprise of literature.

Driving around Salinas, I was reminded of a time not so far back when I was flat broke, and without any health insurance. I spied a car with a bright red bumper sticker emblazoned with a common AA slogan amended to read: EASY DOES IT IN STEINBECK COUNTRY. I was in bad shape and thought of applying for a loan at the Steinbeck Credit Union to get some cash to pay for drug/alcohol treatment. It was my plan to apply to still another local facility with the really unlikely name of the John Steinbeck Recovery Home. When, incognito, I called up to see if they had an open bed, I could barely believe my ears as I was transferred to the office of the clinical director, a Ms. Hemingway. I was sure I was losing my mind. She must have concurred on general principles, as not knowing who I was, she sagely advised me to come on in and get help immediately. Most of their clientele were alcoholic migrant farmworkers from way south and future candidates for membership in *Alcoholicos Anonymoso*. After some consideration, and feeling sure that the credit union would never believe my story, my disease and I took a pass on the whole thing, and swallowed another percodan with a tequila chaser. It was all very strange. I was very strange, but my predicament was anything but new to the area.

The Civil War had brought laudanum, and soon codeine and morphine into wide use, thus introducing the possibility of controlling all sorts of pain and despair from physical or situational difficulty. Self-medication was common, and with the help of the village pharmacist it became ultrastrong folk medicine. Opiates had a powerful and revolutionary effect on the way people began to deal with outrageous fortunes. We can follow this trail in letters from Coleridge, to Cocteau, to O'Neil to Burroughs.

Of course, these things were old as man, though they were not as available as alcohol, the barbiturate of Ferment and the potion that could often cause it. *That* was the real stuff that satisfied a bunch of repressed German Protestants. It had also heated the Welsh-Irish gene pool since the days when we painted each other blue and wore seductive fur on our backs, as well as our tongues. In my particular case, adding further to the Welsh-German-Irish brew, my mother, Gwyn, also brought some Indian blood to my family's outrageous potlatch.

When I close my eyes I can summon up my mother's face and the tide of her moods a little more quickly than I can my father's. People have always said that physically I resemble Gwyn more closely than I do John, though, with little effort, I can feel both of their departed beings move inside my own. As a child growing up in her household, there were many moments, indeed whole weeks that filled me with terror and surprise. However, there is a singular episode that has always stuck with me like the bubble gum I use to fall asleep with, only it was possible to have *that* cut out of my hair in the morning.

On a beautiful spring day in 1953 I came skipping home from the Allen Stevenson School which was barely a block away from our house. I remember the year because even at six years of age I had been struck by the impact of the adult world's reaction to the death of Stalin. I had watched the funeral over and over again on our new Sylvania TV, which, with its special glowing border, made nearly everything that appeared on it indelible in the vivid crèche of childhood memory.

Gwyn Conger was a bright and witty Wisconsin girl who had been a big band and radio singer in California before my father married her in 1943. Then, after their divorce she had her own fame as the ex-wife of one of America's most loved authors. With this dubious credential and the traditional *half* of the couple's sympathizers, my mother had begun her new life. At this particular point she embarked on the slippery career of a socialite and community organizer. For important widows or the celebrity divorced, this role was the standard then as it is now. Though she was quite brilliant, my mother was not from a particularly sophisticated background. I don't think she had a clue as to what this type of society figure would actually be like other than what she might have seen in the feathers-and-patent-leather movies of the thirties and forties. Also, by 1953, bitter about the choices she had made, she was a thorough alcoholic. When under the influence of spirits, my mother became somewhat grand and pretentious. This trait is shared by others in my family and it is common to many alcoholics of a certain type. She also could become rather troublesome when she drank. To put it mildly, eventually I would understand the awful pith of this phenomenon from the inside out as it ripened and rotted in my own life and behavior.

As I ran up the stairs to the living room this day, I stumbled in on my poor mother's latest Titanic adventure; the doomed maiden voyage and grandiose first meeting of what they called the Albert Schweitzer Brownstone Committee. They were gathered to try and arrange something in support of the celebrated humanitarian's clinic in Africa. Enthroned on the huge divan under the many oil paintings by her drinking buddy Luigi Corbalini, darling of the social set, sat my mother in a beautiful silk caftan. She was surrounded by recorded organ music and six or seven neighborhood patrons and matrons of the arts.

As she fixed me on top of the landing, I could tell by the slack line of her jaw and the "you better not blow this" look in her swimming eyes that she was positively plowed under with screwdrivers or some other *polite* beverage. I should have known when I didn't see the family Siamese basking in the downstairs kitchen window that the cloudless spring afternoon would be dismantled in one way or another. In a voice that was completely unrecognizable as that of my mother, she introduced me to the assembled company as "Young Master John," who had just returned from my "studies at the Academy." The only way I can describe it was that she had that theatrical European accent, like some tortured Hungarian-Irish-Spring-Mueslix commercial, with all the false tones of a bad *Mission: Impossible* episode. Then, to my horror she began to speak to me in what she thought might resemble French. Now even at six, with only a little Babar under my belt, I blushed with embarrassment at this sad attempt to be Continental. Perhaps sensing this, she turned to the assorted members of the Albert Schweitzer Committee and explained that she had told me to express my gracious farewells and then retire to my room to continue my studies in Latin. Getting this cue, I happily squirmed away with what I thought would be a helpful *Au revoir*, and ran for my life upstairs to the third floor. After I shut my door loud enough so that it could be heard, I crept back to the top of the long curved staircase to watch with morbid fascination for what would happen next.

Mom had obviously tried to vanquish her deep-seated self-consciousness much too early in the day. She had begun to soar, and was becoming enthralled with her own jokes and the increasing bite of her insight. As I watched and listened to her tongue get thicker and begin to repeat its stories over and over again, I sensed a change in the atmosphere of the room. I saw the people begin to look sideways at each other and become uneasy, even as they laughed with polite enthusiasm.

Though very drunk now, Mother was no fool. That same self-consciousness made her wary, and she sensed the dead sea change too. She was caught in a situation where she was not in control of her behavior but conscious enough to see its unwelcome effect. Then, a fury came rushing in to satisfy the gap. Like a scorpion stinging itself in paroxysms of self-hatred, her humors turned darkly sarcastic and corrosive. Projecting the rapacious demons inside on to anything that moved, she began to openly disparage the folks in the room as if they were but feeble ghosts spoiling at her stabilities.

Soon, the committee began to excuse themselves. Her American vernacular had returned like a squad of Marines. Mother's language and temper had now turned really foul. When the synapses shorted out and finally erupted into a full-blown brainstorm, her adult dose of Flathead Indian blood caught fire. With that potential engaged, anything could happen. Within a few minutes, I saw an old-fashioned glass explode against the wall near the head of the last of the Schweitzer group to beat it down the stairs and out the kitchen door to the street. I watched as my mother continued to curse and scream and begin to break up furniture and throw more things. That continued on and on to the majestic background of Notre Dame's monumental organ with Dr. Albert Schweitzer himself performing Bach's "St. Matthew's Passion." But now, even that, too, had begun to malfunction and skip on the 78 RCA record player in concert with the increasing havoc.

After a while Mother collapsed in sobs and I ran quickly to my bedroom. I had learned that it could be dangerous to try and console her when she was in this condition. Just in case she came to and went hunting, I locked the door and slipped under the bed where I was greeted by the huge eyes and tense hiss of Dr. Lao, the Siamese cat.

What appears to serve justice or even humor in some situations can be experienced as genuine cruelty in others. I for one am often appalled and perplexed at some of the "inventive" and hazardous nurturing that I received at the hands of *both* my parents. But when I look back at this with self-pity, or reach for my preferred uniqueness, there is also something vaguely insulting in the realization that in so many ways, my family, with all its maniacal behavior, was not too much different from other folks that I know.

After Prohibition, the Depression, and the happy conclusion of World War II, the majority of Americans, including my mother and father, were like grown-up kids, gleefully dancing on broken eggshells and gobbling the shards in a brave new world. Part of their generation had escaped drudgery into the life of the mind. Art, writing, humor, and just plain thinking was now a fine and proper birthright. The Depression had forced my parents to become extraordinarily creative. Mother's family relied on her precocious beauty to generate the income she received from her performances on radio and in nightclubs. Accompanied by her mother, fifteen-year-old Gwyn came to Hollywood from Wisconsin, where, in 1939, she met Dad, who was riding high on the acclaim of *The Grapes of Wrath*. Mother was twenty years old and Dad was thirty-nine when they fell in love.

America was at the end of its greatest expansionist era. World War II intensified nearly everything, as wars will, and when it was over the ticker tape only signaled the *beginning* of our sundance.

We were the richest country in the world. Floating on a mixed genetic alloy in the melting pot, we were a powerful recipe for great assets and heroic joy. Anything was possible and everything was fast, but now, thanks to Hollywood, it was even in technicolor. It was to get a lot faster in my generation, but at the end of the war in 1946 when I was born, the short-term-goal ethic had already been institutionalized as the essence of modern living at its best. Things like ecology took it on the nose of course, but no matter; there were new and great things ahead. We were certainly a lot more enjoyable and just plain more fun than our real ancestors or the Teutonic and Slavic types that we had sent scurrying into the endless winter of Eastern Europe.

Life was sleek, and in the postwar euphoria Americans were destined to be slick. Though a bit dated, Nick and Nora Charles defined intelligent affability in their *Thin Man* movies. Maybe it was something in the martinis, or were they whiskey sours? Whatever, it was very impressive and urbane stuff for country folk who caught on quickly and adapted a veneer of sophistication.

Alcohol was the leading character and even the hero of a number of movies that I loved along with my parents. I don't mean just the green whiskey westerns, but films like *The Philadelphia Story*. Why, if Katharine Hepburn had *not* gotten drunk and embarrassed everyone at her high society wedding, she would never have gotten back together with old Cary Grant, now would she? People really thought along those lines. I know I did! We were rich and right and free and not to be contradicted.

With a mixture of zeal, ignorance, and fear, many of my parents' generation also felt that they must swim for their lives in this basically immature and bruising society of ours. Of course they called it opportunity instead of the blind panic that America's new power carried with it. The seeds for today's ethical predicaments were deceptively optimistic, even uplifting in a Deco sort of way. Like Sea Biscuit, the famous racehorse of the day, America was coming up fast on the outside, with lots of opinion and lots of style. We had also become the self-appointed spokesmen for social, though not individual, morality. But this was all still long before the days of "personal issues," or even much reflection for that matter. All anyone knew in the late forties was that Lucky Strike had gone to war and come back a winner, but it had come back with little patience for reflection, and less foresight.

There were also all of the new babies and we whippersnappers had better not contradict too much either. After all, we had not lived through the Depression or known war. Democracy, the Founding Fathers, GI Joe, *and* our parents were the source of our lush success.

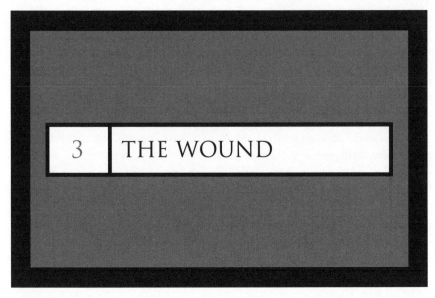

3 | THE WOUND

JOHN

In what increasingly feels like a lifelong search for equilibrium in these matters, it has occurred to me more than once that *everyone* is the child of a famous father. When you are little, he is the opening to the outside world and he actually begins to represent it. No matter if he is the postman or the shoe salesman or whatever. If he is the shoe guy, the postman knows him and can't work without knowing him. If father is the postman, the shoe salesman gets his mail, maybe even all those boxes of shoes from *your* dad, and so on. When I was a kid, the other thing that amazed me was that at least in the other kids' minds, *their* mother was the prettiest woman they knew. I know mine was, and when my best friend told me that his mom was the prettiest, I was struck dumb. He wouldn't lie about such a thing, you know. Somehow his dad was more famous than mine, too; perhaps because he was a painter, and his grandfather was famous, too. This stumped me. I didn't know anything about that, but then again I wasn't hurt or anything since nearly everyone was essentially famous to me.

Realistically, I have found that there are different ingredients involved in being the son of John Steinbeck than were first considered when the doorman who worked the apartment building next to our brownstone told me that my daddy was famous and that *everybody* knew who he was. The attendant repercussions extend out and snag me like vines on different planes all of the time. Often when I just say my name I get back, "Yeah, and I'm the queen of England." Twice, a lady at my father's literary agency just hung up on me, and this was years after he was dead. Maybe that was the problem!

I'm not really sure how hard I've tried, but my father is a tremendously difficult person for me to get away from, particularly when I am being haunted by my usual coincidental reality routine. For instance, just this morning I went into a small "Foodierie" in the nowhere coastal town of Encinitas, California, to grab a bite to eat, and the cash register is sporting a cartoon of an angry French cook with the caption "The Crepes of Wrath." I have seen my father dolefully staring up at me from strange wastebaskets, his likeness celebrated on fifteen-cent stamps. In drunken or drugged states I have seen his name fly by me on papers in the wind, and bumped into statues of him while innocently looking for a quiet, private place to vomit.

In 1983, my wife, Nancy, and I traveled with our children overland from Nepal through the Himalayan foothills to the mountain kingdom of Sikkim to visit the remote monastery of Rumtek. We went to pay our respects to the then recently deceased Karma Kargu Lineage Holder of the Tibetan Vajrayana Buddhist Teachings, His Holiness the Sixteenth Gyalwa Karmapa, the beloved Rangjung Rigpe Dorje. We had received his blessing and teaching many times in life and had traveled far to bid his remains farewell. After meditating very late in the main shrine room that looks over an enormous valley through these mountains to a silent, snow-covered infinity, Nancy and I gingerly found our way in the starry night to the little hut where we had been given shelter. Trying not to wake our host, out of curiosity, and half expecting to hear from the planet Neptune, before going to sleep we turned on the tiny shortwave radio, just in time to hear some histrionic voice from the BBC World Service intone, "And now . . . chapter 1 of John Steinbeck's immortal story, *The Red Pony*." When this sort of thing happens enough, my incarnation as "Son of . . ." takes up quizzical new meanings.

It is my fate, and perhaps my disease to be considerably self-involved, with a head full of thoughts about myself, about my ignorance and the probable mistakes in how I interpret things. It feels like I'm always translating something to myself: the news, the weather, its symbolism, and especially other people's moods. I have always tried to make sense of the world around me as if, by way of understanding it, my confusion would be transformed into wisdom. This is possibly a clever case of putting the cart before the horse. I also believed that if this desire for comprehending life's predicaments was unselfishly motivated and came from my version of kindness and fairness, I would be protected from the terrors that my confusion could bring. I guess I still believe part of that.

I believed Laura Huxley when she wrote *You Are Not the Target*, and in the cosmic sense I think this still holds true. But I have to tell you, by taking this panoramic stance in Absolute Truth, I have often hidden from myself many important relative truths along the road to this ultimate view of things. I think that much of my attachment to a sweet, pacific, and perhaps reductive nirvana was due to my fear in facing the more common and coarse weave in the tapestry that ordinary people toil with. This is not to say that I am "sweet." Instinctively abhorring that silly fabric, sometimes enshrined in notions of "Love and Light," I have also invariably tried to give my philosophies a good test-drive on difficult tracks, like dropping LSD in Vietnamese war zones, or just before being manacled to a wall for an indefinite period of time in a Thai jungle prison. (I took a two-month rap for a woman who had transported a small amount of heroin over the Thai-Malaysian border.) But now all that seems to be merely radical, and today it doesn't appear to say much of anything about what actually counts in the real world of gradual spiritual experience. Consequently, I feel that along with so many other things, deft transcendence became just another painkilling habit.

I find that every day now I have to give myself permission to *not* understand and be genuinely frustrated by what I see. In trying to prepare this book, my vacillations between a seemingly profound and compassionate view of my formative life, and the sad powerlessness of my actual experience, sometimes make me ill. It's awkward. So, I try to dose it down with some sort of desperate comprehension to dispel the motion sickness of impermanence on any scale.

For many people this cognitive approach of constantly interpreting what goes on around them might be all right, but for me it feels like I've worn it out, and the other approach of *nothing means anything* feels like dope. In truth, I'm generally all over the damn place. Especially when I think back on the really bad things that happened to me, I start looking for a reason, for the "good sense," and then I begin to envelop myself in metaphoric pardons of all kinds. Then an attitude might appear and masquerade as if it had, or could beg for, a rational at the Geneva Convention in my mind. This is entirely my own self-consciousness; I have to continually remind myself that even *these* filaments and elliptical reflections are dignified as thoughts and feelings, and that they don't have to make sense on the hard turf of logic or be metered out with Republican prudence. As feelings they are legitimate and can stand on their own, alone, and even apart from themselves. Many of the crosswinds swirling from my head and my heart cannot be followed objectively, especially by me. And though sometimes I might want to, the idea of defending them then becomes truly ludicrous.

For the sake of my greater ease, I have concluded that these oscillations of opinion and emotion, ignorance, and intellect are in themselves part of a legacy that I was given. I don't think I'm alone. Of course much of this depends on one's point of view, and as I've said, mine never stays the same for very long. Though some would say it is terminal ambivalence or indecision, I will say it is a gift of equanimity, and so I am willing to share some of this without too much fear of the perpetual contradictions inherent to my nature.

On the emotional platform erected by my parents, there were many and various planks that served to cripple as well as support me. But despite the copious mix of messages I received from both of my parents, the inheritance, whether stolen or bequeathed, was more than just a rat's nest of neuroses. In its way, it contained the map for survival through the sacred and profane aspects of my life. The aberrant behaviors and the mechanism for coping with the results all came in the same package. These are the deep autonomic styles behind the wisdom of DNA that allowed me to grow my hands and also mend some of the things that they broke.

I've come to think that in many families, the holders of that clan's special knowledge must pass away before the next generation can actually get at the signals being sent. This was definitely true for me. The reasons are sad but simple. Sometimes my family's wisdom was garbled by my father's peevishness or my mother's drunkenness, or sometimes it was delayed by the static of our mutual anger camouflaged as disinterest or plain boredom.

When I say wisdom, I don't necessarily mean something wise or good in a moral sense, but rather just what works. When I sharpen a pocketknife the way my father did with hands similar to his, it is not because it is the right way to do it, but it is the way that he discovered kept the stitches and the Band-Aid bills down to a minimum. There is always room for improvement and rebellion however, so the few scars on my hands could be seen as rings of evolution as I hasten to add that I can get my knives a lot sharper than he could.

When people are guided by their own defensiveness, they are by nature left ignorant of the other's emotional needs. These days, important transmissions from father to son are usually grotesque. The presumption on both sides is that someone here is an asshole. Often the situation is so self-consciously painful and the lessons so harshly applied, that something strong like time or anger or, in my case, chemicals is needed to cushion the fractured exchange. This was true for both me *and* my father, and my brother and mother.

It seems that when all is said and done and in spite of all intent and schooled purposes, the most identifiable quality of what I have come to think of as the Father Principal is anger. That type of anger is in itself, an energy that is intrinsically unconscious, but, when met with pompous or conscious application, it inevitably goes the way of the best-laid plans of mice and men. In other words, burdened with a false sense of power in shaping young lives, most modern-day paternal tutorials go completely awry. This leaves the children confused at best, and the father with terminal disappointment in what he imagines to be *his* creation. Then, the Father Principal becomes associated not only with anger, but with a festering disappointment that feeds on itself. Indeed, for my brother and I, this myth/fact of life was confusing as hell. It is even probable that my father, the creative artist, had a genuine problem distinguishing between what should have been manageable in shaping *our* characters and his masterful and successful efforts at developing literary characters. For the most part, they cooperated from the ground up as his creation. The comparison between his real children and his literary children was no doubt a painful difference for him. Our real-life response or lack of it, when it came to his sculpting and his often shaming goad, was rarely up to snuff, at least not for long.

In some modern homilies, fathers are traditionally called the provider, but what does the father really provide? It has taken me nearly forty-five years to come up with an answer that satisfies my need for equanimity, and eases the little horrors of recollection, and I must say that I've had a lot of help mining for it. On one special level, the helpless father has the thankless task of acting as sort of a representative of the world. This is not a political role exactly, but rather, he is the courier of both extreme engagement, and also cold-blooded indifference; literally reality's agent. And guess what; though it isn't the last word on creation, the world hurts. It even kills, often quite accidentally.

Despite the efforts of poet Robert Bly and the men's movement to help males understand their roles as parents, husbands, and members of a larger society, this is a real problem. This mythic principal defies interpretation in our society. The father is the bad guy if he does or if he doesn't participate in his role as father in the Hallmark card sense of the word.

Within the contemporary notions of neglect or abuse (both of which we deem as abuse), the father *must* be the bad guy. It feels like there are at least two different planes operating here. Though I believe what we all know as abuse to be always unacceptable, whether or not the child feels abandoned by a negligent father or abused by an overbearing monster, as an ignorant representative of the phenomenal world, the father is a bastard, and a wound inevitably occurs, and that wound, those hurt feelings and the scars that they leave, is the mark of initiation into the real world.

For me, and for my older brother, these things were felt in a terribly— and I mean *terror*-bly—personal way. Without a doubt this business could be made only more insufferable if the father consciously knew what was going on and was really guiding the process. Most of the time, my father really did think he knew what was going on. The father as "The Fool" tries to teach: "Let me tell you about life, son."

So, I see that along with anger, fathers are significantly ignorant people. I speak from experience here as a father. In fact, as it happens, I am the same age as my father when I was born, forty-four. However I have a twenty-two-year-old daughter, a twenty-year-old daughter, an eighteen-year-old son, and a one-year-old grandson. In short, I have been on more sides of more parenting than my father could have dreamed of as he set out to address *East of Eden* to his two little sons when he was about my age.

My father was not very good at all in the role of mentor. Looking at other cultures, this seems to be a rather common complaint. Native Americans give that task to an uncle or some other elder in the tribe. The father has a duty to protect and provide for the family, but as a teacher, he is often as not a washout. Predictably, he is too busy with trying to resolve the deeper issues inherited from his own father to be of much use in teaching his son about life.

No one is particularly happy about what's going on here. Not me. Not in either role. Neither the patriarch nor his issue seem to have a terrific ride. The father doesn't like being angry and can't figure out why he's acting like his father, something he promised himself he would never do. The young sons don't even have that perspective to confound them yet. All they know is that the father does seem to do good, but can also do very bad things to them. He acts cruelly. He seems to be always indignant or mad, and always moving away from contentment and happiness to a state of irritation. He is never satisfied. He is demanding. In other words, he is like the goddamned world. Worst of all, he doesn't seem to ever be able to *recognize*, or acknowledge that the son is actually learning and growing. And then, what he does see you learn, like sexuality, somehow threatens the hell out of him. So he wounds you some more, and a scar begins to grow. It grows until it's an angry red, like the one he wears from his father.

Though nobody likes it, this nasty scar is the father's gift. Actually it is really all he has. Even if it is the father's fate to commit suicide, he has left the son, indeed the family, with the reality of death, and facing it. Even that terrible scar is an organic gift spat out from his role; and what I am talking about here is roles, not what is or is not "appropriate" behavior. From my memory, such things as that are purely for gentlemen and not part of my experience.

Today, we try to talk a lot about all of this in terms of an initiation that must take place between fathers and sons, and as we all know, most initiations are painful and disorienting by design and definition. Sometimes I think that perhaps it's the knowledge that there is so much that *can't* happen between people which turns out to be the real essence revealed within the lack of recognition that only a certain few things can be shared directly, and even these only by outrageous, nonsensical gesture that might include all sorts of unconventional, surprising, and even shocking behavior. The meaning? There are no straight lines in life, and the phenomenal world is unconditionally unconditioned. It's raw and wild. With Dad out of the picture, this is the dreadful wisdom of the wound. From this ugly cut of primal insult comes oozing the immensity of one's loneliness and total separation, and then, if you have survived and have been rendered haplessly honest by this trauma, you are finally set free into a world of your own determination.

No doubt, this all may sound rather dramatic, and when put in mythic terms it is. But you know, I think the spirit of life really has much slyer dynamics than are contained in mere tribal campfire tales about this chimera of growing up. Notwithstanding a genuine poetic and collective unconscious, modern family evolution is less dramatic and thus even more insulting in its galling demonstration than a white man's reconstruction of an aboriginal dream. Though myth helps to organize our romantic image of ourselves, in real life, it is about as useful as a bidet in a gorilla cage.

It was a long time before I actually read my father's work. I had to read him in school, of course, and I liked and still like the short stories. They were fun, but it was all rather like hearing him talk after dinner. I accepted his genius for storytelling as an environmental given, bordering on the pedantic. This now happens to me with my children, and it kind of hurts.

Though he would never say it, I know that not taking his work as completely seriously as even a stranger might, hurt my father. But what can you do? Take away your kids' allowance if they don't read your stuff? Still, it hurts. It creates a stew. Though I don't do it as long or as deeply as my father, I can begin to brood about it sometimes. I think what a waste that my kids don't know the exquisitely wise and subtle techniques of mind that I use just to get through the day. If they did they would be so impressed, so proud. They would show me so much respect and wonder out loud at my many accomplishments. They could learn so many wonderful things from me. I could teach them much if I only had their undivided attention. But no, the ingrates think they know it all. They will undoubtedly be sorry after I'm dead and unavailable to them; when they realize what treasures they were missing. Just being close to me was a blessing that went the way of broken toys.

Yup, I know what it was like with my dad. I read his letters and see how his resentments closed in on him. The fact is that I am sorry, and I probably did miss a lot. But then again my father's temperament couldn't handle anything like undivided attention. Certainly I can't. That kind of scrutiny might reveal that most the time we are full of shit, running on fear and educated lucky guesses, in art as well as life.

Some things did get through though. Today I feel that sifting amongst the little things, the almost unconscious things hold as much meaning and usefulness as the grand lectures and pronouncements that mostly served to point out the vast hypocrisies of parenthood.

The main problem in living out the convoluted setup of fathers and sons is that neither of us can know the exact character or mode for the transmission of family wisdom. On the average it is just as likely to be the least flattering and heroic exchange; not at all like some Hemingway-esque dialogue on an elephant hunt. After all, both my father and I were sensitive and easily injured. We were also mutually disrespectful and suspicious of the other through past experiences. Ours were reincarnate feelings resounding back and forth through dysfunctional generations and radiating in every direction.

My father and brother and I actually did go fishing together a lot, around Sag Harbor on Long Island. I learned a great deal, but not the things that Norman Rockwell might have had in mind. The signals were subtle and not intentionally sent, but they were picked up invisibly like a skin disease. These queer potentials and tics are the kinds of things that now my brother sees in me and I in him, though we only catch the shadows in ourselves. I learned, for instance, what a bad and really sloppy fisherman my father was, but most importantly, despite his earnest facade, I also learned how little he cared about being a good one. That was great stuff.

There were times when Dad just loved to catch things, and like all fishermen, he would talk to his slippery prey; scolding and advising them, sometimes complimenting them on their wily intelligence, or gloating at their foolishness for taking on such a keen mind as his; a storied master of predation. But slowly I learned that this alliance between fish and fisherman, even the so-called thrill of the chase, was not really the reason or the point of this, his almost daily endeavor. Basically it was a fraud, a fine and elaborately feudal style of daydreaming.

Sometimes Dad would work out problems he was having with his writing or his characters, or even his hysterically silly inventions, almost all of which he covered with glue and leather. When he thought I was old enough to understand and had my own little skiff, I remember that he told me that if I had something important to puzzle out, and if I was clever, if I didn't bait the hook even the fish wouldn't be able to bother me. Buying bait, on the other hand, was very, very important. His favorite was bloodworms.

My father would also wander around his workroom and whistle tunelessly with a whispery quality that was neither whistle nor "phew." Now I had inherited from my mother a near-perfect pitch and a fine musical sensibility, so this sort of thing would drive me absolutely crazy. When I asked him what he was doing to "The Yellow Rose of Texas" he would say defensively that he could carry a tune if he wanted to, but if he whistled in this way the melody wouldn't distract him. Distract him from what? From looking aimlessly for some sandpaper that he would use to mangle a piece of mahogany, so that he might free up his mind, or so he could figure out some new way to design a lure he could then cover with leather and glue to catch some fish, the hook of which he would not bait so the fish wouldn't interrupt his concentration.

With the exception of the business with the high chair, and a memory of him rubbing my face in dog shit when I was about three (I apparently let Willy, Dad's sheep dog, in the house when Father/trainer was out), I have many wonderful memories of my father when I was a child. In many ways, he was a secretive man, and this made him privy to the secret world of us kids. He could be extraordinarily helpful when I was in a special kind of trouble. For instance, right up until my late thirties I was a bit of a firebug, and once as a child I nearly burned my father's house down. Near the fireplace was an old-fashioned oil can that my dad used to ignite wet logs. I was forever playing with it, making designs in the dancing speculum of the flames which seemed to speak to me in black and orange calligraphy. At one moment, I tried to douse the little burning tip of the oil can out on the floor. I guess I had done this before successfully, but this time a lovely, almost invisible blue flame began to swiftly spread across the fine nap of the wall-to-wall carpeting. After admiring it for a second or two, I tried to stomp it out but the violet tide was too fast for me. I ran downstairs where my father was inventing something in the basement.

Despite the fact that my father had told me over and over again not to play with fire gods (my weakness for conspiring with them was infamous), I blurted out the truth of what was happening in the living room. With his help, we managed to get the situation under control before it had begun to eat the drapes as an offering. Relieved and exhausted, we sank to the sofa and looked at each other. After just a few moments, an expression came to his face which was almost immediately slapped on mine like fly paper which basically said, "Holy shit . . . Aunt Elaine is going to get home any minute."

Without any time wasted in redress, anger, or apologies, we went for the solution to what we imagined to be a heap of woe. Whether it was attained in his naughty youth or as an adult with a vivid understanding of feminine wrath at any violation of the Hearth Principal I don't know for sure, but Dad had obviously had practice with this sort of emergency. In an instant he had me working at the charred nap with a wire brush while he ran for the vacuum cleaner. Then, after opening the windows to get the smell of a tenement disaster out of the air, he vacuumed behind me while simultaneously spritzing the air with Florida Water, his all-time favorite cologne which he referred to as "Stink Juice." Almost miraculously, the red color of the carpet began to come back, though it was a touch too light. He solved this defect by going over it with a wet sponge mop which amazingly made it darker. As for the side of the leather lounge chair which had fairly well been melted up to the armrest, he spray-painted the frame a similar brown with a kind of camouflage stroke known to desert warfare. He then put a low brass table beside the chair blocking a clear view of this mess, and was sitting there smoking his pipe in feigned serenity as we heard the front door open at Elaine's return. I was to be seen flipping through the funny papers and stroking the poodle, Charley, in front of the new warming fire as if we were expecting Mrs. Kris Kringle to stop by for tea. When Aunt Elaine sniffed quizzically for a moment, and then left the room to start dinner, a breath of relief was the only statement my father *ever* made to me about the incident.

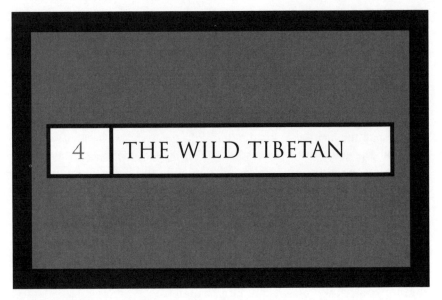

4 | THE WILD TIBETAN

NANCY

I met John in Boulder, Colorado, during the summer of 1975. I had been living a chop-wood-carry-water existence for the past seven years with my husband, Paul Harper, in the wilderness of British Columbia. We had left San Francisco and moved to the back of beyond to insure that our acid trips would be totally undisturbed. We lived on a commune while raising our two children, Megan, age six, and Michael, age three, and a seven-year-old indigenous foster child who had fetal alcohol syndrome.

As a native San Franciscan, I had shunned the Haight-Ashbury ritual of dropping acid around hordes of people. Paul and I longed for nights of endless LSD communion with the *Tao*, the Source, and the assurance that there would be no intruders to bring us down. So we lived two miles from either neighbor, which meant long treks during the winter when the logging roads weren't plowed. Snowed in for weeks at a time, we had all the comforts that didn't require electricity or running water. Stacks of firewood and spiritual books. Horses, goats, kerosene lanterns, and a propane stove. A battery-operated phonograph to play Traffic, the Doors, Dylan. A community of friends who lacked boundaries and sensibilities, but shared equally fried senses of reality along with the responsibilities of children, gardens, and animals. Unlike the media's caricature of the freewheeling hippie, we were on a rigorous spiritual quest that called for the destruction of our egos by severing all attachments. That meant letting friends borrow chain saws, vehicles, husbands, and wives. Often they would return broken, defective, unwilling to work again. Sometimes you had to go looking for them. *Have you seen my drill bit? Did my wife sleep here last night?*

I was the daughter of two award-winning San Francisco journalists. A musical prodigy from the age of six, when an IQ test explained the boredom I was experiencing, I skipped the second grade. At the age of thirteen, after refusing the opportunity to become a concert pianist (I had discovered boys), I made weekend pilgrimages to North Beach with my friends. We hung out at City Lights Bookstore, rapping with Lawrence Ferlinghetti and hoping to catch a glimpse of Allen Ginsberg or Jack Kerouac. Having received the finest public education possible at Lowell High, which is still among the top ten in the country, I was steeped in literature and the arts. I was going to be a writer.

In high school, nuns in the street would cross themselves when they caught sight of our black leotards and leather sandals. Flabbergasted, the jocks and social queens didn't know what to do with us. All they could come up with were unimaginative whispers of "whores." They were so unhip, we'd just roll our eyes. The school administrators sarcastically called us "The Lowell Intelligentsia" in the same way the Cultural Elite is sneered at today. Despite the bravado over Lowell's reputation, our academic rebellion threatened the administration. We rejected pep rallies and football games; we wanted to study poetry, art, and music. The girls' dean declared it illegal to wear the handmade sandals we bought in North Beach, feigning concern lest we get our toes stuck in a door. So we'd don tennis shoes to walk the halls, and wear the sandals in class. If we dressed too outrageously in handmade tunics, they sent us home, claiming we looked pregnant. Confident we were part of an epic in the making, we survived humiliation by sticking together.

Only one teacher, Maurice Englander, really understood us. He quietly approved of our plumage and offered his classroom as a safe haven during sports rallies and lunch periods to study poetry and classical music, thereby escaping the ubiquitous ridicule that echoed through the halls. Later, when the rednecks came to town wearing dashikis and love beads, looking to get laid, we resented the price we'd paid in bloody tears for those fashion statements.

At San Francisco State during my freshman year, we met other baby beatniks and gave birth to the hippies. My kids teased me about that. "How can you invent the hippies?"

"Someone had to and besides, I read it in *Rolling Stone*. Ben Fong-Torres said the first hippies used to gather at a table in the Commons at State." Kids think if it's in *Rolling Stone*, it's etched in stone. We were a bunch of rebellious, angst-filled teenagers, absorbing Kerouac's *Dharma Bums* and *On the Road*, along with the incredible magic that backlit San Francisco in the early sixties. Distilling the creative fervor of the Beat Generation with our Boomer adolescent laziness, we created a societal sea change. I was there for that, for the drugs and the psychedelic music, the Charlatans, Janis Joplin, and the Jefferson Airplane. In 1964 I transferred to Berkeley just in time for the Free Speech Movement, majoring in philosophy.

I met Paul Harper at the San Francisco Juvenile Hall, where we worked with hard-core delinquents. Disgusted with the Haight-Ashbury pond scum that surfaced after the Hell's Angels grisly debacle at Altamont, we were wary of the counterculture's assimilation. Visions of love and light were disintegrating into drug overdoses and runaway tragedies. We fled the city and spent a year living in an abandoned cabin on a mining claim two miles up a dirt road from Callahan, a tiny lumber town near Mt. Shasta in northern California, where Paul spent his childhood. That taste of country living sparked a yearning for unspoiled wilderness. The following spring, in a 1942 Ford truck loaded to the hilt, we immigrated to British Columbia. "You look like something out of *The Grapes of Wrath*," my mother said prophetically.

For the next seven years, we built our own houses and tended horses, goats, chickens, and gardens. When a social worker for the Canadian government came knocking on our door because she'd heard we had worked with problem children, we didn't have the heart to refuse her request to take in an indigenous foster child. Andy Johnson was a crippled, brain-damaged four-year-old who was barely toilet trained. He had a sweet temperament and a certain magical detachment from the phenomenal world that made him irresistible.

Embracing voluntary poverty, without electricity or running water, we started a commune and wrote our own rules. Rumors about us practicing black magic began to circulate in the Kootenay Valley where we'd settled, spread by jealous husbands and wives who'd lost their spouses to the mystique of our merry band. It was a period of great pain and growth, laced with wild spiritual insights and abject ignorance. We prided ourselves on being so far removed from the agonies of the real world that we didn't pay any attention to the Vietnam War, Watergate, or the moon landing, which we were convinced was a hoax.

Eventually, my smug complacency started to erode. I realized our rigid sanctions against mediocrity had us on the same treadmill as the bourgeois life we shunned. We were as attached to our trips, our tools and plumage, as a herd of male peacocks, or a gaggle of Junior Leaguers. My mother sent me *Meditation in Action*, written by a young Tibetan lama, Chogyam Trungpa Rinpoche, who had come to the States to teach Buddhism during the early seventies. The book resonated deeply in my soul. Increasingly miserable in my abusive marriage to Paul, I decided to spend a summer studying meditation with Rinpoche in Boulder, Colorado.

One of the greatest benefits of communal living was that parents could leave their children in the care of extended family. Our foster child had recently been removed from our home by the Canadian government when they passed a law that indigenous foster children had to live with indigenous families. While I was sorry to say good-bye to Andy, who had spent four years with us, I was tired of merely surviving on the land and desperately craved a new life. After seven years of austerity, although I was still passionately attached to the natural beauty of our four hundred acres, my city-girl nature was starved for more intellectual stimulation than radio and the daily mail run.

Inspired since my beatnik days by the mystical yearnings of Rimbaud, Lao Tsu, and Meister Ekhart, I intensified my spiritual crusade to find eternal truth and wisdom. As if answering a call, every child of that lineage, all the hip quester heroes traveled to Boulder that magical summer of 1975. They came to study with the young Tibetan Rinpoche at his newly founded Buddhist university, the Naropa Institute. Allen Ginsberg and Gregory Corso were there, as well as William Burroughs, Michael McClure, Kate Millet, and Baba Ram Das. It felt like the most happening thing since the birth of the hippies, a spiritual Woodstock. We hadn't felt such palpable magic since the early sixties. We were relieved to find we hadn't lost it.

A magnetic aura surrounded Rinpoche (a Tibetan honorific meaning "precious one" and pronounced RIM-po-chay). Infamously wild, in his mid-thirties, and wearing Saville Row suits, he smoked Raleighs, drank whiskey, ate red meat, and sampled the entire panoply of hippie pharmaceuticals. He'd had a son by a Tibetan nun and had run off with his blonde British wife when she was sixteen. As a holder of the exotic Crazy Wisdom lineage of Tibetan Buddhism, his outrageous behavior was traditionally viewed as teaching. His renegade flamboyance appealed to the artists, poets, and musicians who flocked around him.

Finally, we felt, here was someone who wasn't trying to temper our passions, while proclaiming the possibility of enlightenment in one lifetime.

Every other Eastern guru had admonished us to curb our intensity and deny our appetites in order to achieve detachment. I understood how attachment causes pain. If you encounter a dead dog on the road, you might feel a pang, but nothing like if it's actually your dog. Nevertheless, I could never get behind the command simply to cut desire. Rinpoche's method was to go into the depth of passion to wear out the samsaric impulses. *Samsara* is Sanskrit for the endless wheel of death and rebirth, the treadmill to which we slavishly return in our ignorance. It is the opposite of enlightenment. We liked his message. It gave us some more time to dally in the eternal youth zone that hallmarked our generation.

We had no inkling that his method would be so mutually painful. Disillusioned by the unhappy stasis of our parent's lives, we were inspired to chart our course far from their moral guidelines. Years later, when Rinpoche's behavior turned criminally insane and too abusive to raise our children under the umbrella of his trappings, some of us would come full circle and embrace the sanity of our roots with tremendous relief. By then, we were educated about the marks of a cult leader. By then, the traditional values of our childhood looked like an oasis of lucid simplicity. When I consider the extraordinary journey of this gifted man, who ended his life as a tragic alcoholic, I ultimately freeze in a morass of ambivalence. Men like Rinpoche and Johnny take you on their roller coaster, soaring from passion's heights to the depths of degradation. It's all a matter of being a spiritual gun moll, game enough to go along for the ride.

It was precisely this license to befriend our emotions that drew John to Rinpoche in 1971. He was living in Greenwich Village with the mother of his two-year-old daughter, Blake, whom he refused to marry. After a particularly ugly fight, he attended a talk by Rinpoche. Johnny lingered in the room long after the crowd left. Rinpoche was speaking with a few other students and finally turned to John, who blurted out, "Sir, I have a lot of aggression and anger that I cannot subdue." Expecting the usual rap about conquering passions with meditation and developing a peaceful state of mind, Rinpoche's reply startled him.

"You have a lot of anger? That is fantastic! Don't try to get rid of it. Express it, make friends with it. That is the only way to tame your emotions." John had been playing with Transcendental Meditation, a technique that attempts to suppress negativity. The problem with that is, where does it go? His friends were flocking to Spain with the Beatles and actress Mia Farrow. They had been admonishing John to control his drunken outbursts with TM and were less than charmed by Rinpoche's tolerance of John's anger. After all, he was supposed to be settling down now that he was a father.

Unfortunately, he flared with defensive rage at the suggestion that his emotions needed to be curbed. It takes maturity to harness the volcano that erupts from the soul of a true artist. Thanks to the alcoholic adults in his life, John's emotional growth had been arrested during his childhood. For temperaments like ours, Rinpoche's technique worked better than TM's amputation of desires. He urged us to explore our dark sides. By illuminating the shadows, confusion would dawn as wisdom. He warned us it was not a path for the fainthearted. To a standup guy like John, this was a challenge he could not resist.

Rinpoche's patience touched him deeply. That meeting was the breaking point of Johnny's old relationships. A wedge was driven between those who favored the Maharishi's blissed-out state and the Tibetan's barbaric technique of exhausting negativity. "Don't try to escape your emotions," he taught. "Wear them out like an old shoe." Later, when he wasn't allowed contact with Blake due to his drinking, John would claim "Indians stole my daughter."

We learned basic Buddhism that summer, starting with the Four Noble Truths. "The essential fabric of life is suffering," Rinpoche claimed in a lecture that summer. "There is an element of pain in everything. You cannot even begin to experience the notion of freedom until you acknowledge this background of suffering. It comes from nowhere, yet it's everywhere, because we want so much to like everything and be happy. We think that is our birthright. Suffering only ceases when we reach the realization that pain and pleasure are one. This one taste, with no duality, comes from the discipline of sitting meditation. Enlightenment lies beyond good and bad, past bewilderment and sorrow. It's different from happiness. The important thing is to connect with the pain, instead of increasing speed and aggression to get away from it, as you do in Western society. Only then can one attain equanimity."

We learned about the Buddha's teachings on the Three Marks of Existence. If suffering is the first Mark, it is followed by the constant presence of impermanence, the second Mark. It takes a fundamental act of bravery to admit this but we really do conduct our lives on very shaky ground. Nothing is intrinsically solid. Chaos and strife, little hypocrisies, never disappear. The problem lies in learning to live with ourselves. Uncertainties and fickleness plague us relentlessly. All that is left is the continuity of discontinuity. And within that lies the egoless state, the third Mark, able to function without solidification or credentials.

Rinpoche proclaimed that learning at Naropa would be based upon a student's experience and state of mind rather than memorization and regurgitation. As veterans of top universities and a variety of acid trips, this was welcomed. Traditional schooling frustrated us, and now Rinpoche, who was supposedly enlightened, confirmed our attitudes as no one else had.

Despite the superstars, Rinpoche insisted there was nothing special about Naropa. Through the process of slowing down, practicing our sitting meditation, and feeling the haunting quality of impermanence, we would develop a new way of looking at things. Newer than acid, with none of the psychedelic fallout? We were ready for that! Many of us were parents with young children and although we were still into peak experiences, we were looking for a little less excitement. All-night acid trips lose their appeal when crying babies wake you early in the morning.

Rinpoche held up a fresh mirror, a way to get to know ourselves. His meditation technique, taught by the Buddha, was simply to sit quietly, follow the breath and notice how thoughts arise and fade. He gave us a magnifying glass to look at all the hidden crannies we rushed to ignore. We were encouraged to slow down and make friends with the process of our thoughts. There was no promise of a magical mystery tour. He scoffed at the aggressive search for religious highs. During his nightly lectures, he would challenge us in an impeccable Oxford accent: "When your mind stops revving, you might feel like a grain of sand in the Gobi desert, majestic and simple. At that point, you can cultivate a sense of precision. Your mind will click into how to deal with the situation at hand with little confusion." For the refugees from Leave-It-to-Beaver-land, we fervently aspired to meet his challenge. Having watched our parents suffocate in their attempts to avoid suffering, we craved the heroic state of victory over ego-driven futility. Rinpoche's brand of enlightenment had a gutsy quality that blended well with our increasingly grim view of the world. In that post-Kennedy assassination era, we were realizing our generation wasn't going to change much of anything. The notion of individual salvation was extremely inviting.

When Rinpoche told us to view the entire phenomenal world as our friend, he appealed to our vestigial love-generation taproot. By transplanting this radically new outlook into our hearts, we could generate compassion, wakefulness, and the ability to be gentle. *Bodhicitta*, the essence of the Buddha, was the fruition of an awakened heart, arising from the confusion of pain and aggression. Enter *Bodhisattva*, that enigmatic term we'd learned from Kerouac, who wrote of mystical saints dwelling in an eternal present, with a Christlike compassion for all beings. We were offered Bodhisattva vows, a commitment to an endless cycle of rebirths, until the last sentient being in the universe is enlightened. As Rinpoche described the qualities of a Bodhisattva, the openness and clarity, the spontaneity and tenderness, we felt like we'd come home.

And then Rinpoche delivered the final coup. History had confined our literary heroes to the *Mahayana*, or Middle Way of Chinese, Japanese, and Korean Buddhism. Rinpoche was the most brilliant pioneer of that passage. He transmitted the highest teachings of Tantric *Vajrayana* Buddhism in a language we could understand. Previously held secret behind the fortress of snow mountains surrounding Tibet, these teachings were considered dangerous if not transmitted by a Tantric Master, a guru who works directly with the student. Vajrayana practice requires the personal experience of initiation and empowerment directly from a teacher who provides an oral transmission of the teachings, the *dharma*, along with secret mantras and ritual practice.

Rinpoche carefully studied his Western students, their particular hangups, their attractions and addictions. Unfortunately, that study eventually caught him in his own wringer. Twelve years later, he would die of one of the worst cases of acute alcoholism and drug addiction I had ever seen. And I knew, because by that time I was working in a silk-sheet rehab center in La Jolla, California, and John was lying in some gutter in the Los Angeles Asian ghetto, having succumbed to *his* inability and unwillingness to curb *his* instincts. As they say in AA, it took what it took. Rinpoche's drinking himself to death served to wake John up to his own hell-bent; shortly after that he got sober for good. So who's to say who was wrong and what really worked? Rinpoche emanated from a lineage called the Crazy Wisdom gurus, commonly misunderstood by the Western mind. In this tradition, the teacher imparts his lessons through outrageous actions. Later, when John and I lived in Kathmandu, Tibetans would tell us in hushed tones how fortunate we were to have Rinpoche as a teacher. "Oh, he very enlightened being. He drink a lot, right? You no worry about that. All Trungpas drank."

Rinpoche was the eleventh incarnation in the succession of Trungpas. However, the others had lived within the confines of Tibetan monasticism. In America, Rinpoche was on his own, in a jungle of Western temptations that the others had never encountered. Years later, in 1989, our friend the Dalai Lama told us privately that he would never trust a guru who claimed, as Rinpoche had, that he could turn alcohol into an elixir. "Changing religions is very difficult," he said. "I do not advocate converting from Judeo-Christian traditions to Tibetan Buddhism. It is very difficult to understand a religion that is not of one's cultural heritage. One must examine the teacher with the utmost scrutiny. There are many charlatans."

In the early days, Rinpoche mirrored our wild ways. As we matured, he lost his hold over us. Eventually John and I voiced strong moral objections about the irresponsibility of Rinpoche's teachings. The story of that harrowing journey contains grave admonitions about the methods and madness of certain Tibetan lamas. Now that Tibetan Buddhism has become chic, the hottest new religion, I have concerns about how these gurus come without operating instructions. Far removed from papal constraints, their freewheeling style usually results in severe abuses of power and sexuality.

I still don't have a clear answer to the paradox of Rinpoche's life and death. Sometimes I think he was just a garden-variety addict who died of his disease. Did he purposely drink himself to death so that we would quit depending on him? Did we kill him with our greed and manipulation as we clamored to be near him? The Tibetan party line is that the guru takes on the diseases of his students, and most of us were full-fledged addicts when we met him. There was a depth to the experiences I had with Rinpoche, similar to the chaos I went through with John, which taught me that sometimes the only answer is a silent dwelling in the grey area beyond right and wrong. Nothing is either black or white. It just is. And that does not excuse anything.

In the end, the final proclamation of a guru's worth can be found in his students. Those who remain loyal to Rinpoche's vision display the pathetic lack of identity found in every cult. They are unhappy pod people who toast his posthumous brilliance with pretentious, self-aggrandizing platitudes. Denying his abuse of power and his rampant addictions (a $40,000-a-year cocaine habit, along with a penchant for Seconal and gallons of sake), they exhibit symptoms of untreated codependents. In order to restore our sanity, John and I had to distance ourselves physically and emotionally. In that heartbreaking process, we were forced to acknowledge those qualities in us that were attracted to the cult of Rinpoche's personality in the first place. Yet Rinpoche's definition of a spiritual warrior is one who knows himself. And so, the fruition of our path was also the point.

5 | NAROPA NIGHTS

NANCY

The first time I saw John, I was sitting in the audience waiting for Rinpoche to show up for his lecture. Playing to the crowd's fevered anticipation of his black Mercedes pulling up to the curb, he was notorious for arriving often an hour late. The frenzy wasn't just about him. There was an equal amount of concern about who was seen with whom. There was enough artistic glitterati that summer to make every night feel like the Oscars. The beats dressed down and the trust-funders, just back from trekking in Nepal, outdid themselves in ethnic chic.

The magic in the air was never purely spiritual. My irritation with that dynamic grew through the years. I was not there to worship in the cult of Rinpoche's personality. I was intrigued by the man, but I was there to study his teachings, not to fawn at his feet. The unspoken competition and jockeying for position in the scene, as they called it, unnerved me. Later, I would learn that fixation is common in many guru scenes. While Tibetans have been trampled to death waiting to receive a blessing from an exalted lama, Westerners merely play out their high school rivalry for the best outfit and proximity to the cutest jock. I assessed that to be a trait of human nature, but it disturbed me. Not that I'm a saint. I didn't mind being in the thick of it, surrounded and courted by beat poets and tantric playboys. We could have all been standing behind the velvet rope outside Studio 54. There was enough money, hunger, and panache to get us in anywhere. As my marriage was disintegrating, I didn't exactly present myself as unavailable, but coming from a Peyton Place scene where spouse swapping was already rampant, my priorities were different. I was seeking spiritual guidance. If I'd been looking to get laid, I could have stayed home.

We never knew how Rinpoche would manifest. Drunk, wrathful, hysterically funny, or gentle and magnanimous. It would take me years to realize that this uncertainty was the normal plight of all children of alcoholics, or students of alcoholic gurus. The chaos of waiting and not knowing which, Lama Jekyll or Mr. Hyde, would walk through the door, resonated with our habitual anxiety and adrenalin rushes. We figured we must be in the right place.

That night, John made a dramatically late entrance with a wasted, frizzy blonde, goose-faced woman. As they walked through the door, John hauled off and kicked her in the shin. She winced with masochistic delight, whining in protest.

"What a charming couple," I muttered. Shocked and repulsed, I made a mental note to find out who the sadist was.

Friends were quick to point out that was John Steinbeck IV, as if knowing made them hip. He and his brother, Thom, were fixtures at the picturesque Victorian red-brick Boulderado Hotel down the street. In fact, someone told me they owned Le Bar, the tiny bistro off the lobby. I wondered why on earth Steinbeck's sons would end up owning a bar in a Colorado college town. Did they lack imagination or education?

Later that week, I ended up at Le Bar. The room was the size of a closet, with space for maybe five tables. It was *the* place to go after Rinpoche's talks, so it was packed that night. You would have thought it was Warhol's Factory, the way people were carrying on, with those peculiar bright flashes glinting off their self-consciousness about being some place special. When I saw John again and someone pointed out Thom, I got an immediate hit off the brothers. Suddenly the room and the noise dissolved as a chill ran down my spine. A voice from deep inside said, *John Steinbeck was a heartless father. His cruelty has crippled these boys.*

I immediately fell into a dialogue with him, as if he were the only person in the room. *What dark qualities caused you to ignore your sons and withhold your love? What is the family secret?*

John and Thom were thirty-something, arrested little boys, larger than life, drunk, raucous, and center stage. Maybe they did own the bar. Horrified, I watched John deliberately turn over his table on the guy sitting across from him, drinks flying everywhere, broken glass and scotch slopping onto the tiny hexagonal-tiled floor. Again, I was not charmed.

In fact, for the rest of the summer his antics repelled me. He'd always show up late, after Rinpoche had started his talk, so he could make an entrance. I learned he didn't own Le Bar, but spent so much time in it that people thought he did. Invariably he would raise his hand during the question-and-answer period. To my consternation, Rinpoche would call on him every time. He would go off on a ten-minute monologue that I could never follow because I couldn't get past my irritation with this guy who was so obviously charmed by his own mind and the sound of his voice. (It *was* uniquely deep and sexy. Paul once said that John's voice sounded like it came directly from his balls. That was before we got together. After that, Paul would have never been so complimentary.) John was always drunk, so his questions would be horribly circuitous.

"Not him again," I hissed to Paul, who was down for a visit. "I hate when he does that."

"No, that cat asks good questions." I was appalled that anyone had the patience to make sense out of John's haze. I only felt exasperation.

Toward the end of summer, on my way to a party, I accidentally bumped into a car parked behind me. It was a new Mercedes and its grill melted like butter. Shaken, I placed my phone number under the wiper blade so the owner could contact me. Upset by the accident, I winced as John gravitated to me instantly as I entered the house. We had never been introduced and this obvious drunk was the last person I felt like encountering. "What a wonderful shirt!" he thundered, grabbing my sleeve. "Where did you get it? It looks handmade. It's fantastic!"

He went on and on about the color and the material, a silky tropical print.

Oh God, what am I going to tell this guy? I got it at the Salvation Army and I'm too flustered to make up a lie. What's Steinbeck's son going to think? That I'm a refugee from the backwoods? Yeah, it's handmade, it's homemade. I paid a dollar for it and he'll probably think I'm just some poor hippie chick from the sticks and oh, I wish he'd just disappear and let me by.

"I got it at the Salvation Army," I confessed, cringing.

"From the Salvation Army? Really? That makes it perfect! You shop at the Sally Ann? That is so hip!"

Suddenly, all my preconceptions stopped. *This guy isn't a snobby rich kid. He has no pretensions. He's funky enough to know that shopping at the Salvation Army is hip, not embarrassing. He groks this shirt. He wants to wear it himself!*

I slipped past him, looking anxiously for a place to collect myself. I ducked into the powder room and looked in the mirror.

What is going on? Accidents don't happen. That crushed grill meant something. And what a surprise to find out this guy who's been irritating me all summer is one of the more real people I've met in Boulder. He's like a wildcat. His life force is megawatts higher than anyone I've ever met.

Bewildered, I felt a strange energy welling up inside me. I recognized fear, but there was a deeper feeling of seeing my future flash in front of me. Sheathed in banter, his sharp claws had swiped clean through me. I didn't know that I had just experienced Johnny's most memorable talent, the uncanny ability to meet your mind. He could stop you in your tracks, like a tiger leaping out from its triple-canopy cover. That is what Rinpoche had been talking about. You're going along with this great discursive story line about your life, and you encounter these mind stoppers and suddenly there's a huge gap in what you've been telling yourself about your world. The secret was to explore the virgin territory in that gap, where you can find your true essence, stripped of affectation and false beliefs.

John had terrified me. I left the party and deliberately avoided him for four more years.

6 | CHATEAU LAKE LOUISE

NANCY

Reluctantly, as Naropa ended and the boys of summer fled Boulder, I returned to British Columbia in August 1975. My world had been blown apart, not only by the young Tibetan renegade, but by lovers and new friends. I could not wait to get back to Boulder. I told Paul I was moving there, with or without him. Weary of lazy, posing hippies, and starved by seven years of austerity and cultural isolation, I wanted to return to civilization, running water, and electricity. Paul had connected with Rinpoche during his visits and was eager to come with me. We sold the horses and chickens, boarded up the house, loaded up the kids, and by Thanksgiving we had moved to a cottage in the mountains above Boulder.

Paul and I survived four years while I progressed in the study and practice of Buddhism. He found a lucrative job selling cars at a Honda dealership. Soon he was wearing three-piece suits and making outrageous amounts of money. We lost our hippie vestiges, drove a brand-new car, and moved to the poshest street in town, across from Rinpoche's mansion.

It wasn't a good life, but there was definitely a thrust to it. Paul's drinking progressed to the point where he was in blackout most nights. He worked fourteen hours a day, six days a week, and watched football when he was home. After our divorce, on Sunday afternoons I'd get phone calls from his second wife, weeping because he forgot her birthday or was ignoring her. It was like looking down a hall of mirrors as I remembered the tears I shed trying to get Paul to relate to the kids and me. I could only sympathize with the heartbreaking bleakness she'd found in him.

I was raised in a family where no one spoke much, which might explain my initial attraction to Paul, who replicated those family dynamics. I never learned how to play with children; no one had ever played or read to me. Raised by a depressed, alcoholic harridan who screamed at me daily for hours, I had few resources for being a loving mother to my children.

My mother, Anna Sommer, had been an intrepid girl reporter in San Francisco during the Depression. The darling of the front page, she chose to abandon her career when she married the handsome crime reporter who wrote at the desk opposite hers. Coincidently, they both worked at the *San Francisco News* when that paper hired Steinbeck to research migrant workers in the San Joaquin Valley, which later became material for *The Grapes of Wrath*.

Like Steinbeck, my father tried to cage the bird. Both men were left with unhappy, creatively repressed women who turned to alcohol and bitterness in order to metabolize their unfortunate choices. Anna was forty years old when I was born; my childhood spanned the years between her raging PMS and menopause. Later, I discovered I had been molested as a baby by my father, until the age of three.

I desperately tried not to replicate those hideous family dynamics. I loved my children deeply and when I saw the fantastically creative, joyous parenting skills John exhibited when he met Megan and Michael, I knew we had a shot at ending generations of dysfunctionality. I learned how to just be with the kids, to hang out with ease. He had a way of making you feel so cozy, like there was nothing he'd rather be doing than lying around, making jokes, being silly, telling stories. He called us The Etruscans, like those you see on vases, in various states of repose.

"It's Giggle-Snort Time," he'd announce, patting the bed. "Come on up. Let's cuddle. Let's pack!" And the kids and I would be like dogs, lying around with those goofy grins on their faces when they pant, relaxed and happy. I think he must have learned it from Gwyn, who had a fabulous sense of humor. John and Thom inherited her comedic genius, with rubber faces, noises, and wicked, pee-your-pants monologues.

In the scene, a woman's catchet was based on a pretty face and her gameness. When asked to take a series of high-profile jobs, I went along for the ride. I started working at the Naropa Bookstore, selling dharma books, along with various Oriental tchotchkes like Japanese ikebana vases for flower arrangement, incense, and Tibetan iconography. Rinpoche encouraged the study of various oriental arts, painting, archery, and calligraphy. His wife, Diana, was training for the Olympics in dressage, and I took lessons at her equestrian academy. She was the only woman ever accepted at the Spanish Riding School in Vienna, where she rode the famed white Lipizzaner stallions.

Rinpoche began urging me to attend his annual seminary. To be eligible, you had to sit a *dathun*, thirty days of rigorous meditation, from 6:30 in the morning until 9:30 at night. They were held at Rocky Mountain Dharma Center, our rugged land in the Northern Colorado foothills. During those fifteen hours, participants were instructed to practice Functional Talking, things like "Please pass the salt." You also had to do a ten-day retreat in an isolated cabin. Retreatants spoke to no one, except for a visit from a meditation instructor, usually a guy who tried to seduce the women. Without saying a word, there's a way you can let them know you're not interested.

Meditating for ten hours a day, I loved the solitude. I took long walks in the back country. Once I ran into a horse in a frozen field and we stood looking at each other, lost in white silence.

You could roam all over the Rockies up there and no one would ever find you. My heart was still in the wilderness then. The seclusion was delicious. Ten minutes later though, back in the cabin, I'd be dreaming about a steak dinner at the roadhouse in the little town an hour away. My mind bounced around; one minute I'd be raving on about how much I love being alone, and the next I'd be sobbing out of loneliness. Someone carved ALONE above the door, and someone else put a B in front and a Y at the end so it also read BALONEY. That said it all about how the mind works.

Having fulfilled the prerequisite classes, *dathuns*, and retreats, I was ready to attend seminary. Each year, seminary was held at a different deserted-for-the-season hotel willing to accept revenues from four hundred Buddhists who could pay well for the facilities. *Vajradhatu*, the Buddhist organization, had not found a hotel yet. I remembered passing Chateau Lake Louise with Paul one winter, boarded up like something out of *The Shining*. I suggested it as a possibility to Rinpoche and shortly after there was a phone call from him saying they'd gotten the place.

There were usually three hundred and fifty students and a staff of fifty older students who did all the teaching, administration, and cooking. Although Rinpoche's lectures and the classes were the framework, the primary focus of seminary was on partying and sleeping around. If a husband or wife went alone, they would invariably have multiple affairs. John used to say, "You could power all of New York City on the calories it takes to sweat out those three months, if you happened to be the one who stayed home." Those who remained faithful, and therefore abnormal in our jaundiced eyes, were often miserable and lonely. Monogamy was an anathema. Couples who attended together (and didn't sneak around behind each other's backs) were considered pitifully enmeshed. They treated parents who brought their children like lepers, and relegated them to a separate dining room. It all seemed blissfully acceptable then, but now I shudder at the unspoken dynamics of our cruise through the sexual revolution.

Recent studies about cults show that control is gained by the encouragement of either celibacy or promiscuity. Rinpoche implied that extramarital affairs were a direct path to enlightenment. His underlings claimed the practice of monogamy was foreign to Tibetans, as was jealousy. That is simply not true. When John and I later lived in Kathmandu, I watched the wives of lamas who fooled around. I saw the women's wistful pain.

As our role model, our guru had a wife and a different woman every night. If a student were upset, sometimes Rinpoche would tell him to either meditate, drink, or get laid, as if any of the three would liberate equally. It was a razor's edge that cut both ways. We were supposed to be ridding ourselves of clinging ego trips in order to cultivate detachment. The desire for stability, trustworthiness, and peace of mind was dismissed as unenlightened weakness. Eventually, like many women who survived the sexual revolution, I woke up to the insanity. When I found fulfillment in John, I had no need to wander outside my marriage to satisfy my intellectual, emotional, and physical appetites, as I did with Paul.

Rinpoche did not attract me; I refused his advances. I had enough men in my life. Right from the start, Johnny and I decided we were through with affairs. "When your wife sleeps with the guru, you both get screwed," he'd laugh. Other men paled in comparison to John, so there was never any temptation. Ironically, it took someone as outrageous as him to tame me.

A month before my departure for Lake Louise, I started to make arrangements for the children, whom I would be leaving for ten weeks. I found a nanny to care for Megan and Michael, who were six and nine years old at the time. I worried about leaving them alone for three months. If I knew then what I have since learned about child development, or realized how much they'd miss me, I would never have gone. Rinpoche encouraged us to cultivate detachment toward our children, another mark of a cult. My meditation instructor once accused me of hiding behind my kids when I refused to leave them with baby-sitters and do volunteer work. You were supposed to practice meditation, attend classes, and then do a lot of feudal peasant-type work for the organization "in order to progress along the path." I hated working for no pay, and I did use the kids as an excuse to avoid answering phones or stuffing envelopes at the community center. They acted as if the more enlightened you became, the better the volunteer jobs would be.

Rinpoche succeeded in the monumental undertaking of transplanting Vajrayana Buddhism from Tibet to the West. However, the foundation of his practical experience was based on a primitive, patriarchal, monastic tradition that was completely ignorant of Western values. Wisely, he didn't try to force us into the narrow confines of a monastic lifestyle, as some gurus did. Instead, he created a secular practice. Unfortunately, he presented himself as an authority on areas over which he had no expertise, such as child rearing and family dynamics. We blindly followed the piper. His dalliance with Western pharmaceuticals soon blossomed into full-fledged addiction that clouded his judgment. Although his drinking and sexual exploits were never kept secret, his staggering coke habit was well concealed from his students. Huge mistakes, too many broken hearts, far too much abuse would all trickle down like toxic rain on the heads of those children we so blithely left at home. Having no idea what lay ahead, I was on my way back to Canada, completely unaware that my life was to change forever.

As was John's, who was coming from a Hollywood burnout, where he pretended to make movies, but was really doing not much more than drinking a fifth of scotch a day to cover up a burgeoning inadequacy. He was beginning to notice that his youth was flying away and things would never again come as easily. Of course, he had to arrive fashionably three days late to create a stir. I was walking through the dining room after class and saw him huddled in a corner with Johnny Meyer, another infamous bad boy with an equally wild reputation for breaking hearts. They had their heads together, snickering. I took one look at the energy between them and thought, *Damn John for being here. He is going to ruin everything.*

Johnny Meyer's room was directly across from mine and John spent a lot of time there. When I'd walk down the hall to my room, they'd invariably emerge from Johnny's. I dreaded meeting them. John would always

ogle me and I felt uncomfortable. His glances were penetrating. They conjured up the fear he'd sparked in me four years earlier when he grabbed my
shirt. His reputation did intrigue me, however, so I'd send back a wash of
coolness mixed with hostility that said *I dare you*. I never gave much thought
to his famous father; I sensed he had been cut from his roots, orphaned.

Johnny Meyer's father owned the first failed California S&L. He and
John Steinbeck IV had haplessly adapted an idle rich lifestyle. They were
black sheep scions, wealthy when the inheritance checks came in but comfortable sleeping in gutters when the money ran out. Those funds, combined with their alcoholism, prevented them from ever getting their lives
together. Cynical about their birthrights, John and Johnny were unimpressed by wealth or fame. The knife cut both ways; they had also turned
their backs on tremendous advantages. They shared the disapproval of their
successful fathers as well. Johnny's family was extravagantly eccentric. He
once gave their pet chimpanzee a hit of acid. After that, the chimp attacked
him on sight.

The first month of seminary was lonely. I ran the bookstore that sold
textbooks, so I met a lot of people and I knew everyone's name. I flirted a
lot. Flirting was encouraged in the scene. "Flirt to be real," Rinpoche often
said. We would dally after his late-night lectures, a prelude to going upstairs
to your room or his room, if one of you could get rid of your roommate. A
chosen few had rooms of their own. I thought I'd died and gone to heaven
when I discovered I was one of those. Students who had major responsibilities like running the bookstore got preferential treatment.

There is a traditional party at seminary between the Hinayana and
Mahayana periods of study. By the end of the Hinayana session, which
emphasized individual salvation and the solitary path of a yogi, students
are notoriously ready to break loose from the discipline of no drinking,
functional talking, hours of sitting meditation and memorization. They
bussed us into the nearby town of Banff for the day, where we could shop
and have our minds blown by the real world. The plan was to meet at a
disco that evening and then be bussed back to the Chateau.

I felt dressed to kill in red that night, dancing with abandon. Breathless, I sat at one of the tables to rest for a second. I'd closed my eyes and
when I looked up, there was John standing above me. "You're really hot,
Mrs. Harper," he said with a twinkle. Flustered, I recalled the last time he'd
accosted me over my Salvation Army shirt. *Oh, God, is he going to start in
again? What does he mean by "hot"? What does he want? Why can he reduce
me to a driveling idiot?*

"It is rather warm," I said defensively.

"No, I mean hot, like the best dancer here. Don't you know every man watching you has a hard-on?"

Blushing, I laughed into his eyes. Then he made a very peculiar and symbolic gesture that always touched us in later years. He knelt beside me and buried his head in my lap. He left it there. *What is this? What do I do now?* Suddenly, coyness and flirtation dissolved. The room disappeared. I found my hand stroking his hair and then his back. It was just the two of us, with time stretching infinitely. *This man needs your love in order to fulfill his destiny.*

Delirious for a few seconds, I had no idea what hit me. Later, John's brother, Thom, told me that when knights surrender their colors to their fair ladies—Lancelot to Guinevere—they kneel and bury their heads in their beloved's lap. An ancient chord of memory was struck between John and me, of many shared lifetimes and the thread of a common myth that ran through them all. It was a sacred gesture met with deep emotion, a symbol of our eternal love.

Then John asked me to dance, which surprised me. I thought he'd be way too cool for disco gyrations. I was right, he basically stood in one spot and held me, pinning my eyes with his twinkle. Several times, guys would try to cut in but he refused to let go of me. I could tell music affected his senses, which I took as a good sign.

And then, as if we were on overload, we parted. He went back on his assigned bus and I went over to mine and chose to sit alone in the last row. Staring out at the night sky, the moonlight on snow mountains, the laden fir trees flying by, I suddenly felt an unearthly sweetness sweep over me. I thought about love all the way home, love as a sacred emotion, love of sentient beings, bodhisattva love. I wasn't really thinking about John specifically, just the spiritual ideal and definition of love.

During the next several days I decided to check John out before I made any decisions. Watching him walk across the shrine room one rainy afternoon I sensed that *this guy has seen war. He's seen death. He is uncomfortable only with life. There is deep despair in him and there is a quest.* I sensed shame, vulnerability, and abundant humor. I wanted him.

Fortunately, I was not predatory by nature, and I soon learned that John did not respect aggressive females. For the past decade, his feminine ideal had been a lovely older Vietnamese woman whom he'd met in Saigon. She was a recurring compensatory fantasy when his girlfriends became insane reflections of his drunken mother's tirades and promiscuity.

He valued demureness, grace, and reticence in a woman. "I have never been so drawn to a woman since Thao," he proclaimed six months later, and I knew I had won his heart.

Every afternoon, I could feel John watching me from the hotel lobby as I chatted with customers in the bookstore. Sometimes he'd come in and leaf through the books, eavesdropping on my patter. "You had a fast mouth and an easy laugh. I knew you were my kind of girl."

A few nights later, John walked up to me while I was seated at the tables and flashed his most charming smile. "Do you have a quarter I could borrow? I promise to return it at two o'clock this morning in your room!" He told me later that he thought that was a pretty good line and sometimes it even worked. Bemused, I gave him a quarter, chuckling, "Don't bother waking me up." Whereas all the other guys' come-ons were painfully awkward, John's teasing was intoxicating. There was something deeply sensitive about him, simultaneously vulnerable and wary. Intrigued, I silently let him know it would be safe to come closer.

The next afternoon I was selling tickets to the formal banquet as part of my bookstore gig. I was seated behind a table in the lobby when I looked up and saw John standing in line. It was an event where people were encouraged to go as couples. *He's the only one I want to go with.* He approached me with that seductive grin.

"Since you're selling the tickets, I'll only buy one if you will be my date."

The banquet was a week away. I was delirious with anticipation. A few nights later I was sitting at the tables in the dining room, where everyone gathered after Rinpoche's talks. A guy named Gordon asked me if I wanted to go for a walk but I declined. John must have been listening. He strolled over and said, "I hope you don't turn me down for our date the way you just turned Gordon down for that walk."

"Not a chance," I laughed. "In fact, let's go!" The icy path around Lake Louise was slippery, so I had to hold on to his arm. The magic was instant. He clowned around and teased me. We laughed till we were dizzy. As I clung to him, he pressed my arm with every step. We were tight from the start. There was no awkwardness, no sense of getting to know him. It was easy and familiar and delicious. We made friends quickly and deeply. *This man has an enormous heart.*

I was wearing a red fox jacket and he asked me what kind of fur it was. When I told him, he took me in his arms and laughed, "You're my fox!"

"I called my grandmother and told her where I'll be for the next two months," he announced.

"Lake Louise?" she'd shouted. "That's where I spent my honeymoon. What the hell are you doing there? There is nothing to do there but fuck!" John painted a picture of her flamboyance, this maternal grandmother who seemed to be on very intimate terms with him, but he never mentioned his parents or brother. I didn't ask. We laughed a lot about the personalities of our fellow seminarians and discovered that the same traits irked us in similar ways. Though he could make merciless fun of the ones he called "pompous asses," his warmth, his capacity for intimacy, his unpretentiousness and spontaneity were startling.

As he walked me to my room, I wondered if he'd try to come in and what would follow. I really wanted to savor the courtship and apparently he did, too. He kissed me briefly and left me at the door. I was charmed by that old-fashioned touch. Later he would confide: "I wanted you to feel respected. You were, after all, a lady. I was very proud of my restraint." Considering that his friends had dubbed him "The Sex Czar," I was flattered that he hadn't tried to make me a notch on his belt.

We were assigned jobs on the day of the banquet. I purposely found myself in the kitchen with John, who was washing pots. I heard the conversations going on around him. One woman asked, "What's it like to be the son of a famous father?" I didn't hear his monosyllabic answer, but I sensed his discomfort. I was tearing up mounds of lettuce, lost in a bracero fantasy of the Salinas Valley. My mother was born in Monterey and we vacationed regularly in Carmel. I'd spent college summers living in Big Sur and loved Steinbeck Country with a passion. Although I had a million stories about my experiences there, I didn't mention them on our walk around Lake Louise. I'd played guitar with Jerry Garcia and Pigpen in the Salinas Greyhound bus station when we were in high school. I'd met movie stars and famous writers in Big Sur, but John and I didn't need to play name games. More than anything, he needed to be appreciated for being uniquely himself. I wished he could be in that kitchen without having his father dragged in. It was my first hint of how tiresome those encounters were for him. Through the years, as I watched hundreds of people ask that same question of John, I deplored their rudeness. Raised with a sense of old-world manners, I had been taught and learned on my own to treat fame as an unmentionable, like an affliction, or wealth.

During my seventeenth summer, when I worked at the Big Sur Inn, I often hitchhiked down to the hot springs, now known as Esalen, twenty miles south. One afternoon, an anorexically thin woman struck up a conversation with me as we sat in the baths. She asked about the local guys, whom she'd classified as mountain men types. I explained that they were mostly wounded loners, except for Henry Miller, who visited the inn on his motorcycle, and the guy I was madly in love with, who claimed to be the son of a French viscount. When she found out that I was hitching back to the Big Sur Inn, she offered to drive me. That was back in the days when they taped new car registrations to your window. As I was getting into her yellow Mercedes convertible, I noticed her name.

"You didn't tell me you were Jane Fonda!"

"You wouldn't have talked to me so freely if you'd known," she laughed.

Later that summer, as I wandered out on the patio on my afternoon break, I discovered a very attractive older man waiting to be served. When I offered to get him a cup of coffee, he asked me to join him. We sat for ages, talking about his race cars and what it was like to be seventeen in Big Sur. I went inside to get more coffee and my coworkers swarmed around me to ask what I'd been talking about with Steve McQueen. I was surprised, but when I joined him again, I never let on that I'd found out who he was.

Several days later, he returned for dinner with Jackie Gleason and Tuesday Weld. They had been filming *Soldier in the Rain* in Monterey. Tuesday asked me to give her a tour of the grounds, and Steve left me a huge tip. I never acknowledged their identity. Kim Novak became a regular and she, too, just wanted to be treated like one of us. Those experiences helped me cut through the awe that others felt about John. He seemed so alone, devoid of any connection to his father; all I could see was the pain it brought up.

Just before we left the kitchen, a guy staggered in. He drunkenly begged me to go to the banquet with him. John heard the commotion and came over. "Cool it, David. I'm taking her."

"Aw, come on, John. Let her go with me. I see this woman in the shrine room and she drives me crazy."

I sensed David's outburst was an omen and an indication of John's burden, which would eventually become mine. Over the years, people constantly tried to cross the boundaries of our relationship. I watched countless men and women get swept away by the headiness of charisma and fame. Forgetting their own good qualities and accomplishments, they wanted to *become* John or me.

I sang "Some Enchanted Evening" in the shower before I slipped into the long strapless silver evening gown that Megan called the "mermaid dress." We'd agreed to meet in the lobby, where everyone was gathered. I spotted John, elegant in his tuxedo, across the crowded room. I started to walk toward him but before I reached him, Sarah, my meditation instructor, strode up and hissed, "Be careful of John. He'll break your heart." I slipped away from her. *I don't think so. He's going to marry me.*

As if he'd overheard, another guy caught me and said, "John won't marry you. He has a girlfriend in Boulder."

"You're wrong, Ashley. Dead wrong," I laughed and flitted away.

That night set up an F. Scott Fitzgerald-type ambience that followed us through seminary and then for the rest of our lives together. Partly, the magnificent old Canadian Railway hotel and mostly John's old-fashioned style of courtship created a fabulous, romantic setting. We found ourselves in a long dreamy corridor of rapture, so deep was our enchantment. His charm, his wit, his urbane manners were hypnotic. We lingered in the lobby hours after the banquet was over, wrapped in each other's minds. People would join us and drift off, sensing the elegant web we were weaving between us. Toward dawn, we wandered up to my room. He sat on the bed and began telling me about his blonde seven-year-old daughter, Blake, whom he hadn't seen since she was two. He spoke about her birth in Vietnam, how he'd mixed her baby formula with water from the Mekong River. I was surprised to discover he was a father. He obviously had deep paternal feelings toward her, and a great deal of pain about the separation.

Something about the way he spoke of his daughter touched me to the core of my maternal instincts. I knew this man would become the father of my children even though they were already born. And something at that core told me to get naked and take that man into my bed without wasting another precious second. The silver mermaid dress slid to the floor.

NANCY

A seminary is traditionally ten weeks long. We fell in love with six weeks to go. Johnny moved in with me immediately and our room became a source of great curiosity. We were supposed to get up early and meditate all morning, which I usually did, but he slept till noon. While everyone ate lunch in the dining room, I would fix a tray for us and sneak up to the room. He loved waking up that way.

Candles, music, and sensuous delights were wasted on Paul, but John was enthralled. As a teenager, he fantasized about having a wife like Myrna Loy's Nora Charles in the *Thin Man* movies—intelligent, savvy, and insouciant. "You're a real man's woman," he'd crow with delight. Mystified by the girl-next-door appeal, I feared it led to a sexless marriage. My Russian blood and a steady diet of French and Italian movies created a more global sense of glamour for me. I did not fight the battle to become liberated simply to slap a girdle on the soft curves of true intimacy. Johnny and I were both romance junkies. We had a knack for making the world go away, especially in hotel rooms. We'd get so far out that an elevator ride to the real world was culture shock.

At seminary, after we'd finished eating, we'd stick the trays outside the door, as though we were expecting room service to pick them up. There was no room service, only fellow Buddhists who prepared the food and washed the dishes. Eventually we would carry the trays back down to the kitchen. Sometimes there were several stacked outside our door. We rapidly established the reputation that we were way too busy doing other things in that room to engage in mundane activities like taking the trays downstairs, let alone leave the bed.

We talked up a storm through languid, velvet nights and glorious dawns. I couldn't even stop to sleep. No one had ever talked to me like that, so intimately, with such depth. And the laughter! John made me giggle hysterically, especially at myself. After class, we could hardly wait to get back in the bed, make love, and start talking all over again. Endless stories, infinite comparing of notes taken on life. Theories, poetry, quick sketches of people we saw every day. It was as if we'd seen things out of the same eyes before we even met.

We drove the guys crazy on the other sides of the walls. They couldn't sleep because we never shut up. Sometimes at three in the morning, Johnny would shout a Martin Luther King-esque "I have a dream. I *have* a dream." It would echo down the hallway. That would usually elicit thumps on the wall from our neighbors but we were too convulsed in our giggles to hear or care. Ordinarily, I would have cared. But something had come over me and for the first time in my life I ignored all constraints. Johnny's insouciance made me feel deliciously wicked, totally alive. His love made me feel immortal. Experts make all kinds of predictions now about how long that heightened sense lasts in a relationship, but after twelve years of constantly being together, it never died. He always had the marvelously nurturing ability to wrap me in his arms and make me feel like a well-loved baby. There was a maternal tenderness about him that left me breathless.

On the morning before our first date for the banquet, I was standing behind the door to the meditation room, signing in, when John and Johnny Meyer walked by. They didn't see me. John started singing "Putting on My Top Hat" and he did a Fred Astaire soft-shoe for a few seconds before walking into the shrine room. I melted into a puddle. He had a black and white, forties movie-type charm, straight out of an art deco Manhattan apartment set, with a curved staircase and ice tinkling in crystal goblets. It was partly due to the way he'd been raised, but also he had an innate grace, an aristocratic nobility. His magnetism was extraordinarily captivating.

Our room became a gathering place for the curious, lonely, and sociable at odd hours, any hours. They said it was like a cross between visiting John and Yoko's Bed-In and the set of *Tom Jones*. By keeping the window open a crack, we created a windowsill refrigerator, complete with Brie, fresh fruit, and champagne. People commented that they'd never seen a couple have so much fun falling in love.

When we'd make the bed together, we'd start to feel sad, knowing the pink cloud would dissolve at the end of seminary. "I've never missed someone before saying goodbye," he'd say. "It's such a peculiar emotion. We've got to figure out a way to continue this in the real world." We weren't sure we could. He worried about breaking up my family and I waited demurely for him to ask if it were possible.

There were ominous notes, which I chose to ignore. One night I had gone back up to the room to study during a movie. I heard John and Johnny Meyer going into Johnny's room several times during those two hours. I couldn't figure out what they kept coming up there for, and then it dawned on me. How could I have forgotten their reputation? They were refilling their glasses. A chill crept over my heart. I recognized compulsion for the first time in my life and it scared me. But, what did I know? Did that mean John would be compulsive tomorrow? Foolishly, I thought probably not, because I loved him enough. Back then, we thought only skid-row bums were alcoholics; we knew nothing about the syndrome. It took three more years before I was driven to educate myself about alcoholism. By then, I had learned the hard way that women who are raised in alcoholic families continue to replicate the patterns of abuse until the cycle is broken through education about the disease.

Rinpoche had imposed a rule against drinking during those first two weeks, so I fell in love with a sober John. When the sanction was lifted, Johnny Meyer sang prophetically to me "call him irresponsible . . ." as we walked down the hall behind John. He was trying to warn me. Another friend asked why I was contemplating replacing a husband who worked constantly and drank on the weekends with a man who drank constantly but didn't work. I honestly didn't make the connection. I was so in love with John that I thought he would just naturally change if I asked him to.

Whenever we had an anniversary or on Valentine's Day for all the years to follow, we would repeat the litany of those events. It was the beginning of our myth, and it is in the beginning of every legend that tells a story of love.

"Remember when I came down the stairs and saw you? My heart jumped so violently I staggered?" he'd ask me. "Remember all the dawns, the rapture, the raps? Remember the time we were sitting with a group and someone said it's really hard to let go of an affair if the sex is particularly good."

"It's impossible," I had said, ruefully.

"I was shocked that you knew about the prison of great sex in a miserable relationship," he said later.

"It takes one to know one," I shrugged.

We discovered we had funny little things in common, like feeling anxious if there were no lemons in our room. "You never know when you might want to make the odd veal *piccata*," he'd muse. We were astonished at the subtle depths and amazing heights of our twinship.

John told me endless stories about his past. While he never spoke directly about the war, he spoke of his deep connection with the Vietnamese people. One time, he saw a bomb explode, cutting a peasant woman nearly in half. John held her as the life flowed out of her. He noticed a flicker of embarrassment because her body was exposed. Gently, he told her she was dying and to forget her modesty. That great generosity was the essence of John. When you woke up in the morning with him, you didn't feel like you had to rush out of bed to put on makeup and brush your teeth, acting like you barely had a body. Through the years, he'd often exclaim, "Look at you, without a speck of makeup. You are so fresh and gorgeous! I'm so glad you're not one of those women who thinks she has to put on a face in order to wake up next to me!" When a man whispers words like that, he holds your heart.

Throughout the hotel, the constant question became "What's going to happen after we leave here?" Many of us had been transformed by seminary affairs which were notoriously short-lived beyond those cloistered walls. Though John had a girlfriend in every port, he swore they meant nothing to him. As he revealed his romantic history, I realized he had never been alone for long. This was due in part to his mystique, but he also had a desperate need for a love object.

Thom tells the story of a sad winter day when Johnny walked into Le Bar after a fight with a girlfriend. Forlorn, he pulled up a stool, reached into his pocket, carefully placed a baggie on the counter and stared at it. Inside was a Siamese fighting fish, swimming in water.

"What's up with that?" Thom asked.

"It's the only love object left in my life," John said mournfully.

I had been trying desperately to accept the conditions of my marriage when I arrived at seminary, coming to the pitiful conclusion that perhaps I should quit asking for more than the kitty litter I got from Paul. *Maybe this is all I can expect. If the Buddha says the basic fabric of life is suffering, then I must be doing the right thing, because suffering is my middle name. Long-Suffering.*

And then I met John, who filled all the neglected spaces so beautifully.

He wanted to be with me. He loved being with me. He made me laugh, and best of all he got me to laugh at myself. His communicative gifts heightened the horror of Paul's grunts, snarls, and psychotic moods. When I saw the vast discrepancy between what the two offered me, I was determined to leave Paul. I had to create a space for John to join me and the children.

"I'm going to have a very exciting life and I want you to share it with me," he said. "Am I going to have to try to extract you from your family like a dentist pulling a tooth?" I promised him it would be easy. Beyond hope and fear, of which there were plenty, I could not imagine living one day away from him. It astounded him that I could make that leap with so little conflict, until he realized how starved I was in my marriage.

One afternoon, Rinpoche invited all the parents to bring their children to the shrine room for a blessing. Johnny and I watched the expressions, especially on the babies and toddlers. After it was over, alone in the elevator we exchanged a look that said it all. My children were already John's. Paul could never give me this new level of affection and intimacy, and I would never again settle for less. Later that evening, at the hotel shop, he bought little gifts for me to take home to Megan and Michael, among them toy birch-bark canoes, which he lovingly oiled so they would last in the bathtub.

Johnny had been deeply disappointed by other women. Concerned that I might change my mind once we were back in the real world, I sensed toward the end that he was preparing a tough skin. One morning, Paul called my room. John stormed out, slamming the door. I found him in the kitchen, pouring a glass of milk. He didn't want to admit he was jealous, so I let it go.

On the last night, I started packing while John was making the rounds, saying good-bye to friends. Johnny Meyer stopped by my room, looking totally freaked out.

"It's awful," he moaned. "Everyone is becoming who they were before they got here. It's like the pod people are taking over."

I knew he was right. I could feel it in myself. He was such an eccentric, Little Prince kind of guy. He told me he used to let himself in my room and watch me sleep because it gave him comfort. I never felt violated. He lived in another realm. That's why he was able to join me and John so easily during those precious early days.

It isn't just financial independence that lets you live outside the mundane world. It's a mind-set. It can be artistic genius; it can be criminal; it can be addictive, spiritual, or idly rich. Even before we met, John and I lived in a separate reality, another dimension. For the first time in our lives, we could share our private realms rather than hiding the heartbreak of our loneliness. He could take me along to the heights and depths of his fantasies. He was delighted to be transported into mine. That relief was tremendously liberating, like discovering a playmate who speaks your secret language after a lifetime of silence. We both knew this was not to be taken lightly.

Through the years we became convinced that we were part of a larger soul, a perfect circle, Siamese twins of the heart, our fates stamped with the same sealing wax. Both Geminis, eternally bound by admiration, respect, and awe. No matter how volatile our relationship became, there was always a shining polestar that would guide us back to our bedrock of unconditional love. "*Ye thuong*," John would croon to me. That's Vietnamese for "easy to love."

"I'm going to die first!" he'd tease.

"No," I'd protest. " I want to die first! Why should you be the lucky one?"

"Because you could live without me, but I could never live without you."

John and I developed a velcro twinspeak of language and vision. Through the years, Michael and Megan joined in our silliness, our private language and childlike play. That lovely gift of whimsy, which John inherited from his father, cemented our fractured family years after John's death. Although the kids now live two hours away from my house, we still find time almost daily to be zany on the telephone. Playful interchanges with adult children keep them hanging around for other things as well, like your interpretation of life's complexities. Before going out, we still say very solemnly to our dog, "Watch good the house," just as Steinbeck would say to Charley. We continue the Steinbeck tradition of anthropomorphizing our pets to a ridiculous point, carrying on conversations with them, dressing them in outlandish outfits. That joyous laughter, never heard when Paul was around, is the most precious legacy John left us.

8 PRINCE CHARMING THE FOURTH

NANCY

The last night of seminary, I poured John's clothes into his suitcases. We watched the dawn crown pink glaciers reflected in the morning glory lake. Clinging to each other, we prayed that our tender web would keep us connected after we dispersed like the Tibetan tent culture we emulated. Soon Chateau Lake Louise would be claimed by the tourists who'd peered in the windows and wondered what we were up to. After three months in that magical "Canadian Sunset" realm, we were all afraid to return to the real world and its wheel of monotony. John and I were particularly anxious because we wanted to be together, but we didn't quite believe we deserved it or that we could pull it off. In our hearts, like the song, we believed we'd see each other again, after fire and rain, and when we did, we would be just as close.

Johnny left early in the morning on a bus to the Calgary airport. I had to stay for several more days to break down the bookstore. I fell asleep to numb the pain of separation and freeze-dry the warmth of our bed. In the afternoon I went reluctantly down to the hotel lobby, dreading to see the changes. The silk-brocade shrine was dismantled. Our blissful, hermetically sealed world had disappeared, leaving only a garish floral pattern on the long empty stretch of carpet and the bright glare of glaciers outside.

John had promised to meet me in Boulder soon. I could tell he was terrified, already hardening himself to the possibility that I might write off our interlude as a fling and return to Paul, who was driving up to Canada in a new Mercedes he'd bought to woo me back. Paul had heard about my affair with John and he was trying to Band-Aid the past years of conflict. When we first met, he was a pistol, full of ideals and a natural leader. Excessive drinking had turned him cantankerous, killing my love for him. I had wanted to leave him for the past nine years, but I was afraid of being financially on my own; I wanted to stay at home to raise Megan and Michael. When John offered me a way out, I did not question whether I was going straight from the frying pan into his flame.

The ride back to Boulder with Paul was excruciating, except for listening to rock and roll after three months. John had warned me "that kind of media abstinence makes Barry Manilow sound like Puccini." Just before we parted, he showed me a *New Yorker* cartoon. Under a picture of a man driving a car and a woman staring out the passenger's window in abject despondency, the caption read: "Irreconcilable differences."

"Is it going to be like that?" he asked. It was, for a thousand miles, except the times Paul exploded. When it got particularly ugly, I called John and asked him to talk to Paul. John was terrifically cool. "Calm down and be a man about it," he told Paul. "You've got seven hundred miles ahead of you. Make sure you both arrive in one piece." Testosterone met testosterone and Paul listened.

Megan and Michael had missed me sorely. My absence took a toll on their psyches. They were sensitive, loving children. While I was away, their nanny had nurtured them as best she could, but the separation had traumatized them. I felt terrible; their short lives had already been filled with turmoil from Paul's drinking and our fights. I desperately wanted to give them a better life.

Three weeks later, John came to Boulder to check things out. Although Paul had been warned about our plans, he was not going to give in that easily. I picked John up at the airport, feeling human for the first time since we had parted. We went straight to the Boulderado. After a breathless reunion, he asked me to go to the corner liquor store. I felt like a blues song; my man was back in my arms. Walking barefoot and full of his love, I was on my way to buy him a bottle of booze. My life was complete and I was ready to die to keep it all just like that. When I got back to the room, John announced that he had sent me off on purpose so he could call Paul and arrange to meet him in an hour.

"I don't want to walk around wondering if he's going to attack me with a tire iron. I want to tell him I'm in love with his wife and figure things out, man to man. There's a whole family at stake here and I don't want to be cavalier about it." Impressed with his courage, I wished him luck.

They spent several hours together, while I nervously watched TV in the hotel room. *Suppose Paul convinces John I'm a bitch. Tells him about every knockdown fight we've ever had and blames them all on me. It might be all over between us. Suppose they just slug it out and one of them is dead.*

When he returned to the room, Johnny was excited. "Baby, you've got great taste in men!" he crowed. They had put on their best bravado and agreed to be chivalrous. Paul could see the kids whenever he wanted, and we'd be one big happy family. Paul told me he went home and cried that night. Our twelve-year marriage was over.

That summer of 1979, back in the real world, I started to see sides of John that I hadn't at seminary. One evening at sunset, we drove to the mountains. He was distant. Sensing a case of cold feet, I burst into tears. "Please have faith in us. I'm not going to hurt you. Or smother you."

"I guess it would be strange if I weren't a little daunted by the prospect of an instant family."

"Hey, I've got the same fears."

"You think I'm going to abandon you in a supermarket aisle while we're shopping for diapers," he teased.

Damn right. Here was this wild cat who had managed to stay unattached for lifetimes in his thirty-odd years and suddenly he was going to be a father and husband? Believing in him more than he did, I knew we could do it, especially when he met Megan and Michael.

We had gone to the annual Buddhist Mid-Summer's Day celebration, held in a mountain meadow above Boulder. Since I was staying at the hotel with John, Paul brought the kids. I had wandered off and found them sitting under a tree. Megan was playing with Ganesh, Rinpoche's enormous Tibetan mastiff. She was crooning to him, her fist buried in his drooling black mouth. Suddenly John appeared by my side. He studied them silently for a few minutes. I loved the way he would put his entire being into the Other, as if he were receiving a printout from his intuition.

"Megan's ease with that monstrous dog made a deep impression on me," he said later. "So did your utter lack of concern." It was an auspicious sign to him. Crystal, the mother of his daughter, had been terrified of dogs. "She transmitted that fear to Blake, which really annoyed me."

John was born in the Chinese year of the Fire Dog and he'd had wonderful relationships with them all his life, including his father's Charley. The thought that Crystal had taught his own daughter to fear Fido was a source of consternation.

"If I'd played a stronger role in Blake's life, I could have countered her mother's fear," he said ruefully.

Megan recalls that meeting vividly. "I felt that John was totally interested in *me*. Not *Oh, you're just a kid. I'm going to fake talking to you and then dismiss you.* Rather, it was *Who are YOU? What are YOU about?*" She had experienced her first hit of Johnny's unique style of communion.

After he'd met Michael and Megan, all the pieces fit together. John had fallen in love with my babies. "Your children are Bodhisattvas. Do you know how lucky we are?" I could have wept. While Paul treated them like annoying bugs, John had gazed into their souls.

Things were different the next day, however, when he invited us all to breakfast. They tested him with every bratty kid trick they could pull. They behaved abominably. When he bought a newspaper from a vending box, they caught the door before it shut, ripped out the remaining newspapers, and stood there expecting him to chastise them. He merely turned away and walked into the restaurant, ignoring the bait. They fought over the menus and what to order. Curious to see how he'd handle them, I kept quiet and let him take over.

John responded uniquely. Instead of becoming punitive or critical, he got real cool, with a punkish kind of detachment. He didn't make any ineffectual attempts to control them. They were given plenty of room to test this guy whom they sensed would play a huge role in their lives. He sat there like a papa lion watching his cubs, disinterested but very present. When they saw they weren't going to get a rise out of him, they quit. I had never seen anyone treat kids like that. Along with an appreciation for his parenting skills, I sensed we were in for an interesting ride.

Tibetan Buddhism has a particular level of enlightenment called *Ati*, which means "Old Dog." At a certain point on the path to enlightenment, the practitioner sees life through the half-raised eye of an old dog, lazing around, thumping his tail occasionally, never very excited. Johnny could be like that. He had seen so much of life and death that nothing really surprised him. I loved his rock-steady confidence.

John asked if I thought it might be best to wait six months before he came to live with us. Touched by his caution about starting a new family, I felt protected by his concern. He had a thoughtful side that treated affairs of the heart with deep respect. His wisdom bound me to him. It felt as if we had done this for lifetimes, danced these steps for thousands of years. The still, calm space in our hearts knew our union was inevitable.

I went home and told Paul he had to find another place to live. John went back to Los Angeles, ostensibly to pursue his "movie career," which, I later discovered, meant he periodically shopped a screenplay around Hollywood, based on his time in Vietnam. I did not know how he spent his days and never thought to ask, having no idea that he drank all night and slept all day and did little else except visit friends. When he began to call me after midnight, obviously drunk, I started to get the picture. But because I knew nothing about alcoholism, no red flags went up; everyone I knew drank excessively. We talked for hours, sometimes till the kids got up. I don't know when I slept. His daily calls were my life's blood. We continued to weave our spells and the magic was saturating the fabric of our souls, leaving us mesmerized and enraptured. The depth of our connection and joy was intoxicating. Megan even picked up on it. She wrote a story for school called "Prince Charming the Fourth."

John's prudence about our relationship felt somewhat incongruous juxtaposed to his free spirit. He came to Boulder several times and started building a relationship with Megan and Michael. As the months passed, he continued to be very precise about laying the ground for the establishment of our family and my new identity. He had escaped a relationship with a neurotic, alcoholic member of the Buddhist community and her two children. He did not want to recreate the devastation from that aborted attempt at family life. While they had lived together, I remembered being at a party at their house. Noticing some rather decent pieces of art hanging on the walls, it struck me that they were a reflection of John's taste, rather than her Midwestern country-club background. A sorrowful yearning welled up inside me for what I had lost in terms of my own upbringing. I had always felt uncomfortable around the ubiquitous mediocrity of the hippie and wanna-be-sophisticated Buddhist scenes. Sensing that John had been into literature and art as a way of saving his soul, as I had, I felt a deep camaraderie. If you clung to Beethoven or Thomas Mann, or a certain style of counterpoint, if the hopeful pastels of French Impressionists saved you from teen suicide, then you know the level of culture I'm talking about. It has nothing to do with sofa-sized paintings or season tickets. It is etched in the soul, and the rarity of finding such a kindred spirit eventually bound us even closer.

Living on the dregs of his substantial biannual Steinbeck royalty check, John had neglected to pay the rent on his sublet Los Angeles apartment. He received an eviction notice. I never discussed finances with him, naively thinking that all adults could manage money. When the royalty check came, he bought me gorgeous jewelry, a $4,000 Concord gold watch for himself, and paid cash for a new car. I figured he knew what he was doing. I didn't know about his indulgent habit of spending money freely when he had it. I was used to Paul's financial management, which, no matter how little we had, always covered our needs. We never argued about money, so I thought couples just naturally figured out how to conserve their income. I had no idea what John and I were in for, but I sensed trouble.

Staring that uneasiness in the face, I thought, *No matter how bad it gets, I am willing to risk everything to make it work.* I sought Rinpoche's advice. "Watch out. John has a lot of neuroses. The karma of fame is particularly difficult. His family is tragic, like the Kennedys. When he starts acting crazy, don't get sucked in."

Michael sat on Rinpoche's lap as we spoke, and suddenly another little boy rushed over and wildly hugged both of them, knocking over Rinpoche's chair with his enthusiasm. I watched him fall slowly backward, as if he were floating, with no fear. He laughed all the way down to the ground, landing on his back. The boys tumbled on top of him. As his attendants helped him up, he looked at me and said, "That's love for you!"

As I walked away, I felt the force of the obstacles that would barrel at us with furious speed, attempting to knock us off our balance. The karmic patterns we carried in our trousseaus would have to be unpacked and resolved. *We're really in for it. Are you sure you're up for this? It's going to be incredibly heavy.* My heart sank. For one brief second I had a choice. I could have walked away. Time moved on, my heart chose John, and I leapt into the raging river, never looking back.

9 | OUTSIDE IN

JOHN

A critical voice inside me has always insisted that what I really needed to do is grow up. This remains the case though what growing up might mean always hovers around a transient ideal. Today, in 1991, it is coupled with a potent notion about nurturing a "child within"; that kid who was frightened, or rejected, or confused, and maybe abused. It is a fairly common understanding nowadays that we must learn to re-parent or at least reassure ourselves and to try to find the connection with who we were when we were small, and then actually communicate with all these historical selves that are frozen like a school of Canadian Black Fish in the permafrost of our shame.

On its face, responding wholeheartedly to that child and trying to grow up seems to be a paradox, but the suggestion is that perhaps you have to do the one to achieve the other. At first it seems like a very irritatingly un-grown-up way of going about things, particularly when accompanying this process is another phenomenon which only the very slickest of journals now refer to as "parent bashing." I love it; "Learn to Nourish the Little Skin-head" within. Personally, as far as I'm concerned, people can bash whatever they like. In the end it all comes back to finding some sense of resolution, which is, after all, the only game in town if you want genuine relief.

If you need it, trying to summon up this child or teenager, whatever the age, is interesting material. Fortunately, regression or accessing a multiple personality disorder is not the issue, but yes, this kind of thing is strange. It embarrasses a lot of people, including me, particularly if it's done too seriously.

I swear the voice inside my head sounds the same to me as the voice that could count to ten on Seventy-eighth Street. Nothing has changed. I can't even discern a difference in the tone or vocabulary. The unchanging quality in my "voice-over," with its constant stream of "I" in front of every thought, always amazed me and compounded the eternal question of, When can I tell that I have grown up?

One thing is inarguable: all through my youth, I definitely wanted to grow up, and I wanted to do it fast. This is not unique, but I think being from New York had something to do with it. People there were supposedly more sophisticated, but apart from that there was also the tumult at home. Though children mostly take note of when things aren't going their way, in my mother's house it often rose to the traditional drunken hysterics of tears and violence. In my father's house it could sink to a brooding sulphurous depression, or the quick wrath of an old dog poisoned by distraction. Like seismic activity, these things were vaguely predictable though the timing and ferocity of their cycles varied. So, I thought that through "grown-upness," I would be able to orbit off this wheel of potential disasters and maybe even avoid further catastrophes by putting some distance between myself and the people who scared me. Since I also loved and looked up to both my parents, I suppose I should be more clinically precise and say that I wanted to be away from the feelings in me that scared me. Those feelings had a particularly sad and painful tenderness that only got in the way of what I thought being grown up was like. As it turned out, my solutions weren't those of an authentic grown-up, though by example I see they were a lot like the adults with whom I came in contact.

Since I really didn't want to savor more of this erratic, emotive world than I had to, and I couldn't just grow up and get out, I usually went in the other direction: womb reentry. I liked small dark places. I wanted to escape into something. As a very young child I liked places like the bottom of the bed under the sheets, or even just under the bed itself would do in a pinch. It was particularly good if I was in a hurry. It really was the cat who had pointed this out for me, as he went there the instant he heard the ominous tinkling of ice cubes. Dr. Lao was as smart as his name. I liked closets and basements too. I didn't really want to feel that I was hiding, just sort of getting away—vacating.

Later, I developed a strong affinity for rooftops. In this regard, New York City was empyrean, a veritable wonderland like the Himalayas. Instead of down and out, they were up and over. Then I discovered the marriage of the two worlds. I started going into the rooftop boxes where the elevator mechanisms of the big buildings were housed. I particularly liked this. You could climb in, sit on a grate, and watch the gears and cables pull the cars up and down thirty floors or more. There I would daydream of what I would do when I did grow up. Vertigo actually felt great. It made me a little dizzy, but then this business of making yourself dizzy brought up a lot of possibilities all by itself. Perhaps there were even three possible worlds: up and over, down and out, and outside in.

As anyone could guess at this point, there were more than just a few reasons why I became interested in altering my consciousness. I love that phrase. It is such a lofty-sounding, even scientific term. It has such a nice ring to it, like my purpose was as benign as some sort of casual psychic tailor. This was not really the case with me. What I wanted was to be able to be the captain of my boat and be able to negotiate the wild sea of my fears and others' moods. I was an innocent I suppose, but I wanted control. I was terrified by my feelings and the jagged coastline of my surroundings. If I could steer those feelings or distract them, even into base neurological confusion, well, that would be better than being left adrift in the capricious uncertainty of Mom and Dad.

Eventually, as an adult, this almost primordial lack of humility (sometimes known as survival) became a big problem. But like most kids I was too aware and very sensitive to all of the contradictory instructions and skewed examples that I was left alone to decipher. My parents were equally sensitive. Without any doubt, I see how strongly they reacted to their own inherited dilemmas, but the remedies that they chose to give them refuge, like anger or alcohol or shamelessly experimenting on us kids, by making us jump off high chairs, only added to mine.

When I discovered that literally spinning around in circles disengaged almost everything into a world set askew by a neutral dizziness incapable of registering even the direction home, I found another sort of home. I was more than simply amused. I was set free from the tyranny of time and boredom and what was becoming a borrowed shame—since my parents didn't feel any for their shameless behavior.

Then, I learned how to faint by hyperventilating and pressing on my jugular veins with my thumbs. Coming to from this sort of blackout, extremities tingling and not even knowing where I was, became a sortie that I would fly hundreds of times a day, anywhere. I would hit the deck in the park, on the street, in the gym, in fact right in the middle of class behind my books. With this magical technique, I could soar away beyond any need for an imaginary friend. "If happy little bluebirds fly," etc. Why, Harold Arlen and Dorothy were right! Slap it to the head and the irksome phenomenal world with its tiring dimensions of anxiety and guilt would disappear into something beyond a normal gravity.

In my mother's household I discovered that there was also a lot of pharmaceutical support for this predilection for self-propelled transcendence and escape. From my point of view there was a real need for it. It was the age of miracle drugs. Why, penicillin had only really come into use four or five years before I was born. When my brother and I were just teething, instead of Dillworth's Gripe Water, Mom dosed us with codeine. If we couldn't sleep, barbiturates would do the trick for sure. Thom and I even had practice drills on how to take pills so that we would swallow them "like a grown-up." We had to put them at the back of the tongue and swallow them quickly before they could start to dissolve. We practiced on aspirin, of all things, which required extremely quick reflexes. Every adult we knew was talking about something called Miltown, one of the first tranquilizers. The way they talked about it made me wonder where the hell that place was, and why *we* never went there on vacation!

Eventually I found out where the codeine lived in my mother's medicine cabinet. When she had given it to me for whatever reason, I remembered that I always had a terrifically warm and safe feeling and wonderful dreams. Now that was the kind of thing I was after for sure. Maybe if I just went to sleep long enough, I would wake up and most of the growing would be done. The story of Rip Van Winkle fascinated me.

Neither of my parents believed in small supplies of medicines, and so I hooked about forty of these deceptively tiny pills and secreted them away in my bedroom. That first night, being an instinctive addict, I took three of them at once. The warms came, and indeed the night was full of flying dreams in amniotic oceans. The next morning, however, found me vomiting my little heart out. It was sure painless though, and it had the added benefit of making my mother think I was sick and unfit for school. I didn't have to go to the trouble of having to heat and break any more thermometers over the light bulb. This was real, I was spontaneously retching and it was great. I was tucked away in bed, given coloring books, and brought warm broth, the whole works.

The next night I did the same thing except I upped the dosage by a pill, and the warmth and dreams increased proportionally. I kept on like this for about two weeks. The good Doctor Craig, our pediatrician, came and all that, but he was hardly looking for codeine poisoning in spite of the fact that my pupils had become the size of pinheads. He left mystified after prescribing paregoric for my upset tummy. Yummy, more opiates! I stole more pills.

One day there came an abrupt end to this routine; something a junkie never likes. I had begun to lose a lot of weight and so without warning, I was transported to Lennox Hill Hospital, the place of my birth, for observation. The doctors there knew of my spastic stomach when I was an infant. Perhaps there was a connection. Maybe I had cancer!

And so I began my first withdrawal from opiates at about age seven in the children's ward. Though I had some stuffed toys, these could just barely save me from the meanest bunch of kids that I had ever encountered in my short life. En masse, sick city boys are monsters. They soon ripped the head off my toy frog, and basically terrorized me for three solid weeks. One kid in a cast and on crutches had the physical movement and behavioral motivation of the Terminator. Another liked to strap me gagged into a wheelchair and then shoot me out like a friction car racer to see me bounce off walls. I was in hell.

Not looking in the right direction, the doctors obviously could find nothing wrong with me. No cancer, no virus, no childhood disease. They then sent me to a hospital psychiatrist. That was just becoming a somewhat "in" thing to do, and after all, I had been sick. As I know now, I really *did* have a disease despite what I considered to be my innocent, if secret collusion with Morpheus.

The psychiatrist smelled strange, and he also showed me some grainy pictures called a Thematic Apperception Test which I found terribly embarrassing; particularly the one with a half-naked woman in bed and a man in the foreground holding his head in an attitude of what I took for grief. It looked like something having to do with sex or murder or both!

These sessions with the shrink made me extremely nervous. I was afraid he would be able to hypnotize me and find out about the little pills.

After some inkblot work, he concluded that part of the problem with my condition might have something to do with my family life. Actually I thought my family was essentially fine. At least my friends' families weren't much different as far as I knew. On hearing this diagnosis, after first taking the opportunity to briefly attack each other, my parents furiously agreed with me. I was fine. They were fine. Why I hadn't thrown up but once since I first went into the hospital. True, I couldn't sleep for about a week and was often found wandering the wards in the wee small hours, but I was eating, getting better; that was the main thing.

When I returned home the pills were in the same place that I had stashed them in my room. This near-opium den was interestingly called the "chocolate room" because it had been painted that curious color. In its brown darkness, it had been the perfect womblike environment for my occult narcoleptic purpose.

I hadn't been to school in a long time and I was really in no hurry to go back. Like any addict, lacking all regard for timing the very first night home I popped four codeine pills, and the next day I was again to be found vomiting into the toilet. Well, my mother was often drunk, but she was no fool; she knew then that something perhaps similar to her own agenda was occurring up there in the chocolate room. She didn't know what and never did to her dying day, but puke or not, she sent me off to school.

Fear of eventually being found out helped me stop. Also, I didn't relish the idea of another trip to the gauntlet of the children's ward, and after all, the bottle was getting lower. Anyway, summer was just around the corner and that would be the end of school for the time being.

As I look back at this period, it occurs to me that with me home all the time, it must have been very hard for my mother to maintain herself. Even though I slept the days away, my habits were getting in the way of hers.

The next year, after the hospital stay, I more or less stopped going to school. On the rare occasion that my mother got up to check if I was still in the house, I slipped into my spot under the bed for a little more sleep. I needed the sleep too since I was up most every night till 4:00 A.M., reading under the sheets at the bottom of my bed, or listening to popular love songs or mystery dramas with a little crystal radio shaped like a rocket ship that I had sent in for.

This wanting to be finished with growing up included the pursuit of just how to do it. If the movies were to be believed, facing danger was an important element. Even by the time I was six, I had begun to get into some exciting trouble running in and out of that same church where I had tried to get the appointment with God. With my own gang of hoodlums, a modicum of danger could be arranged by blowing out the votive candles on the altar to see if we could make the old ladies in there chase us. But by age eight, this had grown far too tame. Real danger was needed. This could include rooftop jumping from building to building, running up and down fire escapes past startled people's windows, facing down rabid building superintendents, or as I said, just making yourself dizzy by any new means possible. Of course since this was New York, one could always manage to get chased by what passed for gangs in those days (boy choirs compared to today) or the more generic choice, the police.

Eventually I guess the police caught me enough. My career as Batman in Brownstone Gotham ended. The water-bomb king of the tenements had gone too far. My mother had gotten word of my daring exploits and started looking under the bed. She even hired an off-duty cop named Robert to escort me to school a few blocks away. Since she drank till very late with her friends, or "uncles" as we called them, neither she nor they were able to see to this task themselves. But even after the patrolman escort service started, I used to walk in the school's front door and out the back to go riding the subways or buses to the end of their routes. Then I would turn around and go back the same way, back and forth until school was supposed to be over, at which time I would rejoin Bob the cop for the short walk home.

This was like traveling the Great Trunk Road in Kipling's India. I think I rather fancied myself as Kim. I began to really love the sights and sounds of my city. There were so many tribes and casts in Megalopolis. I began to hear and understand a lot of different dialects and unique tongues that were never heard in my part of Manhattan.

Sometimes I would spend the day in the Museum of Natural History. Now this was a great place. It had whole whales and dinosaurs, and dioramas of Africa. They even had a room that looked like the rain forests with what I thought were stuffed pygmies. There was also the room with the huge war canoe of the Indians of the Northwest with beautiful and mysterious eyes on the bow, as well as the great totem poles with wonderful pyramiding animal faces. There were fantastic things here to see and I read the signs, and I learned. The museum also had its own roof that I could sneak up to and look out over Central Park. When I discovered I could do all this, ditching the cop became a really serious business. Of course, in the end I was caught. My brother, Thom, had been gone for a couple of years by this time, sent off to boarding school, and my parents thought that it was time to get me out of town, too.

10 | BOARDING SCHOOL

JOHN

For reasons that were never made clear, at least not to us, my father felt early on that it would be good if my brother and I were separated. Since we didn't actually live with him, this idea smacked of those old Spartan theories that were fast becoming his trademarks as a part-time parent. You had the feeling that if it was good enough for Hector or Agamemnon, it would do wonders for us. Though my father had a cruel streak that varied in width depending on the extent to which his feelings were hurt, these theories were not part of that sort of backlash. He truly reveled in the abstraction and possible range of technique when it came to us. Some of them worked out quite well, like his great endeavor to get me to stop reading *Reader's Digest*.

Judging correctly that I had the heart of a felon, he placed books that he wanted me to read very high up in the bookcase, or even went so far as to lock them up behind a glass case on the second-floor landing. After threatening my little neck, he hid the key where he was sure that I would find it. Thus was I delivered up to the "wine dark sea" of the *Iliad* and sailed even further to meet Circe and the wonderful Cyclops. But not ever hearing the reason, looking back at his rush to separate Thom and me fills me with suspicion.

Nonetheless, in the fall of 1953 at age nine, Thom was sent away to the Malcolm Gordon School for Boys up the Hudson River near West Point. I remember being taken there to watch him play ice hockey on a flooded field that first winter. He was built like a little Samoan at that age, and ice hockey was definitely not his thing. Rather than actually being able to skate, he moved around with his ankles splayed out like little seal flippers as he tried to outwit the mocking puck. Unfortunately, without skating skills, they had made him the goal keeper which made him personally responsible for the many goals that continually slipped through those sad flippers. I remember that people laughed a lot at him, and though he tried to act like a tough little guy who was just having a bad day, I knew that he was really cold and wet and miserable. I thought the whole thing was abominable and cruel. And then later when at lunch he wore his little red-felt waistcoat, which he thought was quite dashing, the teachers giggled and called it his "menu" because it had food stains on it.

By the time lunch was over I had seen enough of winter in Sparta and couldn't wait to get home. Thom cried when we left, and I knew from my own experiences at summer camp, where we had both been shipped off to since age five, just how he felt.

Though by his own admission Thom was often mean to me, I missed him horribly. In the bedroom that we had shared, there hung a painting of my father and mother holding my brother as an infant. Using this romantic graphic as a target, I vividly remember putting myself to sleep alone in this room with a ray-gun flashlight which I used to selectively indict my parents for the loneliness that I felt, and what I perceived as their uncaring brutality toward my big brother. Spotlighting each of the three faces, I would say out loud and ever so dramatically, "How could you, and you, send him away?" I would continue with this circle of light, over and over until I was almost hoarse. I fell asleep with a mixture of exhaustion from this soliloquy to separation, and exhilaration at my brilliance as the avenging Flash Gordon with my terrible accusing "killer beam."

I had been able to escape to the rooftops until about age nine, but eventually the bedroom was completely empty except for the old portrait. I, too, was sent away to school.

I immediately managed to find the dark comforting places there as well. There were boiler rooms in the basements of dormitories, or woodsheds, old attics, or better, the woods themselves. Always I questioned what was supposed to happen later. These places, at least the ones that catered to really young children, were called pre-preparatory schools. In other words,

Gwyn Conger Steinbeck—Hollywood, 1938

Steinbeck, Thom, and Gwyn, 1944

Steinbeck at Thom's christening, 1944

(Left to right) John, Gwyn, and Thom, 1946

Steinbeck and John, 1946

(Left to right) Thom and John, 1949

Steinbeck, Thom, and John—at Sag Harbor, Long Island, 1951

(Left to right) John, Dr. Lao, Thom, and Gwyn—Manhattan, 1959

Nancy—Lowell High School graduation, 1962

John Steinbeck IV, 1962

John in Vietnam, 1966

John, Steinbeck, and LBJ at the White House, 1965

Steinbeck in Vietnam, 1966

John and the Coconut Monk—Vietnam, 1969

schools that were going to prepare you for life in the schools that would prepare you for college, where somehow all your dreams would come together
and you would be prepared for your real life. I was already pretty cynical and
felt that obviously, all of this was somehow designed to help me create a
plan which might give me a handle on how to amass enough money to die
gracefully and perhaps endow all my prep schools. I didn't like this path at
all. I wanted to just get on with it, whatever *it* was. Perpetual preparation was
not the life sentence or even the parenthesis that I wanted.

As I said, neither Thom nor I were quite sure why we were being sent
away. Not really thinking too much about my delinquency from day school
as part of the cause, it seemed to me at the time that it was possibly due to
a new wardrobe. I knew there was some connection there, as the Lord &
Taylor's clothing store had sold Mom or Dad several pairs of special long
pants. They were grey flannel and came with a blue blazer complete with red
piping and a patch with a furious bird that keened, *The Eaglebrook School.*

The boarding schools of the day were truly special little worlds unto
themselves. These gulags, which were to be more or less my home for the
next eight years, were at the very height of fashion. They may still be today.
They all seemed to have been established sometime soon after the War of
1812. Some of them were extremely beautiful, and well outfitted. Parents
could be forgiven for thinking that they were providing their son with a
sublime academic setting, replete with ponds and gardens, and what
approximated the playing fields of Eaton. The Eaglebrook School even had
two little ski jumps, for chrissake.

The schools were brimming with tradition and headmastered along
nepotistic lines. In fact, school management was a sort of family trade.
Often they were the creation of some inspired and kindly man of learning
who probably loved boys, and books, and his own childhood adventures
as he learned about the varied richness of the world. But I think that even
this sort of kindly patriarch was probably unprepared for the dumping
ground that affluent parents could make of the finest of visions.

Some of the parents were alumni, but of course they had long since forgotten that their own glorious boarding-school memories were singular in
their dedication to the various ways that they had tried to escape, either
psychologically or actually. Many a child from these schools with enough
allowance to hit the tracks was recaptured at Grand Central Station.

If you were an inmate, the old New England boarding schools were
scary places full of men with long brooding eyebrows. To me, they were
sad, musty places that mixed higher learning with even higher anxiety. A lot

of my friends at Eaglebrook were the spawn of remote, workaholic business-types, and what we now call dysfunctional parents of one sort or another. They rarely saw their mothers or fathers except on holidays. Some boys were perpetually nervous and tail-down, like field dogs that had been shot over too much as puppies. I remember one eight-year-old kid who just plain died of an asthma attack within the first week of being plopped down in one of these bastions of tradition. It was not just a matter of artistry and creative intelligence that made J. D. Salinger's *The Catcher in the Rye* a popular book. These schools were hothouses of prepubescent alienation, and later an increasing suicide rate.

As institutions, they also seemed to follow a common pattern. There was always the gay English or French teacher who would invariably be caught diddling his "A" students, or the alcoholic-manic-depressive headmaster who would disintegrate, disappear, and then reappear after spending long months or years in a sanatorium somewhere far away from the board of trustees. Fittingly enough, *Catch-22* was to replace *Catcher* as the Bible and basic manual for boarding-school existentialism.

I want to be careful here and say again that there were many teachers and "Old-School" educators whose main love in life was to try and guide young boys into a world of learning that had made their own lives a wonderment. Today, teaching is one of the most thankless jobs in our society and I would hate to be guilty of any sort of easy dismissal. But within the truly warped framework of most of the families who could afford to send their sons to these boarding schools, the emotional and cognitive availability of these wounded kids was not great. Also, for all children, no matter the background, the kind of real mentor connection that the good teachers might have yearned for can only really be made with one or two very special people in life, and we all remember this if we have been lucky enough to have had that experience.

The dominating fact was that in my day, boarding schools had for the most part settled into the fifties to become gilded holding tanks. They were guaranteed, guilt-free receptacles for the abjured children of the rich and the CEOs of America. Tuition rivaled the most expensive Ivy League colleges.

Eaglebrook was a case in point. With perhaps the exception of the actor/producer Michael Douglas, I was the only son of an artist. My first roommate's father was the president of TWA. Little Tom Watson of IBM was there, as were the two Kaiser boys whose father invented aluminum, I thought. There were two kids named Crane. One's father made among other things, most of the toilet bowls for our great land, and the other made the paper that dollar bills were printed on. Then there were the kids from Wyzetta, Minnesota, and Lake Minnetanka. Their parents were the Daytons and Gambles who owned competitive department-store chains that were like the Neiman Marcuses of the Midwest. There were many other children whose fathers ran the steel industries and oil industries of Pennsylvania. Even the American Can Company had its junior representative. Olivetti was there as were a posse of fabulously wealthy gaucho-types from places like Venezuela, Colombia, and the Baccardis of Cuba. All these kids took Spanish for their foreign-language requirements.

Since the tuition at these schools was so high, parents could easily feel that they were sacrificing enormously for their ungrateful sons, and I think to a large extent, that was part of the unspoken bargain. But there was another advantage: they could also lead their unique and powerful lives without the responsibility of any undue parenting.

For my mother, this meant that she could have her many suitors and drink, too. Her alcoholism had matured into far more than just a good time. She absolutely needed to drink.

In fairness to my father, he probably thought by sending us away that we would not only be assured of enduring the kind of classical educational environment that he never had, he was removing us to a "safe" environment. It also allowed him to appease his lifelong sense of inferiority by sending his sons away to where the "best" people's kids went. Certainly his income was a minute fraction of my school chums' families. Like many people with a certain kind of insecurity that comes from being smart enough to hang out with the elite, but too broke to hang out far, my father could sometimes be very sensitive and terribly aware of his image. It got him into a lot of very expensive posturing.

There came a point when my mother's behavior became too much for me. I would come home from boarding school on vacation with a friend only to find her passed out naked on the floor, or something equally bizarre. The strange thing was that my friends took this in their stride, which gave me somewhat of a clue as to their situations at home.

After I finally had too much of her, I locked and loaded my .22 rifle and pressed it to the temple of one of Mom's boyfriends while he was sleeping next to her and twitched him awake. Shortly thereafter I packed my bags and went to my father's house on 72nd Street. Thom, who had been making model airplanes in his room for years (enjoying the glue, I presume), was out later that afternoon.

Shocked, but exonerated, we were welcomed into Dad's lair. Now he would have his chance at showing the world what a great man could do with his sons, since after all, my mother's condition made the question of custody academic. It was also his wife, Elaine's, chance to *relate* with "the boys."

Dad stopped trying to compete with the CEOs and we went to a city school for the rest of that year. At one point, we traveled through Europe with Dad, Elaine, and a young aspiring playwright named Terrence McNally, whom Dad hired as our tutor. That trip broadened my horizons significantly. It was, for the most part, Dad at his best. Certainly he tried hard to allow us to learn about language and our culture from Roman history, through the Italian Renaissance and English history. We toured North Africa, Sicily, Crete, Athens, the works. In ten months I was trilingual and had a taste for travel and learning that has never left me. It was a great gift, and one that I also passed on to my own children in Asia and Europe when they were old enough.

11 | TROUBLE IN PARADISE

NANCY

After Paul moved out, I never missed him. Since he usually worked past their bedtime, the children adjusted to his absence. I'd had all the burdens of being a single parent with barely any of the benefits of being married. Paul was angry over the separation and caused some ugly scenes, but I knew he'd stop, out of cowardice, when John joined us.

That summer of 1979, Michael ran his bike into a wall and bruised his face so badly it looked like he'd been beaten. I could tell the separation bothered him and my heart broke. He didn't have the conceptual framework to talk about it. At the tender age of nine, Megan understood exactly why I asked Paul to leave. She had witnessed his rages and felt the pall of unhappiness that hung in our house. "John makes you laugh, and Dad makes you cry," she observed wisely. But a boy misses his father. Michael was too young to understand that I needed more than Paul could give me or that he deserved a loving father. It is so sad the way kids have to go along for the ride, no matter what. They don't have a choice and in their innocence they try so hard to support you with their enthusiasm.

When John heard about Michael's bruises, he suggested I paint designs on Band-Aids to make them look like war medals, so Mikey would feel proud of his bravery about the pain. He responded exactly as John had predicted. Impressed by John's capacity for empathy, I began to feel a security I'd never experienced. He approached everything with the creative mind of a genius, so you never knew what to expect. Over the years, he nurtured and fretted about Michael and Megan as much as I did, especially when they were teenagers. With tremendous care and concern, he poured a lifetime of attention into them. They adored him. Several years later, when Paul bellowed his usual belittling humiliations at Michael, I said coldly, "If you even wonder why the kids took John's last name and consider him their father, remember what you just said to your son."

Early one morning in October, I woke to the sounds of an intruder climbing through my bedroom window. Screaming like a banshee, I scared him off. The police found him hiding in a neighbor's bushes. I called John in terror.

"Honey, you've got pheromones that would cause a man to bore through a brick wall," he quipped. "You need a dog until I get there. Thom's been keeping George, my standard poodle, since I was at seminary. He can bring him to you." He asked me to keep an eye on Thom till he arrived. "I'm worried about his drinking. Don't let on, or he'll bolt. He's very skittish." And so, a few days later, I met Thom and George, the wild white standard poodle.

I couldn't decide who was more unruly, the boisterous brother or the dog. Thom and I went out that night, to Le Bar at the Boulderado, for drinks, of course. I liked him immediately; he had the same uproarious humor and spontaneity that I loved in John. He was warm, exuberant, and alive.

I'd been cutting apples that afternoon for the children at the Buddhist school we were organizing. As we were walking back to his van, I discovered I'd left a carving knife in my purse.

"Oh, I get it," Thom teased. "You're such a tough chick, you can't just make due with a switchblade." As I look back on it now, it symbolized the protection we would need to guard against this incredibly wounded man, just to keep Johnny alive. Reluctant to sacrifice his lifelong drinking buddy for the sake of his health, Thom would mindlessly undermine John's every attempt at sobriety.

We sat playing with George under the canopy of maple trees on the lawn. Suddenly, Thom's mood swung from gaiety to menace. He held the dog's white cotton head in his hands.

"Do you have any idea how easy it would be to snap his neck?" I froze in terror. The eerie ring of the telephone broke the silence. I ran toward the house. It was John, psychically sensing his drunken brother might be getting out of hand.

"He's got a mile-wide mean streak," John said grimly. "Put him on the phone." He sounded disgusted, but hardly surprised. I sensed a strange sadistic tension between the brothers that would take me years to understand. Although I found the incident disturbing, the chaotic intensity was familiar. These were my kind of guys, dog and all. If I met Thom or John or even George today, I would heed the red flags. I am no longer charmed by living on the edge, but back then I was game for adventure, even danger. When Thom left, I resolved to domesticate all three of them.

John flew in for Thanksgiving with all his worldly possessions and ensconced himself in our home. That Christmas was the most memorable yet; we still talk about it. John embodied the holiday spirit and the children basked in the warmth of his sunny generosity. As he lavished carefully chosen presents on us, the joyous celebration shone in sharp contrast to the dreadful past holidays ruined by Paul's drinking. We sang and laughed, and frolicked like puppies. John kept playing Kenny Loggins's "Please Celebrate Me Home."

"I feel at home for the first time in my life," he told us. He wasn't cool about it. He cried.

My parents decided to buy a home for us. Johnny and I had already fallen in love with a sprawling house surrounded by an acre of lawns, an apple orchard and a beautiful view of the mountains. The master-bedroom suite, with a fireplace in the sitting room, was separate from the children's wing. We could have privacy from Saturday morning cartoons and they would be spared our late-night talks.

John and Thom had a huge moving truck deliver the family antiques that they'd kept in storage since their mother's death in 1975. We spent three days unpacking the treasures, a cherry-wood armoire, flown over the Hump by General Stilwell who'd picked it up in Burma from Dutch missionaries; Queen Anne tables and chairs; Venetian glass, family portraits; and dishes from Napoleonic times. Suddenly the Steinbeck legacy filled our house.

Thom spent hours lovingly unpacking everything, lingering over each piece, explaining the history to me, but Johnny eyed them coldly, claiming they held sad memories of his childhood. I sensed the tension as we opened each crate filled with objects that reflected Gwyn's exquisite taste.

"Mother developed Dad's sense of aesthetic beauty," Thom told me. "She also threw the heavier objects at Johnny's head when she was drunk." There were gifts from every "uncle" the boys had to suffer through after the divorce, along with cocktail-party props and an endless silver service they'd had to polish repeatedly at her whim. Although our house looked beautiful, the elegance was permeated by a slight uneasiness, as if ghosts were unpacking their baggage as well.

With the arrival of memories, Johnny began revealing his painful family secrets to me. Sensing the wounds were too tender, I had never asked about his parents. On one of our first nights together at seminary, lying in my arms, he told me about his relationship with Steinbeck. Feeling safe enough to finally speak the unmentionable, he suddenly burst into heartrending sobs. As I soothed him, I vowed to get to the bottom of his sorrow. Vats of scotch and bales of marijuana later, John finally found the courage to stop anesthetizing himself and learned how to heal those old wounds. After his death, several Steinbeck scholars told me they cannot imagine how Johnny survived his childhood. I wished I'd been able to talk to them in those early days, instead of being locked into the tight-lipped trap set between him and Thom.

As I grew to know John, I discovered many unique parts of his character, such as his distaste for name dropping. Unimpressed by the famous people he'd known, he took them quite for granted. When William Burroughs asked John to write the preface to his son Billy's posthumous autobiography, *Speed*, I heard for the first time about the months John and William had lived at the Boulderado while tending to Billy's liver transplant. Johnny adopted William as a father figure and he felt close to Billy because he was a fellow son of a famous father. Born addicted, Billy wore out his liver with drugs and alcohol. After the transplant, he couldn't stop drinking, and soon died. John saw a prophecy in Billy's life that frightened him.

We wanted to create a refuge for our family and our love, a home filled with harmony and joy. Johnny relished tending the grounds around our house. He created beautiful tanks of tropical fresh- and salt-water fish, decorated with ferns, sunken ships, and pirate treasures. One night, Thom turned up the thermostat, making bouillabaisse from a fortune of exotic creatures.

"I thought they looked cold," he said, abashed and then blamed the scotch.

John was proud of his new family and our beautiful home. He loved hosting dinner parties so he could show off his spread and preen in front of friends who invariably took me aside to whisper, "How did you tame the monster?" They'd ask the same thing about George, who had been notoriously unruly. I really believed my love could domesticate their bestial natures. In the long run, I was right, but I had no idea how long that run would be.

For two years, Johnny drank and smoked pot every night. I drank, too, though never as often nor nearly as much. Gradually, the skeletons started coming out of our closets. Although his drinking didn't affect me strongly at first, there was an underlying uneasiness as my denial slipped. I knew nothing about alcoholism, the signs, the symptoms, the effect on the family. I noticed that sometimes John would get nervous when he hadn't had a drink. He would keep his scotch in the kitchen, which I later realized was a way of controlling the flow. If he wanted another drink, he'd have to get up for it. In my ignorance, I filled Steinbeck's antique crystal decanter and kept it near John so he didn't have to get up. Now it sounds like an Enabler joke, but by that time I was developing the desperate pattern of a codependent, trying to prop up a sense of order like a corpse.

I don't know when the transition happened, when the avalanche of alcoholism hit our safe house. One day there was the joyous fruition of our seminary dream and the next day we woke up to find all our genetically impaired ancestors camped in our backyard. At first, there was the inspiration to create a family that was vastly different from our childhoods. All too soon, pain and confusion had buried us. There were no guides, no signposts. Consciousness about addiction had not yet been raised to the popular level.

Things turned ugly and it broke our hearts. Our first fight started during a trip through the southwest to San Francisco. We planned to see Thom in Austin, their grandmother in Nogales, and then my parents in San Francisco. John also wanted to introduce me to a previous girlfriend's family in Texas. I wasn't looking forward to a tour of old relationships, but since Paul was welcome in our house and often spent holidays with us, I tried to keep an open mind. Old girlfriends can be great if they at least treat you like you're visible. The ones I can't tolerate are those who act like you're not there and the guy who dumped them to be with you is really still interested in them.

By now, I had seen scores of women throw themselves at John. I was beginning to get a taste for the invisibility which often plagues women in celebrity relationships. You become an appendage as these hungry, predatory females pretend you just wash his socks. They smell stardust and suddenly they act like it's just them and him in the room. With the scent of blood in their nostrils, they go for the jugular, that hit of fame. Appalled by their rudeness, it took me a long time to learn how to deal with them.

For example, a well-known New-Age anthropologist was once the guest du jour at a friend's party. She must have known John was coming because when we walked into the room, she honed in on him like a laser. Everyone noticed. It was downright embarrassing. She tried to entertain the whole room with one of her "There I was, out in a kayak with a bunch of Tibetan lamas, chasing a killer whale . . ." stories, but the whole time she spoke only to John.

"I wanted to punch her," he said with disgust. "It's so rude. She acted like you were invisible."

I began to wish Johnny came with handouts for those women: *Just because this man is polite and charming, it doesn't mean that he wants to sleep with you. In fact, when he goes home, he'll probably dissect you mercilessly and rail against his people-pleasing cowardice which prevented him from shutting you up.* We ran into the woman years later at a spiritual conference in Newport. When she cornered Johnny for his phone number, he wrote it under both our names. "She'll never call when she sees your name next to mine," he smirked.

There was an incident over a mustard jar which epitomized those ghouls. Another one of those types, who positively drooled whenever Johnny was around, managed to finagle an invitation to dinner at our house. She was standing in the kitchen when she spotted a crock of imported German mustard on the counter.

"Look at that," she crooned to John. "Who else would have a jar of gourmet mustard?" She raved on about his sophistication. Actually, my mother had sent it, and it was the kind I'd grown up with, but she would never consider it was my choice. Only Johnny could possibly be so special. For years after, whenever one of *Them* started to drool, Johnny would lean over and whisper to me, "Love your mustard, dahling," and I'd snicker.

In a quandary about those situations, I started asking other women in my position. We'd all reached the same conclusion. Married to a charismatic husband, after several dozen encounters like that, you start cringing when you see the signs. You even go through a period where you hate to meet new people, especially single women, because it's so predictable. It helped when we stopped socializing with other alcoholics, but good manners are rare these days in any circle.

Johnny had an uncanny effect on women. He had what singer Van Morrison calls *railway-carriage charm*. Graciously European in his bearing, he made women feel like he was genuinely interested in them, and for some, that was highly unusual. Given the choice, he'd rather hang out with them than most men. "Don't leave me in the other room with the guys, talking about chain saws and studded snow tires. I want to be with your girlfriends, talking about emotions and interesting things."

When the company of men grew too boring, I could feel him listening across the room to what I was talking about with the women. I loved that.

Soon he'd wander over and plunk himself down amongst us. In spite of his macho, stand-up guy persona, he could tap deeply into his feminine side. Frilly bedrooms never made him nervous. He'd snuggle in, prop his feet on the lacy pillow shams, and spill cigarette ash on the pastel duvet.

Some women aren't accustomed to being treated with respect by men; they interpret it as a come-on. Especially the lonely single ones, with no life. You could predict it like clockwork. After we were married, we had dinner at the house of Sam Brown, the guy who started the Peace Corps. Seated at separate tables, John found himself next to one of "those women." Several days later, a perfumed letter arrived. "John, I had such a delightful time with you the other night." Her phone number appeared casually below her signature. Johnny wafted it by me as it sailed into the wastebasket.

Johnny called it *eyelight.* "They're missing eyelight. Nobody's looked in their eyes for years." For him, it was never about being emotionally available. He had a genuinely curious and gregarious personality. No one feared that a dinner conversation would lag when he was around. After he died, I hated going out. I had forgotten that people can be so boring. I was used to a certain comfort zone, knowing there wouldn't be an awkward moment unless he allowed one. The man dripped savoir faire and je ne sais quoi. Not many guys have his qualities these days, not even movie stars. So many men are frozen in their monologues, as if they're these great mythical beings. They start talking and all they want is for you to nod periodically and say "Really???" Johnny's conversational skills left me channel surfing through most men. I remember him often teasing, "I'm telling you, I'll be a hard act to follow."

The first few days of our trip were filled with excitement and romance. Then John's history began to seep in. I watched him become agitated in Austin over the offhanded way Thom treated our visit. "He does it every time. Dad was the same way. They act like they can't figure out what you're doing in the same town. Neither of them could handle intimacy, so they cover it up with bluster."

Thom found his equilibrium by playing Older Brother, goading John into the younger, disadvantaged role. It frustrated and enraged John. When we were alone, he brooded with resentment.

"Why don't you say something?"

"He'd just laugh. He's been cruel to me ever since we were babies."

The cognitive dissonance of Thom's sadism was a disturbing contrast to his tremendous warmth. Knowing nothing about dysfunctional family loyalties, I wondered why John bothered with Thom if all he got back was condescension. Remembering Cal and Aaron in *East of Eden*, I began to realize what a self-fulfilling prophecy that novel would be for the Steinbeck brothers and me. I felt like the character Abra, mediating between the two. Thom had actually been married for a brief time to a woman named Adra. It was my first glimpse into the ancient blood rivalry between the brothers.

One evening, I went for a walk while John sat paralyzed with anguish about Thom's brutality. *It's as if they are acting out a childhood curse. Did Steinbeck foresee the primordial competition between his own sons, or did he just think he was spinning a good tale? Did his failures as a father, his withholding of love and approval, pit brother against brother in a fatal, sickening struggle for dominance? Was the book written out of ambivalence, a favoring of one brother over the other?* Ironically, Thom seemed just as desperate to win his father's posthumous approval as Johnny.

When I got back to the hotel, John was napping. Thom asked me to join him for drinks and he opened up to me, as if sensing my confusion. Keeping secrets is the hallmark of a dysfunctional family. When your father wins the Nobel Prize for literature, it raises the ante. "One wants to be loved and accepted by their parents," Thom explained. "I realized that if the world loved Dad and looked to him for his opinion, and he didn't love me, then there must be something wrong with me. If the whole world says this is a great man, who am I to argue with them? If his opinion means this much and he gets the Nobel Prize for it, then when he tells me I'm full of shit, he must be right. When we got into similar trouble, Dad would say 'You're unhappy, but Johnny's crazy.' He could allow me the usual teenage angst, but to him, Johnny's was a sign that he was emotionally defective. And so I bought into that."

As the eldest sibling, Thom played the role of the family hero. "Johnny was the scapegoat and mascot. I was the 'yes' man. I had to get along with Dad and Mother and our stepmother, Elaine. My job was not to defy. My job was to be loved and accepted. That was my survival. It caused Johnny to rebel. He pulled unbelievable stunts that had nothing to do with the payoff, which was mostly negative attention. It had to do with the fact that he could stop time for these people. I loved him for that. He was always in trouble, always testing the boundaries, and so he was always the first one to be jumped on."

Johnny had told me how his mother physically and emotionally abused him after the divorce. At the tender age of four, she would wake him in the middle of the night by smashing scotch bottles on his head, drunk and sobbing. "It's all your fault. If you and your brother hadn't been born,

I'd still be married to your father." When the boys got up in the morning, before the maid arrived, they'd find the Picassos slashed and the walls smeared with blood from her fights with various boyfriends. Johnny couldn't stand the sound of ice tinkling in a glass because it would remind him of his mother's drunken slurs, just like as a vet he couldn't stand the sound of helicopters. It took years for me to understand these complex emotional undercurrents.

"Mother loved us to the extent that she could love anybody," Thom told me. "She never copped to her abuse of us. She conveniently forgot anything that was remotely embarrassing to her. She did do one thing that was meant as pure torture, and she was a torturer, believe me. If she wanted to get to Johnny, she would tell him how I was loved best. She'd say, 'I understand why your father liked your brother better,' and Grandmother would back her up.

"Their attempt to split us up began to work. Convincing Johnny that Elaine and Dad loved me best and didn't love him, giving me all the privileges and he got all the shit, only split us up even farther. Then we met in Vietnam, on separate ground, where we could recreate the relationship based upon the madness around us during the war, as opposed to our parents' insanity. Mother and Dad couldn't influence us there. I bless the war for saving my relationship with my brother. There's no doubt about the fact that he was cursed in that family. By the time we were in our twenties, I was sick of trying to justify that to him, as though I was in charge of our parents' conduct. Johnny always felt that I was yessing these people so they'd treat me better. He was right, but had he been given half a bloody chance, he would have done the same thing."

I felt we were being held hostage by Steinbeck's solidification of the sibling archetype in the book he'd dedicated to his sons. As I watched *East of Eden* with Johnny that winter of 1979, I tried to view it through their pubescent eyes. It made my skin crawl to think of those two impressionable boys watching the movie without any parental guidance. Steinbeck's portrayal of Kate, the mother figure, as a malevolent, depraved whore confused the issue further, just as Gwyn's increasing debauchery was deepening their mistrust of women. This was one of the many flagrant examples of their parent's irresponsibility. While the critics pondered the significance of Steinbeck's characters, the boys were left like feral children in a maze of neglect. In letters, Steinbeck worried about Gwyn's influence on the boys. In reality, he did little to protect them and he might just as well have worried about the effect he was having on his sons.

"Thom and I always wondered which of us was the James Dean character," John told me. "We figured Kate was a repository for all the vicious things Dad thought about Mother after the divorce." Later, when I watched the 1981 miniseries with Thom and John, I noticed the chilling effect Jane Seymour's vicious portrayal of Kate had on them. When it was over, we said nothing. An undercurrent of despair ran deep through the bottle of scotch they consumed that night.

Earlier, John and Thom had been asked to review the galleys for Jackson Benson's biography *The True Adventures of John Steinbeck*. Benson had unearthed a rumor that when she decided to divorce Steinbeck, Gwyn had taunted him by raising the question of Johnny's paternity. The brothers were simultaneously angered and convulsed with laughter; one had only to look at John to see the striking resemblance to his father. Thom told me, "Toward the end of their marriage, Mother had an affair with a neighbor. She was lonely because Dad was always traveling, but he certainly wasn't Johnny's father." Much to Benson's consternation, they refused to let him print anything questioning John's paternity. He always looked huffy around John whenever they met socially.

To add insult to irony, after Johnny died, Benson made the fact public in a subsequent book and in an Arts and Entertainment Network Steinbeck *Biography*. Both he and Thom are seen calmly discussing the insinuation that Johnny was not Steinbeck's son. That's when I realized you can't win for losing. John spent his entire life trying to life up to a myth, an archetype of biblical proportions and now that he was no longer able to defend his birthright, the remaining experts were fighting over his DNA. "Who, me?" Thom seemed to be saying in the interview. "I'm not my brother's keeper." Although the program outraged our friends, it only confirmed what I saw that summer afternoon in Austin, Texas. Each brother saw himself as the good son, but those of us who knew Johnny's talent, character, and compassion would cast our votes for him.

For the rest of our visit, John and Thom played out their genetically encoded mood swings and Pavarotti chest-poundings. The ebb and flow, swirling around their mutual double helix and mainlining into their veins, was always in direct ratio to the amount of scotch consumed. The pink cloud of my romantic dream was turning green around the edges.

While we were in Austin, Johnny took me to meet the old girlfriend and her five sisters. On the way over, he filled me in on their family history. One aunt had been lobotomized, their father lived with a demented woman who defecated all over the house, and their mother, who was in her seventies, had recently taken a young island lover in Belize. Liz Carpenter, Lady Bird Johnson's former press secretary, was also an aunt, which segued into the Steinbeck ties with strong Texican women, like Elaine, John's step-mother. In 1994, Liz Carpenter published a book about raising the children of the demented woman, subtitled *Confessions of a Seventysomething Surro-gate Mother*. It sounds tragic now, but that afternoon the sisters acted as if it were all very amusing and eccentric.

Unbeknownst to her, Thom and John's private nickname for the old girlfriend was Trigger, which had as much to do with her looks, they claimed, as her Texas roots. She was less than thrilled to meet me. I don't know why I went except I could tell Johnny wanted to show me off. He'd had such a hassle with Thom that I felt like obliging him.

The five sisters, who had previously been eying Johnny as a prize stud, hoping for a Steinbeck heir, sat like lemons and gave me dirty looks. Nobody talked to me but they made a big fuss over John. Frozen on the inside, I managed to limp through the ordeal. As we were leaving, Trigger suggested we meet that night for a movie, along with Thom. She and her date came up to our hotel room. I purposely was lying on the bed looking ravished, just to stick it to her. She was definitely one of those old girl-friends who wished I'd drop dead. She'd write John a note after a meeting like that saying "Sorry it was so *social*."

"Excuse me?" I said when Johnny showed it to me. "What did she expect? You already dumped her once!" It's like they keep hoping the guy will wake up and come running back to them, even years later.

Thom pulled me aside after the movie to ask about the afternoon. "How did you ever survive? I can't believe Johnny put you through that." I made a crack about either having too much or absolutely no self-esteem.

The best old girlfriends are the ones who know what a pain the guy can be sometimes and they're more interested in getting to know you. Rachel Faro, who sang that commercial "in the Aaaarmy," was like that. John had run his you-have-to-meet-my-old-girlfriend number on her, so she knew it well.

"God, he had terrible taste in women," she shouted. I treasure the ones who know sisterhood can be delicious.

Our next stop was John's maternal grandmother's house in Nogales. She was ninety-two years old, bedridden for years with a colostomy. Filled with painkillers, she clung to life like a pit bull. She adored Johnny, and had driven him and Thom crazy for years by threatening imminent death and insisting they fly to her side, which they always did. This was Gwen, mother of Gwyn. Both had contributed to the brothers' misogyny. In her younger days, she'd been imperious in grand style, driving a canary-yellow convertible, asserting her way through life generations before feminism, in dramatic picture hats. She had the touch of St. Francis and taught Gwyn and then Thom and John about the secret life of animals, wild and domestic; of the sweet love and innocence in each silent creature. If a baby cried too long in a restaurant, she'd yell, "Put a sock in it!" She had a mouth on her that got passed on to her daughter who passed it on to her sons. The curse of alcoholism had traveled so far down the family food chain in its diseased genetic structure that it mutated into lewd obscenities.

"Mother could make a Marine blush when she drank," Thom boasted. With enough scotch, Johnny could make a Marine blanch, duck, and cover.

As we were leaving, Grandmother sent Johnny out to the kitchen to fix himself a snack. She drew me to her bedside. "I've been waiting for you to come along. I can tell he loves you with all his heart. I've been afraid to die and leave him, but now that he's found you, I know he'll be safe." It was our secret and she finally did let go a few months later.

Gwen's fourth husband, Stanley, was a broker of Mexican tomatoes, a consummate salesman who'd started in shoes. He was twenty years younger and looked like he could hardly wait for her to die. Not that he had any great plans, but he was getting tired of Grandmother ordering him about. When Thom was twelve years old, he'd worked all summer in Stanley's packing-crate factory, making tomato boxes. He'd saved one hundred dollars and just before he was due to fly back to school in New York, Stanley snookered him into a poker game. Stanley won, and he took every cent of Thom's savings. They hated Stanley.

I felt sorry for him. It couldn't have been much fun being married to a woman who selected her houses according to their proximity to the best hospitals so she could spend every holiday there. This was another charming trait she'd handed down to Mother. Gwyn would stage some illness that required a hysterical ambulance ride over Thanksgiving or Christmas, and the boys would be left to the dark and bleak holiday spirit of hired nannies who nipped at gin bottles. Once, Thom was so upset, he found Gwyn's little revolver, and climbed up on the kitchen counter, aimed it at his presumed terrorist, and declared, "I'm going to *toot* you." She was fired, but the holiday spirits never improved.

When Grandmother died, John and Thom went to her funeral in Tucson carrying the ancient ceramic chicken that held Mother's ashes. They'd kept it in storage along with the other furniture, not knowing what to do with her remains. As the moving men were unloading the antiques for our new house, they drew me aside and asked, "Are those guys really related to Steinbeck?" Then they whispered, "What's in that chicken? It says *Mother's Ashes*." John and Thom had hauled them around until Gwyn was finally placed next to her best friend and ally in perversity. We doubted they rested in peace.

I was starting to see parts of my gentle Johnny that shocked me. He began to take the strain of being around Thom and Grandmother out on me. Refusing to believe I was at fault, as he seemed to imply, I silently blamed his stress. This was the start of a dynamic that was to become a mantra for every woman who lives with an alcoholic when he's unhappy: *denial and blame*.

Johnny was becoming a monster and alcohol was the teratogen. While he seethed with rage, I oscillated between disgust and vulnerability, trying to figure out what was really wrong. I knew I hadn't done anything, but suddenly I was the bad guy. After a few hours of pain and insecurity, I opted for the wrath button and I let him have it.

A fight erupted on the first curve of the Pacific Coast Highway and lasted for six hours till we hit Monterey. I had held it in all week and assassinating his character was the only way I knew how to vent. This was years before any of us would learn to gently express our feelings in "I" statements. He pulled up in front of the Greyhound bus station in Monterey and ordered me out of the car. He suggested I take a bus to San Francisco to stay with my parents and he'd meet me back in Colorado or see me in hell. He threw my suitcase onto the sidewalk. I refused to leave the car and insisted we go to a hotel.

I wish John had come with an owner's manual, something to make him user-friendly. Or some kind, concerned family member could have sat me down and said, "When he hits boiling, don't push anymore. You'll never get what you want; he can't be pushed." It took me ten years to learn that. I was a pusher. Johnny was a pusher. It was part of that mirror thing we saw in each other. Eventually the pain became too great and we stopped pushing and learned to stick out our tongues at each other when we wanted to get a point across. Ten years it took for us to let go of the napalm brought on by the hounds of hell. By then, a fight would last three minutes, tops. We reached a level of enlightenment few couples achieve. But the path getting there was a battlefield, a very uncivil war.

Once settled in a comfortable hotel, I asked him if we could just drop the whole fight. It was important to me that he meet my family and I didn't want to break up the trip. Maybe he was nervous about meeting my parents, maybe he was flexing his childhood habituation to operatic fights in order to feel alive. I noticed that being in Steinbeck Country made him extremely squirrely and so I let go of the whole thing. John softened, the magic returned, we became entranced with each other again, and our world went back on the half shell.

Being around certain people created tremendous stress in John's system. He was driven to maintain a charming public persona, and after a while his nerves would be on edge from the strain of posturing. "When you were with John," a friend once said, "he held you close to the flame of fame. He could elevate you to the heights of that rarified air and make you feel like you were a star, too." While I was furious with him, and hurt by his insensitivity, I also knew that I was the only one who would consistently give him a place where his heart could rest, where he could drop the posturing and facade. Years later, when he finally got sober, Johnny became a wonderful curmudgeon and he refused to play that old role. But it took a monumental effort on his part to achieve enough self-confidence to lose the need to appear larger than life.

John hadn't produced much since his first book, *In Touch*, published a decade earlier in 1969, about his six years in Vietnam. He was drafted when he was twenty and served for a year over there in Armed Forces Radio and TV. Shortly after returning home, while he was still in the army, he was busted for possession of marijuana, which was very upsetting and embarrassing to Steinbeck. Although he was acquitted, Johnny told me Steinbeck's last words to him were, "They should have put you in jail."

When he was twenty-two, John testified before the Senate Armed Forces Subcommittee on Drug Abuse as an expert on marijuana after writing an article titled "The Importance of Being Stoned in Vietnam" for the *Washingtonian*. Johnny was the first journalist to reveal the fact many soldiers were using drugs over there. As usual, he was not afraid to speak the truth and he used *In Touch* as a vehicle for his honesty. When he got out of the army, he was so enamored with Vietnamese culture, their women, and their drugs, that he immediately returned as a civilian. Along with Sean Flynn, Errol's son, and several other Saigon Cowboys, John lived in a brothel called Frankie's House, where they learned street Vietnamese, which made them privy to local stories before they were translated for prime-time news. John and Sean started Dispatch News Service which broke some of the most important stories, including the My Lai massacre of three hundred innocent civilians by U.S. troops on a search-and-destroy mission. Sean disappeared on a photo shoot in Cambodia, another son-of-a-famous-father fatality biting the Asian dust.

John also spent time living on the fantasy Phoenix Island in the middle of the Mekong, governed by a whimsical yogi, the silent Coconut Monk. This tiny, stooped mendicant adopted John as a spiritual son and invited him to live on the peace zone he had created in the midst of the raging war. Howitzer shells were hammered into bells by the four hundred monks on the island. There were seven tiered pagodas, reminiscent of Watts Towers, symbolizing harmony. The relationship between John and the monk was the start of John's search for a surrogate, spiritually evolved father.

While he was in the army, he fell in love with an older Vietnamese woman whose husband was a high-ranking general. Later, he had an affair with an American woman and their daughter was born in Saigon. In the course of those six years, John became a junkie, first on opium and then heroin. He also won an Emmy for the work he did on the CBS documentary *The World of Charlie Company*, which filmed the soldiers in action. When you achieve that much success at an early age, you become a hard act for yourself to follow. A few *Playboy* or *Travel and Leisure* articles and barrels of scotch later, he had to pump up the volume just to keep people from noticing that he wasn't producing. Growing up around famous people made both John and Thom feel that they had to spread a cloud of stardust wherever they went. The stories had to be scintillating, the humor razor sharp, Uzi quick. It was wearing on them, and it wore me down, too, but other people were dazzled, and that was everyone's reward for all their sleights of hand. No one but the three of us noticed the toll it was taking.

I had no idea how deeply John's Vietnam experiences had wounded him. Earlier that fall, he had been asked to write an article about Post Traumatic Stress Disorder in Vietnam vets for *Denver* magazine and that was an education for both of us. The Disabled American Veterans published a list of traits which included sleep disturbances, emotional numbing, loss of interest in work, survivor guilt, suicidal feelings, the inability to talk about war experiences, alienation, cynicism and distrust of authority, and emotional distancing from loved ones. Johnny's favorite was "concern with humanistic values overlaid by hedonism." Four times the number of vets have killed themselves than were actually killed in the war, and now statistics claim over 40 percent of the homeless are Vietnam vets.

I felt like I had been given a topographical map to the Grand Canyons and Himalayas of Johnny's shattered psyche, with the staggering invitation to explore those uncharted depths and heights if I wanted to know this man. I was terrified and felt so alone. How could I navigate through his scarred memories when he refused to face them himself? There seemed to be so many things wrong. He was alcoholic, drug addicted, a Vietnam vet, an abused child, and to top it all off he was the son of a famous father. There was no one I could even discuss these things with. All of these issues were far removed from the collective consciousness at that time, whereas now the talk shows have run out of things to say about them.

You have to understand this thing about being named John Steinbeck. I would watch John flinch on the phone when asked his name. It always got a reaction. You couldn't just call up and make a reservation for dinner that night, or even order Chinese. And John felt he had to be gracious about it, if only to encourage people to read more if they liked Steinbeck's work. He was always heartened by the sons of famous fathers who achieved success, like Jeff and Beau Bridges, or David and Keith Carradine.

"I think their fathers really loved them and encouraged their talents, instead of being threatened," John said. "You get a sense of closeness and support. Their fathers look so kind, like they really knew how to talk to their sons and guide them in their careers. They didn't see them as a source of competition, but rather as a reflection of their own talents, as opposed to the distance and grudge holding that Dad was so good at."

"Dad was jealous of Johnny, because he knew Johnny saw right through him and it would infuriate him," Thom said. "Dad was jealous of Mother's intelligence for the same reason. They didn't act like he was the Great Man. Elaine catered to that need in him, because she knew which side her bread was buttered on. Though don't get me wrong, they fought frequently."

There was the answer to the turmoil I'd felt in Austin. When Steinbeck examined the ancient struggle that pits brother against brother in *East of Eden*, he forgot to take himself out of the equation. He shaped the duel into an unwieldy triangle with this autobiographical revelation. The real issue at hand was his refusal to let either son surpass him with their talents, wisdom, or courage. By dividing and conquering with his favors, he rendered his sons impotent to grow beyond the parameters of what he would allow. I saw the work that lay ahead and once again was filled with resolve that John would not succumb to his paternal curse. If a father does not transmit his encouragement and blessing to his son, he holds him frozen in a flight pattern of resentment and negativity, daring the son to evolve past the limits he has set for himself. In this grudging resentment of the betterment in each generation the son must self-sabotage in order to win the father's approval. I vowed in the name of Abra to beat the old man at his own game.

When we got to San Francisco, John charmed my parents. They didn't seem to notice how much alcohol he drank. Although my mother had quit drinking by then, his consumption of two pints of scotch didn't alarm her. Johnny entertained them with famous-people stories, like the time he was sixteen and drove Myrna Loy home from one of Dad's parties. Just as she was getting out, he asked her for a kiss because, as Nora Charles, "she was my first love when I was in short pants."

My mother told me later that she thought he was fatally attractive. And in spite of the semaphore of red flags going off all around me about his drinking and mood swings, I was still in a swoon about this guy. We told my parents we were going sightseeing and we spent the whole day wrapped around each other in our hotel-room bed. That was our idea of doing San Francisco.

12 | REVOLT

JOHN

Though we both wake up considerably more clearheaded than we have been for a couple of decades, when sifting through buried and drug-dampened memories, my brother and I still find it hard to recall the "facts" of the next two years following the European trip of 1961. For me, I think that this is because of a basic numbness. But oddly, I think it also has something to do with the other fact that I have my own grown children now. In the course of raising Megan and Michael, I have at times manifested some of the same sensitivities that my father was prey to, and I know that I've also harbored some of the same feelings of abandonment by my kids. Usually we think of it as being the other way around, but really, nobody can give life to the concept of being used like a parent spurned.

After our trip through Europe, North Africa, and Greece, in 1962, I once again returned to the familiar boarding-school system at the age of fifteen. For the next year and a half I was away at another one of those New England holding tanks called Hebron Academy.

Over Christmas vacation there was finally a break in the chain of parental control and the hypocrisies of filial gratitude. Ideally, we like to think that sort of thing should come about spontaneously, organically, and in a way it did. It is impossible to instruct a teenager that he should be grateful after all, and in my own bitter state, constantly listening to my mother and father maligning each other, while Elaine and Dad fought far more than I'm sure Elaine is happy to remember—the validity of such a lesson in gratitude was sorely wanting. Dad and Elaine seemed to mostly fight after a lot of drinks the way most couples are likely to do, and as for Mom, well . . . !

The tension inside of me was building. I rarely did well in school, and the letters that I got from England or wherever my father was reminded me that I was letting him down badly. Finally, after his return to America, over Christmas vacation, there was a fierce seismic change in me that initiated a period in which it was my turn to explode. By this time *I* was drinking, too.

Because of my intransigence when it came to not doing any homework in study hall, which I considered a parlor for light reading or letter writing, Hebron Academy had expressed some exasperation and had written my father suggesting that perhaps I should go somewhere else. I had not been an untamed monster, I was well liked, and so on, but my grades were a disgrace.

Thus challenged, my father wrote them back as only he could, and charmed them into taking me back. I wish I had the letter as I forget his irresistibly earthy approach which cornered and flattered their patience into such a blind alley of education vanity that it was impossible for them to *not* take me back. Some cold cash may have changed hands here, too, as a donation toward a future dormitory or something, I'm not sure.

The very day that I was supposed to return to school filled with gratitude that my father had managed this piece of grand manipulation, I had this tremendous fight with my stepmother, and then of course with El Patron. I said fuck it, and refused to return to the school in Maine. Of course when children who have been supported for fifteen-odd years make these kinds of decisions, the hurt and anger that flies back and forth is immense.

If I remember correctly, my stepmother began the contest while hung-over herself, because she had found a bottle of rum in my room, and my father quickly came in to it to tell me that if he chose to push the issue, I could go to jail for such an offense. On an earlier occasion during our trip, on a Greek liner he had informed both my brother and me that he could arrange a similar fate if we were caught fraternizing with the opposite sex in international waters. This seemed especially unfair since when he was drinking, he liked to flirt with our girlfriends if he could, even to the extent of telling them what pale shadows of men we were compared to him; altogether an insensate and embarrassing piece of work.

Though Thom and I discussed it all the time, it was probably the first time I had fought back by telling them about their behavior, rather than just being the object of a general inspection marshaled by them. I had eyes in my head, they weren't such hot shit either, etc.

Since both he and Elaine drank to character-changing, mood-swinging proportions themselves almost every night, I felt that this new threat of jail was cowardly at best, and hypocritical at the very least. In retrospect, it is clear to me that the fuse for this fight had been lit before I was even aware of it. The easy details of our mutual misbehaviors were only the enchanting decoys, but from the moon it would have been starkly evident that the argument was over deep wounds. The somewhat hypocritical theme about the manner and extent of the preferred methods of how we each had chosen to alter our consciousness was mere subterfuge. It was cogent only to the extent that this was how we had chosen to overcome the floating pain of life, and the revulsion we experienced in seeing ourselves in each other's mirror. The disappointment was infuriating on both sides.

So the argument quickly deteriorated to a list of all the toys that I had broken as a young child, and after that I had enough. I took a big drink, and left. After all, it *was* Christmas.

My brother followed suit later that night. He was smart. He moved in with a girlfriend, but I moved back with my mother who had been out of our sight, and thus seemed comparatively sane and friendly through lack of exposure.

Though his experiment at active parenting had not been a great success, even with the help of subletting us most of the time to boarding schools, tutors, aunts, cousins, and camp, my father naturally felt betrayed by us, and when later we sued him in family court for child support, he was mortified and, of course, delirious with anger and hurt.

His position about any support was that he had paid for our "upkeep" in boarding school, and if we refused to be there, then we would have to fend for ourselves. Not a bad point really, but the court disagreed and in the spring of 1964, Dad was ordered to pay $22 a week to both my brother and me. This was obviously not a major financial victory, but our vague point about the vicissitudes of his parenting and our freedom of choice had been made.

Almost immediately, my mother provided her usual alcoholic dramas which only encouraged my drinking as a palliative. I returned to a city school called McBurney for a time, but mostly I hung out with my music friends, and girls. I smoked pot for the first time listening to Stravinsky's *Le Sacre du Printemps*, and immediately realized that pressing on your jugular veins and even drinking were child's play.

On my sixteenth birthday—June 12, 1962—I returned to my mother's apartment to find her drunker and meaner than usual. I went into my bed-room to try and escape her fury, but there was no real cover there. She came in and with a powerful "straight-arm" proceeded to push the heavy TV set over onto my shins. I literally saw stars, and then something snapped in that house too after all the years of being woken up at night, being pum-meled by her fists, and ducking scotch bottles.

I jumped up and threw the television out the twelfth-story window of the apartment down onto York Avenue. Then *I* started to break up the fur-niture in the same manner that I had been raised to eventually imitate. Finally, when my mother protested but also railed Macbethian prediction of this outcome and my "true nature," and then tried to stop me, I punched her in the mouth as hard as I could, and hammered at her body for God knows how long.

After I got hold of myself I watched trembling as she lay on the floor. Unimpressed, in her stupor, she was just barely interrupted with her ongoing drunken epithets about her children and the cruel fate of the world.

Shaking violently, I took the Siamese cat and went to stay with friends. For a month or so I stole food from stores, and lugged the cat around for fear of reprisals on *it*. When eventually we saw each other, despite the fact that she was still horribly black and blue, we were silently contrite, and the incident was never mentioned.

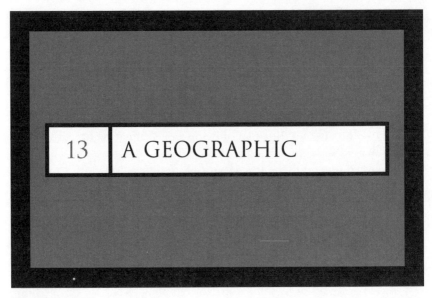

13 | A GEOGRAPHIC

JOHN

E ventually my mother decided to take what is known in the alcohol business as a "geographical cure." She was now in the sweet wedge of her cycling shame. By trying to use willpower to rescue herself yet again from yet another series of disasters and the evident "bad luck" that lay at the root of her unmanageability, she was, like all of us alcoholics, going to metamorphose. She knew what the answer was, so she tried to become a person who would defeat her outrageous fortune. She became at least outwardly optimistic and full of resolve. Neither of us knew that she was suffering from a disease and was well beyond the point where strength of character would do any good. I, too, was optimistic as I helped her move out of New York City to the high desert of Palm Springs, California, for her "asthma." After the events of my sixteenth birthday, we both felt guilty as hell. So the curtain went up again on another fresh start; new beginnings with the old solutions of regret and reform.

Though I didn't know it, my needs were becoming the same as hers. But I was still young, and my only discernible addiction at that point was to cigarettes and the ever-shifting vicissitudes and emotionally chaotic situations provided by others.

There were a lot of good reasons to go to California. My mother loved the West. She was really a lot more comfortable there than in New York.

She had spent most of her time in California when she was a singer. She had met my father there. They had romanced during the filming of *The Grapes of Wrath*, and went on to spend a lot of time in Cuernavaca while he was writing *The Pearl* and a little screenplay called *The Forgotten Village*.

My maternal grandmother lived in the San Bernardino Mountains just west of Los Angeles. When we weren't sent off to camp, my brother and I had spent many summers with her. She was a great lady and perhaps the only really functional adult I knew in my immediate family.

A far as I was concerned, an abrupt move was just what the doctor ordered. In fact, the doctor was the late Milton Brothers, Joyce's husband, and like most doctors back then, knowing very little about the real underlying nature of alcoholism and addiction, he advised the move as well. And what a benefit to me. At last, I would finally be near blonde girls, cars, and sunshine. My father and I had become essentially estranged since I had left his care and the dubious protection of various boarding schools. The sting of family court was also an injury not to be easily suffered. I was more than content about the prospects waiting for me in California. At age sixteen I was ready to begin my adult life.

With a deep voice and an East Coast flair, I gave myself a headstart and told everyone that I was twenty-one. Since I loved music, this fantasy kid was a graduate of Julliard. After first scooping ice cream at Baskin Robbins for a while, and working as a stock boy at the Palm Springs Bullocks Department Store, I started working in radio. Because we were raised on *American Bandstand*, being a disc jockey was a goal for anyone from the rock 'n' roll generation. After doing that sort of thing for a while, I fell in love with broadcast news.

Since I worked in radio news, I was also friendly with most of the Palm Springs police force. In fact, they comprised most of my drinking associates. That proved to be fortunate since Mom's *new leaf* fell quickly with the last of autumn and the cops were often called to my mother's address to quiet some drunken tirade.

It was a new twist for me. Police coming to the house was more of a California phenomenon than a New York City scene, to be sure. Sometimes, loving any sort of vexing engagement, she would call the cops herself, and they would now and again find her brandishing a gun like Annie Oakley, at some invisible foe. Eventually, she knew each of the cops on a first-name basis. After all, it *was* Palm Springs. To me, her behavior was as scary as it had ever been, and made what was to come in the mail that summer of 1964 look like a cakewalk. GREETINGS: We've drafted your ass.

The draft blew my cover. On my twenty-third birthday I turned eighteen. It came as a big surprise to the police I was used to drinking with, especially the one whose wife I'd shacked up with for a brief while. As for me, I had always wanted to see the Orient, and what's more, found war movies stirring. Even though I had totally emancipated myself by then, and had my own apartment, my life was actually beginning to get quite boring. Living alone with my dog and pretending to be older than my years just wasn't making it. I was already drinking a lot by that time, but I rather felt it was only to obscure my mother, who was acting more and more like a trapped animal when *she* was drunk. The alcohol seemed to help me deal with a murky legacy and the fear of some unnamed failure insinuated by my father.

Actually, as far as my father was concerned, my deficiencies were not entirely unnamed. They were the usual failures of sons. I was a lazy, ungrateful, self-centered bum; probably unworthy of his name; and, of course, "just like" my mother. In some ways, he was right, but I don't think he appreciated how badly I wanted to get out from under the barrage of everyone's hysteria, including what I thought was his less-intoxicated style. Little did I know how he had long been medicating himself and passing his ups and downs off as righteous indignation or the license of poetic depression.

I wasn't particularly afraid to go to Vietnam. After all, I like to travel! I even became convinced that the war might help me where I couldn't help myself. Though it was an incredible idea, for a while the war did help. However, the pressure-detonated issues of Vietnam with their multiple time settings would continue to explode in mine and other people's faces for decades to come. Nonetheless, the war presented a somewhat unique solution for the impasse in the two John Steinbecks' relationship.

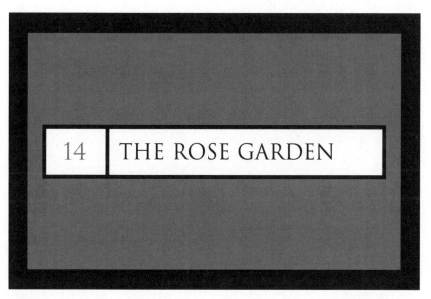

14 | THE ROSE GARDEN

JOHN

I n retrospect, it seems that within moments of bending over and coughing for an army doctor, I was on my butt in Saigon. This swift move is not just the compression of hindsight, but directly due to the fact that on receiving my draft notice, I had reopened talks with my father and asked him to use his influence with President Johnson to get me out to "Our War." This attitude so stirred my dad that a détente immediately fell in place. Now here was the sort of son he wanted, goddamn it!

After basic training at the improbably named post of Fort Bliss, in El Paso, Texas, I went east to New York to visit my father and tour his personal study of the psychology of war and manly patriotism, mostly based on John Wayne movies.

Dad had been sort of a correspondent during the Second World War, and compiled a book called *Once There Was a War* that was full of the kind of absurd human detail that he loved and was famous for.

I remember one story in particular that always appealed to me as an inveterate escape artist. Apparently there was a disgruntled Italian American soldier who dearly missed his girl back in the Bronx. One day on the beach south of Naples along with some other grunts, he was charged with guarding and loading a battalion of Italian Fascist troops onto landing craft to be taken out and put on bigger vessels where they would be taken to POW camps in the United States. Being awfully homesick, he became suddenly inspired. He stripped down to his skivvies and bolted away from the beach, screaming Italian obscenities. He was immediately apprehended by the MPs, thrown into the line of captured soldiers, and boarded for home!

Whether or not this really happened was never the important part of getting a story or even veiled political advice from Dad. Not being too literal in deciphering the message was. He would not have found it amusing if I managed to escape from Vietnam or even the draft, so one had to be very careful as to just what was being advertised when it came to following the thread of what he did or did not approve. He thought of both my brother and me as "goldbrickers," which is something that we are both sore about. If he only knew the energy it took being *his* son! Hell, I was volunteering to get killed over it.

He took me to Washington to meet the commander in chief. I was photographed in uniform in the Oval Office shaking hands with President Johnson, the only man who could rival Dad for jug ears and that larger-than-life stance that some men of that generation seemed to have the patent on. Father's relationship with Lyndon Johnson was anchored not just in Democratic politics, but also in the fact that his wife, Elaine, and Lady Bird had gone to school together at the University of Texas. After our visit with the president, we went back to Sag Harbor, Long Island, where now I was treated as sort of an equal by my father and we drank and talked politics and war for a solid week.

Sleeping very little and grinning at each other like fools who had never had any differences about anything, I felt that this was the way it always should have been. Past behaviors were erased by the masculine import of patriotism.

My father was a master of implicit bonding and charming lies; and even if we both knew them to be lies, well, one had to suppose that, too, was part of real war and a warrior's passage in a kind of tribal bullshit humor. He bought me a lovely Colt derringer as a personal sidearm. For close-in fighting, don't you know. I mean two lousy shots for chrissake! We were obviously in some reverie of war fought in the mists of make-believe, groping toward a kind of manhood embroidered only in daring dreams of childhood glory. It is sad to say here, but fantasy, particularly heroic fantasy, can be a really terrible thing to have to negotiate when enlivened by the mind of a noncombatant.

Later, my brother and I (he became a helicopter door gunner through a similar "bonding experience") began to believe that at this point Dad had probably placed an order in his head for a new piano to pedestal the picture of whatever son would be killed overseas. I mean he could be *very* romantic. But then of course, so could we.

The war turned into a moral quicksand for Dad as for many others. Though he himself knew better, he was somewhat blinded by the heady association with power. Not since FDR and Adlai Stevenson had he been so near a presidency. But he did know better. Some years earlier, during the Kennedy administration when Pablo Casals accepted an invitation to play the cello at the White House, my father had written a piece about the danger of artists getting into bed with politicians, no matter how benign or lofty the atmosphere might appear. He was not snowed by that Camelot, but the many invitations to spend weekends with Lyndon at Camp David were irresistible to him.

These two men prided themselves on being rough-hewn, as compared at least to the East Coast establishment. Of course, Johnson often preferred to be downright vulgar, which was not exactly my father's style, but both of them had a need to exaggerate the difference that they felt separated them from their more "sophisticated" critics. They were both good men who more than anything wanted to be liked, but they also had a tendency to overcompensate in order to bathe their sense of inferiority as country boys. I think that at least part of their friendship was also due to the fact that they unconsciously recognized how easily hurt they could be despite their braggadocio. This was true in spite of the fact that by then the president of the United States and the Nobel Laureate were in charge. There is no doubt that they genuinely liked each other and it *was* a plus that they could share the sometimes hilarious burden of being married to Texas women as a binding factor of real consideration.

In the face of what he considered Communist aggression, my father was becoming more and more conservative. He actually identified I. F. Stone as the voice of Hanoi, and the man's venerable newsletter as the party line. That was about as extreme as he got though, as he preferred dark disagreement to real political argument. He also liked the peasant disputes he could have with his Russian writer friends. He naturally felt more comfortable with that sort of poetic guttural passion than wading in against the critical bite of sharp political scientists. Someone like Susan Sontag would have killed him.

In any case, with me now sporting my army uniform, we whipped each other into an extraordinary sentimental froth. By this time in the visit, patriotism had turned downright Darwinian. The hegemony of the tide pool, the amoebae's thrust to the sky was the real issue here, by God! We took lots of late-night walks, drinking and giggling to near oblivion in the starlight. We had huge impassioned conversations about things that neither of us knew anything about. Indeed, this really is what men like to do. We reviewed the mythos of our civilization back to the slime, and on up to what I would discover "Over There." And after all, that was why I was going to Vietnam, by God: to observe, to learn, perhaps to die. Perhaps to dream? Of course, the extreme foolishness of the war sank any such vainglory or romance.

I didn't know what would happen then, but now, in trying to understand and still appreciate the past, it has became very hard for me to surmount the assault of time and what feels like the perpetual disillusionment of this our age. For a variety of reasons it sometimes seems like so many of my experiences and the once-cherished moments of young adulthood are somehow missing in action.

I had never known anything like stability, and I didn't pursue it. I was young and durable and not very sensitive to the subtle fears that were by now deep inside me. So I of course liked this adventure, the best distraction. However effective in the short term, the technique of derring-do was inevitably to cause further numbing. Perhaps that was the idea. But before I would come to any real conclusion about that, this war and national agony took all precedent under the usual banner of responsibility and glory.

And so, along with so many others, my golden youth was aroused and then served up to the Asian crucible where the major amalgam was death and destruction and where any hint of personal regeneration was subtle if not impossible to measure. In the end, like the rest of the walking wounded, I came home to a country filled with anger and shame. The general population tried to hide its killing with ignorance, thus killing many more of its own with neglect.

I spent almost six years in Vietnam, and in a way, So what! So I've been in a war, I've flown a plane, and I certainly learned that given my background, a taste for ashes is easily acquired and one that doesn't quickly fade. Though the war coemerged with so many other things in the middle of this century, it remains singular in its illusive moral. Even now, I try to fathom something of the purpose of this minefield which tore so many lives apart. For so many of us, Vietnam was like a spiritual concussion grenade. For some the ringing in the ears will never clear. Still, I was to go back to Vietnam many times; from California, from India, Cambodia, Laos, from Hong Kong, and Thailand, but it was my first trip there in the army that sank the barb. It also encouraged a variety of behaviors that nearly killed me. War is dangerous; especially in a world where even love can kill, quite accidentally.

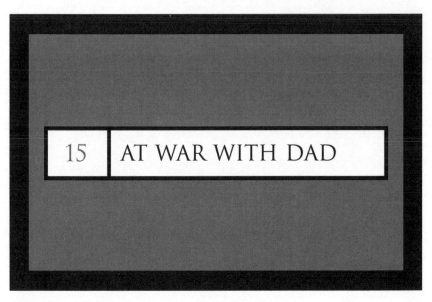

15 | AT WAR WITH DAD

JOHN

When I arrived in Vietnam, the newness of the Asian noises filling the air and the smells that mingled jasmine and shit, French bread, opium and incense completely thrilled me. I was wide open, and here, every minute was crammed with more seconds, more milliseconds, than an entire day back home in the states. Though I had traveled a lot for my age and felt rather worldly, I turned my head to take in everything with the dizzy focus of a four-month-old bird dog.

To be sure I was naive, but hardly anyone knew much about Vietnam when I first arrived in the summer of 1966. Well, people like David Halberstam, John Paul Van, and Daniel Ellsberg did, but they knew nothing about us, and we understood nothing about the war.

When I write about these times, it permits things to come out and lets them melt under my tongue, like sublingual vitamins. Now they are safe to examine, even play with. I don't think that I reacted to my circumstances the way most soldiers did. In fact, I'm sure of it. As the first days rolled by, the Vietnamese sunrise brought me even more things for my mind to grab and savor, and I did it with an avid panoramic awareness, like a child memorizing all the shiny metal objects worn into the asphalt of his neighborhood like they were jewels. Smooth and small, they don't exist for most of the people who move over them thousands of times a day. The Vietnamese themselves seemed oblivious to the textures. They laughed politely at me. I was charmed.

Because of my radio background, I was able to become a journalist for Armed Forces Radio and Television in Vietnam; a war correspondent for the Department of Defense and the people who brought you *Good Morning, Vietnam*. It was the early days of the electronic entertainment business in this ancient nation.

The ground for a huge station was being bulldozed and prepared, but when I arrived we were still broadcasting our FM/AM radio signals out of the basement of a Saigon hotel. The TV operation was literally up in the air as we went flying around in circles over the jungle in old prop-driven airliners, beaming down *Love American Style,* or the *Dean Martin Show.* We had plans to cover the entire country with ground stations to accommodate the big buildup. Within a year, there wasn't an inch of the conflict that couldn't enjoy that goofy girl Carol Burnett, or venture out of the jungle with *Star Trek,* and for the really gung ho, there was always *Combat,* with Vic Morrow. (I always thought it was weird that this poor guy would eventually be killed pretending to be in Vietnam during a *Twilight Zone* remake.)

Zone was also very popular with the troops, and why not? The basic idea for my unit's mission in Vietnam was to try to convince everyone, including ourselves, that we weren't really there at all! And if it turned out we were, well, the war was really just sort of Research & Development and maybe at worst, an exciting nine-to-five job with a few nasty occupational hazards. If our network mission succeeded, then after shutdown, one could just kick back with a cold beer and listen to the radio or watch the tube. The PX made sure to sell all the booze and paraphernalia you would need to support this idea. They also had the TVs, stereos, and refrigerators, and even Weber barbecues. Nothing was going to spoil consumerism in the abstract, though it turned out to be US that got consumed.

After I had been in Vietnam a few months, my father couldn't stand it anymore. He had to come, too! He asked my "permission," whatever that meant, and before Christmas 1966 he arrived at Ton Son Nhut airport in Saigon with my stepmother, Elaine.

After a few months, I had been removed to the field, as they say. But now I was permitted to come down to Saigon from my mountaintop station near Pleiku to visit my father the VIP. It was quite peculiar seeing him in that environment, outfitted in dashing camouflage ascots and drinking with generals and colonels while extolling the common man; the technique that was his trademark.

The army was getting to know me a little bit so I was only allowed to spend a few days with Dad, and then I returned to my mountain where he would come visit me in a fortnight or so after touring the front. Of course, there was no such thing in Vietnam, so basically VIPs were shown the toys and technology and maps and zeal of a military caught in a situation that it did not understand at all. Since our leaders were oblivious to our doom, there was a lot of nudging and confident winking that punctuated the sort of briefing that my dad and other visitors received.

From the South China Sea to the Cambodian border in the west, the Central Highlands of Vietnam represented the most beautiful, varied, and dangerous real estate of the war. This had been true for the French as well as the Americans. My little twelve-man unit had put up a small television station in an eighteen-wheel trailer. The site was on top of "Pussi Mountain," so named because of a vague significance that its sensuous curves held for love-starved soldiers. From its crest at about 3,000 feet, it overlooked the Fourth Infantry Division's base camp sprawled out on the plain below us. The countryside looked more like the African veld than what we think of as Southeast Asia. Getting up in the dawn light, I almost expected to see zebras and gazelle crossing the vast grassy expanse that led to the low hills of Cambodia in the west. This was also Montagnard country where the men dressed in colorful loincloths and carried crossbows and the women were bare-breasted as they slashed and burned for their crops in the ancient way.

Dad arrived at a small, dusty airstrip near Pleiku City where I picked him up by jeep. When I was just a little boy, he used to drive me around the moors of Nantucket in a jeep he bought from army surplus and memories of that time came to me as he climbed in, now dressed in his new combat fatigues.

It was a forty-minute drive through the countryside over roads covered with potholes, mortar craters, and deep furrows from previous rainy seasons. If I close my eyes, I can still see all of its snags. With the exception of the occasional convoy bracketed front and back with helicopter gunships, there was almost never any traffic on it. As a result, the road made you feel very exposed, so the technique was to drive very fast in a zigzag to avoid obstacles and possible bullets. For young and old alike, the drive was forty minutes of torture, but I couldn't help being amused by my father yelling at me to slow down as if we were on the Long Island Expressway or somewhere normal. Here, I was able to look at him and just grin as I pushed down on the gas peddle. Yup, this was *my* jeep, on *my* road, leading to *my* mountain in *my* war . . . Pop.

Eventually we careened up to the top in a cloud of red dust. My father gingerly climbed out to meet the commanding officer, Captain Luckey, and the rest of the boys. Immediately he began to regale the unit in that special way he had that made them feel part of something very manly and full of ironic adventure, something almost secret. His "aw shucks" humility was very engaging and warm. Again, it made people feel as if they were part of a wonderful conspiracy of imagination and action that might be a little risky, certainly to be kept private, but the right thing to do in the eyes of those who knew the secrets of real life. He could pull this off with just the lift of an eyebrow, and all my life I saw hundreds of people tumble for it and be tamed into a submissiveness a sheepherder would admire.

As the first nightfall crept over the plains, my father and I stared out over some bombing far in the distance. It looked like the kind of fake thunder and lightning you see offstage in an opera. After checking our trip flares and claymore mines for our night defensive positions, we broke out the booze. With a nudge and a wink, Dad slipped me a couple of pink pills which I of course took immediately. Practiced as I was with survival kits, I soon realized it was pure speed; something very close to methamphetamine to be more precise. I would eventually learn the underlying significance of this gesture when it was later revealed to me just how long and often he had been taking these little beauties. For the moment, however, it was just part of this undercover fellowship that he transmitted through his bright eyes. We all talked late into the night.

The next day and evening, our little festival continued. Though one cannot discount the effects of speed and booze, war itself delivers an altered state of consciousness of the most compelling and bizarre variety. I've often thought that when a child or cadet looks into an old soldier's eyes, even if the war has been horrible, the younger man sees a queer faraway look on the veteran's face when he is asked, "What did you do in the war?" Survivors of combat have seen a bluer sky and a greener tree than most mystics. Glimpsing this, the kid knows that something very important had gone down; something more scary and unutterable than even sex, though it is mixed with something like that, too. Later, when I worked at the Pentagon around hundreds of professional soldiers who had never heard a shot fired in anger, I used to get chills knowing that more than anything, they wanted a taste of that look and would eventually, without any doubt, help perpetrate more wars to get it.

Our little unit was small and intimate and Captain Luckey, outside of being charmed by my father's presence, was a kind and loose commanding officer. But this second night was much different than the first. At about ten o'clock, the field radio started going efficient on us, reporting an attack on Pleiku City. Then we were probed by something as a trip flare went off in our outer perimeter wire.

With a shout we all flew to our combat stations. I had an M-79 grenade launcher, and Dad picked up an M-60 machine gun. As I jumped into my hole, the man in there before me set off our claymores with a roar, and I started lobbing grenades out towards the tripped flare.

Captain Luckey immediately got on the radio and called in the Fourth Division artillery which started laying illumination rounds over us as well as walking fragmentation up the slopes of the mountain. Time does funny things in these situations, but soon after the first illumination popped, I looked back over the edge of my hole. I saw my father behind some sand-bags overlooking my position with his M-60 at the ready. There was nothing particularly awkward here. We both knew and liked guns, but there was something so incredibly touching and hilarious about the consistently operatic quality in which all our metaphors had crystallized. I mean, who, in God's name, was producing this movie? And what an amazing feeling to see him ready in his helmet and flack jacket protecting my back as I then continued to lob out more grenades. Despite the grandiosity that we were both capable of, this was a rare and oddly distinguished moment in our lives, and one that I continue to interpret in revolving waves of symbolism and flat-out caricature. For just a few moments it seemed that the entire North Vietnamese army and the American military-industrial complex had conspired to let us see through the parody of our true relationship, using perhaps the only tools that could nauseate our sentimental, overcompen-sating temperaments into a genuine clarity. The result of course was laughter. The probe turned out to be just that and of no consequence, but it had been enough to bring us to a brief moment of nondiscriminating awareness for each other. I saw the mirth in his eyes and felt a brotherly love in my heart. When I recall it into the forever present, my greed and longing for a feeling of connection with my father disappears. In those moments, everything is enough.

16 | HOME—1967

JOHN

When I landed back in California after my first year in Vietnam, having been discharged, it was the same eighteenth day in June it had been the year earlier. As I wrote at the time, the weather, the air base, even the hour was the same, yet everything had changed for me, for my country. About half the soldiers were the same ones who had been with me going in the other direction that 365-day circle back around the Sun. We had all separated to different units. I hadn't seen any of them for exactly a year, but here we were again. Though I really didn't know them, they were obviously the same people, and yet they didn't look the same. Their faces were no longer the faces of boys. Grim experience had replaced any innocence. An odd mask of unsettled sureness that probably went back to the Trojan War sat where pure anxiety had once flashed. The other half of the men, well, they just weren't there, and the hushed presence of their absence was partly responsible for the new look on the faces of those of us who were left. I went into the jet's lavatory and looked at myself in the mirror. I started to cry, though probably not long enough, for the child I had lost somewhere. Then I went back, tightened my seat belt, and tried to go home.

Back home, things had really started zipping along. Within the first month of my return I was being chased around in the midnight Pennsylvania woods by an aged hippie wielding a bowie knife. He had discovered that I was a GI, and he felt a duty to eliminate me as a baby killer. "Ecology," he said. I was on my second acid trip ever, and boy, was I surprised. I felt a bit misled by the flowers in his hair. Maybe this was the New Left that I'd heard so much about. Though he was certainly a lunatic, he surely represented some unclaimed point man in the moonlight. In any case, I was resilient. The war had been bad.

I remained in the army for about six months after my return to America. It was like being dropped from one war zone into another. I went from a hell realm of bullets to a realm of confused and jealous gods with their "living room war," and bad-to-worse news bulletins. Once again though, I was eager to immerse myself in the "whatever," and it was obvious, at least to me, that in either theater, I was a volunteer.

As a reporter for the army in Vietnam, I had gone out looking for a good human-interest story, and I found instead more marijuana than Cheech and Chong's best dream. My research soon stopped being objective. The irony of it all: this amazing dope was right there where they had sent us to win hearts and minds. My square mind was immediately vanquished, and then my heart broke.

Now the counterproductive nature of the serendipity which found us slogging through a garden of sheer escapism was a pretty well-kept secret until I got back to the States. In 1967, people had somehow concluded that, quite apart from your domestic variety Communist-drug-addict-hippie-vermin, we in the service were high-minded scouts who were defending the integrity of our shores and interests with sobriety, M-16s, and probably Jesus. Hearing that, strictly speaking, this was not the case, an editor friend of mine asked for more detail. I wrote an article for the *Washingtonian* magazine called "The Importance of Being Stoned in Vietnam," and the cat was out of the bag.

My attachment to sincerity has always been a serious impediment. I was foolish enough to have written and talked about these things before I was actually out of the military.

After almost being court-martialed, I was called to testify in front of the Senate Armed Forces Sub-Committee on Drug Abuse. Though I testified in depth to a number of written questions, I basically told them that there was a lot of dope around, a lot of people were smoking it, and I didn't see that there was really any problem. I was careful not to bring up the Age of Aquarius or anything like that. Astrology was to wait in the background for another administration to bring it into the firmament of government and policy.

After this testimony, I felt a noble sense of solidarity with my peers, but I have to admit to a few shaky moments. Just a couple of days later, while driving my car, I turned on the radio and was immediately zapped with, "Today, Four-Star General of Army, General William Westmoreland, issued a statement saying, 'Private First Class John Steinbeck's comments on the use of marijuana in Vietnam are baseless.'" Talk about the long chain of command. Fortunately, a week later, on Pearl Harbor Day, my hitch was up and I was honorably discharged with a Good Conduct Ribbon.

Somewhat inadvertently, *I* had become news. It seems that I had become a spokesman for dope and its place in our society. So, *ad*vertently, I wrote a small book about my year in Vietnam. *In Touch* was nothing if not earnest. The war was ugly and ill-conceived, but I thought that the rift in the generations was due to simple misunderstanding, and that much could be healed with my unheated declaration of the facts. I knew nothing about the pathology of control and the substance abuse of power. I was too young to know, much less understand, that rage was an excruciatingly specialized style of addiction. Pressure and conflict were like alkaloids that offered a unique sense of well-being to whoever might develop the habit.

To be honest, I really didn't know much of what had been happening "back in the world." As I began to reconnect with my friends, it became obvious that my stint in the army, especially in Vietnam, was truly time spent somewhere off the planet.

America had become extraordinary. It was bursting with excitement. I had gone to Vietnam as a Hawk, and though I had turned into a veritable Turtle Dove, I still had a conservative streak. My love for history was one of the things that had kept me sane during the war. For some sort of cover— and protection—I became a student of the scene, a meteorologist for the changing wind, a wind that sometimes knocked you down, but once again, I was basically eager. This was my time, and I was a quick study.

17 THE SCENE

JOHN

In the spring of 1989, Abbie Hoffman died; on accident, as my kids used to say. I felt that I had lost a good friend, and so had my generation. He was a surprisingly kind and gentle person who also loved to shout a lot. He provided an enlightened and rousingly important sort of misbehavior.

I remember running around the West Village with him one summer in 1973 trying to unload zip-lock baggies of frozen mushrooms before they melted down and turned into a disgusting mottled swill. But then, after they inevitably did, his perky question became, "Was the value increased?" Of course this kind of question, as well as most all others, got more serpentine the more of the product that we ourselves consumed. Eventually there was nothing left but a wet stain on the floor of my car. As anyone will tell you, including the FBI, as a dealer in drugs, Abbie was a complete washout. As a provocateur of conscience, he was one of the sweetest and best.

I thought about him a lot the night he died. He had been a remarkable and totally energized commentator on the conditions of the day. With him gone, it will be like missing an important trick card in a Tarot deck. I had a hard time getting to sleep, and the next day, as if ambushed, I woke up to the fiftieth anniversary of the publication of another social commentary, my father's book *The Grapes of Wrath*. More death and coincidence, I suspect.

I don't necessarily want to sing a paean to Abbie Hoffman, but he was a force for an awareness that had not been mine before I was drafted. I don't know what would have happened to me without him or others in the sixties like him. I might have become just another button-down soul and grown prematurely complacent. I know for sure that the times would have been dumber and duller. He was a hard man to satisfy and it is sad that he is gone. For the most part, despondency was not one of Hoffman's public trademarks. It took just plain bad medicine to take him from us.

When asked once by the "Authorities" just what the hell he thought he was doing, Hoffman said, "I'm just shouting 'theater' in a crowded fire." It was a fire, but for many of us, the fire was also on the inside, and it would smolder for years, camouflaged as rage toward the fixtures of any discerned official oppression.

As this book has me casting backward and forward trying to figure out who I am and where I come from, to be honest I need to begin to get into what kind of person I began to make of myself, apart from the torque of my parents and childhood. My natural environment stretches from those formative days to the present, but despite my upbringing, I'm now responsible for the majority of the stretching. It's a bit like the journalistic quandary of when does the story become part of the event?

Definitely, when I was a young teenager, I felt dispossessed and betrayed by forces beyond my control. These feelings come cruising back from time to time. Without a doubt, a lot of this has to do with the crazy episodes that defined my childhood as well as the events that were compounded by the ricochet of my own erratic solutions. With Abbie Hoffman's death, however, I'm forced to remember that though I may have been clever, I wasn't really all that smart. I didn't have a lot of information to go on outside of the reactionary snap of witness abuse. I just knew something was disarranged.

At first I thought perhaps the chief problem was with me. That's how a program of borrowed shame frequently translates and transfers itself anyway. You witness people acting shamelessly and then you take it on as your own stuff. Typically, its starts with witnessing your parents acting out, and pretty soon you're carrying around a load of shame that was transferred from their shoulders onto yours, while they continue to blissfully ignore their abuses.

Then, right on schedule in the early sixties, my youth and opinions really began to mount as I grew into a "know-it-all" adult. It wasn't until later that I experienced the possibility of real conscious blame upon my perpetrators. Along with my peers, I knew something was about to break open. I didn't know what, but I began to feel nameless discontent just before the spark of articulation. And even when it started to happen, there wasn't a breaking open of floodgates, but just the bestirring of complaint; the old generic type of institutional anger that starts by way of a slow under-chorus, like the way babies begin to cry while parked next to each other in their baby carriages. First, they hear the noise of one comrade crying. Then, by way of imitation, one or two more rise to the wonderful sound of pure emotion, and before you know it, twelve babies are screaming bloody murder.

By the time I first returned from Vietnam, a curtain of betrayal hung everywhere. We were way past the gripe stage by then. From *our* side, it was largely due to what we felt were patriotically enforced lies about America's actions throughout the whole of the past, compounded with other crimes that were born of a decrepit white horror and a facile sense of superiority. We soon realized that even Saint JFK had been jerking off to his ballad of the Green Berets, or screwing Marilyn and reading James Bond every night, for chrissake!

Biologically, a seemingly drastic "punctuated equilibrium" happens all the time, and as the word implies, it's hardly ever a smooth transition, even for a mollusk. In freethinking people, the big lurch forward has the distinct sensation of a real double cross. Perhaps it was inevitable and maybe essential. Then bitterness and anger became ornaments that were pleasing to wear.

Our parents weren't really all that stupid. They suspected correctly that we were about to abandon them to their vanity, their fear, and their dusty domino games. So, by 1966, though we didn't know exactly what was going on, young people definitely *felt* something, and in my generation, the likes of Abbie Hoffman and Bob Dylan were some of the first babies that screamed foul.

Today, I get a little worried wondering what is going to happen in a world where a lot of younger people think that the Holocaust is a Jewish holiday, and the DMZ was a pre-rap rock group who performed *at* Vietnam, an unpopular but famous antiwar demonstration somewhere near Woodstock. I have met people who think that the Black Panthers were some sort of an expansion team, and the Dalai Lama is a Peruvian newspaper. I know that before his death, Abbie was somewhat dazed about this sort of thing, too. Without a blink, I saw him say on TV that now he didn't trust anyone *under* thirty. However, the twinkle in his eye was soothing, as if to say we could educate the young and give them some more time to see what a pickle they might really be in.

Because of the many habits that began to overwhelm me in the seventies, it had been a while since I thought about all of this, but shortly after Hoffman's death, my sixteen-year-old son, Michael, was sitting in the back of the car with his Walkman on, trying to compete with whatever it was that I was blasting over the other system. As I glanced back at him atonally mouthing lyrics, I saw a look of what seemed like rapture and certainty. His jaw was set and his eyes moist. His face was transfixed on a vision floating somewhere just over the horizon of his experience. Curious, I turned off "Hotel California" in time to hear him fervently declare (in that self-centered à capella Walkman way), "The Answer my friend is blowin' in the wind; the Answer is blowin' in the wind." I got a wonderful lump in my throat. At his age, the proclamation of truth is fearless, and the assumption of a basic goodness is basic in itself. It is unconditioned by the questionable kindness or the gauged decencies portioned out from the adult above.

At times, I've seen younger generations look at mine with the hilarity and slightly embarrassed terror of a high school football team from Nebraska watching a serious Japanese porno movie. The sixties and our fine youth recede into caricature as the "No Longer Suited for Prime Time Players." A realm of the senses perhaps, but it was no movie. It was our lives, and it was so tangible; the very Life of Life.

Everyone who was there remembers the burst of energy that brought us the likes of Abbie Hoffman, though they now remember it with varying degrees of fondness. Memories sometimes suffer. For a while it seemed the only way to grasp the era was to pick it up by its shoulder-length hair and dangle it, a sour and silly morsel, over the maw of the eighties. But euphoric recall aside, I can remember the energy and goodness of the time. Our society is still permeated with many of the holistic values and qualities that were distilled in my youth. They linger like the fragrance of perfume in an empty bottle. There were flashes of serenity, and perhaps even an inevitable enlightenment. There was also a notion that happiness or even mere Being, would or could suffice. Maybe, in its quiescence it was superior to action! This was not entirely laziness or hesitation, but a fine caution as the message we were getting was that even excellence seemed apocalyptically suspect. The mastery of science looked like it could be the route of pollution, madness, and nuclear destruction. So . . . "Let It Be."

The social and political stops along the way to the present might just seem like a convoluted game of Hippie Trivial Pursuit, however the movements of the day hadn't come out of nowhere. It is true that the little eddies of revulsion and revolution looked like they were coming from youngsters like myself, but a deeper maelstrom had really been a long time swirling and coming, way before Berkeley's free speech movement or Vietnam. Neither did the unmistakable vortex have an epicenter other than the human heart of dissatisfaction. Baby doctor Benjamin Spock and psychologist Abraham Maslow were no kids; and New Lefties like David Dellenger, feminist Betty Friedan, and San Diego's Marxist philosopher Herbert Marcuse weren't either. They had all spent decades shouldering the Old Left's rugged cross. The Beats, with their Emerson-tinged Eastern religion, had been "on the road" for some time already.

Before I was drafted there were lots of counterculture seniors, though some had an obvious need for musty control. At first, professors Timothy Leary and Richard Alpert, spun round by the double helix, fairly patronized their followers from their Harvard psychology chairs. With mostly good intentions, they imagined a generation locked like pigeons in a Skinner box. They held out a free radical, a key, a chemical/molecular possibility for early liberation, or a least a sugar cube worth of parole. By micrograms we might just forget the box . . . dose . . . and "break on through to the other side." Such easy fruition was out of sequence, of course, but what a sensate, delicious solution.

Like flies in a fly bottle which had been dashing against the glass, en masse we began to realize that the top was mostly off. The perceived jailers were in the *real* prison, dumbly guarding the "Outside." We on the inside were free. The fact that there might be bigger bottles ahead that might demand more, even real work at the lid, we didn't exactly foresee. We were very young, and that had its own sweet virtue and leverage.

Though everyone wasn't eighteen years old in 1965, it *was* the youth(s') movement. It was the kids in their late teens and early twenties who picked up the ball and ran in dizzying circles from goalpost to goalpost, leaving the Keep-the-Faith Old Guard panting and just a little bit worried. For some, it was for the sheer contrary delight of it all. For others, it was far more than just coltishness. A renaissance of organic politics and philosophy were let slip past and through the "dogs of war" at a perfect moment. The millennium by happenstance was colliding in coincidence with the mass adolescent rites of the most populist and reflexively utopian generation in American or world history. If you had survived to this point, it was really great to be alive.

Now "adolescence" is what anthropologists amazingly call a "high-context" culture; a spontaneous medium in which intuitively shared assumptions and formal nuances are so densely packed that every gesture speaks volumes. Overlooking the bloodless sound of it all, this was definitely true. When Bob Dylan sang about people like T. S. Eliot, he wasn't talking about literature; he was reducing progressive demigods to a Saturday night tag-team wrestling match. He could also sing, "The birdies in the trees go tweet-tweet-tweet," and the poetry and the gall were sublime. It was scarcely even the voice of a singer. It was some kind of antivoice, shamanic, invocative, used for sending complex, compelling messages over long distances to anyone with wit to hear. And by the way, if you could read cold lips, Liberalism was dead. The posture of this disregard and indifference that we began to display toward the worn-out righteousness of our immediate elders, also squared the mass family resentments wafting under the surface like a kelp forest.

Without the army to wake up to, my beard grew, I carried a stash, and learned how to tell long meaningful stories about my smallest possessions, like where I got a hole in my clothes. For now, I was becoming a socialized hippie. We hippies felt distinctly abused because of our soft views, and abjured for no good reason whatsoever. For a time, we tried to legitimize ourselves with examples from history. Though I couldn't manage it, there were long-as-you-could-grow-them locks of hair defended as really American, like, you know, Native Americans, the Founding Fathers, the Apostles. No matter the foolishness, what now seems like only style, set off deep, immensely powerful resonances among us.

It was a while before I really "understood" LSD. I had received a liberal education from inspired family sources. I was familiar with the Elizabethans and their King James Bible, as well as the knots and loopholes of Western psychology and philosophy. I loved paradox and Plato, e.e. cummings, and Wallace Stevens. That is to say, I loved the words, but I only understood the meaning in a jazzy, superficial sort of way.

One day, as I was sitting in my bathtub, amicably confused on a certain amount of acid, I began to look at a friend's copy of the Tao Te Ching. This was the jewel in the crown of Chinese thought. My father had exposed me to the works of Chuang Tse and Lao Tse, and I had found the topsy-turvy logic direct and amusing, if bewildering. But as I sat there this day in the clear water, trying to focus on the vibrating point, much less the sense of this Taoist comic book, I was distracted by a bird in the sky, and BAM, I suddenly "got it." Just like it sounds, the scales fell from my eyes, and that was not all. The bathroom exploded into dripping colors, and all the dumb metaphors I had ever heard danced around the room as holy truth. My mind seemed to become absolutely still, and then to fly up, like that bird in the empty sky, happy and free and away from its ancient prison. Oh boy, our species was actually well programmed for transcendence, but there was also the deep mechanism of ego provoking us to grasp and forget.

Looking out the window at the town, all the streets were actually rolling, like a yellow brick road leading to the Emerald City of my primordial being. My God! In my Father's house were many mansions, and they were all suddenly right here in the bathroom. Everything that I had ever read by the Christian mystics, the Taoists, the Sufi poets, the Concordians like Thoreau and Whitman, the Vedas, Vedanta, William Blake, William James, Buddhist Sutras, Ludwig Wittgenstein, Bertrand Russell, Carl Jung, Joseph Campbell, and the Book of Common Prayer, all of these things were pointed at the same damn thing that was luminescing all around me. It was something, *that* thing, that was inexpressible, but whole and real and eternal. In its ineffability, it was the answer to the suffering of the world.

Yup, I had gotten it, but within a few hours of trying to discuss it and own it with words, I lost it. I dearly wanted to share all this with my dad, but my gushing enthusiasm no doubt made it seem like I was "on drugs" or something. A true double bind. Nevertheless, I was stunned, and my life was changed forever, and like the dead Pascal's "This morning, fire everywhere" note found pinned under his hair shirt, I sit here even today, meditating on the fullness of the present to keep the memory green.

All in all though, I guess I was not unique. Why, every head shop in town was testament to the fact that a lot of my contemporaries had been in a bathtub or two themselves. The lyrics to the music of the day, though not referring directly to the Blue Cliff Record of Zen Buddhist transmission, were distinctly pushing the core ideas of instant enlightenment. You know, Satori . . . the FLASH.

Some things were profound, and also very funny. While still stationed at the Pentagon after returning from Vietnam, I'd already started calling in "well." Innate happiness often made it absurd for me to go to work, especially for the Defense Department. It now seemed necessary for me to "Drop at Dawn" at least twice a week, just to stay in tune with a micro-macro cosmos. One had to wonder how it ever got along without me knowing it was there before.

I began to comport myself with the air of a full-blown mystic. Mind you, this was not just vanity. What I had seen, I had seen. It was worth contemplating forever. I also liked sex and rock 'n' roll.

With my new hippie friends, I appreciated what was becoming a family that would play with me, and one that I didn't have to fear would be blown away at a moment's notice. In Vietnam, getting close to someone was risky business. For the time being, it was actually American to try and "love one another . . . smile on your brother . . . come on people now . . . etc."

And we were Americans, after all. No matter if the Swiss had invented it, even acid was American. Certainly the electric slam of it was much more like football than, say, curling or grouse hunting. We were for and about revolutionary change, both inside and out, and we had all sorts of other electric toys as well. With these we could implement that change. We *had* the technology and the drugs to manipulate our psychobiological view. We could communicate with Arthur Koestler's "Ghost in the Machine."

There seemed to be a chance to erase centuries of Western mind-lock with one protracted burst of amplified feedback. Yes! *Amplify the feedback!* Everything became louder, brighter, more overwhelming. Make art, music, love. Make yourself free. Sometimes we all had the feeling that maybe one mighty thought blast of wild-eyed, god drunk sound would tumble the walls. It was the beginning of music becoming impossibly loud, and speeded up or else stretched out, with languorous drifting musical figures. These were shades of yet more things to come: make politics, make language. Make more love. Make new drugs as battering rams against the old order.

The new culture of the sixties was bursting forth from the main body in a megamitosis. Tired of neglect, our "true" nature would now explode out of our own subconscious. Also true, it looked like it could get a bit freaky on the edges, maybe even a bit messy; the timid might get splattered, but at least the blood would be Day-Glo, like in the *Iliad*, or like in the *Upanishads*. Yeah . . . like that.

The stars were changing positions, perhaps swirling up enough centrifugal force to throw off everything the Western world seemed to represent to our simple prejudice and complex frustrations. I don't think hardly any of us really knew it, but what seemed like sociology or politics was also a surge of emotion of such proportion that the increasingly loaded dope-receptor sites were perhaps the only fit landing zones for the anguished and minimized concepts of the new order.

Despite the bliss-inducing psychedelia, and the copious painkilling, our anger, though it was almost always obscured in smoke, was alive and palpating our unconscious family dreams. There was real hatred for the mad conquest of nature, the worship of inhuman technology. By 1968, the Chinese Year of the Monkey was upon us with all four thumbs, and rage and grief were to eat our spines from the inside out. It was the year of the Têt Offensive, where children of both sides foddered and salted Vietnam's soil as if the fucking Hittites had joined the fray. The Democrats at their convention in Chicago goose-stepped on the bodies of their natural heirs, and it was also the year that Martin Luther King's and Bobby Kennedy's assassins would make us question any sort of providence and the value of human evolution. It was also the year that I returned to Vietnam as a journalist.

18 | SAIGON AGAIN

JOHN

Using my definition of things, returning to Vietnam in 1968 was probably the first really adult thing I had ever done. It fit all the requirements of my long-ago dream in the elevator shafts of Manhattan. It had danger aplenty, which now, as a civilian, was of course voluntary. It had romance and love in the form of Vietnamese womanhood and the abundant blessing of a matriarchal society, and then of course it was history in the making.

Sometimes memories can or should be obsolete, but though I have tried from time to time, it's impossible to forget Vietnam. In any case I spent such a long time there—far more than a normal person might—that to try and get a grasp I have to go back there as surely as a vet sometimes must board a plane to revisit the battlefields of his youth. But for me, the fields of Vietnam had a wide variety of meanings, the symbolism of which colored my life in ways that are probably different than most.

There has been so much misapplied pathos and sloppy thinking (confused as "the Brightest") both before and after "our war." This arrogance derailed us into Southeast Asia in the first place, and we then tried to impose our limited and linear thinking on an ancient world with seasons that could last a decade apiece. So, even today, America is stuck with a

Vietnam that won't decode easily and a sensation of quicksand between our toes no matter where we go.

Still, I was struck by a tremendous jolt of inspiration while in Vietnam. Among other things, the Vietnamese saved me from the certainty that technology was supreme. This inspiration included a growing political sophistication. Certainly, the John Wayne war movies that had been the real basic training for my age group had lacked much in preparation for the lethal truth of American sanctimony.

Often when people ask about the war, I glibly say that I grew up in Vietnam. I think many Americans shyly feel the same. Since my first year there more or less kept me bound to the U.S. Army, when I returned to Vietnam I tried to "find" myself by way of doing something different from what one normally does in an army at war. And again, to be truthful, the women of Vietnam and the sweeping gardens of *cannabis sativa* had as much to do with the pull of returning as a drive toward conspicuous good works or an affectedly bleeding heart.

Saigon was once called the Paris of the Orient. Come to think of it, I believe Phnom Penh was, too, or was that a Pearl? In any case, there are probably more Paris and pearls of the Orient than fleas on a poodle. This was due in part to the old colonial French municipal architecture, which had a wonderful way of accommodating the climate and soul of the people who lived in these towns. There was a sort of built-in decay with a comforting feeling that smoothly supported the ceaseless human pastimes of birth, romance, commerce, old age, and death.

Though at first I didn't really notice it, the Saigon that I returned to held out a different bouquet than the city that I had left in the army. Though I had only been gone for about a year, the city was choked with two million more refugees from the countryside. The Tet Offensive had just finished its roll through America's notion of invincibility and had now left even deeper scars on the people and the architecture.

As a soldier, I had found myself in bars a lot. These were the requisite relaxation spas for military boys, even if you preferred to smoke dope. There one could find the jubilees of male bonding stamped with the fear-driven sexual preening of the condemned. This class of business was quite often cloaked in a self-conscious walkie-talkie-radio-procedure chatter designed to distance its users from all feeling; "Baby-Stumper, Baby-Stumper, Friendly zeroing-in at two-o-clock . . . Roger?" The reply would be "Roger that Tango, I'm loaded with 'Nape & Snake'!" This means something like, "Look at that pretty girl."

Though times had changed in so many ways for me, my impulses set in motion by the scenery returned to their old grooves. Scarcely stopping to feel my way, the very first thing I did when I got back to Saigon and checked in to a hotel near the main bar street called Tu Do, was to lose all my money in a sleight-of-hand exchange on the black market. The amazing thing was that I had watched this sort of back-alley shuffle go down dozens of times and yet I fell for it anyway. I just stood there in the shadows fully aware of what was going on, and watched like a toad blinking on a hot rock as my $400 in greenbacks miraculously turned into about $7 of wonderfully manicured newspaper with just a taste of real piasters on the top and bottom of the stack. After the numbness wore off, the second thing I did was to look for some old friends so I could eat and have a place to sleep the next day.

The first past acquaintance that I ran into was an old, and I mean old, prostitute who went by the name of Monique . . . of course. She had been a dance-hall girl who had performed various wondrous routines for the French army. She still thought of herself as something of a chanteuse, and had fascinating gruff stories of those long-lost Foreign Legionnaires. Monique had been a friend of mine since my first days as a green private. In times past I had lent her money as she was rather poor herself, and I had gone shopping at the PX for her. She liked Chanel No. 5, and had considered changing her name to Coco. Now her age, or rather vintage, had given her a certain dignity, but also a look that wasn't all that popular with the free-spending young GIs. I liked to speak French and she had taught me a lot about the romance and ambiance of the previous war in what the Europeans preferred to call Indochina.

Having seen it all, the span of Monique's charity was limited. The blessing of a good-hearted prostitute is perhaps eternal in archetype, though brief in function; I had a day to crash—tops! Friendship got in the way of business. Short as the benefaction was, I thought that Confucius should have allowed room for a hexagram in the I Ching dedicated to this eternal icon and protectress of foolish boys like myself. Anyway, such was the life of a wandering mendicant, or so my finances forced me to assume.

Looking around my old haunts, I found other friends from the year before who had volunteered for further duty. They had stayed either for the money, or to get out of the army earlier, or because they were in love. The latter was a strong pull. In a couple of years, GIs were staying because of the comforts of another lady, another heroin far more demanding than your basic girl.

For a week or so I hung out with these old army friends, sleeping in their hotel billets, borrowing money, and feeling my way in my new civilian guise. After recovering from a lot of reminiscing, I started getting my freelance press credentials in order. My status as a tourist had a seven-day time limit. However, I had managed to get letters of accreditation from my friends at the *Washingtonian*, on the strength of the marijuana article that had launched my infamy.

After receiving my press card and my visa, I cashed in my return ticket for money to live on. Back home, my mother was drunk, my father was emotionally unavailable, and my brother was somewhere in the army. The last time I had seen him he had been miserably stationed at Fort Knox, Kentucky. I, on the other hand, felt happy and alive with all my bridges burned in the existential vacuum of youth, immortality, and careless self-propulsion.

There was a certain lawlessness that I believe had to appeal to anyone beyond the reach of the California Highway Patrol, or the Connecticut State Police. And though we were to lose the war, in the cities that we financed, it appeared that we round-eyed Christians were the privileged boys on the block. In truth, any Vietnamese civilian could have killed you in a heartbeat, but on the face of it, colonial arrogance was met with the genuine politeness of Confucian people. It also helped to form the illusion of personal sway over the population. This was very intoxicating to young men with guns, both in the cities and the countryside. It also sometimes led to tragedy.

The nerve center of all journalistic alliance and dalliance was on the veranda of Saigon's Hotel Continental. From this lovely perch one could watch the main boulevards of the town intersect in front of the National Assembly and drift with the monsoons over gin and tonic, argue the distinctions between the French war and ours, or commiserate over the tides of network benefits or the per diem. Just a couple of blocks away, the daily afternoon briefing known as the Five O'Clock Follies gave out onto this same veranda where interviews and lies could be swapped before dinner.

One day, lonely and a bit shy during that first week, I ordered a beer and sat at the hotel trying to feel the transition in my identity, the new view from the vantage point of personal recognizance. For most Americans, Saigon was a very small town. They traveled by taxi, frequently not knowing the location of where they were going or how to pronounce the names of the streets anyway. Generally, Americans had only three or four destinations in their entire stay: the PX, the airport, their hotel or villa, and the veranda of the Hotel Continental. I actually knew the neighborhood well. I had worked mere yards from this veranda at the first Armed Forces Radio station before it had moved to its vast complex on the other side of town. I had been deeply though unrequitedly in love with a married woman who had lived around the corner, and when my father had been "in country," I had slept in his suite at the Hotel Caravel across the street.

Soon after I ordered my second beer, a very friendly man looking somewhat like a blond bear came up to me and asked if he could sit down. He introduced himself as Dick Swanson, a *Life* photographer. He had recognized me from photographs that had been taken during my notoriety and arrest in Washington, D.C.

I was something of an anomaly. Though I knew nothing about the legitimate $300-a-day press world, I had been "in country," in fact all over the country as long as most of the reporters who flocked to get their wings singed in Vietnam. And, of course, I knew the military in Vietnam better than most, having just been in it.

I ran into some other young Americans who were not aligned to any particular enterprise other than the curiosity of conscience and a mutual resolve to immerse ourselves further in this bloody passion called Vietnam. We all spoke the language, some extremely well, and we shared a common love for the Vietnamese and their culture.

Trying to understand Vietnam is a task that is beyond the Vietnamese themselves, but just learning some basic things about Vietnam is also an involved project, and one that most Americans were unwilling to take on. This was made evident by the way we Yanks tried to prosecute a war in this already mysterious bamboo forest of contradiction.

As a country, we never made much of an attempt to locate even our position in the cultural terrain, if only for convenience sake. I mean, why were we there? James Kunen, the author of *The Strawberry Statement* and other documents of the era, once went up to the MP guard in front of the American Embassy and asked him "Why are we in Vietnam?" Jim was referred to the guard's sergeant, forever onward and upward, all the time taking earnest and diligent notes, until he found himself in front of General Abrams who referred him to the president. Needless to say, no one had a very satisfying answer.

For many of us critics, there was a distinctly racist component to the conflict. So it seemed that in trying to defoliate the truth of our real instincts about racial equality and our desire to "help a yellow democracy," we got snagged by a far more rugged relationship with our projection. We tried to con the Vietnamese and ended up conning ourselves in a quicksand war.

This is nothing new. Not under Kipling's sun, or even Joseph Conrad's for that matter. Why, it has taken us fifty years to be able to just focus a little bit beyond our prejudice to see how the Japanese function. In short, even though understanding the East (or now the Mideast) will probably never be the forte of American diplomacy, just trying to learning some basic facts about the people and the countries where we think our interests lay should be obligatory for our leaders.

Our small group began to coalesce and gather itself together around the little soup stands in backstreets and the world of shoeshine boys, shopkeepers, and beggars. Before we knew it, we had become sort of an American counterculture phenomenon right in the heart of a volcano. Again, it was all very street level. This was sympathetic and great for the little city boy in me who had traveled alone as a child through all the backwaters of my own old city.

Vietnam was a magnet. It also had the kind of bohemian, revolutionary cafe-society style that students love to get all worked up about. Indeed, this sort of refreshment was Ho Chi Minh's mother's milk, though he had a different agenda. Our hatred for the war, and our particular disgust in the way it was being reported eventually prompted us to start Dispatch News Service. Because of our simple language skills, this news agency quickly became completely independent of the flow of information dispensed by the Joint United States Press Office or the various embassy spokesmen. It wasn't just a problem for reporters to get past the political bias of these sources, but the texture of the air-conditioned foreign correspondent's life also made it next to impossible to grow beyond the "compound mentality" that governmental Public Information Officers provided and typified.

We at Dispatch were soon joined by defectors from various volunteer services, such as CARE and others who knew the country and had been duped into converting their cultural acumen into military intelligence. With their talents, Dispatch developed into a reliable, if amateur news agency. We were the first to disclose the My Lai massacre and the Con Son tiger cages, as well as other stories now long forgotten. How many people remember the Vietnamese spy who was shot out of a canoe by the CIA like a scene out of *The Godfather*?

Since I was the only one who knew anything at all about Eastern religions, that became my beat. As I have already hinted, the literary fascination that I had for many years with Buddhism and Taoism had been supercharged with the psychedelic advantages I never had as a child. Thus, with a kind of lysergic warp-speed, I returned to Vietnam as a more or less fully blown acid mystic with a postmodern, nonspecific Aquarian view of what was metaphysically on line, so to speak.

To be fair to myself, as much as I may have liked the Doors and Jefferson Airplane, I was not much of an "Oh Wow" recruit when it came to what people use to call transcendentalism. Though I have always managed to associate with them, I was not a very gooey guru junkie either. My conceit spared me much of that. Then, I was mostly a student of the highly literate mystical view of people like Meister Ekhart, the Sufi poet Rumi, or passionate nuts like Sri Ramakrishna, St. John of the Cross, and of course the industrially iconoclastic Sixth Zen Buddhist patriarch, Hui-neng, who founded the notion of instant enlightenment.

As fatuous as it may sound, for a kid who didn't practice much meditation in favor of dope, I knew or at least had read a lot of stuff. And after all, this was more than a hobby. I genuinely felt and still feel that the solution to the entanglements set forth by a discursive and egocentric mind and the emotions that carry its painful though powerful argument could only be set free through spiritual principles. Every culture I had studied knew about this, and each had its own style of bringing about or recognizing the tension necessary for this radical awareness to break free. I was even sometimes smart enough to remember that scholarship alone wouldn't do it, but it helped. In fact, the more you knew, or thought you knew, the greater the release when the conceptual world was turned upside down leaving one dumb in contemplation of the unthinkable. Though this all seemed pretty simple, I already "knew" that pursuing the unknowable with the lantern of knowledge was a wild ride on the Mobius Strip, much like trying to hang on to the dizzy context of this very sentence. It was this kind of tricky business where I felt some professional guidance or example might be helpful.

With all this in the back of my mind, I set off to work. The Buddhist riots in May and June of 1966 allowed the monks of the powerful An Quang Pagoda in Saigon to become a major political force and a tremendous embarrassment to the then South Vietnamese Premier Nguyen Cao Ky. The two most imposing figures were a young firebrand named Tich (Venerable) Tri Quang, and an older monk, Tich Tien Minh. I set out to find out whether or not they were politicians or spiritual leaders, or both. It wasn't until years later that I realized that there was no such thing as one without the other, but at the time my confusion came about because of the violence of the riots in the city of Hue, north of Saigon.

Many monks, with mortars and machine guns, had blasted away at the government opposition. A friend of mine, a photographer for *Time*, had been shredded by a venerable old monk with a grenade launcher. They had their reasons, but from my understanding of the traditional nonviolent Buddhist point of view, this approach seemed odd. Also, self-immolation was not really a Buddhist or even an oriental way of doing things.

I spent a good deal of time studying and interviewing the leaders of the An Quang, and came away feeling that they were in fact more master organizers than master mediators. However, within the precincts of the war itself, and given the political strength of the An Quang Pagoda as a third force, there was no question but that these men were an extremely compelling crew. Yet, despite their achievements at political activism, my notion of Buddha activity, at least in the blissful realm of Absolute Universal Silliness or even "right action" was not appeased.

19 | THE COCONUT MONK

JOHN

In the spring of 1968, a few months after interviewing every Buddhist and Catholic leader in sight, a Vietnamese friend of mine told me about a large peace conference on an island in the Mekong that was hosted by a silent yogi called the Coconut Monk. I bussed the seventy kilometers south from Saigon to My Tho City with a party of novice monks. Arriving with a lot of pushing and tickling, we all climbed into sampans at the My Tho quay on the Mekong.

The river here is about four miles wide, segmenting the delta between little My Tho and Kien Hoa City. Phoenix Island was hidden by other small shreds of land that seemed to float like peach slices along with a salad of coconuts and mango, garnished and strewn together with palm fronds in the swift brown water. As we came around one of these spits of land, what I saw made me almost fall out of the boat. There, like a hallucination floating in the middle of the river, was what resembled a Pure Land Buddhist Amusement Park built on pilings. At the prow of the island, a towering pagoda rose from the top of a seventy-foot plaster mountain. The summit was crowned by a Buddhist swastika, a triangle and a cross, which looked down on a huge terrazzo prayer circle, separated by color scheme and the elegant sigmoid line of yin and yang; duality in motion. Sporting neon lights on their heads, the nine dragons of the Mekong sprouted a full forty feet high from the prayer circle. The dragons were ancient and revered figures, symbolic of the nine fingers of the Mekong River's alluvial fan that had in fact created the amazingly rich delta.

While we got closer, the noise of our little outboard motor began to fade and disappeared beneath the din of large wind-bells that hung from the corners of the seven-tiered pagoda. There were hundreds of them. Their size was oddly familiar though and I later learned that they were made out of the brass casings of 175mm howitzer shells. As we came around in front of the island to a landing quay, I saw an extremely large and elaborate relief map of Vietnam, fully seventy feet from end to end, suspended horizontally above the flowing Mekong. The map was complete with little toy towns and cities, mountain ranges and jungles. Sprouting out of the North and the South were pillars that were at least five feet in diameter which rose to the sky to support two ends of a rainbow bridge more than a hundred and fifty feet above the surface, with a little hut on each end.

When we finally edged up to the docking area, I saw about two hundred monks and nuns doing prostrations in the main prayer circle, bowing toward the funny plaster mountain that supported the ascending tiers of the pagoda and looked like something designed for not-so-miniature golf. In a little alcove near the top of the central plaster mountain the Coconut Monk sat grinning. Without a doubt, he was the true embodiment of the classic "Don't Worry—Be Happy" posture that is eternally endearing and mystifying in a world gone mad.

On this particular day, the little community of about four hundred was choked with tourists and guests for the two-day peace festival. With others I made the pilgrimage up the micromountain to receive a blessing from the master. My friends introduced me as an American Buddhist. His eyebrows rose comically and he began clapping. For a silent man, he was a most communicative person. I somehow understood him perfectly when he questioned in a gesture whether or not I ate meat. I did, and he sort of unclapped, and sent an attendant running down the mountain to the kitchen area. The attendant quickly returned with mangoes and coconuts. The master made me eat. He watched intently until I gobbled the juicy fruit down completely. My genuine enthusiasm was applauded by all as a sign of conversion, or at least sympathy.

I explained to the Coconut Monk (*Dao Dua* in Vietnamese and pronounced Dow Yua) that I was very interested in Taoism and of course Buddhism. The day before, when I had sat stoned in the Dispatch office staring at a map on the wall, I noticed that if one drew a circle around Vietnam, a simple yin-yang curve appeared. Ton Le Sap Lake (yin) in Cambodia and Hi Nam Island (yang) in the South China Sea, separated by the curved coastline of Vietnam itself, made a perfect, classic yin-yang symbol. The center of the completed visualization lay smack on the infamous DMZ.

When I told him about this discovery, the Coconut Monk's eyebrows jumped up again and he stared at me seriously. After a very long moment, he suddenly sent another monk scurrying down to a little library in the grotto/heart of the pagoda mountain. When the monk returned he had an exquisite map of Vietnam highlighted with the exact same circle around it which Dao Dua had drawn himself the day before. He was going to release this meaningful cosmo-geographical discovery to the guests later as a kind of explanation for the Vietnamese predicament; and here this round-eye had stumbled on the same thing, perhaps picking up the master's vibrations. It was a tremendously awkward moment. The surrounding monks and nuns started clucking their approval, and whispering to each other about my prophetic perceptions. Dao Dua and everyone began complimenting these friends who had invited me. No mere coincidence this, which had brought the American Buddhist to Phoenix Island. Within an hour of being there, I had become a sign, of what I'm not sure. Nonetheless, I was to pay for that little exchange of symbol-awareness with a mixture of pride and embarrassment for the rest of the years I was to be associated with Dao Dua, as the incident eventually spread on the Taoist tom-tom circuit throughout the delta.

I didn't see it happening at first but an increasingly deeper understanding of the life-and-death lessons of Vietnam were to be miraculously furthered by this jungle monk, whose eccentric attitude indicated a compassion and humor that made pathos and simpleminded commiseration unworkable. For me this lesson has never become obsolete.

My year in Vietnam as a soldier had left me with the memory of being a very realistic target. I was always frustrated by my army role and the desire to be near the people without my olive-drab identity. Soon I started going down to Phoenix Island every weekend on my little motorbike. I felt happy in the countryside and that I was no longer such a juicy bull's-eye in the dress of the foreign invader. My shoulders were light as I motorcycled through the flickering sunlight on my little bike under the palms. I felt very secure with the people and as my accent got better, I began to lose the notion of what it was to be non-Vietnamese.

On Phoenix Island, the mutual grief about the war was honest and penetrated all cultural barriers so that I felt like just one of the million carp swimming along in the silt-rich brown water of the Mekong, whose bounty travels all the way from Central Tibet to fan out here in the delta and on into the South China Sea. I was happy here. Perhaps happier than I had ever been in my life. The island became my refuge for the next five years.

Any sort of happy equipoise was Dao Dua's play. He was the father figure I'd longed for and we forged a deep affection for each other. Inversions, centering in chaos, transmutation, and a hilarious annihilation of negativity, were seemingly possible here. An incestuous exhibition of symbols swung around on a pole in the wind. A sign pivoted there, displaying Buddha with his arm around Christ; the flip side, the Holy Virgin, Mother Mary embracing the Bodhisattva of Compassion, Quan Yin. Always, bells out of bullets, inverted aggression.

In response to this extraordinary display of concrete pacifism, and to his Harpo Marx impression of a Buddha, my commitment to the Coconut Monk grew.

One day, the Coconut Monk summoned me. He asked me to stay more permanently with him on the island. He handed me his coconut begging bowel, and I accepted. That night, in the small hours I was woken up, and all the monks took me into the large cave in the plaster mountain and handed me the maroon robes (pajamas really) of the community. Having accepted the robes and the rules of the community such as they were, I moved into a tiny hut which we built on top of an old wooden river barge.

No war and a dragon's roar of nonaggression were the most tangible, and often mysterious part of Dao Dua's influence. It seemed to rule the environment, and I mean this quite literally. It is one thing to emanate kindness or manage to deflate a kitchen quarrel, but there was something deeper going on here. There actually was *no war*, or the jagged vibrations of war on this island. Above and around it, yes. Many evenings I used to sit eating pineapple under my thatched hut in the moonlight, watching both banks of the river rage at each other with howitzer shells and tracer bullets whistling back and forth over my head, while the colored lights of Dao Dua's prayer circle embraced the sadness and the huge bells of Phoenix Island slammed, exchanging and diffusing the suffering.

From a logical or pedestrian point of view, Dao Dua was quite mad. His presentation was beyond ridiculous, though in fact he danced in a desperate political world surrounded by an electronic battlefield. He made one's mind spin, but his style penetrated the heart. A purely analytical mind could never get purchase on his vision.

Whether or not the person you take teaching from is completely out of hand or represents the truth is often an unavoidable problem. This is more and more the case as we have to spiritually grow up and have to take responsibility for our own truth, rather than hide behind a dead doctrine or any old emperor's new clothes. But in Vietnam, with everyone else in sight trying to slaughter each other, I found it easy to be relaxed about Dao Dua's debatable relevance.

Dao Dua was the epitome of his creation. When I met him he was well under five feet tall. He used to be taller, but he had fallen out of a tree that he was meditating in and broken his back. He asked his disciples not to worry, and get him back up in his tree. His lower back became fused in a sitting posture. His arms seemed to sprout out of his chest instead of his shoulders. His expression mixed a mock-seriousness with a huge approval of everything, except the demonstration of war. The fact of it, however, didn't phase him.

Dao Dua was special. He normally wore his ponytail wound around the top of his head with the tip tucked in at the back. He thought this could symbolize Christ's crown of thorns. Sometimes he let the ponytail hang down in back, which he said represented Maitreya, the coming Buddha. Then again, he would pull it full around like a beard under his chin and stuff it over the far ear. This one always eluded me. Abe Lincoln perhaps? Symbols are always good advertising, but Dao Dua's knees and the overall shape of his body reflected years of really industrial sitting practice and prostrations.

The Coconut Monk always wore a large crucifix over the saffron robe of a Buddhist monk. It rested on a large round saffron collar, similar to what a clown might wear. I'd never seen anything like it. I studiously asked Dao Dua its origin. He scribbled a note which when translated said, "It's really a bib. I invented it. I only eat vegetables, but I always seem to spill my food."

Having discovered the peaceful eye of the hurricane, I felt a little selfish abut my niche, but Dao Dua's generosity compelled me to invite friends from Saigon to come down and spend a few nights on the island and enjoy his peace. Most of my friends were combat photographers working for the networks and wire services. They, too, found Phoenix Island and its master the only refuge available when the succor of gallows existentialism ran dry. Quickly Dao Dua realized that he had a built-in public relations department through me and these new war-orphans. In some way the Aquarian age had delivered AP, UPI, *Time* and *Newsweek*, CBS, the BBC and French television, as well as *National Geographic*, into his lap.

One full-moon night Dao Dua decided to make a move. I was awakened at about 4:00 A.M. by my friend Dao Phuc, the Coconut Monk's only English-speaking devotee. The wind was blowing small ripples across the Mekong and Phuc threw his cloak over me against the chill as we walked across the wide prayer circle to the plaster mountain. The morning star had risen over the river palms but the moon was still up and Dao Dua was eating his breakfast of coconuts and hot red peppers. He wanted me to go to Saigon and arrange for my journalist friends to come to lunch as his guests in Saigon's Chinese suburb of Cholon. My motorbike was already strapped into a sampan waiting to take me to the mainland. When we hit shore I started out nervously for town. I knew that if Dao Dua were to meet his luncheon date and leave the island, he was risking imprisonment. As for myself, I was risking my visa and general credibility. In a way, it was really like being Soupy Sales's press attaché.

I contacted everybody I had ever brought to the island, many of whom had grown to love the Coconut Monk. The lunch was a huge feast prepared and served by some of Dao Dua's Saigon-based devotees who ran a Chinese pharmacy. Dao Dua did not appear at first, but about halfway through lunch he arrived in a 1954 Buick Century with a saffron-painted roof. Though he wouldn't leave the backseat of his car, he handed me an outline of his plans. He wanted my friends in the media to know that on the following day he would arrive at the presidential palace, and then march up the boulevard to the U.S. Embassy to present Lyndon Johnson's emissaries with his updated plans for peace.

After lunch we all went our various ways. Dao Dua had disappeared in his car, leaving us all apprehensive about the mess that we knew would follow any public demonstration on the streets of Saigon. Dao Dua had managed to get off his island by meeting the car at a secluded part of the river, but his presence in the backseat of his car on a Cholon street had started a buzz through the city.

Having seen the head-smashing methods used to break up street demonstrations in Vietnam, I was worried about him. People were passionate and the police often cruel. The solution I thought was to go to the U.S. Embassy right away and warn them that a peaceful monk wanted to drop by and deliver a letter for President Johnson. The political section treated me politely, and after informing them of the next day's activities I left feeling that this little bit of diplomacy would smooth things over. I was very naive.

The following day my friends and I rendezvoused in a side street near the palace. Everything looked fairly normal except perhaps for me—a Westerner in maroon pajamas. Dao Dua's car came around the corner and when he stepped out, half the people on the street stopped and stared and began to giggle among themselves, or make prostrations of obeisance to the jungle holy man. The other half turned out to be plainclothes policemen, many of whom had apparently been following me since leaving the U.S. Embassy the day before. Police jeeps quickly tore in, blocking the way to the palace, so Dao Dua started strolling towards the embassy. He had brought one coconut with a naturally formed peace sign on the bottom. Actually, *all* coconuts have this, but he thought that there could be the outside chance that the American president might be moved sufficiently to halt the war though this lovely organic sign of universal harmony.

Our corps of friendly photographers and journalists snapped away, as the small band of ten monks and nuns made its way up the street toward the U.S. compound. The police were actually very delicate with Dao Dua. The central command had made a faux pas by sending a captain to lead the operation whose family was from Kien Hoa where the Dao Dua was most revered as a saint. In fact, the old man knew him as a boy. Anguish and confusion covered the captain's face as he tried to persuade the Dao Dua to please go home to his island and not make any trouble. The Dao Dua just kept walking and grinning and as always, pointing his finger to the sky with huge approval as if complimenting the weather or heaven itself.

As we approached the embassy, a company of marines surrounded the building and locked a huge linked chain around the main gate. As I looked up I saw about forty more soldiers on the roof with quad-barrel 50-caliber machine guns staring down at us. Helicopter gunships began circling overhead to defend U.S. soil from my four foot eight inch teacher. At this show, the Dao Dua sat down on the sidewalk and refused to move. After twenty minutes someone in the embassy began to realize that a little old man was making a ridiculous spectacle out of the police and American military might, all with a single coconut.

Since the old man seemed to have half the press corps cheering him on, the atmosphere began to change into a weird sort of party. The Dao Dua started preparing his lunch on the street. By this time the Vietnamese crowd, past their nervousness, were howling with laughter. Eventually, a tall and typically sweatless diplomat came out and accepted the letter through the bars of the gate. He refused the coconut on the grounds that the president of the United States could not accept gifts from foreign dignitaries. The Dao Dua was satisfied and moved off. Once again with police escort, he was taken back to Phoenix Island with the threat of more severe imprisonment if he ever set foot on the mainland again. To help make the point, a raid had taken place in his absence, and thirty of the Dao Dua's closest monks were arrested.

In his letter the Dao Dua had asked LBJ for the loan of twenty huge transport planes to take him and his followers, plus building materials, to the Demilitarized Zone on the Seventeenth Parallel between North and South Vietnam. There, in the middle of the Ben Hai River, the Dao Dua would build a great prayer tower and deposit himself on the top without food or water. Along with three hundred monks on one side of the river and three hundred on the other, he would pray for seven days and nights. He assured the American president that this project would bring peace to Vietnam.

In the following years the Dao Dua and I played many games together. I was nearly thrown out of the country on several occasions, and it was probably the aura of his wackiness that saved me. Anyway, after this first incident and test of my commitment, I don't think I was ever really taken seriously again as a serious journalist. I, too, was transformed into a nuisance and a nutcase. *Time* magazine ran a picture of me in my robes with the caption:

John Steinbeck IV
A yen for Zen?

In the course of the next few years, with the help of myself and his other new friends, the Coconut Monk escaped his island many times, always to be carted right back by the police, who eventually kept a flotilla of patrol boats circling the island. A police station was established on the edge of the community and soldiers began little patrols on the island. Once in a while, U.S. helicopter jockeys would drop tear gas in the middle of the prayer circle during prostrations, but never once did a bullet penetrate the Dao Dua's domain.

It's all over now. Ho Chi Minh is in his grave, and so is Dao Dua. At first I heard that Dao Dua had left his island and moved back to Seven Mountains. This was in 1973. Then later in 1986, in a Vietnamese restaurant in Paris I overheard my name and his mentioned by some Vietnamese exiles. The Communists had tried to turn the island into a tourist attraction after the war. Later I learned that the Coconut Monk had been put under house arrest by the North Vietnamese and eventually killed. When I saw him for the last time we didn't say goodbye. He touched his eye, indicating a rare tear. Then grinning, he pointed to the sky where he lived. Memories are obsolete and I can't forget.

20 THE TURN OF THE SCREW

JOHN

Toward the end of 1968, I found Thom in Saigon standing right in front of me at the PX. I didn't even know he was *in* Vietnam. One night, flying on Romilar cough syrup (I got everybody drinking it to the point that we bought out all of Saigon), Thom had a vision of Dad dying. Unable to convince him that it was the dope, he went home on emergency leave and naturally, was accused of goldbricking. However, he did spend time with our father who, though supposedly sick in bed, was actually Dad very alert and in bed; clearly not in pain, reading the galleys of my book *In Touch*.

My father never spoke to me after my dope bust two years prior, which I believe was set up by the U.S. Army to discredit my testimony about the use of drugs in Vietnam. Dad's last words to me, when he heard I'd been found innocent, were, "They should have thrown you in jail." However, that day he told Thom that I was "a damn fine writer."

The next day, Thom went back for a chat about the war and what was going on with him, and was told by Elaine that it's all over. Dad was dead. Apparently he had gone out on a purposelessly suffered overdose of morphine; this before Dad or anybody else considered that it just might be important to say good-bye. Thom and I are to this very day left completely adrift about all of this, without any closure. Elaine had been carrying around a vial of morphine with strict instructions to administer it by needle if Dad asked for it because he was terrified of suffering a painful death. This practice was secretly quite fashionable among their posh Manhattan brownstone set during that period. However, Elaine was not the one who overdosed him. Neither Thom nor I have a clue about Dad's situation and state of mind at the time of his death. I want to examine the underlying dynamics of his family of origin, the seeds of which were carried forward to create, with Elaine, a really unfair and even disgusting display of irresponsibility, and, in her case, greed. Thom is the only witness I have to the darkness that runs through our veins. Readers can find it in my father's stories, but we live with it daily.

Thom returned to Vietnam marginally out of his mind on some THC pills, complete with a highly defensive altered personality, i.e., like Artie Johnson's old man routine from *Laugh In*. It was days before he came down. In fact, in some sense part of this whole book is because neither of us have; we are bitter that this maneuver took place.

With my father's passing, my brother's eventual rotation stateside and the monsoons coming, I felt it was time to return to America for a brief visit in the spring of 1969. It had been six months since my father's death. I wanted to look into the family affairs of the estate, see my mother, and attend the wedding of my old boarding-school friend Ali Rubottom.

By this time, my mother's unmanageability had just about edged her out of Palm Springs. She was fighting with everyone with the exception of a few aging queens who were ripping her off and exalting her alcoholic tirades as sublime bitchiness. Her ventures in dealing art had all blown up in her face, in part due to her desperate grandiosity and her inability to distinguish between honorable business associates and cirrhotic drinking buddies. These lower companions had robbed and flattered her into virtual bankruptcy. Even her anger had shrunk into little spasms. If by describing her in this way one only gets the picture of an alcoholically churlish woman, I am doing her a disservice. Little Gwyn (my grandmother was Big Gwen) had a lot to be angry about. Her history wasn't a happy one. It wasn't till much later that anyone bothered to figure out that she had been sexually abused by her drunken father. In the light of today's understanding of the pathology of sexually abused women, she had always been right where she ought to be. Haunted, drunk, and pissed off.

She now smoked a little marijuana to be hip, but it didn't sedate her resentments and fears as well as rum and coke. It was more sad than difficult to be around her.

To my way of thinking, the really big event of this return to America was my friend Ali's wedding. Friends of the bride and groom were coming from all over. Though I probably came the farthest, the fabulous Anonymous Artists of America band, America's oldest commune, were going to drive their magic bus from Novato, California, to Newton, Connecticut, for the gig. Their bus had obviously copulated with Ken Kesey's. In fact, they had originally paid for their musical instruments with proceeds from acid sales donated by Richard Alpert, aka Baba Ram Das, and hung with the Merry Pranksters, the Grateful Dead, and other infamous characters of the time. Most of them had been graduate students from the University of Chicago and were among the first to actually "drop-out and tune-in." Indeed the Triple A gave real meaning to those words. Outside of being hippies, for the most part they were actually brilliant.

Ali's brother Sam and I drove across the country in a brand-new "You Deliver-it Drive-Away" Cadillac. This Drive-Away system, where a car owner handed the keys over to a perfect stranger, had been our preferred mode of transportation, though why anyone would have turned over their new car to the likes of us was a testament to auto insurance advertising or desperation.

Arriving in New York, I went to my father's apartment on Seventy-second Street. Because of my arrest in Washington, more than two years had gone by since I had been there. It was so odd seeing his things, knowing he was gone forever. That sounds extremely simpleminded, but even after witnessing so much death in the war, just smelling the odor of his Florida Water cologne made it hard to imagine that I would never again see his lower lip jut out as he polished a knife, or began the process of covering whatever was at hand with leather and glue. Though I tried to be a "grown-up" and hide the fact from myself, I actually missed Dad terribly. But Elaine's apartment was not the place for me to share my sadness even if I could have found it. With the exception of the devastating anguish that overcame me when a pet died, my survival skills and then my homegrown cosmic attitudes had never allowed or prepared me for grief. With my mother's thrashing about and Dad's more saturnine style, there was no model, no proper way to relate to grief. This was not lacking just in my family either. Most Americans are completely lost in space when it come to grief. As usual, all anyone had was the movies! One of the alternatives, for which I did have a model, was anger. Though it didn't yet apply to my father's passing, when it did I liked to think it was on the "warrior" level. Though I may talk later about my walk with grief, during this period my ancestor's genetic proclivity for mood alterations would mask that process before I could get any of it in focus.

At Tower East, over lots of cocktails with Elaine, I was quickly told that my father's will would be in probate practically forever, though I could already see in its content that my stepmother basically inherited everything except a small percentage of some of the domestic copyrights. Thom and I were assured "that your father never wanted you to inherit money." And in truth, the lawyers' fees would far exceed anything that my brother and I would see for decades to come. Blinking in good faith, Thom and I signed all that was put before us. Anyway, as nonmaterialistic hippie types, this was all "cool"; why, this was the first New Age and a revolution taking place, and who knew what role mere money would have in the days to come. Better, I thought, to inherit the wind than fight over more of my father's character-shaping routines from the grave. Anyway, my brother and I could be easily convinced that we hadn't "earned it." And yet, we had a society that all of us were given to shape, and with our own sense of betrayal as legacy enough, try and shape it we would. Later, when we woke up to the fact that we'd been cheated, we hired a lawyer and went after the estate with a vengeance, ending up with a larger share than Elaine had originally intended.

I would soon discover it wasn't just my family that was topsy-turvy. Things back in "the world" had progressed dramatically by the tail end of the Year of the Monkey, 1968. In New York, boys from City College had started hopping Canadian freighters to Cuba to hack sugar cane with the campesinos on the Isle of Youth. North Vietnamese kids who knew the lyrics to "Purple Haze" were there too! If this was a zephyr of collective consciousness, considering the murder, the international foul play, and everything else that was going on, why stop?

And so, around the world the people of my age began the first active deconstruction of our old societies with their gold standards and love and sex standards; in fact any standard was suspect with perhaps the exception of the hashish standard.

In France, a bunch of students chanting "All Power to the Imagination" nearly overthrew the government. Though it had first started as an academic strike, it quickly spread to the workers and after a few days, nine million people stopped going to their jobs.

There was a growing feeling that the whole thing, and I mean the whole thing, was about to topple. In Washington, the Bureau of Standards would probably have to close its doors, and like in the old French Revolution when the calendar and nearly everything else had been changed, all the antediluvian rules would just plain disappear.

Less overtly political than the French, the future cream of American society at Yale spilled stark naked onto State Street, dancing like sylphs through clouds of pepper gas. At Columbia, American Red Guards armed with *The Strawberry Statement* locked their professors in their dens. As for the boundaries, were there any lines worth drawing at all? Why not breach the divisions between audience and actor, art and action? Why not performance art? Action painting? Wasn't everyone an artist, a genius, a sleeping god? Was there such a thing as criminality? If one were to talk about the politics of experience as the only politics that really mattered, then surely madmen were political prisoners. "Let the men out!" was the slogan of the Black Panther Party newspaper.

And all along, in the foreground was the draft. Because of my family loyalties and background, I had been too old and was already out of the army by 1967 so I didn't quite get the full thrust of this most visceral part of the general revolt, but to everyone else that I knew resistance was obvious. Cards burned. After all, rather than appreciate the new imagination or our higher solutions, the bastards were actually trying to kill us.

Instead of their missions to search and destroy, but still searching, we looked for a unifying principle that would magnetize the disparate fields of politics, the arts, and the spirit into a solid-state approach; one that would ease our outrage and pain.

When all you suddenly want is to stop participating in the hurt created by others for you to live in, you start asking a lot of questions. Why this? Why that? We became like children woozy with agape. Why clothes? Why marriage? Why work? Did you really have to eat meat? Eat at all? And why did the sky have to be blank or blue when it could be purple and populated with avatars and Alpha Centurions. What if C-A-T spelled "dog"? "WOW" became the first guileless retort in a new Esperanto. Language was becoming less than slang, it was becoming epiphanic, almost placental.

Since we were all pretty well stoned, the logic and lineage of things got a little bit fuzzy around the straight edges. If we were to totally follow the dictums of our noble savage hearts, we would soon be running down wild game with our bare teeth in "back to the earth" zeal. Mind you, some logical extensions weren't yet worth the stretch. With the appropriate attention span, you had to backtrack a bit to get it all in focus. After all, it has been said about the sixties that if you remember them, you weren't there.

Some of the first exuberance of the era came pouring from the gates of the academies. Those nutty professors, Timothy Leary and Richard Alpert, had begun distributing the drug, that drug that could, it was said, turn convicts into saints and make Matisses out of bank clerks; the drug that could disengage the clumsy rational gearbox and send you hurtling to godhead.

Love was a rush, and life was rushing. In a hurry to seed and flower an enduring New Age, it seemed there was just no time. Since everything was essentially questionable, this would be the Omega generation: vision first, reality later. Bands like the Anonymous Artists and the Grateful Dead learned to play their instruments on stage in front of fifty thousand people. There was not time to digest reams of accumulated wisdom. In a synthesis, all the needed answers would surely be laid out with synchronicity like wish-fulfilling gems. Anyway, effort was the probable glue-on to rigidness, and we'd had more than enough of that!

It was to be the passing of poor *Homo sapiens*, the man heavy with knowing, and the birth of *Homo ludens*, the man enlightened by play. Enough with television father figures, this emergent creature was going to be the new steward of the garden, with a sharp eye for previous contradiction. We looked over the cultural savannah and saw a society creating an ever more carcinogenic environment even as it spent more than $100 million dollars on cancer research, and an "atoms for peace" program that was spreading atomic war materials across the globe. A senseless game of chicken was being played, for brittle honor, with the Four Horsemen.

Suddenly, the new tribal spokesmen, myself included, were thrust up out of nowhere. With no credentials, no papers other than disenfranchisement, and sincerity, we began to bob like a flotilla of bright little wooden ships on the ever rising tide.

After Ali's wedding, the usual buggy summer came to Connecticut. Sensing a good thing and tired of their California truck-farm style (that is to say, many trucks, but no farm), the hitherto rolling commune of Anonymous Artists now didn't move at all. This was nothing out of the ordinary. "Flopping" was as much in the posture of all-around Aquarian recline as anything else. So were the little dope deals that were needed to pay for brown rice, lentil soup, guitar strings, war paint, and of course more dope.

Though some Newton cops had actually been at the wedding, some of the local police in this almost antique part of the New England Parkway eventually began to worry about the increased hippie traffic up from New York City and the gaily painted buses whose engine parts began to expand like lichens over the once manicured lawns of the leased estate. The overall petri-dish effect of so many people living on so little land was beginning to become noticeable in the agar of the heavy summer air.

An unusually late rain came that year. It went on for weeks and then the property, which had been so verdant during the spring wedding period, began to literally rot and slide into the central pond which had been sensibly abandoned now even by frogs. Instead of the Dionysian reflecting pool that it had been in springtime, it had turned into a sort of La Brea tar pit. A sewer really. I had never seen actual ground rot before. The concept astounded me.

After scabies took over the management of the band and the sylvan arc of the honeymoon's orbit started to decay into the dog days of August, I began to think that maybe at least some of the things they were saying about us hippies might be true. I thought it was as good a time as any to return to Vietnam. In the delta they at least understood the principles of seepage, and anyway, I missed my island and the Coconut Monk a lot. Also, Americans, even if it be this tribe of brothers and sisters, appeared to me to be too big and ungainly when compared to the plums of my acquired Asian taste. But in the process of going all the way back to the war zone to nuzzle with dragons, I also wanted to make a pilgrimage.

In order to fulfill my long-held dream and my childhood identification with Kipling's Kim on the Great Trunk Road of the Raj, I wanted to walk where Buddha and the great yogis had walked. Starting around the world again, I wanted to go to India. I wasn't exactly looking for a guru, and fortunately I didn't find one. Anyway, I wanted to see and play with them all.

Many of my more practical friends longed for the natural high promised by the Maharishi Mahesh Yogi. Transcendental Meditation, or TM were the initials on a lot of people's minds in 1969. It was not really on my mind. I rather liked drugs, and also there was something about the old goat that I didn't entirely trust. But I had to admit that even though the metaphors of his presentation were extraordinarily cloying, his overall sales pitch toward a measurable (in alpha waves) and drugless encounter with God Consciousness in some ways made good business sense. He was after all appealing to what was to become the spiritual entrepreneurs and prototypical Yuppies of the Western world.

The Maharishi had actually made a remarkably successful march through the Ivy League, and with a stream of lisping giggles he had wooed and won the hearts of many students who had been milk fed on marijuana, Hermann Hesse, and Swami Yogananda's all-time classic, *Autobiography of a Yogi*. Even for this infant New Age where drugs were still relatively harmless and the new intelligentsia had tried and even manufactured most of them, the possibilities for straight-up yoga were tantalizing. The Indian connection and the desire for excursions to the subcontinent was now also fanned by the release of the phenomenally successful book *Be Here Now* by the old Harvard man himself, Dr. Richard Alpert, now Baba Ram Das. His account of his experiences with his guru were wonderfully received and the miracles waiting in India were vouchedsafe in great measure because Richard had helped to start the mind-drug covenant to begin with. He was "one of us."

Though the Maharishi lacked the golden heart of Swami Yogananda or the deceptively self-effacing Himalayan/Catskill humor of Dr. Ram Das, what the old man did offer was technique. "Enough with the 'trip' stories already . . . teach us how to meditate" was the sentiment of functional, pragmatic minds and the searchers who had not yet slumped into marijuana-induced apathy. Those still imbued with the energy and desire for achievement, however sanctimonious, now reached for the subtle bubbles that the "Big M" said were the Perrier of God, expanding exponentially as they reached the surface of consciousness. When the Maharishi then scored the Beatles, for however short a time, it more or less clinched the deal as far as that was concerned.

There is a lot that can be said for Transcendental Meditation as a technique for relaxation and general good health. To be sure, building any sort of formal relationship with one's own mind is the epitome of friendship and patience, not to mention the possible resulting compassion derived from such a slippery endeavor, knowing that other people have the same basic problems with their heads. But the Maharishi claimed more, like levitation and walking hand in hand with him for an interview with Ram or Krishna or other significant nabobs in the Hindu pantheon. That sort of thing remains a matter of interpretation with TM or any other technique. A deeper understanding of what the psychobiological root of what these divine entities really are, or what such a colorful experience might really be comprised of, needs serious discussion. Nevertheless, I felt that the characters along the shore, pilgrims and gurus alike, were often deliriously funny and genuinely touching. As for me personally, suffice it to say that obviously no one on their way back to Vietnam voluntarily could possibly be serious about looking for an offhanded technique for relaxation.

It has been said that pink is the navy blue of India, but additionally it has to be said that grandiosity is also a specialty of that culture. The Maharishi Mahesh Yogi was no exception. He needed lots of instructors to spread his new and improved mantra system over the surface of the globe. Ali had been practicing TM long enough for him to be eligible for teacher training. Fortunately, during this early period in his career, Maharishi's income taxes were still low enough that he could afford to be in India instead of Switzerland, so for pilgrims who wanted to go farther than the Alps, one had to get to the foothills of the Himalayas to take the training course.

Maharishi's ashram lay above the little settlement called Rishikesh, near the ancient city of Hardwar on the Upper Ganges north of New Delhi. This was where the Beatles had gone. Now too, Ali and I and our women set out for India and the Maharishi's ashram nestled in the jungle woods. I was just along for the ride to the old Fatherland as it were. And so it was, as a Buddhist/Taoist mendicant with my eyes set on Vietnam that we started planning the trip.

Like all good dream trips, I seem to remember that this one was to start out gloriously on twin BMW motorcycles which we would purchase in Bavaria with pro-stock sidecars. Ali and I had been friends since our early teens, and with the help of a little hashish and Southern Comfort, we could dream well together. Also, there was something in my memory of going up and down the road from Saigon to My Tho that made this approach to world travel seem plausible. However, by the time we had all of our plans in place, winter had long since hit the Hindu Kush!

As for me, I had my area of responsibility. Since I was surprisingly "happiest" there, I planned to return to Vietnam in short order. It was, after all, sort of my spiritual home, and it stood as the central metaphor for my generation's dissatisfaction with the massive tactics of aggression which had stirred us to loathe the status quo to begin with.

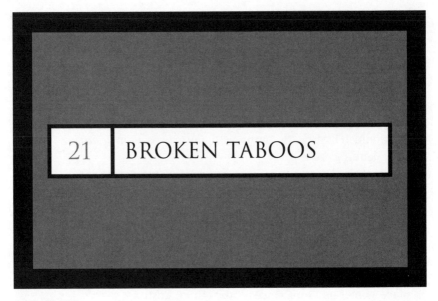

21 | BROKEN TABOOS

NANCY

Of all the secrets John had packed in the dry ice of his shame, the one that bone-chilled me most was the act of beating his mother black and blue on his sixteenth birthday. That mutual rape between mother and son broke all taboos, corroding the boundaries between morality, healthy sexuality, and emotional incest. He was also haunted by a story that his mother and grandmother repeatedly threw in his face.

"They said Dad shoved Mother down a staircase when she was three months pregnant with me. He'd decided one baby was enough."

"Mother was the only one who had the intelligence to see through a lot of Dad's posturing," Thom told me. "He couldn't stand that. He needed everyone to take the seat behind him. Mother had too much fire and spunk to do anything but stand up to him. That's why it appeared that his marriage to Elaine was the final success. She knew how to keep him happy by making him feel like the great man. Don't forget, Dad didn't want Mother to continue her singing career after they married. He wanted to cage the bird, and then protested when she turned on him in frustration." The brothers insisted Gwyn was Steinbeck's greatest love. When they met, she was an immensely talented singer and lyricist. Stifled by the marriage, all her unused creativity imploded into depression, alcoholism, and child abuse.

Recently, while combing through Gwyn's archives, I came across an excerpt from an interview that was done shortly before her death, when she had reached a point of equanimity in her sobriety:

"Christmas came, and, like other years, it was party after party. As usual, we followed the same partying pattern through to New Year's eve and everyone around us seemed to be lovers with liquor and feeling no pain.

"John had completely recovered from his trip to Russia where he'd written articles for the New York *Herald Tribune*. He had begun to become his old restless self again. He became unsettled to the extent that suddenly he decided he did not like New York anymore. 'I want a farm in upstate New York,' he said. So we began a search for a farm. Finally we found one through Burgess Meredith, a great big dairy farm. When we went to look at it, I knew for once in my life I was going to say a firm 'no' to John. I could imagine myself stuck there for the rest of my life. John was always trying to push me away to some corner where there would not be any other soul around. He never realized it, but he was a very jealous man.

"I love the country, but was not prepared to be put away in it. When I climbed back in the real-estate agent's car, I simply said 'I will not move there.' I did not speak to him until we arrived home. It all boiled down to the fact that I'd had it, I was tired of being torn up and dismantled, mentally and physically.

"As we entered 1948, I began to turn away from John. It seemed as if a climax had been building up for years and suddenly I realized it. He was taking aphrodisiacs; he would get drunk and take these pills and then wanted to plunge into his conjugal rights. It is common knowledge that a man who had a little too much to drink will not be exactly at his best when it comes to making love.

"Our relationship as husband and wife continued, but I knew that unless there were some drastic changes in John's attitude toward me, it could not last. He was hardly ever home and when he was he worked in his nest or would say little to me and the children. Always, always there was no reason for his behavior. Only John knew why.

"But I still loved him.

"I got up in the middle of the night at Easter and blew out several eggs and painted them for the children, and for John. He was thrilled to death when I gave them to him the next morning. But moments like that were rare. His attitude, generally, toward me was cold. Like any father he spent moments playing with his children, but rarely Johnny; it was always Thom.

"That summer, his restlessness grew. He was working on the film script for *Viva Zapata!* and had several things running in his mind. He hardly had time for his sons. He was always preoccupied with something or going somewhere and I never knew where. I did know that he was drinking more than was good for him. I became so unhappy as a woman as I lived what had become a deadly routine with my children. At least I had two sons whom I loved so much. Johnny had chicken pox which John did not care about and as usual, he left it up to me to take care of the matter.

"Sometimes during that summer, we would be out socially and he would erupt into screams and yells against me and I would break down and cry and go home alone. When he returned home, he would say as if nothing had happened, 'Why did you leave the party?'

"Then he decided he could not stand the children's nurse, Miss Diehl, or "Platterfoot," as he called her. Nor could he stand the children or anybody else. He left our house at 175 East Seventy-eighth Street and took a suite at the old Bedford Hotel. He had another 'nest.' He took all his notes on *Zapata* with him and said to me 'I think I'm going to write a history of my family.' That of course became the forerunner for his *East of Eden.*

"John's hate for Miss Diehl could only have one ending. She had to go. It was actually a mutual parting of the ways. And when she left, she came to me and placed the key to the house across her hand and said, in soft tones, 'I hope no one ever treats me again in my life as John has.' John refused to write her letters of recommendation, but I did.

"We found a new nurse, Kathy Gunther. She was a very nice, efficient girl. She came at a time when life for me had moved into an unbearable state. As much as I loved John—and I did, very much—I knew I could not live with him anymore. It was just impossible.

"And then, one night as we danced together, I quietly told him, 'I want a divorce.' He thought I was joking, but found out that I was not. He tried hard to stop me, but it was no use.

"I went to Reno in September 1948 with Kathy Gunther and my two sons, and divorced John on the grounds of incompatibility. John went off to Mexico."

After the divorce, the brothers would wake up to various states of horror, bloody shards of revelry gone wrong. They often found their mother passed out in her nightgown exposing body parts that crossed the boundaries of decency. One fight with a boyfriend was so violent that John interceded with a loaded gun. This was the weather system in that posh Manhattan brownstone. It scarred the souls of both boys with a wound that could only calcify, never heal. An oil portrait of a disturbed, four-year-old Master John Steinbeck, looking like a dog that's been shot over too many times, hangs in our living room. By the time the brothers returned home from school, the walls were cleaned, spilled drinks removed, and the slashed Picassos replaced by lesser artists, because the money was running out, but Mother's denial could not mask the stench of depravity. I recoiled in horror as Johnny told me he received frequent midnight visits from his mother's drunken girlfriends, stumbling into his bedroom to fondle him.

"Like all sexually abused males, I thought I had a good thing going. You don't feel you're being manipulated. You think, 'God, this is great.' They're doing what you want them to do."

Rinpoche urged Johnny to make peace with his mother before her death. He and Thom invited her to Boulder where she lived with them until she suffered a fatal asthma attack at the age of fifty-six.

"She didn't die drunk," John told me. "Toward the end she only got very drunk once a month. We had a rapprochement. I didn't get in her face about the past, but she was sober enough to know how bad things had been. By that time, I was drinking heavily and I was worried about myself. I'd talk to her about it, alcoholic to alcoholic. We could be frank with each other about alcoholic breakdown.

"When she was into her drunken Marine mouth, she'd call us names and we became a hallucination of him. She'd scream that Thom was just like Dad. But then again, when Dad was drunk, we became a hallucination of her and he'd say we were just like her. It was like being caught in a cross-fire. The character assassination was directed at us, rather than the other parent. 'You live with the bitch. Don't you know better than to be just like her? But you are, you're just like her.'"

John's therapist, Mark Bornstein, encouraged him to talk freely about the buried feelings. After John's death, Mark and I listened to the tapes of those sessions.

"Why didn't you go to your father for protection after you beat your mother?"

"I'd already given up thinking he would protect me from her insanity. He was into his Great Writer Bubble, so it wasn't like having a dad around, but instead having the Great Writer present. By the age of thirteen, I realized my father was an asshole and this created a conflict. When you read things like *The Red Pony*, you think this guy really understands kids, their dream world, their fantasies, and what it's like to be a child. If he knows that much, how can he be such a jerk to Thom and me? So, in a noble,

Spartan, stoic way, I formulated this sentence: *You can't expect a great writer to be a great father.* As the apologist for my family, it worked for me. It made me feel adult, it made me feel reasonable. If someone else challenged or asked a question about his behavior, I could come out with that sentence and I totally bought into it. But now, Michael and Megan expect me to be a certain way, and I have to think about that. From their point of view, I can't just be a great writer and a lousy father. They won't accept that, because Nancy and I have encouraged them to talk about their feelings.

"I had always thought my father was a manic depressive, cranky person. After he died, Thom and I found his stash of speed. Two huge hospital supply bottles with thousands of pills in them. One was three-quarters empty and one was full. He'd been soaring and crashing on amphetamines all along, but this was a missing piece of information when we were growing up. He thought it was artistic to be temperamental, so he indulged his moods. You see this all the time in people who use their moods to verify the fact that they're real, or really important. It taught me to beware of the creative process. Dad would tell Thom and me that we were getting on his nerves. Well, something was—a huge amphetamine crash. His mouth was always dry, he was peeling his lip, his tongue was raw from rolling it around his teeth all day.

"My father was full of this constant push to make it on our own. He'd put us in situations where he was too chicken to go, like the army. He got Thom reassigned to a fucking helicopter door gunning unit on a whim. He used his influence with his great friend, Lyndon Johnson. He himself drank his way through the Second World War in London during the Italian campaign. Thom was terrified and I'm sure it contributed greatly to his Post Traumatic Stress Disorder. He was supposed to be working for Armed Forces Radio and TV and suddenly Dad gets him switched to a door gunner's gig, one of the most dangerous posts in the war. Where was his head at? I think in his darkest subconscious world, he would have loved to have pictures of his dead sons who were killed in the war sitting on a grand piano, to fill out his image. Meanwhile, we were lucky to be alive.

"He wanted sons who could be stevedores and at the same time read Latin and Greek. Who understood all great things but could work on the railroad like hobos out of *Tortilla Flat*. It was a projection of what he himself wanted to be. Very funky, tough, rough-hewn, masculine men who were great lovers, sensitive, multilingual, and courageous. We tried to be what Dad expected us to be, regardless of our basic natures. I'd say we actually turned out to be those people. But we couldn't understand it. We were constantly threatened by his expectations.

"I speak four languages. I'm a very funky motherfucker, a two-fisted drinker. I spent six years in a shooting war. I've been wounded, scarred. Everything that I've put myself through growing up, and what makes up part of being me, was something he pushed for, so that he could claim it for his own. There weren't proper boundaries between his life and ours. He wanted to live heroically through ours.

"Dad had a real dilemma, which I think is interesting not just for him, but for fathers and sons and parents in general. This 'famous father' thing is a smoke screen. The real underlying myth is not whether your father was a speed-freak-abusive-alcoholic-famous-son-of-a-bitch. When all that is resolved, what is most significant is how the generations forgive each other. You get your microscope down onto that and it would be like discovering the structure of DNA.

"I found out my father was famous when I was really young. The doorman said, 'Do you know how famous your father is?' and I asked him what famous meant.

"'Well, everybody knows him.'

"I thought that was quite natural because I knew him and everybody I knew did, too. Those kinds of things, for people who don't have famous fathers on the level of press, radio, and film, are very organic to the people who do. It's like growing your fingernails. When people ask, 'What's it like to be the son of a famous person?' you actually have to do this kind of thing where you answer the question in a way that you think it will be helpful for them to understand. You don't have a contrast. If you're born to a famous father, you don't notice.

"I remember the day I realized my father was an asshole. It was out at the house in Sag Harbor. He'd hired a local sixteen-year-old to mow the lawn; a good old wiseass Long Island punk who didn't give a fuck if this guy wrote books or what. My father barked a couple of orders at him which were very similar in tone and quality to what he'd say to my brother and me. The kid just looked at him and said, 'Fuck you.' He threw the gardening tools in the garage where I was standing, mouth agape, and said, 'You know, your father is a real asshole.'

"I sat there in shock and suddenly everything hooked up and I said, 'Jesus, you're right.' It wasn't me, it was him! I saw his feet of clay. He was no longer Jehovah. I remember the summer afternoon so vividly. I was half in and half out of the garage. Dad was striding out of the house toward his workroom, perhaps to work on the carburetor of his outboard motor. When he heard the kid swear at him, he said, 'Get out of here.' Looking back on it, if you know anything about my father and how he was raised, or as any kid with a summer job yourself, these kinds of dramas happen all the time. My father probably remembered what it was like being a kid with a summer job, saying 'Fuck you', too. This kid had seen a lot of assholes and my father had been around a lot of kids that did yard work. For them, it was everyday stuff, but I was young. It was a new world to me.

"I swear my father picked up on my rite of passage, because our relationship was seriously strained from then on. I became special fodder because I was a threat to his caricature of what he wanted people to see. Just my existence was a threat. I never really listened to my father straight again. I didn't know what was wrong, but I knew something wasn't right. I noticed that he'd surround himself with people who adored him or thought of him as being the word of wisdom on all things. He was involved in a literary circle, but he never quite made the Algonquin. He wouldn't hang out around someone like Dorothy Parker and have her check him out. He was not available for penetrating insight. He was very self-conscious. He knew he was a phoney. He was a total bullshit artist on some levels, and often that makes a great writer. But if you don't walk like you talk, it's not a great character trait.

"After serving in Vietnam, I got busted for marijuana in D.C. and hired my own lawyer, who got me acquitted. I had beaten the military by having the trial postponed till after I was out, so I didn't end up in Leavenworth. I got an honorable discharge and Dad's last words to me were, 'They should have jailed you.' Juxtaposed to the closeness that I felt with him in Vietnam, that experience was a mirror of my whole life with him as a little kid.

"Dad was soundly criticized by his peers for his ridiculous saber-rattling routine. He was touring around and got photographed pulling lanyards and 175 mm artillery toward the enemy, or in helicopters with guns. The Writers Guild said, "Come on, even [Yevgeny] Yevtushenko doesn't do that for the Soviets." But being alcoholic and surrounded by totally admiring army men, he did his usual insecure number which started with *The Grapes of Wrath*. He had a knack for imbuing people with strengths and nobilities and powers that they didn't know they had. In fact, maybe they didn't have them, but they would be so flattered they wouldn't argue. On Long Island, for instance, there'd be some Mafiosi who bought some land up on South Hampton. Dad would drink coffee with them in the morning and say 'Boy, you can really catch fish. I wish I could catch fish like that.' They'd start talking to him, not sensing the bullshit. It was his own way of calming the waters. He was good at keeping people at a distance by flattering them, and it worked well for him.

"Thom and I are convinced that he never talked to any of those people in *Travels with Charley*. He just sat in his camper and wrote all that shit. He was too shy. He was really frightened of people who saw through him. He couldn't have handled that amount of interaction. So, the book is actually a great novel.

"When he, as 'the Conscience of America,' and his generation realized that the Vietnam War was wrong, his reputation was at stake. He couldn't let go of his belief in the war, and when he finally did, he didn't do it publicly. The M16 he'd been given that had hung over the fireplace ended up in a closet along with the green beret. All those John Wayne symbols melted away and I think being wrong killed him. One thing I've noticed about a certain variety of addicts is that bottom line, they don't like being wrong. It's a threat to their very existence. Dad believed his own press. He was treated like an omniscient philosophical person and he forgot that came from his ability to be humble at one time. It's somewhere in the 'power corrupts' mode. I think that's why he chose the overdose of morphine when he did. He was broken from the Vietnam thing. He didn't want to be alive in a world where he wasn't right.

"He never realized that he'd been an asshole to his family or that he'd messed up as a father. But then, we hadn't messed up enough for him to think he'd messed up. We would in time, but not when he was alive. It was more about him, his reputation, his ego. He was conflicted about us. He didn't delight in our iconoclasm, although he loved the Arthur legend. He knew that the king must die and that he'd be the first motherfucker to get it. We'd topple him first, and that pissed him off."

22 | DECENT

JOHN

By 1971 I was living with my own one-year-old child on Morton Street in the West Village in New York. Blake and her mother, Crystal, and I had moved into an apartment leased to journalist Michael Herr's wife, Valerie. My little nuclear family had returned to the United States from what seemed like a lifetime in Vietnam where Blake had been born.

As a witting soldier, then journalist, most of my stay there had been more or less voluntary. However, with others of my kind, I had tried to elude the spectral fear that floated around in that crucible of agony called "Nam," in the soft, warm glow of the opium lamp. It seemed to help to numb the feelings of remorse and pity for myself and missing friends.

Back home in the States, I had begun to drink heavily, and mostly alone at night. The only people I could relate to were people a bit like myself; people with the odd *malaise de corps* of the literate walking wounded. Many were journalists like Michael Herr, and a lot of us were "living" in New York. Most of my friends were ex-volunteers from agencies like CARE and the Peace Corps.

One night a group of us met at this little one-room apartment in the Village with the arguably perverse intention to celebrate the Vietnamese lunar New Year at Têt, and call another comrade who had just made it out alive to

California. He was back from the land of the dreaming dead after ending *his* opium habit and perking up in Hong Kong. With one of those little suction-cup things I decided to tape the call for everyone's entertainment.

All things considered, it should have been a loving night of grace and gratitude that we were all reasonably whole and well. The problem was that I wasn't. Not long after everyone's arrival I began to celebrate our special togetherness with a half-gallon of cheap scotch. Soon things began to turn to the inappropriate, and then downright ugly. I remember referring to my dear friend Scott's Chinese girlfriend with some skewered and out of character racist/sexist twist, as if she would be amused and amazed at the cavalier power of my raw expressionism. That was just the beginning.

The technology had changed since my mother's day. The phone call was a disaster of filthy, rambling interjection by me. Afterwards, for some strange reason I put a fresh cassette in the slot. The ensuing two hours of madness went on tape and were waiting for me like a mugger the next morning when I woke up abruptly at dawn from a blackout. I gazed at the infernal machine with what had become an increasingly familiar sense of dis-ease.

Timidly, putting in the earplug, I began to listen to myself and my world go insane. I heard my friends excuse themselves to Crystal and leave under the hostile fire and unprovoked ground assault of my surging abuse. I heard my child begin to cry and go mute when I yelled at her to shut up. I heard myself storm out of the apartment toward a neighborhood bar, only to come right back screaming at the top of my lungs from the street for the keys that I had forgotten. I heard the scuffle on the stairs with the landlord who was protesting about the hour and constant yelling in my apartment. I heard me curse and threaten his life as I nearly pushed him over the banister. I heard my family shift around in their silent fear of my increasing violence. But most of all, I heard my mother, and then, turning off the tape, I heard my own tears.

That cold morning I was dreadfully and irrefutably awakened to the family disease of alcoholism. The experience did nothing to reform me. Indeed, it made further drinking seem the only straightforward escape from the depression of this terrible inheritance. Though I knew that I had not invented the disorder and neither had my parents, and though it took me almost another eighteen years of struggle to come to grips with my "unique" personal expression of this most ancient lifestyle sickness, it was on that morning that I realized I was enmeshed in something far more powerful than just myself.

23 | BILLY BURROUGHS

JOHN

After leaving Crystal, I traveled back to Asia again, this time motorcycling from southern India to Nepal. I spent two months in a Thai jail, having taken the rap for a woman who transported a small amount of heroine over the Thai-Malaysian border. When I returned to the States, I decided to spend some time with Rinpoche in Boulder.

In 1981, I was drinking with my friend Ken Kesey at the Boulderado. I don't remember what we were talking about. Indeed I don't remember a great deal of that period of my life. But one thing did register. As I slipped deeper and deeper into stupor, Ken brought me up short and said, "What the hell's *wrong* with you, man? Your dad must have been a real jerk. My children are the sons of a famous father, and they're nothing like you. John, you better start looking squarely at some stuff and get your shit together or you're going to end up dead meat like Burrough's kid."

In truth, I inherited two life-threatening diseases from my parents. Hemochromatosis filled me to overflowing with iron. But it was the other one which was cunning, baffling, and the most powerful, the one that could speak in tongues of reason or comfort, that held my spirit for ransom. It took me multiple relapses as an extremely "low-bottom" addict and a lot of enlightened care from veterans of dependency to get me into a condition where I had the clarity of mind to be able to receive the help of other alcoholics and addicts.

Despite my lifelong dedication to spiritual pursuits, intellect blocked the road to surrender. But fortunately, just like they say, when I truly accepted my powerlessness over my disease, the drama was over, and I could begin to understand the source of some of the behaviors that had taken over my life apart from the fact that I am just a plain old alcoholic-drug addict.

I was once asked to write some words on the occasion of the reissuance of William Burroughs Jr.'s book *Speed*. It's a bit awkward. I was not an old friend of his, in the sense that I've never been to Palm Beach, Florida. I filled my arms mostly in Asia and first met Billy in Boulder, Colorado, in 1976. By this time we were both beginning the completion of our advanced course in alcoholism, and first-stage cirrhosis. Thom had met him the year before in the same town on a painful car ride one night: he had told me about meeting this obstreperous bastard, who with intense prodding from a goo-goo-eyed girl, held forth, screaming back the million answers to what it was like to be his father's son. According to the story, my brother, the elder Steinbeck pup, kept his lips scientifically sealed. Apparently the distance of obscure sociology quickly shrank into "there but for the grace of God go I" land, and Thom couldn't wait to get the hell out of the car. When I met Billy a year later in a bar, I found him almost demure, though definitely excited about slow things like glaciers, granite, or sand on beaches—things like that.

Like some others of the generation, Billy was driven to look at things as clearly as we could judge clarity at all. Probably things were constantly something. This group of people was not particularly select: to wit, hippies. Some of us suited up for the joust by reading a lot of John Rechy, *Last Exits* of all kinds, not to mention Bill Senior. As heroic kids by nature with some sense of birthright, we also washed down hours of green-whiskey westerns and sagas about existential gangsters and time travelers. For Billy and others, the flavor of that straight drink was not exactly love and light, respectable as that might be. There are always mountain men and pinnacle men. Junkies are always the latter. Beyond a mere haze, many of us knew that the universe was not so pat a phenomenon. Straight shots had to be created or you'd go bonkers. Truly there was no such thing as a free brunch or even a naked one for that matter.

At this point I have a problem in trying to distinguish for the reader the difference between Billy and any other drugged-out kid. His work, and his nonegocentric approach to sharing his often hapless derring-do, is one hint. As I reread his books, and as I remember him, everything was an oddball dance of coincidence. I don't mean those flaming quizzical connections perceived by speed freaks and acid heads. There things wear off and become silly morsels, as Billy delights in showing us over and over again. For Billy, warm charnel coincidences kept leaping up, and it was to those little deities that he dedicated his nervous system, body, and his life.

Bill Burroughs Jr. would go through trash cans in strange cities looking for and *finding* the map of his life. Doubtless he was on to something. Not so coincidently, he and I shared a number of similarities born of a common habit, not the least of which was cirrhosis. Billy died after his body rejected a donated second liver; the seat of some young girl's soul, we thought. His coincidences obviously coincided with hers. As a pursuit, the onslaught of so many beads on a thread exhausted him pretty early. He was like a fagged-out tobacco hand, but he had a nervous sort of languor as he translated things into long and short southern humor that always left you with the feeling that you'd missed something important. In the best of times his fears made him chuckle for its wonderful humanity. He seemed to feel that there were a lot of creative possibilities in panic.

I do not know to what extent Billy was cranked by his own measurement to his father. We never really spoke about it and he probably didn't know. In any case, it was tacitly understood that William Senior had his own death-defying dedication to vision. Thus Billy never experienced the curious liberation of seeing his own father as a fraud. And he was never shunned by Dad for finding writing necessary, if not handy. But things haunted him. Possibly it was the morgue picture Allen Ginsberg allowed him to see: a picture of his mother's bullet-hole third eye oozing its black pineal blood. Perhaps this flooded Billy's emotional pain receptor but I don't think so, lurid though it might be. However, speaking of Mom, Billy had a few strikes against him to be sure. He had tried to grow his fetal brain cells in a swirl of Benzedrine-eucalyptus amniotic fluid from her habit during pregnancy of shooting the soakings of nose inhalers. The first liver cell he ever owned was put to indentured servitude even as it tried to mesoderm its way into mere helpfulness. Speed and booze were constant birthday presents when you look at it that way. Still, willing and forgiving as that old liver was, it remembered the world of existence that dares not to exist, and shrank into itself in Bill's twenty-ninth year. Remember, he was in hot pursuit, so he borrowed a sixteen-year-old girl's bile-maker for a few rounds of beer and life. Things got worse.

By now, Billy had a very good nose for when the magic of the world was afoot. At the first whiff, he would search out its cloud-chamber tracks like a bum or a magpie looking for shiny stuff in the street. With his speedy birthright, significance could be found in bent pins when he was on the hunt. With his new liver, most drugs were replaced with powerful antirejection steroids and a modicum of postoperative painkillers. He developed a fistula that wouldn't close and with great embarrassment learned the dubious yogic art of shitting out of the middle of his chest. It eventually closed, though only with heroic doses of wacky prednisone. As mortality winked at him, Billy saw and talked to his creator a lot. It could be freaky to be around during one of these tête-à-têtes, but down-to-earth guy that he was, he didn't forget how to whine and make you feel guilty. He certainly made no bones about his love for sympathy.

One last thought for you. The energy that I got from Billy was not an arrangement of tedium or even brilliance particularly. But I say again that there was always this nagging feeling that what he experienced was important for us to be always aware of. For many of us he was too silly, or we were too busy to pay proper attention to the husk that surrounds us all, or to the game that his innocence didn't have enough constitution to describe fully. His compassion was due wholly to what he had seen in his adventure as well as giving a "thanks and tip of the hat" to simple meanness.

I saw him last at a Halloween party. His being looked swollen and sore but his eyes twinkled a "Shucks, who me?"

24 | KISSING TRAINS

JOHN

The mountains and gorges around Boulder, Colorado, are exceedingly beautiful. They surge like a frozen tidal wave and then stop abruptly to project their sharp witness over the broad high plains. There the apparition of millions of migrating buffalo would often wander across my mind. Long ago, it is said that it would take weeks for a single herd to drift through the yellow grassland. In winter, the cobalt blue sky almost shatters the eye and the naked aspens on the mountains stand out like oxidized steel on the rare grey days. But even in winter, when the dry chinook winds blow down from the north, even the deepest snowfall is soon puffed away from the streets of the town like baby powder. To some Vietnam vets the word "chinook," which means "snow eater" in Arapaho, had an unwelcome ring to it as the name of an ungainly and sometimes dangerous troop-carrying helicopter.

Boulder and its environs were actually a magnet for Vietnam vets. Though during the war I heard a great number of GIs swear that they would never go camping or even fishing in the woods again, now others felt forced out to the hinterland. Choked with depression and an overwhelming feeling of strangeness, along with their dogs, maybe a rifle, and some booze, they left the townships in search of higher and less wrenching ground. Sometimes in small groups or all alone, they secluded themselves in the mountains near Boulder, or other less fashionable hamlets all across the Rockies, the Tennessee Mountains, the Appalachians, the Ozarks, or any other range that was as inhospitable as the people they felt they had come home to.

In 1979, after attending a Buddhist seminary, I moved back to Boulder from California to be with Nancy and her two children. Midway through that first summer with my new family, I found myself crossing the street with one of my closest surviving friends from Vietnam. He had come out from Pennsylvania to do some trout fishing and to take a look at the Naropa Institute Poetry Department. The Third Annual Red Zinger International Bicycle Classic of Boulder was in top gear. In the middle of the course, which lay in the middle of *our* course to the Hotel Boulderado bar, my friend stopped and asked me to answer him yes or no—did I think Vietnam had fucked us up? Since John Balaban was an English teacher, there were a number of other ways that he could have framed this question. For that matter, we were both men of many words and sophisticated shields. If for no other reason than that, I said yes and hurried on before we were run over by the Austrian racing team cornering Spruce Street onto Thirteenth in front of the hotel.

Balaban was so determined to pursue this point that my customary glibness was useless and there wasn't any other available cover in the bar beyond the ordering of stiff drinks. When we went to sit down, John asked his question again. Again, I said yes and surprised, I felt a kind of lightness.

It had been eight years or so since John and I had returned from Vietnam. Portions of our lives had moved forward, but when we met we talked always of the war, about our distant and sometimes dead friends, and about sad and funny memories. John, who is a poet with a bias for life's darkness, had written of these things, describing the leaves of our long calendar in Vietnam as "barbarities, each heaped on the other like stones on a man already stoned to death." Yet the question—What had this done to *us*?—remained unasked. Though we knew better, hoping that a muse might spare our lives, our time in Vietnam had made us squirm into the role of immortal observers.

To new acquaintances we were probably terribly boring: when we got together we must have sounded like two kids coming directly out of an adventure movie saying "remember the part when. . . ." Now eight years later, somewhat numb even amidst the summer glow of thousands of young and enthusiastic celebrants of herbal tea, bicycle endurance, and beer, the permafrost began to melt and we started at last to acknowledged each other as incomplete and part of the brigades of walking wounded.

With this breath of honesty, we won some comfort from the immediate fact that we had at least stopped redescribing and remembering a
bygone Vietnam to ourselves and had begun recounting our lives *after* to
each other. Instead of further layering emotional cysts by encapsulating our
experiences in vain and rugged images of the past, we tried to share the
chaotic feelings which had begun to surface through our peculiar conduct.
John said he found himself crying a lot about nothing in particular. I, on
the other hand, had not drawn a clean or sober breath since 1967.

Sometimes when people asked me to tell them about Vietnam, I used
one of my fifty stock responses and let them fill in the blanks. Often my
audience was not really listening, or just enough to confirm their personal
theories about war and life. When I see movies about our war, I find myself
mostly avoiding the theme and instead I concentrate on criticizing the special effects; wondering how, after thirty-million-dollar .50 caliber bullets
still look like cheap Chinese fireworks, Vietnamese speak like nisei, and
Montagnards seem to come from Fiji. Vets spend a lot of time guffawing
over such incongruities as the only berth to hide from memory. For
Vietnam veterans, a large part of the impact of *Platoon* was because a skilled
technical department robbed us of even that cover.

On the television network I helped build in Vietnam, the favorite programs were *Star Trek* and *Combat*; the super fiction of the one and the thick
melodrama of the other were actually both so hilariously otherworldly that
they were unusually comforting. But even today, a car backfiring or the
sound of helicopter rotors in the Los Angeles night are a bitch. And then
there are the innumerable rock 'n' roll tunes that snare my limbic brain
stem and send me hurtling back in time. My so-called Vietnam brothers
mostly agree that the truly horrible things we saw and felt in Vietnam we
now remember when we are awake; our nightmares (like running around
the living room furniture being chased by VC or something) are just
spooky extensions of the fear we learned to look for over our shoulders.

By the time that Balaban and I began to get honest about all of this,
people had already begun to speak in terms of the effects in a clinical
pigeonhole called Post Traumatic Stress Disorder, or simply PTSD.

When I was a kid, fatigue and stress were things that happened to
metal, especially that of British airliners; now we understand that they also
happened to the people in them. These days, what used to be a tough life
or even just *life* is now seen in terms of stress. The odd measure of this is
such that either good news or bad could actually kill you.

Despite my initial sneer at the new antiseptic filing for wretchedness, the fact that the Vietnam veteran had now come under the calipers of stress "technology" actually amounted to the first gesture of compassion these forgotten or unwanted men had received up to this point.

When I first heard the psychological term *Delayed Stress*, I wondered if the "delayed" part referred to our delay in seeing it, or to our unwillingness to throw off the seventies' television stereotype of Vietnam vets as homicidal maniacs. Eventually I discovered that the condition was real and if not dealt with, it was indeed life-threatening as hell. Its effects could range from bleeding gums to cancer to suicide.

Originally, this "stress" business was not really a bandwagon that I wanted to jump on. To be blunt, I found it *unmanly*. But on encountering my own resistance to acknowledging its existence, my cynicism and hesitation began to fit more and more into the Delayed Stress model. Not all afflicted vets fit under this specific umbrella, while at the same time the list of symptoms is far-ranging enough to splash any number of people who never went to Vietnam; like for instance people who were born in or around New York City, or East L.A., America's answer to Beirut.

Pretending at first to be merely intrigued, I began to look into this affair as a journalist. Just an observer again, you understand. The symptoms that I found on the following list were culled from literature put out by the Disabled American Veterans, though they could apply to victims of natural disasters, prevalent abuse, rape, or any kind of physical or psychological violence. Afflicted vets sometimes like to think that they own this territory as the only ground they ever won, and indeed they won some of it dearly. Certainly I have my favorites:

- sleep disturbances
- tendency to react under stress with survival tactics
- psychic or emotional numbing
- loss of interest in work and activities
- survivor guilt
- avoidance of activities that arouse memories of trauma in the war zone
- suicidal feelings and thoughts
- inability to talk about war experiences
- alienation
- fantasies of retaliation and destruction
- cynicism and distrust of government and authority
- hypersensitivity to perceived injustice
- emotional distancing from children, wife, and others

And my all-time favorite:

- concern with humanistic values overlaid by hedonism

Of course, some of these reactions make for basic good sense and others could be attributable to the pervasive midlife crisis in a world seemingly gone mad. There are, however, some startling statistics that exist exclusively within the world of the Vietnam veteran. Figures indicate that the suicide rate among Vietnam vets is 33 percent higher than among the general population. The figure has now climbed. When I say suicide, I don't mean death by "misadventure" like drunk driving. I mean real gun-to-the-head, blow-yourself-away type stuff. In fact, *far more* vets have killed themselves than were actually killed in the war. That number also grows daily upward of eighty thousand men. For life insurance or other reasons, many returned vets preferred to "kiss" a moving train or bus, or for that matter, let the cops blow them away reaching for a nonexistent gun during a domestic quarrel.

Of those soldiers who were married before going to Vietnam, 38 percent were divorced within six months after returning home. More than 60 percent of the veterans had persistent problems with emotional adjustment, and the number of Vietnam vets hospitalized for alcoholism or drug addiction has gone off the charts. And then there are the veterans who became inmates of penitentiaries; men who under ordinary circumstances would have never found themselves in such big-time trouble. And one cannot forget the homeless vet population, which, if you'll forgive the pun, is legion.

Though these figures have been ineluctably trickling in over the years since Vietnam-era soldiers first began returning to the States, the statistics were first lumped together under the rubric "delayed stress reaction" in June 1977, when they were brought to national attention in testimony given before the U.S. Senate Subcommittee on Veterans Affairs by the psychologist John P. Wilson. (His report, *Identity, Ideology, and Crisis: The Vietnam Veteran in Transition*, is but a small part of a two-pound book of his findings gathered during the Forgotten Warrior Project on Vietnam Veterans, a study sponsored by the nonprofit Disabled American Veterans organization.) Assuming that Dr. Wilson, a member of the Department of Psychology at Cleveland State University, used a chronologically and demographically sound cross section of veterans way back then, what comes across as most interesting is not only the identification of a serious problem and its symptoms but a description of the events and circumstances of our times that resulted in a delayed *something*, for approximately half a million GIs.

From the purely psychological point of view, Dr. Wilson's explanations draw heavily on the work of psychoanalyst Erik Erikson. The basic idea runs as follows: Most cultures permit their soon-to-be adults a psychosocial moratorium at about age sixteen. This unofficial grace period, a sort of DMZ between youth and adulthood, ideally allows for the young a space to prepare for and grow into acceptable adult roles. During the years after Korea, in our society this process used to involve motorcycling across the country or hitchhiking through Europe; or it could be a more intense, inner experience involving religion; or it might be getting into food fights and throwing down a lot of beer in college. At any rate, the young adult presumably begins to receive intimations of what he will do with his life. Only when a coherent identity begins to solidify does society apply the screws. Plastics? The Vietnam era, of course, created a different paradigm—it drafted and sent us to Vietnam.

It is not that the particular passage of becoming a soldier is so unusual. For some this role might even have been an appropriate career choice. Eighteen-year-olds and younger fought in World War II and in all previous wars in American history. In fact, in 1965 most young people were reflexively, unthinkingly "hawks" like myself. But in Vietnam, for a lot of reasons, whole flocks of hawks turned to doves, and after another group ended up singed, they were birds with no feathers left at all.

Thanks to the likes of writer Philip Caputo, director Oliver Stone, and many others, the story is now well known. In Vietnam, we didn't really know who we were fighting most of the time. In Vietnam, death and the horror of war in the jungle amidst friendly incompetence was hardly what you could call grounding unless you were to end up under it. Most significantly, when the GIs came home, they didn't come home in a group, but one at a time. Our friends back home had all been against the war; our parents and wives dearly wanted to avoid the subject. My brother got a very condensed version of this when he came home to find his wife in bed with the "friend." When it came to alienation, this was really one-stop shopping.

Many vets couldn't explain Vietnam to themselves much less to others and eventually we wouldn't even try. When forced into a corner, vets could easily fight amongst each other about the smallest details. So at this point, getting help or gathering any political strength and unity was a parody of anger, mistrust, and more alienation that spilled over onto itself. By 1979 many of us were walking around in "thirty-nothing" bodies, lost in hesitation, furiously trying to remember who we were going to be.

In the days when a delayed stress reaction was a hard fact of life rather than a medical syndrome, help was where you could find it. During most of the seventies, it was nonprofit organizations like the Disabled American Veterans that helped vets carry the weight of post-Vietnam despair and emptiness. They started funding the seminal research projects, doing the street-level work, and making themselves available to those vets who managed to come in out of the cold. On the other hand, the Veterans Administration, the organization traditionally charged with ministering to the American victims of our wars, was one of the last places Vietnam veterans would go. It was weird. Everything was so tangled up that we forgot whether it was General Hershey who ran the VA or Walter Reed who invented the draft. Wasn't it the VA where you went to die in your own piss?

The VA *is* a tough outfit, and the then director Max Cleland was in his way the toughest of them all. A triple-amputee Vietnam veteran, he was perceived by many vets as a sort of hair-on-your-chest, you-can-make-it-see-I-did poster child. He was unquestionably an inspiration to some, but also the cause of despair to those with less grievous wounds whose lives now seemed to be in shreds. In fairness to the VA, once money came from Congress to start an "outreach" program, the VA proceeded, finding a number of psychologists who were also Vietnam veterans to man the clinics.

When I first started thinking about all of this after the incident with John Balaban, the sound of these programs made me hugely suspicious. The very word "outreach," the generic term used for most programs dealing with PTSD, reminded me of *chieu hoi*, which means "open arms" in Vietnamese. This term referred to a surrender program for Viet Cong in which cash would be paid for weapons (the bigger the weapon, the greater the money), and then the enemy soldier would supposedly be rehabilitated away from struggling with his oppressor and be taught a trade. This usually worked out in one of three ways: sometimes the soldiers threw down their arms, shouted "*chieu hoi!*" and were shot dead in their tracks. Sometimes, the returnees survived and got something to fill their bellies for the first time in years; and at least once, in a master stroke of sublime infiltration, an entire battalion which used to live underground in a vast delta tunnel system, "*chieu hoi'ed*" and finally took complete political control of the province without firing another shot.

The relevance of these programs, and to American society at large, remains an open question after the Persian Gulf, where Israeli experts predict that there will be at least two psychiatric casualties for every one soldier killed in a high-speed desert land war. And then there is also the personality-shredding specter of invisible gas to contend with as well. That kind of war will make Vietnam look like a South Sea cruise on the Love

Boat. Nonetheless, Vietnam did bring us to a human understanding that was a good deal more refined than the old notions of "shell shock" that had hung around since Verdun.

The main aspect of the "syndrome" approach that I, as a vet, *do* like is its definitive separation from mental illness. This is an enlightened attitude that in any case seems to work out well for the two main parties: the VA gets off the hook of having to pay Service Incurred Disability Benefits for emotional wounds, and the veteran doesn't have to worry so much that he is losing his mind.

Best of all, with a perception of Delayed Stress, the vet doesn't come under the tyranny of the mental-health game, a self-perpetuating system of isolation in which the doctor is always right and, to certify you are cured, he must be convinced you are willing to exchange your reality for his. Few psychiatrists will take the time and pains to try to understand the Vietnam veteran's reality, or, indeed, ever *could* understand it. As I said, vets themselves still rehash it constantly, and they were *there*.

Speaking personally, a great deal of what did happen as a soldier in Vietnam feels like this. I went to war as a hawk. I hated the idea of people who would plant a bomb in a movie theater and force frightened villagers around like slaves. I was very naive; I had grown up watching *Victory at Sea*. I believed our bullets always hit their rightful target. When I discovered in dreadful instances that this was hardly ever true, my political identity was severely shaken. I turned against the war. I never claimed to be a pacifist, but this thing was loathsome. The jumble of any common moral relationship with nature was downright unhinging. It was a crazy world inhabited by little children running down the street on fire, and great golden carp idling happily in pools which were burnished over with a beautiful thin rainbow-colored film of napalm. Your buddies would be talking one minute and become steaming lumps of flesh and bone fragment the next. The world of existence, suddenly, violently daring not to exist, is really shocking to a nineteen-year-old. The light slips out of your friend's eye and there is no longer any ground on which to put your feet. This corporeal impermanence is perplexing enough for a Buddhist monk, a professional. The best we could come up with at such times to keep from falling of the edge of the world was the expression "Don't mean a thing; don't mean a goddamned thing." The truth was that late adolescence in the jungle allotted only a few trails through existentialism: floating terror laced with bewilderment and an aching boredom that had ridden on the back of foot soldiers since Carthage.

When we came back to "the world," the response of many of us was to first celebrate and then stupefy our memories. We were like people building an expensive beach house on a cliff. To no avail, we tried to reinvest our experience and fill the hole in our heart with the girl back home, or the family left behind in the theater of normalcy. When we felt shaky about how tenuous and flimsy the whole thing was, to appease insecurity we built yet another porch jutting into thin air. Numb-a-holics, when the whole thing collapsed, many Vietnam vets unconsciously built for themselves a counterculture of obscured fury. Not understanding, even twenty years later an awful lot were still wondering why we spent so much time in bed watching reruns of the *Mary Tyler Moore Show* and *Love American Style*, spilling cigarette ashes and beer all over what was left of our lives.

There was a time when I thought that victory for the Vietnamese people would be a great leap forward for mankind. Sadly, this has not been the case for anyone in Southeast Asia. By the time of the Red Zinger Bicycle Classic, I could almost taste the grief and smell the killing ground, while the Earth Mothers of the antiwar movement obscenely argued with each other over who the Boat People really were. Another conviction melted in my mouth and desperate cynicism tried to keep pace. I realized that I wanted to cry and not have to feel it. Then I wanted to feel it but I didn't know how. Was this my Post Traumatic Delayed Stress reaction? Boy, I hoped so. So great to have a name that I could joke about at least; great to be able to twitch and grimace at children on Halloween while they squeal, "Oh, no—the Viet vet monster!" Great that it had come out in the open so that people would finally know that it has taken a lot of us a long time to come home. Great that the new psychic amputees of the future will have some basis for being understood.

I spent long years before even really starting the trip, and because I spent so much time with them, my feelings and thoughts have a lot to do with my life with the Vietnamese. They have had about two thousand years of stress and the symptoms have crystallized into folk poetry:

> *Sad, I blame Mister Sky*
> *When sad, I laugh. Happy, I cry.*
> *Not a man in my next life*
> *I'll become a rustling pine*
> *On a cliff in the sky.*
> *Fly with the pines, cool and lonely.*

Not since the First World War has there been so much written by soldiers, but it would be nice if still more GIs wrote poetry. Perhaps someday we will be able to retranslate life that has been turned into "stress" back into life. But for a while to come, many men who began to recognize some of the symptoms of delayed stress in themselves soon became catharsis junkies of a sort.

In 1976, my dealing with Vietnam had really just started. Of course I preferred the total anesthetic approach as did many others. If I thought Vietnam had fucked me up, I had an even greater fear of what facing it with lucidity might hold. Upon just a little exposure to the "syndrome," I found out how hard it could kick once one started to let it in. And then, unbeknownst to me, any foraging through my pain *without* anesthetics was bound to turn up not just one battle, one war, but my whole fucking life.

For the most part, I surrounded myself with intellectual friends and was deeply involved with searching and sifting through my consciousness in the more polite realms of meditation and the fine points of Buddhist theory concerning things like the nature of sense perception and the objects of perception. The meditation practices were best suited for shrine halls, and retreats, but the theory part traveled well in bars. I was becoming more and more facile with this spiritual approach for dealing with feelings, and this kind of transcendental denial was terrifically absorbing and thus perfect for bull-shit drinking. But as I mentioned, the bars of Boulder, though often crammed with Buddhists, were also sometimes home to the descended angels from the Vietnam war. They would periodically come down from the mountains and junkyards of their loneliness to get drunk and angry at strangers. They could get wonderfully malevolent and resentful in a clean, rich college town like Boulder.

Every once in a while I would literally run into one of these guys. At this point my own increasingly aggressive persona always seemed to attract the dangerous and belligerent type, never the shy, scared sort. I had begun to fight a lot in bars, and it always seemed to end up being another vet tumbling through the tables with me. Magnetized, it was like we were cats. There was the combative frozen staring and subtle yowling at each other until there came a sudden burst of attack, neither side knowing what was the cue that set the contact off. Perhaps it was the mirror on the other's face reflecting some mutual dismemberment of the spirit, the ignoble sight of which was unbearable and only worthy of additional destruction. Sometimes, in a "Don't mean a thing" trance, it felt like a shade of a spent friend passing by and whispering through the booze to join it, passing further, beyond the stink of survival.

Because of these fights and their resulting "night wounds," it wasn't very long after being faced down one too many times by an unhappy vet with a loaded revolver, that I looked at my erstwhile research into the old syndrome business and started going to vet groups. At the very least, I would know more about my adversaries. I also talked to my brother about it. We agreed to try to get some help despite our feelings of uniqueness. He was living in Austin, Texas, at the time, and had to drive all the way to Waco to get onto a group. Though not getting into fights, he was having real problems with dark anger and a private humiliation which had turned more torturously inward. But in Waco there wasn't much for him to identify with. Most of the vets around that neck of nowhere were what he termed Texican cannon fodder; sometimes double and triple amputees with little or no education other than some grade school and what they had managed to pick up in the army. He began to feel like he was the "toy" thinker, encouraged by his regular army counselor so that *they* could have someone to talk to. Thom started to feel that he was making the long Texas drive for this sad group instead of for himself. It was a point that became moot when the VA counselor himself blew his own brains out. Thom felt that these were possibly not the right people to go to for help.

In Boulder, I was more fortunate. For one thing or another, the police with whom I now enjoyed a first-name relationship had often thrown me into a county-funded overnight detox, and there I met up with an ex-Marine named Don Roth. He was among other things, a board-certified alcohol counselor, but more importantly he was a Marine Vietnam vet, recovering alcoholic, and an all-around regular guy from Pennsylvania who had once gone into the woods himself with a rifle, a lot of hooch, and the grim intent to call it a life and hop on the next train to another world. Don Roth was the genuine article, and best of all, he was alive, sober, and laughing in my face.

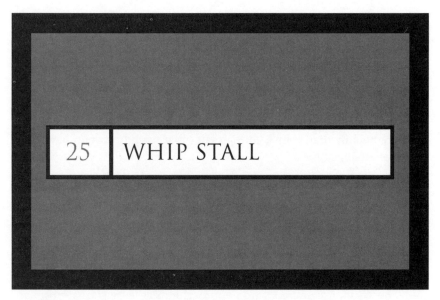

25 | WHIP STALL

NANCY

A s if it were his last chance, there was a dire urgency in John's attempt to create a sane family with me and the children. He knew it and I knew it and we shared that truth wordlessly, in our lovemaking, in our laughter, in our play. Although our fights over the mood swings caused by his drinking were becoming more frequent, this weather pattern caused little concern. Because my mother, my first husband, and everyone else I knew drank alcoholically, I was accustomed to bizarre behavior. Along with Megan and Michael, who were similarly acclimatized, I thought the roller coaster of constant crisis and drama was normal.

Fortunately, when a bond is strong, when two souls are seamless, the real healing of childhood wounds can take place. John's drunken excess held a mirror to my enabling codependency, and my outrage reflected his craziness back to him. That simple act became our salvation. Although the journey was often ghastly, it served us well. Eventually we arrived at a breathtaking detente simply because we wore each other down to the bone and thereby found a core of truth and authenticity. Later, as popular literature emerged about alcoholic family dynamics, we were proud of the trail we'd blazed without any road maps.

John and I had suffered tortured childhoods; our developmental needs were never met. Two inner angry babies drove our emotional lives, scream-ing for the attention and nurturing we never received. The task was to trans-mute the rage into the maturity of two emotionally intelligent adults. At the time, I had no memory of my father's repeated molestations. These did not surface until after years of therapy. So, my family of origin appeared to be more healthy than John's, though later that would prove to have been an insidious illusion.

My father, Ernest Lenn, was a well-known San Francisco journalist, active in the political scene that spawned Diane Feinstein. My mother, Anna Sommer, had also been a talented journalist for the *San Francisco News* who, like Gwyn, quit working when she got married. Frustrated and depressed, she became an alcoholic as I was growing up. Like John, I was the family scapegoat, though my brother suffered equally. My parents imprisoned us in separate parts of the house, the same divide-and-conquer tactics by which John and Thom were raised. I won approval in that tense Nazi atmosphere through academic and musical achievement. My only emotional outlet was playing Beethoven sonatas. The passion and catharsis they evoked preserved my sanity, but when my piano teacher suggested that I become a concert pianist, I balked because it meant I would have to be tutored at home. I had discovered that boys could provide an escape from the tower in which my parents held me; their attention breathed air into my tomb.

Later, the memory of my father's molestation of me as a baby, which con-tinued until I was old enough to find words to express my anguish, was vali-dated by my brother. He recalled that I had found it safer to blame him than my father for graphic acts that were way beyond the ken of a three-year-old.

John and I began to realize how clearly the scattered shards of our childhoods mirrored each other. Incest; physical, emotional, and sexual abuse from alcoholic parents; toxic tension; and to some extent, I knew about the famous thing. Mine was on a smaller scale, but you could men-tion my father's name to any San Francisco policeman and a traffic ticket would not be written. All the cops and politicians knew him.

For the first time in all my relationships, I didn't ask, *Is this all there is?* Previously, I had always felt trapped by the limitations of the men I'd chosen when they abandoned their impetus for personal growth. Johnny and I shared a transcendental chemistry, in the same way a beautiful sunset can bring you back from an afternoon of despondency. Certain people are like that; their presence makes colors more vivid, music more intense. A snack at a fast-food joint with John could be as enchanting as a picnic by the sea. A friend once observed, "There is a stream between you and John, a natural current, that synchronizes your lives." Ours was a love that transcended obsession, one containing such a strong gravitational pull that neither indignity nor abuse could tear it asunder.

When the fights over his drinking started, I understood why John was so fearful in the first stages of our commitment. He worried that I would abandon him when alcohol turned him from a courtly suitor into a monster. We both became wary of each other. Shortly after we moved into our new home, Thom came to stay with us and the primal tug of war between the brothers kept us all on edge. In their competition, they pushed and pulled, forgetting to blame their parents for their professed wounds; ultimately beating on each other for the lack of attention and nurturing they howled over. I never questioned the abnormality of a brother moving in with a couple just beginning a committed relationship. It wasn't like he needed a place to stay. He just acted like it was his right to be there. Because he was rootless, there was nowhere else he was supposed to be. They didn't have parents to rely on, but they had each other, even if their relationship was combative. They often told me that they depended upon each other for reality checks about their abusive childhoods. I gave them plenty of room, but the litany of ancient injustices got old pretty quick.

One night they started in on the usual drunken argument over who had it worse when they were kids. And who had more delayed stress from Vietnam. And who drank more or fought less with their girlfriends. Even, which one Mother loved more. Johnny picked up a chair and slammed it into the wall. That was the start of the holes in the walls of our house. The next morning Thom apologized to me. "You looked so bored when that happened. How much more of this can you take?"

They'd stay up all night. Once I got up to get a glass of water and they were teaching Sluggo, our beloved Abyssinian cat, to jump from the TV toward the birdcage in one flying leap. He learned quickly and never gave up till he'd killed the parakeets a few weeks later. I went back to bed feeling I had four kids in the house, and I hated it. Megan and Michael, who were ten and seven at the time, couldn't figure out if they were living with adults or very large feral children who had never had any adult supervision. While they were charmed by John and Thom's extravagant sense of life, I could tell that the ground underneath them was starting to be as shaky as when Paul was with us. This disturbed me greatly, but I was at a total loss about making any changes. I found myself reuniting with the codependent pattern of shoring up quicksand with my efforts to maintain sanity when the chaos erupted.

Johnny was on edge because of the attention Thom paid to me. It had been de rigueur for their male friends to seduce their girlfriends behind their backs, and then the game was for everyone to pretend nothing had happened. That was ubiquitous Boy's Club behavior back when the Rat Pack met the sexual revolution. When I returned to Boulder from seminary, their friends informed me that Thom had to sleep with John's girls before they could be accepted and vice versa. Horrified, I asked John point-blank if that was the case. I could tell he'd have died if anything had happened with Thom. I took it as a serious indication of the blurred boundaries between them.

John knew I would never betray him in that way. We'd both been relieved to discover each had sown so many wild oats in our respective younger years that we were not tempted by trysts, knowing they only resulted in the exhaustion of being spread too thin. The first time I went alone to a Buddhist seminar, John sat me down and said, "I don't want you to sleep with anyone while you're away and neither will I. I want you to call me every night before you go to sleep. Let's not waste time worrying." Touched by his expression of vulnerability, I adored that the Sex Czar wanted monogamy for both of us.

Thom left at the end of summer and that's when John decided for the first time in his life to stop drinking. He seemed to have reached the end of his infinite rope. We knew nothing about the kind of support new sobriety needs, we just thought he could quit and that was that, a matter of will-power. He stayed sober for two months and they were glorious. He was consistently relaxed and gentle. Friends were impressed and the children were greatly relieved. Like all members of an alcoholic household when Dr. Jekyll is home, we were delighted with the establishment of a comfortable routine. Michael and Megan were forging a strong bond with John. They were very responsive toward his affectionate nature, which tended to dote on them. They loved to cuddle and talk for hours with him about all sorts of things. Their friends also found John to be an entertaining and compassionate relief from their uptight parents.

Things were going so well that we naively decided to take a vacation on the East Coast. We planned a visit to New York, a fall foliage tour through New England, stops at some major Buddhist centers in Vermont, and ending up in Nova Scotia. Thom was to join us for part of the trip. We never thought to ask if John would want to drink and what we'd do if he did, never suspecting Thom's drinking would infect John's efforts at sobriety.

We left the children with Paul and went off blindly, innocently, into the eye of Bedlam. The first week was heaven. Being in New York with John was the epitome of romance to me, ensconced in our hip Grammercy Park suite overlooking the tiny, time-warped square, wrapped in its black iron fence outlining the scarlet leaves. He was a true New Yorker, walking everywhere. We'd rush through the streets in a flurry or else stay in and order veal marsala from room service. John never wanted to go to museums or theaters; to him the sights were on the street, with the people, the homeless, the smells and groaning banquet of urban disintegration.

After a few blissful days, Thom flew in and we set off for Vermont by car. At first, they kept me afloat on gales of laughter, teasing me mercilessly with outrageous volleys, sailing past the crimson trees on those topaz-colored afternoons. We were a joyous trio and it almost felt like a victory. John remained sober for days. I began to think that our life might continue like that, with sanity and grace and extraordinary humor. Eventually, a bitter edge of wariness began to surface. Sharing me, sharing Thom, and beginning to crave alcohol, every night John watched Thom down a fifth of scotch.

Just before we reached the Canadian border, Thom told our waiter offhandedly to "Bring my brother a double." I sat in shocked trepidation and watched the evening decompose. Knowing nothing about alcoholism, I thought John could control his use with willpower, as did he. If he drank that night, it wouldn't necessarily mean he'd drink for the rest of the trip and the following six months, would it?

Wrong. The ensuing days fell into a black hole. John's hangovers left him unbearably grouchy. He and Thom started on their mutual harangue. Then the triangle would turn and I'd be left out in the cold. Mood swings were indulged in like iced tea on a hot afternoon, guzzled and then drained.

Our destination was Halifax, where Rinpoche had moved the center of Vajradhatu, the Buddhist organization. He claimed that the Canadian soil was more fertile for meditation practice, the natives less aggressive than Americans, and the lifestyle more in keeping with the gentleness of Buddha dharma. Secretly, we were privy to the real reason: he wanted to establish an enlightened society. He had come to the alcoholically grandiose conclusion that the best structure for a spiritual utopia was a monarchy. Indeed, the formation of his kingdom was the latest assignment on our spiritual path.

After extensive research by his minions, he decided Nova Scotia was most appropriate for his vision, a small foreign province with little political influence. He established his own army, navy, and even an air force, staffed by weekend warriors, sailors, and aviators. Former hippies were now being told to find lucrative jobs, buy elegant houses, and dress in three-piece suits in order to build a power base. The more financially endowed were buying boats and planes, and sleek new Mercedes became ubiquitous.

He assigned a battery of henchmen called the Guards, and suddenly large men in pinstriped suits appeared at Rinpoche's talks, flanking the auditoriums like Nazi bouncers. We were told they were there to establish a sense of "container" at all the functions, standing at attention on the periphery. Some students were disturbed by these developments, but the dissenters were cajoled back into the herd by the party line that we were serious students of Buddhism, weren't we? No longer hippy trippers browsing a spiritual supermarket, we needed to manifest in a more orderly fashion. Like many Boomers, we were mutating into Yuppies, but our impetus was at the invitation of our guru, which made us superior to the others, whom we scorned because they were doing it out of greed. Advanced practitioners were told that the plan was to infiltrate Nova Scotia and eventually we would take over, thereby creating the Kingdom of Shambala. Rinpoche claimed this would happen, not by force, but by example. The simple people of that impoverished maritime province would be so impressed by our ways that they would want to join our utopian society. Rinpoche, as the universal monarch, would govern the people with his fearless proclamation of sanity.

Having lived in British Columbia for seven years, I was intimately familiar with the Canadian mentality and I was disgusted at his naïveté. Most Canadians are fifties-types with distinct family values, and they don't like their boats rocked. I once asked Rinpoche in front of a room full of people if he really thought Nova Scotia would secede from Canada to become the Kingdom of Shambala, and he didn't bat an eyelash. He claimed that it would happen perfectly naturally. A few years later the Canadian government placed the Vajradhatu community on their subversive list.

John and I were uncomfortable about the direction in which Rinpoche was headed, and especially by his spiritual chauvinism, which touted his particular lineage of Tibetan Buddhism as having all the answers. Students adapted a sense of superiority based on the access he provided to teachings that had previously been kept secret within the confines of Tibet's isolation. Again, we were helplessly uneducated. The same lack of awareness about chemical and codependency extended to our ignorance about belonging to a cult. Later, we were astonished at how his tactics fit the mold.

Rinpoche played into Western greed. He took fifteen hundred hip students and encouraged us to shed our counterculture plumage for a formal lifestyle, which he claimed would be a reflection of our discipline and exertion. We were ordered to stop tripping and make enough money to support him in the lavish elegance to which we were all about to become accustomed. He began to insist on a courtly style of life. Indeed, his home was now referred to as "The Court." We were to treat him like a king; his middle-class British wife was to be called "Her Highness, Lady Diana." His head honchos were titled "Lords" and their wives became "Ladies." Students who had come off of communes a few years before, or from the sweat of the antiwar movement were now lapping up the very bourgeois lifestyles we had all protested. Livelihoods changed from subsistence to opulence. We were encouraged to study the Shambala arts of ikebana flower arranging, calligraphy, archery, and dressage. Ragged-assed hippies became monkeys mimicking English nobility. It was hysterically funny and perturbing at the same time. There was a *Mouse that Roared* quality, and there was also an underlying oxymoronic undertow, of which John was particularly suspicious. What did this have to do with Buddhism?

When Rinpoche insisted that we adapt European manners, John flew into a rage. "He's got a bunch of ignorant, provincial assholes who won't even listen to the evening news, parading around like Louise *Quinze* fops, crowing because now they know which side of the fork to eat off!" Since that was something we'd both been raised to do, it failed to give us a feeling of superiority. At least our dinner companions no longer commented on our strange handling of utensils.

John had always viewed Rinpoche as the Good Father he never found in Steinbeck. He would write him little notes.

> *Sir, I want to thank you for steering me in the right direction. There is no way that I can do this without the strong connection and presence of you as you guide my steps. My ego is large. Some people bring it out more than others. I think I know so damned much, but as we both know, the light of my knowledge could not illuminate even a flea's glove compartment in your universe.*
>
> *Please help me. I am powerless over the need to have others respect what I have seen and learned and this is such a waste of time. It is compulsive and I know where it comes from, but it does me no fine service. Please help me with this in the cause of your skillful means. People treat me with kindness because they see the light of your face on mine. Please let me keep it there for a few more days. I supplicate you in all your forms. Help me be ever mindful of your living presence, as the entire phenomenal world is your dance and delight, without exception.*

Hoping Rinpoche could heal his childhood wounds, John thought he had finally found a father figure he could trust.

As Rinpoche's drinking increased, we began to see holes in the fabric of our devotion. During a seminar that summer, Rinpoche was so drunk during his evening talks that several guards had to haul him on and off the stage. One night all he could say was "Be kind to each other. Please, be kind to each other" over and over. It was horrible to see him so inebriated, but it was even more chilling to watch the sycophantic fawning of his henchmen. John and I maintained a healthy sense of discrimination during that period, at the risk of being shunned, as happens in all cults when the student questions. Maybe we had a nose for it, because of all the obsequious behavior that manifests around fame, but we sensed a disturbing quality of delusion both in Rinpoche and his yes-men. Still, we wanted to check out Halifax, where many of our friends had already moved their homes and businesses. We were itching to leave the unreality of Boulder's Disneyesque confines, and hoped Halifax could offer a more cosmopolitan atmosphere.

At first glance, John agreed there was no way on earth those uptight Haligonians with their blue blood, or the peasants who had immigrated from Old Scotia, would ever leave their Church of England or Catholic religions. It was ridiculous to think of them ever becoming Buddhists, as Rinpoche predicted. Thom and John reacted to Halifax as if they'd been thrown in a vat of boiling oil. They were appalled at the slowness of the traffic, dismayed by the last-place-on-earth quality, the utter bleakness. John kicked and bellowed like a bull in a pen.

"There's no damn way I'm going to live here unless I have a guaranteed ticket out at all times. Boulder is provincial enough." We feasted on lobster as our friends showed us around the city. I convinced the captain of a pleasure cruiser to take us around the bay. All he wanted in exchange for the trip was a bottle of scotch. To this day, that poor captain still tells people that he met the Steinbeck brothers and they consumed the entire bottle during the first hour of the voyage. He barely got a drop. John drank vodka that week, which always gave him a bizarre, hallucinogenic high. On our way back to the Maine ferry one night, he suddenly ordered Thom to pull the car over to the side of the road. He leapt out and ran out to the middle of a field, as if he were being chased by bloodhounds. Thom and I sat there, incredulous.

"He has become Mother. The same mood swings and violent emotions," Thom said, shaking his head. Silent minutes passed on the dark, empty road and then Thom called out for him impatiently. John came back subdued, insisting he'd had a religious experience. He'd kicked off his shoes while he was running around the field and was magically led back to the place where they lay. This was an omen, a sign of his liberation. He railed to us about his freedom and what he saw out there in that field. At the hotel, when I couldn't listen any longer, he went next door to Thom's room and raved on. We had no idea what he was even talking about.

From then on, especially when we visited old friends of theirs in upstate New York, Thom would flash me a look that said, *"See, now he's where he belongs. You can't touch him here. No girls allowed."* Early on, Elaine told me she was stunned by the jealousy Thom exhibited toward me.

"Don't you find it disgusting that a grown man can be so resentful about his brother's girlfriend?" she asked. "Johnny said to me 'Wouldn't you know Thom would be like that?' and I said yes, unfortunately, I knew he had it in him. Does he think he's going to have John cornered for the rest of his life? It's pitiful."

Johnny told me not to take it personally, that Thom was that way with all his women, but it confused and hurt me deeply. I'd see Thom nonverbally putting out the message that I was excluded, and Johnny would be ignoring the whole thing, exuding his own static about Thom's expectations. When all else failed and there was enough booze, things would fold into the sloppy category of *We're Steinbecks.* I loathed the stale, closed system of Thom's mystique. All I saw were a couple of incredibly wounded bozos posturing like drunken apes, legends in their own minds.

I was starting to lose heart. John's horrible outbursts of anger, which were mostly related to his family, were wearing down my sanity. Not knowing how closely linked they were to his alcoholism, I was utterly confused as to where I fit in. When we were alone, the family baggage would slip off of him like snake skin and he would be at ease, sweet, and loveable.

Years later I saw women making gravel in the streets of Kathmandu, chipping away at a huge stone in the afternoon heat. That's what it felt like. I'd chip and hack and clear away, trying to get to the tender heart I knew was trapped inside John's calcified scar tissue, petrified I wouldn't make it in time. I began to dread that there might be so many obstacles lurking in John's psyche that the task would be impossible. Unfortunately, within the Buddhist community, seeking outside help in the form of therapy was considered taboo. Mediation was touted as the cure-all. When I sought advice within the community, I was given the useless recommendation that I should encourage John to practice meditation, or to sit more myself.

Sometimes his moods manifested as downright sadism. The friends we visited in upstate New York took us to a glider port one afternoon. John put me in the plane and winked to the pilot as he whispered, "Give her a whip stall." I had no idea what that meant, but since Johnny had done a lot of gliding, I figured he wanted to share the experience with me. The plane rose gradually and I was entranced by the graceful airiness of the silent motion. Suddenly, we started going straight up, nose first, tail down and then, without warning, the plane flipped over. As the green fields rushed up to meet us, my stomach felt like it was hurtling through my brain and out the top of my head. Terrified, I said prayers, I thought of the kids, I figured it was the end. And then, as suddenly as the downward lurch had happened, we leveled off easily. The pilot flew on calmly. I broke the silence.

"Did you lose control of the plane?" I cried.

"That was a whip stall, ma'am. Like your husband asked for." I sat stunned, blinking like a toad in hot ashes.

"Have you ever been in a whip stall before?" he asked gently.

"No, I've never even been in a glider before."

"And your husband sent you up without telling you what a whip stall is?" I nodded.

"Lady, your husband is a sadist. That was a cruel thing to do."

I emerged from the plane, seething. It was the end of our fall foliage tour and the beginning of a giant six-year whip stall in our relationship.

26 | CLOSE ENCOUNTERS

NANCY

People still ask me how I managed to stay in the relationship. In those early years, despite John's mood swings and heavy drinking, we clung to the sweetness we saw in each other. Our survival-mode living skills dovetailed beautifully. We had both grown up in a war zone, so we were addicted to a constant crisis and drama. As children, when insanity screamed from the rafters, no one was allowed to speak about it. We learned not to trust or even feel emotions. However, as is typical in recovery, those childhood safeguards eventually stopped working. The strength of our emotions was so powerful that we were forced to deal with feelings directly, instead of using the habitual defense of stuffing them.

As our relationship deepened, we dredged up the unimaginable and unmentionable from each other's psyches. Our psychic Roto-Rooting turned our safe haven into the trench warfare of our childhoods. In his search for recognition at any price, John had become a master manipulator. Abandoned by our parents as they chased after their own narcissistic reflections, we both had self-esteem issues, which resulted in the deleterious practice of people pleasing. Since neither of us knew how to communicate discomfort without anger, our fights became more frequent. And then, strangely, in the midst of our mutual napalm, we could drop the rage enough to give comfort, to search for meaning and hope. We never gave up on each other.

Later, when I became personally familiar with the private lives of my existential heroes, Kerouac, Cassady, Burroughs, and Ginsberg, I learned those guys had grappled with the same painful issues. For many years I have corresponded with beat icon Neal Cassady's widow, Carolyn, who was also Kerouac's longtime lover. She is one of the few women I've known who can truly understand my journey with John. Once Carolyn told me:

"People, especially feminists, ask me constantly why I didn't dump Neal. The circumstances he provided me were tailor-made, exactly what I needed to jolt me out of attitudes blocking my growth. Suffering is necessary in order to change. I pity those who aren't strong enough or too blind to have known such men as Neal, John, and Jack."

Psychiatrist R. D. Laing's widow, Marguerite, has also given me enormous solace about that chaotic period. Ronnie was a consummate alcoholic, yet Marguerite stayed with him because every other man paled in comparison, drunk or sober. She knows the magnetism of a man who reveals the full sweep of human emotions, from drooling drunkard to a brilliant, creative cult hero. We've spent hours talking about what it's like to live out the myth of Beauty and the Beast, as Ronald Colman morphs into Quasimodo.

William Burroughs watched his son die of a failed liver transplant in his twenties because he couldn't stop drinking and wore out the new organ. Born to a drug-addicted mother, Billy emerged from the womb craving a fix. Although William wrote with a tough veneer, the death devastated him. Watching a loved one possessed by the demons of addiction is heartbreaking.

Allen Ginsberg struggled to detach from his lifelong lover, Peter Orlovsky, when he drank. "We made a vow to enter Heaven together," Allen said. "It's hard to break that vow."

The radical feminists and recovery police would prefer us to toss guys like Ronnie, Neal, Jack, and John aside. They would chastise Carolyn, Marguerite, and me for our weakness and lack of self-esteem. But it's never that black and white when you love an addict, especially when you stop pointing the finger at their transgressions and look at your own character defects.

Robin Norwood, who wrote the codependency gospel, *Women Who Love Too Much*, is a pioneer in understanding the nuances of tempestuous relationships. In her subsequent book, *Why?* she explores the link between childhood wounds and an inclination to attract certain events and people into our lives. To toss John's problems out like yesterday's garbage would only have meant I would have attracted another difficult relationship. In order to clean up the mess in my own psyche, I had to develop stronger boundaries to keep from getting sucked into John's maelstrom. That cannot be done in a vacuum; I need to practice in a relationship.

Norwood goes so far as to question whether the prevention of addiction is even desirable. She claims that although the stakes are high and the price one pays for failure can be immeasurable, addiction can create a pressure which results in personal transformation. I am grateful that there are some veterans of the recovery movement who have emerged with such outrageous insight. I rode astride the razor's edge with John, and although we placed our bets on victory, the odds were on insanity or death, mine or his. As a result, I learned about the true nature of unconditional love. There is a bond so profound that it can surpass the ravages of child abuse, a garbage pail of addictions, and finally, even death. Nine years later, when John embraced sobriety wholeheartedly, he made his amends to me. "My drinking must have taken years off your life. Can you ever forgive me?"

Norwood examines the theory that people with AIDS can be seen as a group of souls dedicated to expressing universal laws of sacrifice. Their suffering may be the catalyst that advances the evolution of humanity toward compassion and acceptance. Similarly, in the early eighties, I believe many addicts worked on a soul level to raise society's awareness about the effects of drugs and alcohol. When the dust settled, I felt that we had bitten off a huge chunk of the collective consciousness by striving to heal those ills on a societal level, as well as in ourselves. When the nights are darkest, our souls labor toward a quantum leap in spiritual evolution. I would have walked through fire in order to free myself from dependency, rage, and fear. My quest began when, as a thirteen-year-old beatnik, these words of Rimbaud's *Illuminations* were etched on my soul.

> *Mon am eternal,*
> *Observe ton voe*
> *Malgré la nuit seul*
> *Et le jour en feu.*

> My eternal soul,
> Observe your vow
> Despite the night alone
> And the day on fire.

In the spring of 1981, John and I flew to Monterey to watch the filming of *Cannery Row*. Evenings were filled with cocktail parties, late dinners, and midnight swims. Debra Winger swaggered around like a drunken sailor and bellowed "Hey, Schwarzenegger" whenever she saw John, which only she found hysterically funny. Nick Nolte swallowed his wife's wedding ring one night during a row. Every morning, as the crew gathered at the coffee shop for breakfast, he would report that he'd defecated on a newspaper in the hotel room and dug around until he finally found it three days later.

I could not relate to these people. I didn't like the way the little groupies flocked around John. The minute they heard his name, their eyes lidded over like something that had crawled from under a rock and they went into automatic piranha mode, slicing me out of the water. Away from his relative anonymity in Boulder, for the first time I saw a side of John that I detested. When he was recognized for his name, rather than for himself or any accomplishment, his way of smoothing over the omission was to become extremely charming, almost unctuous. As if that would prevent anyone from noticing that he had done nothing remarkable in the past fifteen years.

The exposure of John's insecurities was a double-edged sword. My reaction and his defense solidified our fears of each other, but it also deepened our intimacy. As more of our hidden tendencies surfaced, we were terrified one of us would give up and run away. Fight or flight was becoming a regular stance. But there was also that stand-up guy in John. He had a rock-solid ability to look the truth in the eye and spit at it, which inspired me to stay the course.

I noticed that I was getting stronger, no longer willing to do the walk-on-eggshells when his nerves were on edge in Steinbeck Country. In the blink of an eye, I saw his ambivalence about being recognized as Steinbeck's son swing the gamut from enjoyment to disgust. Because he'd dealt with the whiplash of his reactions for so many years by himself, he found it difficult to let me in. I wanted to share his emotions, but he was too busy pretending they didn't exist. Rather than simply admitting his vulnerablity, he feigned a false ease toward the onslaught of attention.

The pressure kept building. While we visited the *Cannery Row* set in Hollywood, we got into a terrible fight. He ripped his fingernails down my cheek, leaving four long trails from eyelid to chin. The film's producer, Michael Phillips, who also made *Close Encounters*, invited us to dinner the next night. I wore a ton of makeup and made the excuse that a large puppy had scratched me. I wasn't sure if I fooled anyone but Michael and his wife were very gracious.

After our experience at seminary, Johnny told his friends that he'd finally met a woman who wouldn't tolerate his bullshit. He sang paeans to my strength and the fact that he'd found his intellectual and emotional match. Now the intimacy was cutting too close to the bone. He had never unburdened himself so openly to any woman about the conflict of being his father's son. Fearful of my scrutiny, he resented the fact that I saw through his "playing Steinbeck." He had lowered his guard; if I had gotten that close, then perhaps I would abandon him. His Hollywood pose didn't help matters. Given enough alcohol, you would have thought he was his father in the flesh. I wanted to tear down the pompous facade. Disgusted, I raged about his bombastic masquerade, which other people blindly saw as charm. "Why do you feel the need to be so pretentious? Why can't you just be yourself? When are you going to develop your own talent, something that is genuinely yours, besides your hollow name?"

Although I was clunky and harsh at times, I felt as if I were fighting for this man's life. I knew that if he didn't resolve these issues, he would waste away. It cut both ways, the demand to discover his true nature and find his own genius was also being made of me. Often during those years, my mind would drift back to that night at seminary when John wept bitterly in my arms. We had to heal the wounds in order to save our souls.

I began to wonder about my penchant for saving conflicted men. While their brilliant complexity challenged my intellect, the high-maintenance regime of pep talks and cheerleading detracted from the task at hand, that of developing a stronger sense of myself. When the abandonment issues caused by my father's molestations were revealed, I would eventually understand why my insecurities were heightened when some bimbette came up to John and played like I didn't exist. Who was I, anyway? I hated the fact that my desire to stay home and raise my kids held no cachet in John's world. I was a full-time mother and housewife, but the act of propping up John to face his demons was enormously time consuming. I desperately wanted a stronger identity, a job, a credential, a title, something that was mine that didn't involve our relationship. In order to create a space of my own, I took a part-time position as administrative assistant in the Vajradhatu Office of International Affairs, which governed the worldwide centers. Also, I devoted two hours a day to my Buddhist spiritual practice, *ngöndro* (pronounced NUN-dro).

In the Tibetan tradition of Tantric Vajrayana Buddhism, the purpose of *ngöndro* is to purify body, speech, and mind. It is the foundation of all other practices, meaning "prelude" in Tibetan. The Buddhist path to enlightenment is divided into three stages, or *Yanas*. *Hinayana* meditation techniques uncover the student's hidden neurotic tendencies. I had spent hundreds of hours in sitting meditation, following the breath in and out and labeling thoughts as they arise as "thinking" and gently bringing awareness back to the breath. Grounded spiritually in the Hinayana when we met, John and I had to go through a Hinayana period in our relationship. We had to befriend every nasty, dark, demonic emotion that was buried in our psyches. That awareness would bring enormous humility and acceptance of human nature, our own and each other's, and every other being we encountered.

Rinpoche used to call it "sitting with your shit." Habitual patterns are turned into compost, nurturing your Buddha nature, your basic goodness. Unless you become intimate with the shadow side of your psyche, the characteristics that you are too embarrassed for anyone to see will keep you from knowing yourself and human nature. John and I plowed the ground with fortitude and tenacity until every grotesque rock and twisted root was delivered up to the scrutiny of discriminating awareness. While we managed to conquer all of them, it took our life's blood. Our guts were ripped apart by each other's curious, insistent sword and spilled on the ground for all to see. This was true warriorship, in Rinpoche's sense of the word. He defined a warrior as one who finds authenticity in the search for his true nature. There was an energy between us, a centrifugal force that jet-propelled our quest for self-knowledge.

The second stage in Buddhism is the *Mahayana*. Now that the earth is plowed and charity has begun at home, the practitioner can afford to be gentle to himself and to expand that generosity to others. Realizing the enemy resides within, not in the other, the task at hand is to tame our own beasts and quit trying to change each other. We must take full responsibility for the chaos and discomfort, examining with microscopic detail the part we play when we fight over slights, whether real and imagined. Later, when experts would observe "Codependents don't make friends, they take hostages," we would understand our mutual acts of terrorism.

Within this context, John and I had taken *Bodhisattva* vows, promising we would return with each rebirth for as many lifetimes as it would take for every sentient being in the universe to achieve enlightenment, until the last gnat was liberated. Committed to the benefit of all beings, we renounced all self-serving comforts. Rinpoche gave us Bodhisattva names. Mine was Deathless Turquoise Torch. John's was Egoless Thunder, which he joked could be inverted to Thundering Ego. When I got my black belt in codependent studies, I renounced my vows. I no longer want to save the world. It is not healthy for me to put anyone's salvation before my own. It plays into the codependent tendency to comfort the victimizers in hopes that they will be less apt to flip out and kill you. This is not honest behavior; it's a way of controlling and manipulating the environment.

Scholars may accuse me of missing the point, but this is precisely where I began to depart from Buddhism. I had to define a code of ethics that worked in the real world of addictions, not merely in scripture. As John's behavior pushed the parameters of decency, I had to concentrate on my despair and my dis-ease. I was forced to find comfort for myself, rather than in him. My misery could no longer be blamed on his character defects. I could not change him, only myself. This insight was extraordinarily humbling.

At seminary, Rinpoche introduced us to the *Vajrayana*, the Diamond Vehicle, the most dangerous of all spiritual paths. In this stage, the world becomes free of duality. Things simply *are*, beyond good and bad, black and white. This is where the magic happens, and I believe it is the basis for unconditional love, the acceptance of both shadow and enlightenment in a partner, the best and the worst. At this point, the student traditionally begins *ngöndro*. Using visualizations and ritual practices, it begins with prostrations, which originally came from the Indian Buddhist tradition, and continues with three other equally grueling practices involving mantras and offerings of repetitive chants, jewels, and perfumed rice. We were to do one hundred thousand full prostrations, from standing to lying flat on the floor, to eliminate the schism between the sacred and the profane. This is an act of surrender and commitment to the *dharma*, the teachings of the Buddha. It took me three years to complete them, and the psychological and spiritual states they evoked played heavily upon our relationship. Prostrations hone you to become real, honest, and direct. They knock the stuffing out of you and sometimes you want to knock the crap out of everyone else. The practice does not create love and light. Domesticity becomes an irritant. Rinpoche said one has to be a saint to live with a practitioner who is doing prostrations. He called it "airing your dirty laundry." They bring up ancient psychic dreck and deposit it in front of the entire world. There is no place to hide and everyone wants to hide from you, threatened because you see things more clearly. I once told my meditation instructor that just when things were going smoothly, prostrations seemed to create conflict.

"Why do you always want things to go well in your life?" she asked. "Do you even think that's remotely possible?" Rinpoche encouraged learning to live with chaos, and while I believe it served me well as a discipline, peace of mind is my priority now. I don't always get it, but I believe I deserve it.

Since John never meditated formally, we never practiced together. "My other girlfriends used to lord their practice over me," he said. "I'm grateful you don't use that as leverage to prove you're better than me. And thanks for not nagging like they did." I knew that would never work, and besides, I noticed he did a pretty good job of beating himself up about his laziness. I found a relief and renewal by going to the community shrine room to practice, or closing the door on the one in our house. John was always supportive of my practice time, as if in some way I was doing it for both of us. "I love that you take the time to communicate with the universe on a daily basis."

One winter night in 1982, we rented a cabin in Rocky Mountain National Park, thirty miles from Boulder. Because we had started an instant family with our union, there were times when we needed to get away from the children, in hopes of finding ourselves, and our coupleship. We left Megan and Michael with Paul and brought along Sluggo, our Abyssinian kitten. John drank heavily and started his usual late-night monologue, which had been failing to charm me for months. Something about being stuck out there in the snow with him made me feel bone cold and alone. The next morning he woke up, still drunk, and continued where he left off. As we drove home through the mountain forests, the contrast between the purity of the white snow on the firs, the crackling blue sky, and his smelly, degraded appearance made me nauseous. Gone was my noble, aristocratic lover, as well as his wit and urbane manners. I saw an ape, Quasimodo locked in a belfry of oblivion, and my heart recoiled.

When we stopped to walk in the woods, John carelessly placed Sluggo on a tree limb. As the kitten crawled nearly out of reach, I quickly grabbed him. I was annoyed. Would John have let him climb up the other fifty feet to the top, and then what? Would he have waited three days till Sluggo decided to come down or would he leave when it got dark because it was getting cold and then always miss that cute little guy? Or maybe he would create a drama and call the fire department, miles away. Not only was John no longer so much fun to be with, because no one was home, but he was becoming a colossal bore, a time waster, a nuisance, a fool. I wanted to scream, "Get a grip!"

When we returned to Boulder, I started making phone calls to find help. I heard that some community members had formed a group which Rinpoche named *Sarpashana* (Sanskrit for "peacock" because they supposedly transmute poison) to study substance abuse. I asked John to attend a meeting with me, and I told my story of the ride through the forest that day. I was shocked to see people actually crying in sympathy. These alcoholics had started to face their own drinking problems. They were able to identify with my despair. Several shared that they had heard similar reactions from their loved ones. When they put themselves in my place, driving through the glistening snow, completely alienated from John, they were struck with the depth of suffering they were causing in their own lives. They urged me to seek professional counseling at the county-funded Alcohol Rehabilitation Center (the ARC).

Johnny sat there in his inimitable style, listening to every word in sympathy.

"Yep, I'm an alcoholic!" he announced in his typical stand-up fashion. He didn't notice that everyone looked at him as if to say, *Yeah, and what are you going to do about it?*

"The game is up," I told John when we got home. "I am going to find out what to do about this craziness. I will do whatever is necessary to get some answers, and if that doesn't work, I will leave you."

The fact that he'd recently been arrested for drunk driving kept John from slipping into defensiveness. The judge presiding over the DUI case ordered John to see a psychologist named Carl Sternberg, who specialized in Post Traumatic Stress Disorder. Carl suggested in addition to his sessions with John, that we do some couples counseling with him and his wife, Benta. While they did teach us some communication skills, the Sternbergs knew nothing about alcoholism. They mistakenly thought they could help in spite of John's drinking. Now, therapists know not to treat someone until they're clean and sober. To this day, the Sternbergs admit, "We blew it with the Steinbecks." Nevertheless, the fact that John was being watched by the law and by two outsiders caused him to modify his behavior.

The turning point came when I started attending Al-Anon meetings, where I saw women who had been married for forty years to alcoholics actually laughing! They had developed a sense of humor about their lives. I wanted what they had and I was willing to go to any lengths to achieve it. John went to court-ordered AA meetings and claimed he enjoyed the camaraderie. As they always did during his periods of sobriety, things started to lighten up.

In fact, we felt so buoyant, we decided to get married. We had been together for three years. If I were going to continue to put my children and my life in John's hands to such an extent, I wanted a real commitment before going any further. John felt it was necessary to cement the work we were doing. "I admire the fact that you can stick with me through this process," he said. I wanted to know why I'd developed that tenacity. Why did I feel like I've been fighting for my life *all* my life?

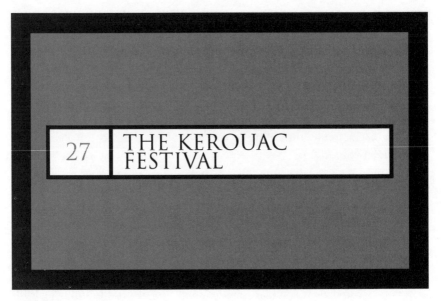

27 | THE KEROUAC FESTIVAL

NANCY

Friends of ours had planned their wedding date for March 6, 1982, and so John and I decided to have a double wedding. These were common, as Rinpoche was urging many couples to marry. The Sternbergs, our therapists, helped us make certain the event would be a peaceful celebration of our love. They negotiated a contract between us that John would be sober for the ceremony, and he agreed to moderate his consumption for the reception. Thom was not to stay too late on our wedding night and he was not to accompany us on our honeymoon. When I asked Johnny if he wanted to invite Elaine, he shrugged. "She doesn't care enough about me to warrant an invitation. Last I spoke to her, she asked, 'Dear, are you still a Muslim?'"

I found a wonderful Victorian white gown and a wide-brimmed hat with a long veil trailing down the back. Johnny and I decided not to see each other for twenty-four hours before the ceremony, to create a sacred moment when we met in the community shrine room. A meek and sober Thom came to town and he and John rented a room in the Boulderado. There was no stag party, no final send-off for the Sex Czar at his stomping grounds. The aura of dignity surrounding the event delighted both of us.

One of those cosmic coincidences occurred on our wedding day, reminding us of the mythic bonds that tied us together. I'd invited a girlfriend to stay at my house the night before, to help me with last-minute preparations. On the way to check the wedding cake, she had to pick up some graphics for her job. To my amazement, we stopped at the house where John had grabbed me seven years ago and admired my Salvation Army shirt. This was a déjà vu of a déjà vu and I was speechless. I remembered backing into that Mercedes, wondering what the significance was. Connecting the dots, I recalled with shock how Paul had brought a Mercedes up to Lake Louise, hoping to woo me back. I totaled that car on an icy road shortly after John moved in with us. I had been driving with Megan after picking her up from a Girl Scout meeting. A speeding car slid on the ice, melting into my grill like butter, just as the other one had done that night we met. As Megan and I examined the damage, John drove up immediately, as if he'd been called. He was the first car to pass on the silent narrow street and he pulled over to comfort us. I felt that time had stood still since that night four years prior when he saw me in that Salvation Army shirt. Had the universe been dancing circles around us, leaving a trail of breadcrumbs in case we got lost, holding its breath to see if we'd make it that far?

For years after, we loved to pore over our wedding pictures. My eyes were backlit, glowing with delight. It was the happiest day of our lives. We were able to stand outside the shadows and celebrate our mutual love and devotion. Many guests said it was the most moving wedding they'd ever attended because they could feel the depth of our commitment. We offered our vows with confidence and pride. Looking movie-star gorgeous in his tuxedo, John wept during the ceremony.

Buddhist wedding vows are not about *'til death do us part.* They are based on the Six *Paramitas.* We promised to extend transcendent generosity, morality, patience, exertion, contemplation, and wisdom and always be a friend to the other.

Transcendent generosity means giving without expecting anything in return. Transcendent morality means working *with* pain, not trying to avoid it. Transcendent patience means staying nonaggressive in the face of tremendous challenge, not trying to avoid the hurt with denial, continuing to work with confusion. Transcendent exertion means never giving up, working and practicing diligently to maintain the vows. Transcendent meditation means practicing mindfulness all the time, remaining fearless of the ongoing journey, like a benevolent elephant plodding through the jungle. Rinpoche called it "Twenty-four-hour awareness." Transcendent wisdom means the clear, continuous perception that results from practicing the preceding five vows. Then you can afford to relax, your psychological state is no longer threatening, because you trust your discriminating awareness and intuition.

Two hundred friends attended the wedding. At the reception, of all the endless toasts, Thom's was my favorite. "Here's to Nancy's courage." I loved that. We went back to the Boulderado for our wedding night and the next morning we drove through the snow to Glenwood Springs, a place Johnny loved because of the hot mineral baths. Our honeymoon was a flurry of black negligees, talks till dawn, and room service. Johnny drank only a little. We had reclaimed our heaven and he was very proud of the whole accomplishment.

My parents were unable to attend the ceremony. My mother had cancer and would die a year later. "I have a wonderful feeling about your relationship," she said with tremendous enthusiasm. "You will inspire each other to achieve the greatest heights of your potentials. He will make you become your true self and you'll do the same for him."

The Naropa poetry department, the Kerouac School of Disembodied Poetics, hosted a weeklong Kerouac Festival that summer. All the poets from the first summer at Naropa were back and this time, Ginsberg and Corso, Ferlinghetti, William Burroughs, Kesey, and Norman Mailer were hanging out at our house. A video production company was filming them daily in our living room. Of all the glitterati, John was most fond of Burroughs. They shared a silent understanding about the pain of being a famous father, and the lethal danger of being that father's son.

"I think it is hardest for writers' sons," William told me, but he couldn't say why.

He touched us deeply. In person, you never sensed the degradation he wrote about. His patrician manners were gracious and understated. Compared with the other macho beat heroes, I found him the most courteous and attentive toward women. He loved to play with our Abyssinian cats and would disappear into Michael's room for long periods, petting and crooning to them. "Yes, you are such a magnificent beast. What a handsome boy."

One evening, after dinner, he lingered in the kitchen as I washed dishes.

"Well, what did you two do today?" he asked.

"Target practice with a twenty-two and balloons. We drove up to the mountains. It was my first time."

"How did it go?" he asked, eagerly.

"Actually, I discovered that Zen thing when I aimed. I hit the mark almost every time."

"Ah, the bull's eye," he rejoiced. "It's the greatest feeling."

I started to agree, and then remembered *this is William Burroughs you're talking to.* Looking down at the soapy water, I thought how strange it was to be having that conversation with the man who had missed his mark in such a disastrous way. *Maybe I'd better change the subject. I mean, I'm standing here in my kitchen discussing the joys of shooting with a man who killed his wife while playing William Tell.*

With his perception and her instincts skewed by drugs and mescal during a sojourn in Mexico, he shot her in the forehead. It had devastated him. Yet, he celebrated my marksmanship without a wince. I looked closely at him, and saw that he was guileless. It was precisely this innocence, in sharp contrast to his desiccated literary voice, that made him so touching.

I loved it when John and William spent hours sharpening John's knife collection, the long, curved Khukuri blades from Nepal, pocketknives, paring knives, and meat cleavers. They spoke of everything cosmic and mundane, but their favorite topic was weapons, in which they shared a boyish glee.

After John's death, I visited William at his home in Lawrence, Kansas. His gracious factotum, James Grauerholtz, prepared a sumptuous dinner for us. As usual, William was surrounded by admiring young men. Although he drank copious amounts of vodka-laced Coke, he remained lucid and entertaining. After dinner, he grabbed me by the hand and gave me a tour of his modest cottage. He showed me his paintings, created with a splatter technique achieved by shooting holes in paint cans. He was particularly proud of his koi pond, and an orgone box where Kurt Cobain had sat just days before his recent suicide.

"There's a cigarette he smoked," William mused, pointing to a crushed butt lying on the floor of the box. Then he brought out a primitive, long, and lethal blowgun. With a devilish glint, he deposited a dart in the column and poised the gun on his lips, aiming it at my head. Laughing, I ducked around the corner.

"Oh, no, you don't," I chided him. "I'm not as game as I used to be! Now I know when to get out of danger." In the hands of another man, it would have seemed a gesture of insanity. In William, it was a cosmic acknowledgment of the humor, however black, in every situation.

He told me his theory about World Assassination Day. "That's when you get to shoot all the assholes."

"But William," I protested. "How do you know who's bad enough that he deserves to die?"

"Oh, you know," he said, grinning emphatically.

I remembered a time when my world had gone mad, and the only comfort I found was when Johnny told me sometimes William wished he could put an atom bomb in the Dharmachakra of the universe. His audacity put things in perspective.

Late in the evening, as I petted his cats, I looked up at the stars and felt the old familiar call of infinity that happens in communion with those extraordinary men. For the first time since John's passing, I felt truly at home on Earth. As I drove away, William stood on his porch and waved his arms like a madman under the two o'clock moon. It was the first time I'd been transported to the farthest reaches of the cosmos since John's death and the last time I saw William alive.

Old friends of John's from London, Fran and Jay Landesman, who had been one of the first to publish Kerouac, came to stay with us for the week. Of all the celebrities, we were most fond of Carolyn Cassady. Witty, wry, and beautiful, she was a cool oasis of gentility as opposed to the groupies' dry heat. There was an instant familiarity among the three of us. She was there when John pulled his "I'm the son of John Steinbeck" routine with Ken Kesey. She generously did not catch my eye during any of it. She had lived through Neal's excesses, and she knew what to let pass. As drunk as he was, that night had a profound impact on John. He never forgot what Kesey said, or that Carolyn had witnessed him making a fool of himself.

After John died, Carolyn wrote this in memory of our time together:

> My acquaintance with John was not a long one, but from the short time I spent with him, an indelible memory remains with me. He immediately impressed me by his warm and open welcome as though it were his delight to meet me. He was one of those rare individuals (my late husband was another) who make you feel you could say or do anything and he'd understand and approve, eager to give himself and anything else he had at hand you might enjoy.

This was in reference to an opal ring that John's father had bought for Gywn in Mexico. Inside, it was inscribed "Tu requerdo, J. S." On our last night with her, I took it off my finger and asked John to give it to Carolyn. He was delighted at the idea and presented it to her with a great flourish.

I sensed an inner joy, bursting to be unleashed, to learn, to do, and to give. Such an outlook is invariably accompanied by a healthy sense of humor, altogether creating an aura around him that "beamed you up" to your own increased awareness and inspiration, along with him.

Just before they left, Fran gave me a book of poems and lyrics she had written, including her most famous "Spring Can Really Hang You Up the Most." There was one about John that she was worried might upset me.

SON OF A FAMOUS FATHER[1]

You might have been a writer, musician or a saint
You might have been an actor or told your tale in paint
But now you're just a hustler who travels with the tide
An easy riding con man who never even tried.

Son of famous father, you work hard having fun
Everyone hurries forward to meet your father's son
You started in your childhood to play a special game
Bearing a special burden, your famous father's name.

The people ask you questions about your father's life
His habits and his pastimes, his crazy second wife
You answer them with patience, supply the missing link
The only thing you ask them is buy another drink.

Women are what you win at, you never do them right
Watching the way they wind up is not a pretty sight
Women can hear your nightmares, they love the game you play
Somehow you must destroy them before you slip away.

Whenever you get busted somebody bails you out
With all your charm and talent you only fuck about
You can't ignore his footsteps on any side of town
He's too much to live up to and so you live him down.

You can't avoid his shadow no matter what you do
Though he was loved by many, he had no time for you
How could you ever touch him when all is said and done?
Son of a famous father, you load your father's gun.

John had seen the poem many times before. He had no visible reaction, but the words chilled me. Fran insisted there had been an enormous change in John. "He used to be such a brat. You've helped him grow up." In his younger days, Johnny had been incredibly self-centered and indulgent. It was precisely those vestiges I had kicked and screamed about. Grateful for the perspective of old friends who celebrated the turning of a new leaf, I also knew old ways died hard. As the festival came to a close, I felt the return of that familiar dread. John's burden was so heavy, and now I had formally shouldered half of it with our wedding vows.

NOTE

1. From *The Ballad of the Sad Young Men and Other Verse* by Fran Landesman (Permanent Press, 1982). Reprinted with permission of the author.

28 | APOCALYPSE NOW

NANCY

John never allowed me to be sanctimonious about the discrepancy between his wretched excesses and my practicalities. I could not hide behind a Snow White facade, pretending I didn't know why I had landed in the middle of *Apocalypse Now*.

He's driving me crazy. If only he'd quit drinking, everything would be fine. Reluctantly, I had to admit that was not entirely true. Even if *he* did get sober, I still had to face *my* character defects. What qualities in me caused my attraction to a raging alcoholic? I was too loving, too patient, too forgiving. Why did I feel so desperately empty when I thought of life without him?

One winter night, a year after our wedding, I got a phone call at two in the morning. We'd had a fight about John's drinking and he had gone tearing off to Le Bar earlier that evening.

"Mrs. Steinbeck, this is the manager of the Boulderado. Your husband has had an accident. Can you come as soon as possible?"

I threw on a trench coat and drove down streets paved with black ice. Going the wrong way on one ways, I drove recklessly, in a panic, afraid he might be dead. An Al-Anon phrase echoed in my head. *The only difference between us and the alcoholic is the smell of our breath.*

A fire engine, an ambulance, and two police cars blocked the hotel entrance. Slipping inside the lobby, I stood behind a crowd of bleary onlookers. My precious husband lay crumpled at the foot of a long marble staircase. I heard people say he'd fallen the entire length. The paramedics lifted him onto a stretcher; an oxygen mask covered his demented leer.

I knew if he saw me, he would go off on one of his tirades, so I stayed quietly in the background. For once, I didn't charge in to save the day. Thinking it best if he were left to his own devices, I simply watched. *Let him face the consequences of this on his own.* As I witnessed myself watching, I experienced the nuts and bolts of genuine detachment.

I called Mitchell Levy, Rinpoche's physician, from a nearby pay phone. He laughed as I told him about the fall. People often reacted to John's highwire act with inappropriate humor, the mark of an untreated alcoholic or code-pendent. Mitchell said he would meet me at the hospital a few blocks away.

I pulled up in time to see John's stretcher being taken to the emergency room. Floating down the eerie halls in shock, I peeked into the room where they left his gurney. John was sitting upright; the look on his face terrified me. His features were distorted in a manic resemblance of Gwyn, as if she had taken possession of his soul. True to the alcoholic's poisonous duplicity, Johnny, the victimized child, abandoned by his mother's holiday hospital stays, was now sitting in the catbird seat in her favorite vacation spot. Silently peering through the curtain into the darkened room, I saw that horrible no-one's-home look in his eyes, a one-man freak show. *Ladies and gentlemen, see the monster impersonate his mother and grandmother in the throes of their dementia. Watch his handsome features change into a macabre mask, his brilliance turn to lunacy before your very eyes. Step right up, but not too close, or he'll turn into a snarling tiger.*

I crept home and went to bed. An hour later John came tiptoeing in, meek with chagrin. He wanted to tell me all about it. I begged him to go to sleep, never letting on what I had witnessed. My blood ran cold that night, like the black ice in front of the Boulderado. This was the closest he had come to death since I'd known him. I had heard about the dozen times he had OD'd on heroin, revived by friends. Just a few weeks before, he'd drunkenly run a stop sign and was blindsided by a tow truck which then hauled away his mutilated car. In his denial, he thought of that as an elegant pun.

I saw his crumpled body in my mind's eye as the hours passed into a frigid grey dawn. *He could have broken his neck on those marble steps. I should sue the bartender and the Boulderado's owner. He probably had been captivating someone with his drunken monologue. Talking to strangers, cavalier, frantic for recognition. Where is this going to end?*

In the morning he looked appropriately haunted, and I could tell we had turned a corner into a chilling corridor where some definite choices would have to be made. My mother was reading Betty Ford's autobiography; she explained the notion of intervention. She encouraged me to educate myself more about alcoholism and codependency. The crux of my Al-Anon recovery was to resolve the conflict between their notion of Higher Power and Buddhism's nontheism, no external God, no savior outside yourself. Rinpoche taught that one could only rely upon individual salvation, saving yourself through the practice of meditation and a commitment to discriminating awareness. He laughed at the idea of a God in heaven and claimed Christianity fell short of the truth compared with the notion of emptiness found in Buddhism. One Sunday morning when he first came to Boulder, Rinpoche visited a little chapel in the mountains. As the pastor expressed his pleasure in seeing the Tibetan, our intrepid guru flipped him off. While we laughed at his roguery back then, I now think it was incredibly arrogant and rude.

When John and I left the scene and returned to our childhood concept of divinity, I realized how spiritually bankrupt we all had been. As children, we communed with a Creator, as well as angels, fairies, and lesser gods. To no avail, we had tried to follow the rules of nontheism by fostering devotion to the guru and the teachings, but it never worked. We were greatly relieved when the Dalai Lama explained our spiritual dilemma to us when we met with him later in Costa Rica. "It is not good for a person to change from the religion into which they were born. Very difficult to understand the religion of a foreign culture. Much better to stay with the one you know."

When I quoted a poem by Rinpoche on my Christmas cards one year, my mother was horrified. "Why do you identify with that? It sounds so melancholy." I found it enchanting.

> *The lonely child*
> *who travels through the fearful waste and desolate fields and*
> *listens to their barren tune, greets as an unknown*
> *and best friend*
> *the terror in him*
> *and he sings in darkness all the sweetest songs.* *

---

*From MUDRA by Chogyam Trungpa. © 1972 by Chogyam Trungpa. Reprinted by arrangement with Shambhala Publications, Inc., Boston.

As Rinpoche divulged the dark secrets of his monastic training, I saw what made my mother shudder, a twisted survivor, like John and me and much of our Buddhist community.

One night, Rinpoche told a particularly gruesome story about his monastic training. His ten-year-old best friend had died. The next day, he was passing by a room where several lamas were gathered. They called him in and asked if he were hungry. A typical Tibetan meal often consists of a hunk of yak meat and some barley bread, so he didn't think anything when they cut off a piece of meat and offered it to him. It tasted a bit strange, but he washed it down with the traditional rancid yak butter tea. A few minutes later, the monks indicated he could go. As he was leaving, one called out to him. "By the way, that was a piece of flesh from the arm of your young friend."

"This was a teaching about the nature of impermanence," he explained, with no emotion. While primitive Tibetan psychology may not view that as an abusively criminal act, some of us did, and we were horrified.

I began to sense that under Rinpoche's rhetoric lay a metaphysical landscape of generic junkie desolation, a justification for the bleak inner world of cocaine, alcohol, and sedative addiction. This was not going to help me define my personal spirituality. Parroting cultist doctrine cannot heal the dis-ease, a rehab term used to encompass all forms of addiction; it is too cunning, baffling, and powerful to be vanquished by liturgy and recitation. I had to find a faith that could sustain me through the darkest night, a sense of sacredness that provided solace in times of crisis and heartbreak. Rinpoche's admonition to live "beyond hope and fear" was a bit too existential for me. Living without fear, yes, but without hope? Why?

As I listened to the people in those Al-Anon meetings, I abandoned the attempts to force the Twelve-Step program into the mold of Buddhist jargon. I had to start from ground zero if I wanted for myself the light I saw shining in those people's eyes. They told me it was a selfish program; I had to shift the focus from John to my dis-ease. We weren't there to discuss the alcoholic. *How can you think about anything else? Here he is killing himself and you want me to think about myself? There's nothing wrong with me. Fix him! Why should I change? If he'd quit drinking, everything would be fine.*

I saw that by detaching from the alcoholic, I could create health in relationships smothered by obsession. Alcohol enslaved John, but I was just as consumed by his behavior. Whenever I drove crazy, or called around frantically trying to figure out which bar he was under, I might as well have been drunk. The Buddha said all suffering was based upon attachment and craving. Well, John craved alcohol and I was attached to his behavior when he drank by wallowing in my outrage and self-pity. I used the Al-Anon slogans like mantras. *Detach with Love. Love the person, hate the disease. Live and Let Live. Let Go and Let God.*

I found serenity at those meetings, a peace that I didn't feel among my social-climbing, competitive Buddhist community. Although Rinpoche taught compassion, all I saw were a bunch of people jockeying for political positions and trying to outdo each other with Yuppie aggressive elegance. I watched other Buddhist women come and go, rejecting the Al-Anon program because it referred to God, *as we understand Him.* I didn't know what to say to them. Lonely and scared, I kept going back, trying to define my Higher Power.

I was asked to do public relations work for the Buddhist community. Proud at first, John became increasingly resentful of the time I was spending away from him, threatened because Al-Anon and work were making me feel more fulfilled. My absence exacerbated the hole inside him. I had been his toy; we had gotten way too enmeshed. By detaching, I was questioning the delicate balance of our marriage and it caused profound discomfort in both of us. I knew with bone certainty that I had to find my passion in life, other than loving him.

Although John dripped with wildly creative ideas, he lacked consistency. I struggled to come up with suggestions to channel his energies, but all he did was talk things to death. When I gave up and began to focus on myself, shifting my priority from his happiness to my fulfillment, he became indignant. Al-Anon calls this *King Baby* behavior. He was upset with himself because he couldn't find the motivation to occupy his mind with anything else but alcohol and me. No longer willing to be a source of entertainment, the greatest gift I could give John was to be an example of how a sane life is lived. When he finally got sober, John thanked me for my courage to pursue the Al-Anon program. He acknowledged that my inspiration penetrated his denial more than any previous attempts to control his drinking.

I was concerned that John was taking attention away from Megan and Michael, as the addict always does. The focus was always on him, which interfered with the children's development. I had to put their needs before all else. I finally got up the courage to tell John if he didn't get professional treatment, I would leave him. To my amazement, quite docilely, he immediately checked himself into an outpatient program without a fuss. It was a simultaneously excruciating and liberating process, a birthing, for our family. Along with all the other participants, we had to look at our denial, justification, rationalization, minimization, and enmeshment. When John graduated, he maintained two years of sobriety, and we created a life that did not revolve around my fears and his abuses.

29 | MAGICAL THINKING

NANCY

As the dust settled on our home front, we could see more clearly into the toxic dynamics that were boiling in the Buddhist community. We began to understand the dangerous trap of magical thinking that surrounds many offshoots of Eastern religions. As my fearless compatriot Andrew Harvey writes in *The Direct Path*, the "temptation to transcendence is the last, subtlest, and most dangerous of all the temptations to power that appear on the journey to the Divine." Andrew claims that the initial temptation to use occult powers in the domination of others develops into a habitual pattern of "signing off from every kind of earthly responsibility in the name of 'ultimate awareness.'"

Believing that practice and discipline protects them from reality, both students and gurus act as if they are above the law, both civil and universal. Five years later, when Rinpoche's spiritual heir, Tom Rich, revealed his HIV diagnosis, he claimed our guru had told him that if he meditated properly, his unprotected sex would not endanger his partners. Rich proved that theory wrong when he infected a student's son, who died a year later. When Rich died of AIDS in 1990, we heard it was reported in the *New York Times* that he admitted having over a hundred sexual partners of both sexes, after learning he had AIDS. Senior Vajradhatu officials who knew this did nothing to stop him. According to the *Times*, Rich said that he thought his sexual partners were protected by the magical power he had received from his lineage.

Another form of magical thinking can be seen in Rinpoche's coked-out fantasies, which were responsible for turning the scene into a *Mikado*-like parody of courtly intrigue. He created a political mandala, with himself as king, surrounded by his henchmen. The all-male board of directors were adorned by their wives and secretaries. Only one woman had managed to rise to the highest rank, and I was her assistant. The source of a woman's power was her beauty or her husband's position. We were supposed to be building a utopian community. How was this different from corporate America? Fluent in a variety of languages, cultures, and religions, John and I shared an international consciousness. We considered ourselves to be citizens of the world and he raged against the provincial atmosphere.

Unfortunately, when there's a center, there's a fringe. Those who couldn't be at the hub because they didn't have the right stuff were comforted by the party line that a mandala needs people at the periphery. Secretly, they were called Fringies, derided in sneering whispers, like high school nerds. They were promised that if they practiced and volunteered enough, they could ascend to huddle near the chosen few who had the money, glamour, and panache.

According to Tibetan prophecy, *When the iron bird flies and horses ride on rails, then the Dharma will come to the west.* Rinpoche's pioneering efforts transplanted Tibetan Buddhism to North America. While he did not believe that the feudal monastic model was viable in the West, he couldn't come up with anything more original than the archaic mannerisms of the British monarchy for his "enlightened society." As courtiers, we were encouraged to give lavish dinner parties, fund-raisers, and formal affairs. He urged us to develope livelihoods that would give the community a strong economic base. Just as I'd deduced in my hippie days, our trappings camouflaged a bourgeois small-mindedness as the lemmings struggled to top each other with expressions of elegant opulence. Every house was a replica of Rinpoche's Court, with white carpets, white walls, and the requisite amount of calligraphies and Tibetan art hanging on the walls. While I loved wearing formal gowns and Johnny looked gorgeous in tails, it was like an endless beauty contest for who had the most exquisite clothes, luxurious houses, and extravagant dinner parties. The lack of spirit and conversational depth began to bore us. Once again, we had sought utopia and discovered dystopia. John and I were tired of the petty bureaucrats, phoney yes-men, arrogant intellectuals and their materialistic wives.

Naropa became an accredited university and Rinpoche continued to hold seminars. A program of Buddhist social services was created and any involvement with Boulder community services was highly discouraged. Problems such as alcoholism or mental illness were to be dealt with by the community rather than by outside therapists or AA. The party line was that unless we approached these issues from a Buddhist perspective, we wouldn't find help. This only served to seal the communal pain and family secrets. It was the blind leading the blind, with lay people claiming meditation could heal every problem. Now there is evidence that meditation can actually exacerbate emotional problems, and may even prove dangerous.

Our lawyer and friend, Duncan Campbell, was grappling with the same issues. He recommended Alice Miller's *Thou Shalt Not Be Aware* as the necessary Draino for our collective denial. She wrote about children who have been disempowered by abuse, growing up in a system where the parents punish them for making the smallest critical observation. Just as their rebellion is met with parental ostracism, this dynamic is later replicated when they attach themselves to a cult. We were attracted to a system that appeared to be antithetical to the rules of our childhood. We learned new customs, rituals, and languages that were completely beyond our parents' reality. As Miller points out, members of the group experience a sense of maternal warmth never felt before. This is how it should have felt had there been a healthy symbiosis with our own mothers. However, every form of addiction, instead of fulfilling the old longing, merely perpetuates the tragedy by repeating the dependency, which in our case was the community and the guru.

Then came the savage blow. We discovered our church was replicating the exact harmonic of our original families. Only this time, instead of our parents, the Buddhist community silenced anyone who questioned with the threat of ostracism. This created a similar anxiety to the infant who risks losing love by inappropriate behavior. This dynamic keeps even the most intelligent members from leaving the group. In our community, questions were often met with a condescending sneer. "How much do you practice?" Dissenters were told, "You're solidifying your ego."

Some guy would flip out because his wife was having an affair and six Buddhists would take him aside and lay that one on him, which always appalled me. I preferred the reaction of the great Tibetan translator, Marpa. When his son died, he wailed and moaned for days.

"Marpa," a puzzled student asked, "you claim the phenomenal world is an illusion, including suffering. Why do you let this bother you so much if it's only an illusion?"

"Because, you idiot, this is super-illusion," he roared.

So you wake up one morning, on a hippie commune or a Tibetan spiritual community, and suddenly you hear the same words your parents used to exert control. Someone else is telling you they know better. They have the answers. They got your power and you weren't even looking. *See, you've always been a mess. You'll never get the point. Just do it our way, and you'll be fine, because ours is the only way.*

Recovery from religious abuse requires as much courage and tenacity as recovery from drug abuse. When we understood the scene's fascist tactics, we experienced a profound existential crisis that eventually led to our spiritual maturity. Using the perseverance which spilled over from our efforts to hold our family together, we applied the reserves to heal the wounds from our toxic community. But the withdrawal process and subsequent discovery of our personal spirituality was a long and painful journey.

Tibetan Buddhists believe that a student cannot progress on the spiritual path without the guru's blessing. Even if you never practice or study, they claim that obstacles will be cleared and you can attain enlightenment solely by remaining devoted to the guru. However, even if a teacher is guilty of murder or sexual misconduct, once you have become his student, you cannot slander him, examine his qualities, or do anything but treat him with reverence and devotion. This primitive belief system teaches that if you criticize a guru, you will go straight to hell. According to scripture, those who lack faith in the guru will be seen as enemies. They will be everyone's target of abuse.

Initially, John was valued by the community for the feather his name put in their caps. He overheard one of the directors tell a fund-raiser, "Kiss up to Steinbeck. He's got money." They found intriguing similarities between John and Rinpoche, their drinking, the way women threw themselves at both men, their brutal honesty and compassion. John acted out the communal shadow side in his drunken escapades. As long as he was out there, walking point, dancing on the edge, they didn't have to face their darkness. When he began to question the politics, he was dismissed as recalcitrant. And I was often blamed for corrupting him.

When we quit playing the Emperor's New Clothes, many longtime friends turned on us. One of John's drinking buddies, Jack Niland, had previously treated me like Yoko Ono for removing John from the Sex Czar circuit. Jack didn't have the courage to confront John directly, but he confided to me that he was appalled when John told him he got down on his knees and prayed every morning and evening after joining AA.

"Buddhists don't pray!" Jack sputtered. "What does he pray to?"

"That's what keeps him sober," I explained. "He's talking to a power greater than himself and he's finding out exactly what that power is."

Jack's alcoholism was clearly threatened. "I can't even hang out with you guys without breaking my vows," he ranted, referring to the edict that it was dangerous to listen to heresy about the guru. "You say terrible things about Rinpoche."

"Like what?"

"That he's an alcoholic."

"You mean a medical diagnosis is not allowed?" I asked incredulously.

When I repeated the conversation to Johnny, he rolled his eyes. "Just ignore him. He's been invaded by the Body Snatchers. It's pitiful." They never spoke again.

30 | MOTHER

NANCY

In the winter of 1982, at a gathering of courtiers in Pennsylvania, Diana, Rinpoche's wife, invited us to move to the property adjoining her farm in rural Nova Scotia, where she was training for the U.S. Olympic dressage competition. While I had been studying with her in Boulder, and might have loved the proximity to her riding school, I told her it would take a papal injunction, a command from Rinpoche, for John to consider moving up there. She said she would work on her husband. The papal edict was proclaimed and we were summoned to meet with her and Rinpoche to discuss the offer.

"Oh, I get it," John said humorously. "Rinpoche's going to say, 'Won't you be my neighbor?' "

In our search for a new way of living, we decided to check out the situation, though we doubted that Nova Scotia would appeal to us any more than it had the last time. We wanted a fresh start, what AA calls a geographic cure. Painful memories of John's drinking lurked on every street corner in Boulder and the town was turning into a white ghetto of Yuppie consumerism.

We flew up to Diana's farm, north of Halifax. It consisted of a large barn for her horses, a miserably bleak farmhouse, mismatched wallpaper, and a bitter, freezing wind. John was downright insulted when he saw the house she wanted us to buy.

"It looks like a girls' boarding-school dorm," he said with disgust. "How could she even think we'd want to live miles from nowhere?" I hated the house, with its narrow upstairs hall that opened into tiny, pinched bedrooms. Diana's promise of proximity to Rinpoche did not entice us. He would be bored there, and we predicted Diana wouldn't last long either. She sold the farm the following year.

So there we were. We'd seen the house. The bleached sun was barely warming the frigid December afternoon. To kill time, we decided to visit a friend named Dorje. We found her in the depths of depression. She hated everything about Nova Scotia. The neighbors were suspicious of the ringing bells, drums, and chanting when she practiced. They thought it was devil worship. Years later, she heard voices that told her to slice off both her ample breasts. Someone found her before she lost too much blood. She was not the only psychological casualty among us. A fellow student committed hara-kiri with a wooden sword. A woman, convinced she was a Tibetan deity, walked naked down a Berkeley street. Another woman purposely walked through a plate-glass window after an intensive practice retreat. She firmly believed the glass would not stop her.

Suddenly, John and I felt like we'd hit a wall. Stopping at a Kentucky Fried Chicken on the way back to Diana's, I was despondent. I desperately wanted to go somewhere, preferably another country, just to get away from our Yuppie Boulder sandbox. We sat glumly with our neon chicken.

"What do we need?" John asked.

"A spiritual community, but not this one, and not at the end of the world. I want to see more of the world."

Johnny drew me close. "Let's take the kids to Nepal. We can spend a year traveling around the world. My father did it for me and I'd like to do it for my children." I looked at him incredulously. He was adamant. "We need to celebrate the work we've done. Lets go back and tell Diana we're not going to buy that damned house. Then we'll start planning our journey."

Eight months later, we headed in a westerly direction and circumnavigated the globe for a year. We often remembered that Kentucky Fried dinner in the most exotic places, Tibetan refugee camps, monasteries in Darjeeling, Hong Kong ferries, at the Louvre, dining alfresco in Positano. As we turned our backs on an era, on Rinpoche's kingdom and that tiny provincial world that was about to implode, we embraced the entire planet.

While we were planning the trip, my mother's uterine cancer, which had been in remission for the past seven years, settled into her body with a death sentence. In 1975, when I returned to British Columbia from my first summer at Naropa, my parents had visited us just before she was initially diagnosed. A month later, the discovery of a tumor explained her fatigue. The doctors gave her six months to live. The day before I flew down to San Francisco to comfort her, a dashing fellow with movie-star good looks and waist-length blond hair drove up to our house. Sent by a Buddhist organization in Vancouver, he heard we might want to turn our land into a retreat center. He had made the long trek up the logging road to survey our four hundred acres. When I explained the necessity of my trip to California, he left me with the number of their affiliate in San Francisco. Once there, I discovered my mother's nurse was a member of the group, and she invited me to join them for evening meditation.

Devastated by my mother's ill health, I decided to attend their meeting. After an hour of sitting meditation, I slumped in a chair, feeling crushed by the weight of the doctor's prognosis. Suddenly, a graceful dark-skinned woman in a red sari entered the room. The atmosphere became charged. She had thick black hair swept up in a bun and laser-sharp eyes. Without hesitation, she walked directly up to me. "You look so unhappy," she said with concern.

"I just found out my mother has cancer. They have given her a few months to live."

"Bring your mother to me tomorrow and I will help her. She won't die."

This was Dr. Rina Sircar, a revered Burmese nun who practiced traditional healing and taught Sanskrit language classes at Stanford. Her sisters are all highly respected surgeons and gynecologists in India; one brother had trained with the famed Dr. Christian Barnard. In a magical instant, she lifted the pain from my heart. That single auspicious meeting gave my mother seven more years of life. Rina's treatments consisted of passing her hands over my mother and whispering mantras. Astounded by the instant remission, doctors and family members developed a new respect for alternative healing methods.

My mother had always known she would die at the age of seventy-six, so when the cancer came back in 1983, just before that birthday, she was at peace. I left the kids with John and flew out to San Francisco. Armed with a copy of *The Tibetan Book of the Dead*, I was prepared to usher her into the *bardo*, the state a soul enters after death. In spite of her drinking and harsh emotional abuse, we had formed a loving friendship after chemotherapy forced her into sobriety. She would often call me just to say, "You are my best friend. I can tell you anything and I know you'll understand."

However, my father was a wreck. Upon my arrival, even before I saw my mother at the hospital, he confided that he had rekindled a relationship with a woman he had known at Stanford. They were going to live together after my mother's death. My reaction was neutral; if he had carried a torch all those years, he deserved to resolve his fantasies. Unfortunately, this was a man who had never dealt with his emotions, and within a few hours I could tell he was in need of psychiatric help. Clinging to the hope that his lost love would spare him the grief over my mother's death, he was emotionally volatile, headed for a crash. Still unaware of the incest issues between us, I felt very uncomfortable in his presence since my mother was no longer there to run interference for his inadequacies.

John flew out immediately and we moved into a hotel, which infuriated my father. He railed about my abandonment. Why wasn't I staying in the family home, caring and cooking for him? I tried to make his favorite stew, but I left it boiling on the stove as we went to the hospital. I had to turn around and drive the half hour back to turn off the pot that was simmering in the silent house. With no regard for the pain I was experiencing over the impending loss of my mother, he thought everything should revolve around his needs.

I never had a normal life, so whenever something ordinary happened, like my husband being with me when my mother died, I counted my blessings. Commonplace events hung on my belt like scalps, like the way John took me out to quiet, elegant restaurants every night after I left the hospital. He had brought a new Abyssinian kitten to charm my mother and for me to cuddle when the grief struck. Those gestures helped keep me sane. In spite of previous friends, lovers, husbands, and kids, I had felt alone all my life. Yet now, at the end of every day, as long as John was sober, I could regain my sense of pride and faith. Disgusted with my father's blatant jealousy, I was fiercely protective toward the sense of normalcy and companionship John gave me.

Although we took my father out to breakfast and lunch, it was never enough. The black saliva spewing from his twisted soul finally burst the dam. While my mother lay dying, he whispered vile epithets under his breath about my abandonment. I begged my brother to come down from Sacramento to intervene, but he coldly refused. I wanted to spend a few hours alone with my mother each day without my father's obscenities. In desperation, I asked the hospital administration to arrange a session with a social worker so that I could confront my father's behavior. Seething with rage, I was determined that he would not ruin my last hours with my mother.

"She had a lover when she was married to her first husband," he hissed. Incredulous, the social worker asked him how on earth that related to providing a peaceful passage for my mother. Holding my ground, I rode out threats of disowning me and silently vowed a bloody triumph on his assault. He finally sneered and said, "That's all you want? Some time alone with her? Take it."

Already in a state of shock, as my Daddy's Little Girl role turned into his distorted projection of frustration and impotence, I was heartbroken. John was extraordinarily tender with me, as he always was in times of great need. He stayed sober during those weeks, except for one short trip to Monterey to visit Thom. Of course, he drank the whole time he was down there, returning disheveled and reeking, his arms full of apologetic red roses. I continued the sacrament of sitting by the deathbed as my world cracked apart. My mother was dying, my father's psyche was in shards, my husband was in relapse, and my guru was perpetually drunk. Was I suffocating or springing forth from a new womb of liberation? One foot in front of the other, slogging through the maze, I was determined to reach my destination, my true self. This heroine was taking no prisoners. Slashing, burning, the days on fire, I held my ground as I watched the life force bleed out of my mother, father, husband, and religion. Sometimes I would falter, but mostly I knew I was going to emerge victorious.

"I love you so much," my mother whispered her last words to me.

Rina performed a ritual at the hospital to ensure her peaceful passage, and the next day she was gone. My father didn't have the courage to face her corpse. He asked me to pick up her things, so John and I went to the hospital. Kissing her without hesitation, John closed her eyes with a quick reflex, as though he had closed a million dead lids. I sensed he wanted to spare me an imprint of the filmy blue stare.

"Thank you for giving me Nancy. I will cherish her as much as you did." Just as I feared later with Johnny, I did not want her cold skin to become a memory, so I refrained from touching her. We sat with her body and I felt her lightness and relief. We were free to start our journey around the world. I clung to John as we drove back to the hotel, feeling profound gratitude for his calm, strong presence. I wanted this man around for all the death I would ever encounter. However, I knew he would not last to see me through mine.

31 OUR MAGICAL KINGDOM

NANCY

John had already traveled around the world four times. He knew which places would be of most interest to Megan and Michael, who were fourteen and ten years old at the time. We decided to spend time in Hawaii, Hong Kong, and Bangkok before setting down for the school year in Kathmandu, Nepal. John had been there, after motorcycling up the length of India, and he had always wanted to show it to me. We could study with the many Tibetan lamas who had sought refuge there after the Chinese invasion. John had a great fondness for Third World countries, and I had cherished memories of the year I spent in Mexico, where Michael was born. Excited about exploring the world as a family, we set off in the fall of 1983 with four suitcases and high hopes. The following excerpts from my journal were written during that year of grace.

October 5

We flew into Kathmandu this afternoon. I was so excited last night, I couldn't sleep. In the Bangkok hotel at midnight, I drew a bath while John sat on the edge of the tub, painting a picture of the enchanting valley we were about to enter, the jade-green rice fields rimmed with towering snowy peaks. When we got here, I felt him watching our reaction, vigilant to see how we are adjusting. With the breath knocked out of us, the children and I kept drinking it in, trying to make sense of sizes and angles and diseases and levels of poverty we've never seen. In the swarm of tiny Nepali people at the airport, we hired two taxis, one for us and one for our luggage which holds a year's supply of things you can't get here (Tampax, spices, prescription drugs). Rickshaws, *tukuks* (three-wheeled motorcycle taxis), women in saris and men in sarongs, beggars, our first sight of lepers, all rushed past in a blur of color, strange smells, and bursts of sounds.

The Rose Hotel, recommended by the government tourist office at the airport, is funky. We said we didn't care where we spent the first night, later we would look for a home base. The green walls of the room are peeling and look putrid in the light of one bare bulb. This morning we had no hot water for bathing, but the brick courtyard filled with rosebushes makes the whole place bearable. John likes funky hotels; Megan and I do not. He was worried that we might be offended by Kathmandu's filth. I see it as primitive; this level of rawness can only be hidden by affluence. Like an acid rush, I welcome that old Third World seduction. It settles in my body, releasing the American toxins from our pretense that life is not really happening. John is relieved; he has quit watching us. He's gotten the reaction he wanted, that we would love it here as much as he does.

Last night we took the children to dinner at the best Indian restaurant, the Gar-e-Kabab, next to the elegant Annapurna Hotel. Located in a neighborhood that caters to the Nepalese upper class, John chose that restaurant because it is sufficiently westernized. He wants to acculturate them gently. This was the moment he had been chuckling about for years, when our designer-clothed children would discover how the rest of the world lives. He started by telling them about the city, the customs, the incredible history of how the Western world came to Nepal. The Rana Princes ordered their Mercedes from India, which had to be disassembled and carried across the Himalayan foothills on elephants, only to be reassembled when they reached Kathmandu. Since there were no roads, they could only drive around the palace grounds. Loving all things Rococo, the elephants also packed in delicate china, crystal chandeliers, and ornate mirrors, as well as Rolex watches and other civilized accoutrements.

Then Megan and Michael started asking the questions John had expected. "Where's the mall? The closest English-speaking movie theater? Any video arcades?"

With impeccable timing, John delivered the punch line he had been rehearsing for months.

"Guess what? There aren't any." When they realized they were thousands of miles from even the nearest television station, they began to cry. As they drowned in culture shock, we reveled in a perverse delight over their electronic withdrawal. This was precisely why we had taken them out of Boulder's white-bread Disneyland, which was turning them into miniature racist consumers who thought the entire world hung out at the mall. John provided cold comfort when he pointed out that there were places you could rent videos to watch on TV.

October 6

We went to Lincoln School today to enroll the children. It is a school for embassy families. The students were very welcoming but the smug looks on some of their faces caused us to warn Megan and Michael about the white supremacy trap that so many Westerners fall into in Asia. We told them to be really careful about feeling superior. "Your pale skin and designer jeans don't make you better. The Nepalese have a lot to teach us." We don't want them imprisoned in a white ghetto in the midst of this exotic culture. Hoping they will establish a new identity as citizens of the world, we want them to learn how to work the town like natives.

"That way, they will feel at home in any country," John said.

Boulder Buddhists who'd been here told us that the Vajra Hotel is *the* place to stay, so we checked in there this afternoon. It is an incredibly beautiful place, at the foot of a hill crowned with Swayambhunath Stupa, a towering monument, where the Buddha taught. Born in southern Nepal, his footprints are embedded in stone near the Stupa, where monkeys tumble around the footpaths, mischievously eyeing cameras and handbags. We were told not to look them in the eye, which can threaten and turn them aggressive. This land abounds with the history of characters from our ritual chants and practices.

The hotel is tall, red brick, with the traditional ornate carved wooden windows, a pagoda roof, rose gardens, an art gallery, a theater, and makeshift room service. Owned by Westerners, it is perfect for us. We have rented two large rooms, one above the other, with modern plumbing. I don't think I can ever face a Nepali toilet, a fetid hole in the floor.

October 10

John's been shopping for a new motorcycle for the past two days. He brought it back to the hotel this afternoon, a bright-red Yamaha 185. He's downstairs in the courtyard putting a padded passenger seat on the back. I'm stunned. Most men would be tearing around the valley, flaunting their symbol of freedom, but he is fixing the seat so I'll be comfortable. Watching him so painstakingly adjusting the backrest, I could cry at his tenderness. He says he doesn't want to test-drive it around the valley without me on the back.

Far from anyone we know, from anyone who recognizes our name, we are cut loose from the curse of fame. We're simply John and Nancy. The Nepalese have never heard of Steinbeck. Sensing we are genuinely enthralled by them, they like us simply for that, measuring how we speak from the heart, not by appearance or money. John has shed the mantle and the weight of stardust and so have I. It's deeply subtle and incredibly humbling. I didn't know to what an extent I had assumed his karma till I felt this relief. He says he loves being free of it.

October 15

Tonight we were walking home from Boris's restaurant in Thamel to the hotel, across the bridge by the *ghat*, a place beside the river where bodies are burned. We left the kids to eat dinner and do their homework in the Vajra dining room. I was wary; it was late and dark. In an American city that size, you watch your back. John stopped me in the middle of the bridge and said, "It's not like New York. You don't have to be afraid. They don't have crime like that here." I could feel layers of conditioning dropping away then. These are gentle people; they don't think of hurting or robbing. I practiced feeling safe the rest of the way home, across the bridge, down narrow dark alleys lit only by the moon. I am shedding so much programming. When we got back to the hotel, a guest was helping Megan with her French and Michael was engrossed in a chess game with a Nepali waiter. It feels like a home.

October 16

We rode out to Boudanath to see the Great Stupa, sitting there like a huge flying saucer in the middle of the plaza. It's an ancient, enormous pile of white stone with a dome top, strung with colorful prayer flags, a place of pilgrimage for many centuries. We joined the traditional circumambulation, along with dozens of Tibetan devotees who prostrate every inch of the way. I could have sat there for hours, staring at them. They seem so wild, like a circus you want to run away with. These pilgrims have crossed the border from Tibet for the winter. They live in black yak-hair tents pitched in the surrounding fields. They have a look in their eye that is so primitive, almost Stone Age, as if they have never seen civilization. When I see that, my heart stirs up crazy feelings and I want to crawl into their tents with them and tend their lavender-tinged donkeys.

October 20

This morning we woke up to the kids talking in the courtyard below our window.

"I smell a body burning."

"No, dummy. That's garbage."

"Nuhuh, Michael, that's a body. I know what they smell like."

There is a burning *ghat* on the river bank below the hotel, a concrete slab where bodies are cremated. Yesterday we attended a Hindu cremation ceremony. Megan and Michael peered into the flames and then started chanting, "There's the rib cage, there's the skull." No shock or horror, quite *Lord of the Flies*, without an ounce of sentiment. With the detachment of a laboratory scientist, they accept the finality. I'm not that blasé. Sometimes I hide in the hotel room, especially after seeing the river-rock smoothness of a limb eaten to the elbow, flake by flake, by leprosy. There are days when I cannot face the beggars. It's the mothers with babies that I cannot resist. I've decided to distribute a certain amount of rupees when I go out. After that's gone, I have learned to say *Pice china*, which means "no more money." Then they don't pester you.

John handles the Asian people with such offhanded ease. I see so many Western men awkwardly posture to prove themselves; it's pathetic. They act as though they're so magnanimous, like *We're all equal*. You can tell by their apoplexy when they don't get their way that they secretly believe dark-skinned people should be subservient. John spent so many years in Asia, he grins at the way it kicks the instant gratification out of your agenda. He's loose around these people, he laughs easily and engages them gracefully with a teasing playfulness. This social tai chi melts resistance; with a flick of his innate imperiousness, he lets them know he has all day, no, all year, and pretty soon they're knocking themselves out for him. When I see those uptight Western wimps, I'm thrilled to be traveling with him. He sets a great example for the kids.

October 25

Nanichuri, the Nepali nanny of the German woman who manages the hotel, has become quite attached to Megan and Michael. Tiny enough to fit into a suitcase, she is fiercely attentive to Kim-la, her half-Tibetan charge. We have entrusted the children to Nanichuri's care and traveled west by motorcycle to Pohkara, a resort at the foot of the Annapurna Range.

It was the most incredible ride. John had often spoken of this tropical lake with Mount Machupichari towering 27,000 feet above the murky green waters. It took us seven hours to drive the 200 kilometers on the twisted highway, filled with beings of all kinds. Mostly water buffalo, chickens, and goats, but we did come across a man lying on his stomach in the middle of the road, reading a book. Nepal has an *Alice in Wonderland* quality, where things look curiouser and curiouser and all you can do is giggle because it's so convoluted. Even the landscape is hard to compute. It's all straight up-and-down mountainsides with terracing on every available inch, which gives everything a rippled, tipsy effect, like when you watch a river moving and then shift your eyes back to the land. The road is chipped high into a mountainside, and below the sheer cliffs plunge down through dark narrow canyons to the twisting rivers fed by melting Himalayan snow.

The orange mud-and-straw thatched huts look particularly elegant at this time of harvest, hung with golden strings of braided corn, creamy garlic, and puddled orange pumpkins. From their elaborate black carved wooden windows, faces peak out at us in surprise. Westerners on a motorcycle are an unusual sight. The winnowing, threshing rhythms of working with nature softens the mind as the body blends into the mountains' curves. You could cry with every passing sight, the goatherd, the rapid "Hello! One rupee? Goodbye!" echoing from the children. Golden raspberries sold by the roadside in paper cones look and taste like jewels. The high mountain air is so intoxicating, I feel constantly giddy. Each moment of the ride held something unexpected, exploding constantly varying textures, accompanied by the rock and roll blasting on our twin earphone'd Walkman. Johnny would dip and sway the motorcycle in rhythm with the music. We felt like we were sailing through Paradise, velcro'd to each other, dizzy in love, and enraptured by the spirit of this magical kingdom.

It was dark when we arrived in Pokhara. I never saw the mountains until this morning, just the smoky town and men sitting on blankets, selling parts of used flashlights and ballpoint pens. John had made reservations for us at the Fishtail Lodge, on the far side of the lake. We parked the bike and signaled for the hotel boatman, who pulled a raft silently through green water, hand-over-hand on a rope strung from the other bank. It was so tropically soft and quiet, we fell asleep soon after dinner. This morning, John woke me and told me to turn my head to the right, but keep it on the pillow. "Now, open your eyes!" The view astonished me. There was the Annapurna range, with Machupichari's crowning peak. Only 15 miles away, the towering thirty thousand foot tall mountains rise so dramatically from the valley floor, I felt I could touch them.

Today I am speechless, just staring at the snowy peaks, from the pillow, from the deck off our room, from the boat we paddled about on the lake for hours. To the Nepalis, the mountains are goddesses and as I commune with them, I feel myself falling passionately in love.

October 28

We have lazed every day away in Pokhara, enthralled by the scenery. Yesterday we took a precarious jeep ride up a dry creek bed to the Tibetan refugee camp to visit a shaman that our friends in Kathmandu told us about. Powa Anchuck is famous among Tibetans and Nepalese for working miracles, especially in the cure of rabies. Without breaking the skin, they claim he sucks a litter of tiny puppies from the patient's stomach through a human thigh bone. The brood is always the exact replica of the rabid dog. Holding the creatures in his palm, they say he then eats them, bones and all.

Upon arriving at the camp, we paid ten dollars for a tiny hotel room where he set up his makeshift shrine, wearing a cardboard crown. After four hours of ritual ceremonies meant to purify the room, we were ushered in. He is old and ugly and rumored to beat his wife. Although he looks quite poor, the Queen of Bhutan consults with him regularly and he salts away her payments.

He didn't look up when we entered, continuing to make offerings to the deities. Suddenly his head snapped back, his eyes rolling, his raspy voice turning into a shriek. He used a small bone to suck out what he claimed were blood clots from the back of John's neck. He asked if John had fallen in the past year. We remembered his tumble down the long marble staircase at the Boulderado. There were five tiny red clots lying in Powa Anchuk's palm and the atmosphere in the room was charged and crackling.

October 30

Our return to the Vajra last night held more surprises. We went straight to the children's room, and found them in bed. They had come down with a fever while we were gone. As they were telling us how sick they had been, a tall woman with long straight black hair, wearing a traditional Tibetan dress, flew into the room. "How do you do? I'm Hetty MacLise. I've just returned from India and found your children ill, so I tended them when Nanichuri was busy."

Hetty is the British mother of one of the rare acknowledged Western *tulkus*, a reincarnated lama. Her son is the sixth highest incarnation in the Kargyu Lineage, with His Holiness Karmapa and the Four Regents preceding him. The child, Ossian, is now fifteen years old. As a young boy, he had spent many years at the Kargyu monastery up the hill at Swayambhu. Hetty has just returned from visiting him in Sikkim, where he has been pursuing his studies at Rumtek, Karmapa's monastery.

Hetty tells us Ossian's father, Angus MacLise, was a beat poet and a drummer with the Velvet Underground who died in Kathmandu many years ago. She is an artist and lives here at the Vajra. She looks like a cross between an Acid Queen and a Tibetan matron, very flamboyant and colorful. We sat up half the night, captivated by her stories.

November 5

We have become fast friends with Hetty. This morning she and I took the children to the King's Royal Game Reserve for an elephant ride. Sailing along twelve feet off the ground to the peculiar sway rocking sway, the beast undulated like a plodding water bed through the jungle. Our heads were level with golden monkeys dangling from sun-dappled treetops. We watched in fascination as the trainer, called a *mahout*, steered with his bare feet placed behind the huge pink-freckled ears. There was one terrifying moment when the mahout's mallet bounced off the elephant's head as he was guiding her. As we halted on a steep slope, she stood perfectly still while he climbed twenty yards down the hill to collect it. We sat there holding our breath, at the mercy of this unattended behemoth, fully expecting her to bolt back to the stable like a riderless horse. Hetty started chanting mantras for protection, and we all joined in, giggling somewhere between giddiness and terror. Patient and still, the elephant stood silent as a mountain. She lifted the mahout gently back to his seat with her trunk and continued past monkeys scurrying out of her way on the trail far below us. We sang all the way back to the barn.

I've asked Hetty if I could tape the story of how Ossian was discovered to be a *tulku*. I've been praying for something to write about. Since we're staying at a hotel, I don't have a domestic reference point. Without cooking, shopping, or cleaning up, sometimes I'm a bit lost about my identity and dismayed at how much it's been wrapped up in being a caretaker. I've also seen how those actions are more than drudgery. They were ways of showing my family how much I love them, by creating grace, beauty, and order. Now that energy is transmitted by spending time listening, explaining, and exploring together.

I found a wonderful room at the top of the hotel to practice my *ngöndro*. I'm just starting the 100-syllable Vajrasattva mantra of purification, and the flow of Sanskrit words comes very slowly. Out the window I can see across the entire misty blue valley, past the medieval city to the mountains beyond. I am so blissed out when I finish, it's heaven. So when I'm not hanging out with John and the kids, I practice, read, write letters, wander through the streets just *looking-looking* as the Nepalis put it. Sometimes I miss "work." Most Westerners are here to study or trek, very few have jobs unless they teach or are employed by an embassy. In fact, it's considered rude to ask "What do you do?" This is to avoid the same awkwardness you feel when you're just a mother or a homemaker and someone asks that; you secretly want to smack them because you don't have a better answer.

Things move at a slower pace here and so little can be accomplished compared with American efficiency. It's very humbling, and many Westerners can't take it. Their egos feed on habitual hurry. Soon they're off, buzzing from one lama to another, then down to India to check out Sai Baba's ashram or the hippie-infested beach at Goa. It takes a certain amount of stamina to make a life here. Interviewing Hetty will be a welcome attempt at creating the feeling that I'm accomplishing something.

December 2

Yesterday was Michael's eleventh birthday. We managed to put together a great party for him, with one amusing mishap. There's a bakery in town where you can order real Western birthday cakes and so we had one delivered by taxi to the hotel this morning. About an hour later we heard a great commotion in the courtyard below our window. Apparently, the wrong cake had been sent up. Unbeknownst to us, you can order cakes laced with liberal amounts of marijuana from that bakery, and a loaded one had been delivered by mistake. The bakery was delivering the dope-free cake and trying to get the other one back from the kitchen manager. We all had a good laugh, but it would have been dreadful if Michael's young guests had bitten into the wrong one. Hetty told us a similar thing had happened to her when she'd ordered a cake for one of the lamas. Often, when you walk out of the monastery up at Swayamhu, a Nepali hustler will whisper, "Smack, cocaine, marijuana?" Since the sixties, Westerners have been coming here for the drugs. I hate what it's doing to the Nepalese, a genocide in the making.

The children played soccer in the courtyard, and then the hotel served them lunch. After the cake, we all went upstairs and watched videos.

December 12

Hetty and I have been getting up early every morning and taking a taxi to Choki Nyima Rinpoche's monastery across town in Boudenath where he is giving a weeklong Three Yana seminar. After his talks, the monks serve a lovely lunch and then they offer Tibetan language lessons. I'm struggling with the letters, which I love drawing. It's considered a sacred language and I feel the energy when I'm practicing.

While Rinpoche lectures, you can hear the high voices of the youngest monk-lets, some of them only four years old, reciting the alphabet. They are so adorable in their miniature red robes, earnest and sincere, far from their homes and parents. I wonder if they get lonely. I remember Trungpa Rinpoche talking about missing his mother "as only a small boy can" in his autobiography, *Born in Tibet*.

December 26

We actually celebrated a Christmas of sorts. A German family brought over some pine boughs hung with handmade ornaments, stuck in a pottery urn, so that we would have a tree. John had been cruising the Tibetan traders at Bouda for the rare perfect pieces of coral, and he made me a beautiful *mala*, a string of dark shiny wooden beads interspersed with fat bright-red round pieces of coral, like cherry tomatoes. A *mala* is a Tibetan rosary, used for counting mantras.

Hetty joined us as we opened our presents. We feel as if she's a part of our family now. The children adore her. Often she lets them do their homework in her room, and then tells them stories. She comes with us to their performances at Lincoln School. With Ossian gone, she showers them with her leftover maternal affection. It's quite touching.

December 30

Just for an adventure, John and I took a taxi ride above valley this afternoon. We told the driver we wanted to do some *mountain viewing,* as the Nepalese call it. He took us over the crest of the foothills that ring the valley. We reached a viewpoint just as pink alpenglow touched the frosted tips of the Himalayas. A hundred miles of snowy peaks stretched across the horizon, towering four miles above me, culminating near the southern end with Everest. This is nature's "Ode to Joy," and my heart burst with awe.

January 1

Last night was New Year's Eve. The Vajra held a dance with a live band which has been rehearsing here for days, mostly by playing "I'll Be Watching You" by the Police, over and over till we wanted to scream. We were up in the ballroom when the dance started. It was packed with young Nepali men. No females in sight. Nepali girls aren't allowed out of the house at night. When the band started up, they only had each other to dance with. There was no awkwardness, they simply grabbed partners and started to gyrate. It went on way past midnight. At one point a gang of boys came from up the hill from the Thamel neighborhood, and whispers went around the ballroom, "Thamel Boys coming," so they all went out in the courtyard to protect their motorcycles. John moved ours just before a whole row of them was pushed over like dominos.

Megan's Nepali boyfriend is a prince in the Newari tribe. His family owns vast amounts of land near the Tibetan border. He isn't allowed to bring her home, or even acknowledge that he's dating a Western girl. Megan is fascinated by this racism. She wants to wear saris and wonders how her copper hair would look dyed black. She and Michael are learning to speak the language and when we're in the hotel dining room, they eat Nepali-style, with their hands. John and I are delighted at their assimilation of the culture.

After midnight, John and I took a ride over to the center of the city. He brought along some trick flash paper, the kind that explodes into a ball of fire when you light it. Within seconds, he had a huge crowd around him. Giggling hysterically, they started chasing him as he rode his motorcycle in circles around the plaza. He had everyone going. No wonder he was a cult hero when he lived in Vietnam during the war, famous among the American soldiers and the Vietnamese. His charisma is magic, intoxicating; it rides the razor's wild edge. Nights like this, I wish we could stay here forever because I know how things are heightened here, and they will inevitably go flat when exposed to jaded Western attitudes.

This is us, this is the epitome of us and it feeds our adoration of each other. Few Westerners know how to nurture this level of delight. Will we have to work to keep it alive, amidst the speed that will inevitably claim us upon our return? Sometimes I wake up late at night while John's reading and he says he's been thinking about how much he loves me. There's time here to do that, to languorously appreciate the Beloved. Because nothing is hidden, not death, or excrement, or disease, everything is relaxed. There is no need to strain at the bit to keep from acknowledging the shadows, the filth, the poverty, the way we homogenize all those negatives in the West and come out desperately trying to look like we're Having a Nice Day. Here there is no Sani-Wrap on pain and so the lid is lifted and joy can soar. I am beginning to savor every minute with gratitude, and for the first time in my life, I feel at home on the planet.

Michael paid us a supreme compliment yesterday. "You guys are so polite to each other, you sound like *Chip 'n' Dale*." I asked Johnny what that meant.

"They're always saying things like 'You first!' and then she says, 'Oh no, you first, please!'" When the four of us eat in restaurants together, the other tourists eye us as they sit silently, having run out of things to say. They wonder what our secret is as they see us jabbering and giggling away.

January 5

This afternoon, Michael and I walked down to the bridge below our hotel. A body was burning at the *ghat* on the opposite shore of the river. We perched on a stone wall and watched a mountain shaman conduct a funeral ceremony for a small child on a sand spit in the river below us. He lit a pile of neatly crossed logs and prayed over the tiny shrouded body. The family sat near him and during their silent mourning, they would occasionally pull out a plastic jug of homemade liquor from the cooling river and pass it around. The mother sat slightly removed and stared at the sacred waters flowing past, her head averted from the body and the ritual. This river, the Bagmati, is like the holy Ganges to the Nepalis.

On the far bank, beneath a towering pagoda, the other body had almost totally been reduced to ashes. John wandered down from the hotel looking for us and we sat on the bridge for several hours, absorbing the two funerals. Huge pigs and water buffalo wallowed under our dangling feet. A Sherpa mountain guide stopped to chat. He showed us where he'd lost two fingers to frostbite on his most recent successful Everest expedition.

As the torch was put to the child's pyre, across the river the other family was shoveling the charred remains of the cremated body onto a bamboo mat, which they then spilled into the slow-moving water. We watched the blackened fragments of bone flow downstream. The huge buzzards wheeled above the pagoda and the snow mountain tips leaned gracefully over the valley in watchful reverence. I felt a simultaneous rush of impermanence and fulfillment, bliss and emptiness.

January 6

John wrote this poem about yesterday:

> Subtly, recognition binds me. Wonderfully
> Isolated this afternoon, waiting like
> A dumb Sioux Indian waiting for a vision,
> I've been sitting on a narrow bridge overlooking
> A tiny river at the base of a Nepali hill
> Crowned by the Buddhist Stupa of Swayamhu.
>
> Marpa the Translator studied some Sanskrit
> Waited and rested here for three years before
> Attempting the convection heat of the Indian
> Plain, and the luminous incandescence of his
> Teacher Naropa.
>
> Today, my view of the Bagmati River is bracketed.
> A small child is burning on a pyre at the
> Prow of a little sandbar. The flames are
> Licking at the rubber shower shoes of a Tamang
> Shaman. He chain-smokes, Bell and Dorje in hand.
>
> As he points the direction for the child's spirit
> To travel, helpful relatives guzzle rakshi, the
> Whitest of lightning from the plastic jug kept cool
> In the river. They totter a bit and toy with the
> Embers. A cheap Buddha Amitabha thanka flutters
> On a stick in the wind.

On a riverbank a few yards away to the east,
An old Hindu woman, dissolving on her own pyre,
Has exposed her rib cage to finally embrace the
Sky. Her scalp has popped open like a lychee to
Offer her shiny skull as a reminder.

Between these curious columns of smoke, naked
Children are playing in the shallow brown
Water, while handsome male ducks quarrel mildly
For the affection of a particularly splendid
Other. She quacks indifferent concern about the
Whole business of her Bagmati.

After many years in Asia, the scene is not
Too strange for me. A peace that long ago
Passed misunderstanding flickers through my
Mind. Still, Sacred Outlook becomes fragile as I watch
The ashes of the dead glide down the river.

Tears from my eyes, nose, and throat
Mix with the green flotsam of this tropical
Himalayan river, slashed clear and open by
Manjushri's true sword. Double-edged wisdom
Rings through this poor man's Burning Ghat.

January 14

We took the kids to Pohkara last weekend. Megan and John went on the motorcycle and Michael and I flew. With the plane at 20,000 feet, the mountains are still two miles above you, which is mind-boggling. I'm so used to flying over the Rockies, where they're two miles below. The children made instant friends with the Nepali kids who live near the Fishtail Lodge and they're gone all day. They've learned to fashion slingshots from twigs and shoe leather, to fish with a branch and twine, floating on rafts, diving from the boats, coming home waterlogged, Third World Tom Sawyers.

We love to imitate the Nepali children's gentle pidgin English. They will sit forever watching John turning the motorcycle headlight off and on for them, chanting "Light coming" as it goes on and patiently waiting till he turns it off, saying "Light pinished" in hushed voices filled with awe. When one of them got in trouble with his father, the brother told our kids he couldn't play anymore that day. "He crying-sing," he relayed sadly, in their wonderfully poetic way.

John and I drove into town today. He wanted to buy me a shawl of purple velvet embroidered with red strawberries. This is a status symbol among the women of the mountain tribes and he thinks I should have one too if I'm going to be completely Nepali. Last week as I was browsing in the gift shop of the Annapurna Hotel, I overheard the owner saying to someone, "You see her, she lives here. Actually, you could say she is a Nepali." That is the highest compliment you can receive from the locals. It's also something John teases me about all the time. Wherever I go with him, I'm not content until a strange town is familiar enough so that I can navigate it by myself. When I come back and tell him about my forays, he then calls those places that I've conquered "My Bangkok, My Hong Kong, My Kathmandu." That's what he meant when he talked about the female duck in the poem, about "her Bagmati." It makes me laugh, but it also makes me feel very pleased with myself, and I know he's proud, too, because that's the way he likes to see the world. It's all about making your oyster wherever you are.

They told us we could buy the material at a tiny shop on the outskirts of town. We parked the bike under a banyan tree and walked in. They did have some of the coveted purple velvet, which comes all the way from Hong Kong. As we were ordering a length of it, I turned around. The shop had suddenly filled with a horde of incredibly silent Nepalis, just watching us. I whispered to John, "If you were blind, you'd never know that they were in here." You couldn't even feel their vibes, they were so gentle, but fascinated that Westerners would want to own one of *their* status symbols.

Sometimes we load the kids on the bike and ride around with all four of us, Nepali-style. They love to get as many people on as possible. When they see us do it, they laugh and point hysterically.

January 18

We're moving into a house. Hotel life is wearing thin. We lost our cover when the Western managers returned from America where they heard from William Burroughs that John and I were living here. Apparently the two women are employees of a multimillion-dollar cult which owns property all around the world. They've told everyone about the Steinbeck thing, as if to gain prestige. Whenever we walk into the dining room now, there are whispers and knowing glances. The regular guests used to treat us in a relaxed manner, but now they want to engage us and there's often that underlying push to prove something, to come away with something. The Nepali staff couldn't care less, thankfully. They still treat us with the same gentleness they bestow upon everyone. We feel like we've fallen from grace, but maybe there's something better in store. We're going into culture shock, slimed with their sicko-sycophantic fawning. I'm disgusted. They have no notion of protecting our privacy, and they don't give a fig about me and the kids, it's all groveling over John.

January 29

I contacted a rental agency in Kathmandu and found a huge furnished house. For $450 a month we have Gopal, the cook; Serita, the maid and nanny; and Krishna, who sleeps in the guard house and seems to live only to open and close our gate. He lazes around the kitchen all day, but whenever we leave the compound or come home, he stands by the huge gate at strict attention. For an extra $5 a month he will grow a vegetable garden. It's a house built for an embassy family, two-story brick with a roof garden that looks over the valley. We just finished eating lunch up there, cooked by Gopal and served by Serita. Now we are *Sahib* and *Memsahib*. They bring us breakfast in bed and ask what we will be wanting for lunch and dinner and what time we want to eat. Gopal shops, Serita cleans the house and does laundry in the bathtub. When the kids come home from school, she fixes them a snack. The Lincoln School bus drops them off at the corner, and you can tell they're coming, because the little kids line the street and shout, "Michael-el! Michael-el!" I don't know if it's his strawberry-blond hair or his equanimity, but he's certainly inherited John's ability to charm and he walks in the door beaming.

This morning we hired a sign painter to write "STEINBECK" on our gate in Nepali, as is the tradition. We stood there watching while he did it and, as he put away his can of red paint, we looked at each other in delight. No one would ever know that strange script had anything to do with our name, and we felt safe again. We would never have written it in English. Escaping the connection is part of the healing that's been occurring here.

February 1

We're on our way to Ossian's monastery in Sikkim with Hetty. Megan decided to stay behind with friends so she wouldn't miss school. Yesterday we flew to Patna, India. The endless boredom of the flat plains is a heart-wrenching contrast to the awake and vertical textures of the magical kingdom we've left behind. Like John, I've already decided I much prefer Nepal to the chaos of Mother India, whose citizens seem like spoiled children compared to my noble Nepalis. Last night, when the heat subsided, we hired a rickshaw to take us to the Ganges in the moonlight. When we arrived back at the hotel, we stopped at a bookstore next door. Suddenly the driver came up to John and slapped him on the shoulder, insisting that we owed him more money than he'd originally asked for. John pounced on him like a wildcat and shoved him up against the wall, yelling, "Don't touch me. Don't you dare ask for more money. Get out of here or I'll call the police." As the driver peddled furiously down the street, his rickshaw tilting behind him, John explained that India was a far cry from the protected enchantment of Nepal. I was impressed by how quickly he assessed the situation. Had he stood there bargaining, a crowd would have gathered, opinions would have formed, and that's how all those Indian riots start.

At midnight, I got violently ill. Johnny heard me retching in the bathroom and called out, "Oh, you poor sweetheart. That's the loneliest sound in the world." It was true, I'd been thinking the same thing. If it weren't for his presence and his protectiveness, I would have felt like I'd been shot into a distant galaxy. India is so foreign and I missed our gentle Nepali home. My heart melted when I heard those words drifting around the cool tile floor. John always knows how to say just the right thing.

Outside our window was the most romantic courtyard, wild with flowers and ancient ruins scattered among the palms and banyans. We sat on the window seat, drinking in the cool moonlight. This morning I felt stronger and ready to tackle Mother India again.

After flying into Siliguri, we hired a leather-lined British taxi to drive us up the vertical road to Darjeeling. Past tea plantations and the small Himalayan people who plow up and down the steep 8,000-foot hillsides like sturdy Shetland ponies, past the most curious Victorian gingerbread houses built during the Raj period, all hidden and then suddenly revealed between thick fog and brilliant sunlight. Tonight we're staying at the Windermere Hotel, complete with a library and fireplaces in the rooms, yet run by Tibetans. I keep pinching myself, to think we're actually in West Bengal. It's so exotic, it's intoxicating. I feel at any moment a tiger could leap from the forest, or a maharajah could ride by on an elephant.

February 2

This morning Michael and I got up at 6:00 A.M. to look at the sunrise on Kanchenjunga, the third highest peak in the Himalayan range, floating over the steep hills and narrow valleys of Darjeeling. We walked around the hotel grounds till we found the best view, and there she was. She had lifted her foggy veils for us, her snows were seeped in the pink tinge of dawn, framed by the dark towering firs. We sat there for the longest time, in silence, in awe.

The distance from Darj to Gantok is 180 kilometers. We descended one steep mountain, followed the Tista River with its innocent sandy white shore; crossed the Sikkim border into a gentle land of fifteen-foot poinsettias, Day-Glo bougainvillea, and thatched huts covered with orchids; climbed another perpendicular mountainside; and there was our destination, Rumtek Monastery. Mostly we traveled in first gear. When we crossed the Tista, Johnny leaned over and whispered, "Someday we're coming back here, just you and me on the motorcycle, to camp out on that sand."

We reached the monastery courtyard at dusk. The splatters of young monks in red robes ran to crowd around us, staring at Michael's blond hair. We set off down a corridor of shadows to find Ossian, and suddenly he was there, beside us. He had a warm, slightly devilish twinkle in his eye. Since no hugs were allowed in public, he could only smile. We all piled back in the jeep for a short ride to the house where we'd be staying, and then Ossian really hugged his mother. The narrow alleys leading up to the monastery compound were filled with whispers about the Western visitors. As we climbed higher, a single sound began to swell from the shadows. "Michael, Michael-el." The Tibetans had seen the golden-haired boy and learned his name. We marveled at the speed with which he could magnetize an entire village.

February 6

We are staying with a Tibetan family in a simple house that overlooks the valley. Tonight, as we climbed into our sleeping bags, John turned on the shortwave radio and suddenly, in this remote mountain village, surrounded by Tibetan lamas and peasants, we heard the familiar lines of a BBC production of *The Red Pony*. We felt lineages of all kinds converging upon us, from the valley below, from the vast stretch of mountains zooming down into India, flying across China to England where some anonymous actors had gathered to read John's father's book into a microphone. Our world feels small and cozy and close to the gods in their heavens.

February 8

We have been privy to the inner workings of the political system of the Kargyu Lineage, in a very intimate way. The lamas have confided in us about their concerns for Ossian's state of mind, considering how much time he has spent away from the confines of monastic discipline. We are caught in the middle, because we know how much Hetty misses her son. We also know how much Ossian misses Western culture—motorcycles, girls, videos, music. Hetty worries that if Ossian leaves the monastery, he will not be able to fit into the outside world. I sense a deep confusion in the boy. I fear he will not stay the course.

John had a man-to-man talk with him this morning. "I told him I was selfish. I want him to grow up and become a great teacher. Ossian knows he's in a tough position. He wants to leave, but he's also ambivalent because he knows about the myth of freedom."

This evening, we had a serious conversation with the Regents about Ossian's fate. They fear his exposure to Western temptations has spoiled him beyond repair. We asked them to give him another chance. They said the only way they could rectify the situation was if he were not allowed to see his mother anymore, because they feel she stirs up too much unrest in him when she visits. There is no easy answer in this situation, and we feel badly for everyone.

February 10

Tonight we're staying at the Tashi Deleg Hotel in Gantok. John and Michael have gone down to the marketplace to sell our tape recorder for Indian rupees to get us home tomorrow. In our Western arrogance, we assumed there would be an American Express office here, in case we needed more cash. The manager has sent up tea and biscuits and I'm looking out the window, down to the vegetable stalls hundreds of feet below the cliff side on which our hotel is perched. The tumult, the energy, shouts, flapping prayer flags, bustling, trading, all blend together in shocking contrast to the tiny silent curve of buildings I can barely see through the mist on the opposite mountain. Like Brigadoon, Rumtek Monastery sits veiled and mysterious, holding our hearts and the exotic story we left behind.

February 12

On the way back from Sikkim, at the Biratnegar Airport in Eastern Nepal, in spite of our tickets, there weren't enough seats available for us on the plane. Rather than spend the night in the funky hotel, John in his infinite Asian travel wisdom told the airline attendant that our daughter had been involved in a motorcycle accident in Kathmandu and we had to hurry home. Royal Air Nepal squeezed us on a charter flight along with a squadron of Ghurka soldiers returning from training in Hong Kong with their wives. Michael sat on the jump seat, which he loved.

Waiting for the plane, we left Michael in the coffee shop of the airport with his Pac-man and strolled out to the empty airstrip. It was there that I really got a hit of what Johnny's nine years in Asia must have felt like. In that thin winter sunlight, everything was utterly simple and unencumbered. No moving parts. I wanted to stop time then. Johnny pulled me against his chest. "You're the only person in the world whose mind I really trust."

"I feel the same about you."

That's the supreme compliment between us. Better than *love you forever* or *you're really good in bed*, it's a victorious, rock-steady love that goes beyond impermanence.

| 32 | IMPERMANENCE |

NANCY

I t took awhile for us to come down from the trip to Sikkim. Things seemed to be going along as usual, but as I look back on it now, full-tilt denial was reigning. John would stay up late most nights, listening to the shortwave radio or reading by the fire. Sometimes when he'd come up to bed, he seemed out of it. Whenever I asked him, he would say he was sleepy.

In the mornings, Gopal cooked breakfast. We'd say good-bye to the children after Serita had gotten them ready for school. John would fall back to sleep till noon. That gave me many hours of privacy to write in my office or practice my *ngöndro*. We loved that routine. One mind could go off on myriad flights while the other one slept close by. One could sleep feeling totally safe because the other was there as guardian of their dreams.

Once or twice while we'd been living at the Vajra Hotel, when John seemed a bit lethargic, I suspected he had been smoking dope. After we moved to the house, a nagging feeling grew as I noticed changes in his behavior. He began to make daily trips to the Supermarket, Kathmandu's funky version of a mall. I hated the rows of tiny stalls that hawked a myriad of Western goods, mostly smuggled from Thailand and Hong Kong. The air was atomized by the pungent aroma of Nepalese plumbing. Supermarket epitomized Western greed, the window displays full of pirated cassette tapes, wristwatches, and electronic gadgetry. It was easy to score drugs there. A sly Nepali would stroll close and whisper, "Hi, you want hashish, cocaine, heroin, LSD?" If you didn't respond, he'd simply disappear in the crowd.

John started buying compulsively. Sometimes he would buy two of one thing, like the tiny Pentax cameras he brought home one day. "His and Hers," he quipped. I began to feel sad, because his life was revolving around long sleeps, visits to Supermarket, and isolated late nights. I didn't know enough about the signs of relapse to call this a symptom.

One night, my dream voice told me, *Get out of bed and go downstairs.* I came upon John as he was inhaling white powder from a magazine into a half-emptied cigarette. When he saw me standing in the door, he deftly flipped the magazine under the couch and smiled hello.

"What are you doing?"

"Just staring at the fire."

"What are you smoking?"

"A cigarette."

"I'm going back up to bed, and when you want to get honest with me, come up and talk." I turned and left the doorway, frozen with panic and fear. My denial dropped like a nickel in a winning slot machine.

He came right up to the bedroom and took my hand. "I'm really sorry you had to see that, but I'm glad you caught me. I've been smoking cocaine. I want to quit." It had been so long since I'd had to think about his abuses. I had been basking in months of heavenly freedom from the cunning, baffling tricks of drug addiction. Horrified and enraged, I mustered enough inspiration for a straight up Al-Anon number.

"You know what to do to quit. So, do it." I didn't rave, I didn't shame, but I let him know it had to stop immediately, foolishly thinking he had control. That's what he wanted me to believe, and I didn't know any better, yet.

Two days passed and he seemed normal. On the third day, I walked into the bedroom and entered a hell where I would dwell for the next four years. John was lying backward in the bed, naked, with his feet propped up against the huge plate-glass window. His legs were jerking spasmodically. His feral eyes didn't register recognition. Hallucinating and angry, like a trapped animal, he looked right through me. There were puddles of diarrhea on the floor. I ran downstairs and called our American doctor. It was Friday afternoon and he was on his way to a wedding reception. I begged him to come to the house immediately and alerted the staff.

"Sahib is very ill. Please take care of the children when they get back from school."

When the doctor arrived, I told him about the cocaine John had been smoking.

"Are there any drugs in the house now?" he asked.

"I don't think so."

"It may be a paratyphoid that's going around. High fever, delirium. You need to get someone to sit up with him tonight."

"Could it be withdrawal from cocaine? Can he be admitted to a hospital?"

"You don't want your husband in the Kathmandu hospital," he shook his head ruefully. "It's filthy and inadequate."

As the doctor gave John a sedative, my heart turned to stone. We were set to leave Nepal in two weeks, immediately after the school semester ended. Since our tenant's lease on the house in Boulder was not up for another month, we planned two weeks of sightseeing in Delhi, Rome, and Paris. How could we travel with this animal thrashing around, shitting on the floor? There was no way I could handle John on my own. Like a blind shark, he couldn't see me, but he smelled my terror and it made him murderous.

Frantically, I thought of a plan. The doctor's American partner was a friend of ours, married to a very tall man who had interviewed John for the tourist magazine he published. That's what I needed, an English-speaking doctor who could monitor John's symptoms and a large man to restrain him. I sensed I could count on them for help; they were ardent born-again Christians.

"Here's what I want," I said briskly. "Ask your partner and her husband to come spend the night here with John. I'm taking the kids to the Sheraton until he recovers."

We could hear him upstairs, slamming into walls. I asked the doctor to wait till Ken and Kathy arrived, packed up the children, and sent Gopal for a taxi. When Dr. Kathy and her husband arrived, we were ready to go. To my relief, Kathy agreed it sounded like drug withdrawal.

Ensconced at the nearby Everest Sheraton, we ordered room service and played cards, desperately trying to establish a ground of sanity in the midst of our shock. I had given the children a brief sketch of John's behavior, sparing them the ugly details. Long after Michael and Megan had fallen asleep, I stared across the rice fields at our darkened house. I was afraid John would die that night, perhaps sever an artery on the plate-glass window he'd been kicking. Filled with rage, terror, and a sense of betrayal, suddenly our safe little kingdom seemed hideously foreign. The exotic trappings mocked me with their inability to speak to the situation.

I prayed for protection and guidance all night. In the morning, Ken called and said it was safe to come home. To my great relief, the minute I walked into the bedroom I could tell John was himself. He apologized for putting me through the horror. Sometimes he had a candid way of copping to a situation. He did it with such bare-bones honesty that you could tell he meant it from the bottom of his heart. Whenever I heard that particular bottomed-out tone of voice, I would find the resilience to stay for one more day.

"That wasn't cocaine I was smoking," he cautioned me. "I'm withdrawing from heroin." When he got honest like that, I'd hear the plea for help, the plea not to abandon him, the plea to stay and fight the demons with him. There was still something so precious inside him. I could not walk away, not yet.

Kathy and Ken told me he had thrashed around the room all night. Thinking the antidote to his confusion was hidden in his glasses, he took a bite out of the right lens. Our wonderful Christian friends had stayed by his side, praying. Toward dawn, Kathy had gone into the bathroom and saw a huge black spider, the size of a tarantula, on the wall. Ken rushed in and killed it when he heard her scream. We looked at each other, but we didn't say it. Something evil had descended upon our home. The Steinbeck Black Hole was back.

"There's a Swedish guy named Ollie across town who runs a makeshift rehab for Westerners," Ken said. He suggested I go over there and see if they could detox John as an alternative to the dreaded hospital. Gopal went up the street to find a cab. I was relieved to have some direction, but it was a useless trip.

Ollie painted a bleak picture about John's condition. "He cannot travel. He could relapse into psychosis at any minute. You will have to leave him here with me." Several vacant-eyed hippies wandered past, lobotomized by street drugs. I remembered the young American Buddhist scholar who had lost his mind during our stay at the Vajra. I came upon him wandering, demented, in an alley behind the hotel. The desk clerk called the police, but even after several days in jail, the young man's mind was nowhere to be found. I arranged to have him sent back to the States by the consulate. It's funny how the universe trains in disaster preparedness. I was often given a dry run for the emergencies I faced to save John's life. Back in the taxi, I knew what I had to do.

This is why all our expatriate friends insist they have to return to the West at least once a year. How ironic that Mr. World Traveler is the first to succumb to Lord Jim jungle rot. We've got trouble in paradise here. We cannot linger under the pagodas a minute longer. Mother Asia is about to boot us out of our magical kingdom like a tigress. We need a clean hospital and a drug-treatment facility, American-style.

I felt myself grow bitter. I had traveled alone across the valley to Ollie's and returned to the house, alone. Alone, I begged John to go to the hospital, no matter how primitive the conditions. It was the only place I could put him where he would have no access to street drugs in order to continue his withdrawal. Alone, I got him a semiprivate room, though the procedure took five hours. During the interview, John told the nurse he had not done drugs since Vietnam. I was incensed. "Why are you lying to her? She's not a cop. She's trying to get you some help!"

John had a down parka with velcro pockets where he stashed his comb, cigarettes, lighter, and pens. When he was stoned, he'd spend hours searching his pockets, muttering to himself. He would start slapping his sides to feel for the item that had suddenly become urgently necessary. Ripping open each pocket, he'd desperately try to find whatever he was missing. You'd hear the velcro scratched apart, but within three pockets he'd forget what he'd been looking for due to short-term memory loss. The rest of the search was merely the death throes of his mind trying to remember what he wanted. He'd go through the annoying routine, first looking for a comb, then a lighter, then a pen ad nauseam. I sat there wondering if he'd be frozen in the Great Velcro Hunt for the rest of his life. He looked utterly demented. I wanted to scream. A handsome, red-robed lama passed by with an attractive Nepali woman and a small child in tow, and I distracted myself by making up a clandestine romance about them in my mind. To this day, the sound of undoing velcro sends shivers up my spine.

Years later, R. D. Laing's widow, Marguerite, shrieked with laughter when I told her that story. Ronnie would do the same thing, often at odd ends of the globe. Sometimes she'd pretend she wasn't with him, or that she was a hired nurse. "A drooler," she'd chortle. "An absolute gonzo drooler!"

John shared a hospital room with a dying elderly Tibetan. His entire family was camping out on the floor, cooking, chatting, grieving. Several days later, after he died, they replaced him with a raving American hippie who was coming down off speedballs. That guy never shut up.

"He's annoying, but he's also a lesson," John said meekly. "There but for the grace of your intervention."

Michael confirmed his words as we left the hospital. "You know, Mom, if it weren't for us, John would be just like that crazy guy." We noticed they had given John and the hippie the same diagnosis, *Psychosis/Diarrhea*, posted on the door.

Unfortunately, the Nepali form of detox was enough Valium to arouse John's disease to full-blown proportions. Although he was quite chipper when he left the hospital a week later, I sensed the desperate animal scratching under his skin. My blood ran cold watching him do his Maurice Chevalier number as he said good-bye to the nurses. Terrified to return home for fear the Black Hole was still lurking, I had remained at the Sheraton with Megan and Michael. As John and I entered our bedroom for the first time since that harrowing event, a terrible weakness possessed me. The demons were still there. I collapsed on the bed and spat out, "This place makes me sick. Once again, you have turned our home into a bedpan. We've still got a week before our flight to Delhi. I'm going to a hotel till we leave Nepal. I am never setting foot in this house again."

Instead of the impersonal Sheraton, I purposely chose the Dwarika Hotel, owned by a stern, no-nonsense woman who was also the Swiss consulate. I knew that the Spartan atmosphere would force John to keep it together until our departure. I breathed a sigh of relief when I noticed she didn't grovel over his name as he signed the register. My instincts had been right; she maintained a suspicious distance from us, and I didn't blame her.

That was when I lost my will. Dysentery swept over me, wringing ten pounds off my body. I lay in bed delirious, filled with hatred and resentment for John. I wouldn't talk to him. I was outraged that he could mindlessly trash our precious time in Nepal. Had I been more practiced in Al-Anon's wisdom, I would not have ranted at him for spoiling my heaven. I would have tried not to shame him. It would take me years to understand that heaping guilt on an addict only prevents him from feeling the full effect of his own remorse. The self-discipline of a veteran Al-Anon is staggering, and I was still a novice.

Just before we left Boulder, I asked Rinpoche for advice about the trip. He predicted that we would be forced to come home prematurely. Throughout the year, part of me had stayed vigilant, wondering what he meant. Now I understood.

John's liver-function tests showed a high level of uric acid, which, along with the drugs, explained his erratic behavior. I was desperate for the comfort of my support group in Boulder. Despite the fact that we still had two weeks to kill until we could return home, I felt that returning to the Western world would ease the burden of being in a country that had no understanding of John's condition. I was also concerned about the color of his skin. He had turned a peculiar shade of greenish bronze, which delighted the Tibetans. "Oh," they'd exclaim, stopping him on the street. "You look just like us."

By the time our plane left Kathmandu, I felt as relieved to be leaving Shangri-la as I had longed every day to stay there forever. I also felt curiously victorious. John often quoted Kipling, something about how you can't hustle the East. I hadn't. Facing the challenge of making myself at home in that relentlessly foreign culture, I had succeeded in finding and befriending myself. I had written, explored, and practiced. I quit smoking because the Nepali tobacco tasted like burning yak hair, and I discovered a wellspring of sanity and cheerfulness in my being. I had learned how to travel the world, and had transmitted that ability to my children, so that wherever we are on this planet, we feel at home. I was proud of myself. Compared to Mr. I've-Been-Around-the-World-Four-Times, I felt grace about my Nepali life, as opposed to his disgraceful undoing.

On our last night in Kathmandu, Khentse Rinpoche blessed our *thankas*, Tibetan scroll paintings. We had seen Khentse many times in Boulder and visited with him whenever he came to Nepal. He was one of the last great lamas, dripping compassion like a fat mother sow. We brought along our Tibetan friend, Tsering, whom we had met at the Phokara refugee camp. He was in awe of Khentse, as if he were the Wizard of Oz.

As Khentse printed the traditional sacred symbols of empowering mantras on the backs of the painting, I thought long and hard about this man's supposed wisdom. *Here I am in the presence of a great lama. What does he know about heroin addiction? What advice could he give me about traveling with John?* He did not dwell in the realm where opium poppies grew. I was on my own.

Where did all that magic and mystery get us in the end? There would be no miracles ahead, not for years, as John's disease progressed like wildfire. What good was any of it, I wondered, as I saw Tsering act as if he weren't worthy to be in the same room with Khentse. He had even gone outside to wash his feet in the dewy grass before entering the shrine room.

Was I hypnotized by the Valley, seduced by the fervid religiosity that hangs in the air? Is everyone in the Silver Jade Kingdom buzzed by a confluence of spirits, high on the realm where Absolute Truth can never bend so low as to touch Relative Suffering? What good has all the bliss and peace done? We are worse off than when we started. In the depths of my dilemma, I forgot how slowly evolution works, like the rings around a tree trunk.

John wanted to stick to our plan of sightseeing until the lease on our house was up. More crippled than any previous time in our lives together, we limped through Delhi. In my grief process, I had moved through shock and rage in Kathmandu. Depression settled in Delhi, where it was so hot, the hotel swimming pool was a tepid soup. One afternoon, friends from Boulder came to take me to lunch as John rested. At last, I could share our crisis with a Western mind. They were appalled at what I had gone through and the unknown territory that lay ahead. Nevertheless, when her Tibetan husband left the table, Betty whispered, "Noedup is having a hard time relating to John because he's not drinking. He feels awkward." I felt surrounded by lunacy.

Wanly, I tried to enjoy the Raj atmosphere at the Imperial Hotel. The children and I set off valiantly every day to sightsee. Unbeknownst to us, that's when John would duck down to the nearest drugstore to purchase over-the-counter Valium. I smelled a rat when I noticed he was buying compulsively again and seemed groggy. Five pairs of eyeglasses and twenty dress shirts later, we were up at 3:00 A.M. for our flight to Rome. On our way to the airport, with a set jaw and a sinking feeling, I did get one last exotic hit as we passed six camels walking down the freeway, bound for the marketplace. As John slipped into the duty-free shop with Megan, Michael and I went on to board the plane. Mercifully, we were flying business class, with long reclining seats and more clout than steerage, as I discovered when I had to ask the flight attendant to hold the plane till John appeared.

If the slogans say "Let go and Let God" or "Live and Let Live," would I be practicing Al-Anon if I let the plane take off without John? Had Megan not been with him, I might have risked it. I could not ignore the aching certainty that if John and I didn't make it back to Boulder together, he would die.

Rome was the worst. The minute we got off the plane, John started playing Papa Steinbeck-on-a-trip-with-his-family. Surreptitiously scoring more Valium, he postured and posed on the boulevards and in hotel lobbies. I wanted to strangle him. As we showed the children the Colosseum, the Forum, the Catacombs, John blamed his grogginess on "Italian vegetable tranquilizers." He fell asleep wherever we stopped, in restaurants, on benches, on the grass near the Palatine Hill. The children were embarrassed and confused. I explained as best I could, and cursed the fact that we were stuck in tourist limbo until our lease was up.

To my relief, I discovered Rome had Al-Anon meetings. In my broken understanding of Italian, the words I heard helped me formulate a plan. One night, a heavy dose of Valium triggered a heroin flashback in John. Delirious, sleepwalking, he arose and pissed in the corner of our pensione bedroom. I woke to the stench.

"What are you doing?"

"Looking for the bathroom," he muttered sheepishly. He stopped midstream, went over to the toilet, and pissed all over it. I reached out to feel his forehead when he got back in bed. He wasn't feverish. He was tripping. I was alone again, except for my prayers. I thought of calling Thom and Elaine, but I knew they'd be of no help. *They'd probably tell me to leave him here and I don't want explain that I can't.* In the morning, I phoned the American Embassy. They sent over an English-speaking doctor. By this time John was drooling, burning cigarette holes in the sheets. The doctor talked him into going to a mental hospital, which he euphemistically referred to as a sanitarium.

We set out in a taxi for Belvedere Montello, in the Roman suburbs. As a discreet attendant took John up to his room, I noticed it was a locked facility. That was not going to sit well with him, but his moods were no longer my problem. As I filled out the insurance papers, the head psychiatrist asked about John's name.

"Oh, the son of Steinbeck!" he crooned rhapsodically.

That and a nickel will get you to the point where you need your own rubber room, you idiot.

"Would you like to go up and see his quarters and say good-bye?" he asked graciously. I could tell he hadn't understood one iota of what I had been through in the last two weeks. It wasn't a language problem. He was so mesmerized by the Steinbeck thing, he couldn't hear me. Disgusted, I had to repress the urge to scream, *No! He's all yours. You can wipe up the drool and the shit and venom. I'm out of here.*

The poor shrink seemed to think I should be kissing the ground John walked on because of his father. "We'll take very good care of him," the good *doctore* promised, as if John were a living treasure. I stood with the children at the gate, waiting for the electronic buzzer to open the lock. It was an old palazzo and the grounds were beautiful, but the empty swimming pool gaped forlorn and abandoned, like the puzzled inmates who wandered amongst the voluptuous statuary.

During John's stay, I was determined the children would not miss out on any of the Roman history, art, or culture, no matter what we had been through. We wandered around the city, trying to be cheerful in the face of grave worries. In the evening we would visit him.

On the fourth day, Johnny wanted to come back to the pensione with us, promising *Signor Doctore* he would return by dinner. John had enough wits about him to sense we needed to spend time alone. We left the children on a street they wanted to explore and arranged for them to meet me under a tall clock on the corner.

John and I sat at a sidewalk café near the Spanish Steps and kept our conversation in the moment, as we always did after those fiascos. My rage was worn to a nub; I wanted to share Rome with my aristocratic Johnny and forget about the gonzo drooler. He asked me to ride back to the sanitarium so we could linger in an embrace. The world wasn't feeling exactly like my oyster, but hope springs eternal in the heart of a rookie Al-Anon.

Terror returned when I couldn't find the children at the appointed clock tower. I had a feeling something was terribly wrong, and I wasn't sure if they remembered the name of our hotel. The taxi driver shared my concern. We drove up and down the long boulevard three times. "Madonna," he would exhale under his breath, praying as if he had lost his own children. Finally, an hour later, he remembered there were two identical clock towers on that street. We found my poor waifs, looking like abandoned kittens. *That's it. I'm not going to be an idiot anymore. We are strangers still, in a strange land, and if I don't stay on top of things, disaster will strike. Nothing is going to come between me and the children during the rest of this trip, not even John's ridiculous flirtation with death. Thank God they are with me again, safe and sound. They are the only sanity I have in the swamp of John's dementia and my own frenzy.*

Upon his return that evening, John finagled a Valium drip. Several days later, he insisted on leaving against the doctor's orders. To my dismay, when I came to pick him up, he was more loaded then when he'd entered. I didn't bother confronting *doctore*'s ineptness in dealing with drug withdrawal. This would not be the first time I experienced John coming out of a hospital detox flying on tranquilizers. Tests showed severe liver damage, which they feared may have permanently affected his brain. His ammonia levels were six times higher than normal, causing confusion and bizarre behavior. The doctors told me if John left, he could go into tranquilizer withdrawal and, combined with the ammonia levels, he might end up in a coma. True to his death-dance, John stubbornly refused further treatment. I knew it was hopeless to convince him otherwise; the animal was surfacing again, scratching at his skin, clawing its way out. He glared at me, daring a confrontation so he could rip me apart with his vicious blame as if the situation were my fault. *Denial and blame is the name of his game.*

I was beginning to understand the tightrope act he played with me, how he watched my safety net with cunning. When the net got pulled, he actually became quite docile. This gave me the courage to insist he find another hotel for the night. I simply could not bear the pressure of being responsible for his health for one moment longer. I needed a break, even if he went into a coma during the night. He meekly checked into a hotel down the block, oblivious to my worries and prayers for his safekeeping through the lonely, sleepless hours. I thought bitterly of all the times Thom had cruelly mocked my pleas for John to stop drinking and drugging. *If I called Thom, he would only protest that he is not his brother's keeper. Why is it solely up to me to grapple with this madness? Let go and let God . . . grant me the serenity . . . the courage and wisdom. . . .*

In the morning, I woke to a knock at the door. Certain it was the police with the worst possible news, a sheepish John surprised me.

"I'm ready to get off Valium. I can detox on my own." I burst into tears, grateful he had made it through the night. Secretly, I noted that a healthy dose of Al-Anon detachment can work wonders.

After several blessedly uneventful days, we felt brave enough to take the train south to Positano. Steinbeck had taken Thom and John there and he wanted to relive the memories. It was a glorious train ride, and I prayed the tide might be turning as our hired car glided along the Amalfi coast, past pink stone villas dappled by the afternoon sunlight.

Unfortunately, our hotel's manager was another one of those fawning spinsters. Like a moth to flame, I watched her fan the dying embers of John's ego. Within two days, he was back to aping his father, parading up and down the village streets as if he had just won the Nobel Prize. To add to the masquerade, when the tourist department filled our room with flowers in memory of Steinbeck's visit twenty years ago, John confused the gesture with adulation toward himself. *For what? An award for pissing in the corners of assorted Roman pensiones?* As I quietly watched John forget where he stopped and his father started, I decided it was time to remove myself physically, come what may. The culture shock of having left our magical kingdom and the burden of John's health was driving me insane.

Once we were back in Rome, I sensed John wanted more over-the-counter Valium. I sought a direction. I had been a Thomas Mann buff in college, and wanted to see the places described in *Death in Venice*. Knowing John disliked Venice's tourist trap aspect, I chose to escape there with the children for several days. Although I was haunted by the chaos of our situation, I started piecing together a sense of reality. We still had ten days to kill before our tenant moved out. It was up to me to orchestrate them. I decided we would meet John in Paris and limp through France for a while.

On the last night in Venice, he called me, freaking out. "I bought some gorgeous Fumi jewelry for your birthday. I showed it to the concierge yesterday. When I woke up, it was gone." He had ripped the room apart and then accused the hotel staff. "I told them I was going out for breakfast and when I got back, the stuff better be in my room." They must have figured he meant it, because when he returned, they claimed to have found it under the mattress.

Although he never made it there, John referred to those final days in Europe as his *Death in Venice* period. To me, Gustav with his makeup and his sirocco had nothing on John's disintegration. For some reason, the missing jewelry incident shocked John into staying sober in Paris. The withdrawal symptoms, along with his liver disease, had exhausted him. The city was crawling with tourists, but I managed to show the children the important sights. We spent hours at the Louvre. After a morning at the Jeu de Pommes art museum, John met us there for lunch. I caught sight of him strolling through the park, wearing an elegant new three-piece suit, lost in the fantasy of being a great writer, swinging his umbrella to the rhythm of his boulevardier strut. When he saw us, he seemed to wake from a dream. We knew only too well who he was, and the familiarity disoriented him.

By the time we arrived in New York, I was racing to get John to his physician. Something was terribly wrong, more than the progression of his addictions. His mind was not functioning. Usually his thought process was stellar, no matter how many chemicals he ingested. His skin had a peculiar bronze cast. It took ten days to receive the diagnosis. They told us he had liver cancer; that it would be a matter of weeks before he was dead. They ordered a biopsy and John immediately locked himself up with a case of Johnny Walker in the Boulderado, hoping to beat death's agenda. His doctor, with the bedside manner of Leona Helmsley, ordered me to prepare for widowhood.

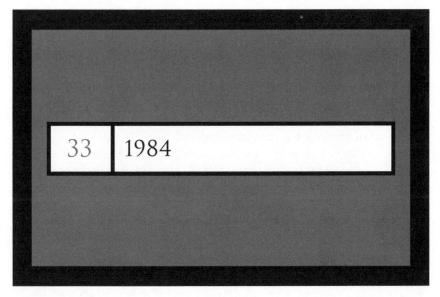

| 33 | 1984 |

NANCY

I t was now midway into 1984, and Orwell's predictions were coming true. Ever since reading this book in college, I felt something prophetic about that year. Sensing danger if Newspeak and Big Brother ever became reality, it would be an indication we were crossing over into a bankrupt lifestyle that would endanger the planet. A collective surrender of individual power would doom the spirit, the artist, and the lover.

Having been abroad for a year, I was more sensitive to Western speed, complaisance, and somnambulism. The signs were eerily familiar. The smokey wisps of thoughts that had arisen in my twenties were converging into the eye of a gathering hurricane, fueled by the ecological predictions of ancient prophecies—Aztec, Hopi, Hippie, Aboriginal, and Marian.

Ten years prior, during the winter of 1974 in British Columbia, I devoured Doris Lessing while the kids slept. Paul was working on the railroad, often gone for days. Imprisoned by blizzards, I melted snow for drinking water, bathing, and washing dishes; fed the woodstove with huge armloads of firewood; and periodically shot at a chicken hawk to protect our hens. Whenever Megan and Michael would go down for a nap, or sleep at night, I'd curl up with *The Four-Gated City* or *The Golden Notebook* and when I put down the books, the visions would come.

I saw a time when adolescent gangsters terrorized society. Driven by tribal instincts, they marauded the cities. I saw the graffiti and guns. I experienced a deep sense of their rage and numbness about the breakdown of a culture where greed and selfishness twisted traditional values. I foresaw a bleakness so horrible that no amount of gentrification or police could stop the spread of their slash-and-burn mentality.

When Megan and Michael woke, I returned to the mundane tasks of baking bread, sewing on the ancient Red Bird treadle machine, carding and spinning raw wool. Dying the skeins with golden onionskins, brown walnut husks, and orange madder root in the glacial waters of Kootenay Lake, I wove blankets to keep us warm under the heavy lead skies.

I had apocalyptic visions of hurricanes, floods, and earthquakes. I kept asking why, and the answer was always the same. *It is the only way to wake people up to the planet's destruction and the severing of their spirit.* Haunted by those visions, I prayed that when the time came, I would be surrounded by a tribe of strong and trustworthy friends.

I dwelt in two worlds that winter and never came out of them. I can cross the bridge between the visionary and the ordinary, but I will never abandon one for the other. I have never married for money, never made a decision solely based on security. Living on the edge of choicelessness, I take things to the limit until a way out appears. You have to know this about me to understand what I went through for the next four years with John's drinking. Beyond the unconditional love, beyond the abject codependent flip side, much of my stick-to-it-iveness boiled down to Johnny's "shit happens" attitude, rock solid in the face of adversity. I wanted him there for the coming rites of passage, the death of my father, the kids' adolescence, watching Rinpoche kill himself with alcohol. As a friend once said, "John had more clarity and creativity in his little finger, drunk or sober, than most people have in lifetimes."

John was in a panic over the cancer prognosis. Since he couldn't drink himself to death at our house, he checked into the Boulderado. When he failed to show up for his scheduled liver biopsy, the hospital called me. I found him in his hotel room, bleary, reeking, and disoriented. He let me convince him to keep his appointment. *If that smacks of enabling, I don't care. God knows when he'll find the courage to face this on his own. When we have the results of the biopsy, he can get treatment. If he's going to die, I'll quit fighting for his life and figure out what to do with the rest of mine.*

This was the start of my bottom. I had failed to convince John to stay sober, and now it looked like death was going to solve that problem for both of us. Outraged in the face of this final abandonment, I was turning another corner, cold as ice, clinical, and dispassionate. As the biopsy needle probed John's liver, I saw the work that lay ahead. I had attracted abusive people, typical of an incest survivor. Al-Anon was teaching me to leave them in the dust if they didn't earn my loyalty, and John might be one of them.

After the biopsy, he came home and soberly waited three days for the result, docile and considerate of my anxiety. Whenever the dust settled between us, John tried to cover all the bases. Mr. Hyde, doing whatever he damned well pleased, gave way to tenderness and nurturing. I felt like a snake charmer, waiting for music to lull the viper.

"You must have been a great yak herder in a previous lifetime," he teased. "You know just how much rope I need to hang myself."

The initial scan had shown a black spot on John's liver that the doctors thought was a cancerous tumor. When the biopsy report came back, it took us a couple of days to recover from the shock, and then we laughed at the results. Fecal matter inexplicably had shown up in the CAT scan.

"It was a piece of shit! They put me through all that anxiety over a lousy piece of shit!" he groused, half humorously. So much for his tumor and imminent death. They did have a diagnosis, however. They called it *hemochromatosis*, a genetic condition in which the body absorbs too much iron, leading to potentially fatal complications by damaging tissue and organs. Amazingly, the iron deposits can cause cirrhosis of the liver without any alcohol abuse. The doctors bandied about life expectancies, a 60 percent chance to live five years and 30 percent to live ten. The treatment was laughably primitive, a series of phlebotomies.

"Bloodletting! We might as well go back to Nepal and live among the leeches," John quipped with tremendous relief. In order for new blood to replace the old, he would give a unit of blood at least twice a month. Finally we understood why he had turned such a peculiar shade of greenish bronze in Nepal. Iron stores in his heart, liver, and other organs had effected his pigmentation.

Later studies of hemochromatosis would attribute John's bizarre behavior to iron overload. Disorientation, mood swings, and other personality changes, such as severe depression and anger, are now considered symptoms of what they used to call "bronze diabetes." While the drugs exacerbated the dementia, his mood swings convinced me something else was to blame, although I fought my intuition with self-deprecating admonishments about my codependency. Ashamed that I had stood by him, I considered it was a measure of my low self-esteem. When the research recently confirmed my instincts, I forgave myself for saving his life. I knew if I left him in Asia or Europe, he would surely die. I have come through the eye of a terrible codependent paradox, and the experience has left me with little patience for people who give black and white advice.

"Why didn't you just leave him in the Kathmandu hospital?" my Al-Anon sponsor asked condescendingly when she heard the story.

"It didn't feel right."

"You are addicted to him. You can't live without him."

Remembering that Al-Anon sponsors are not supposed to give advice, I challenged her. "Look, the doctors have just diagnosed my husband with a terminal illness. We've got two children who love him deeply. I can't just throw him out. I may be in total denial, as you say, but I have to answer to myself. I can't take your advice on blind faith."

"Nancy, I cannot support you if you stay with him."

"Okay," I thought for a moment. "Then you know what? I'm firing you. I may not be very far into my recovery, but I have to take Al-Anon literally. Your insistence that I leave him goes against the program's traditions, and I cannot accept that." I hung up the phone and felt terribly alone, yet confident that I had done the right thing. This was my introduction to the syndrome of Al-Anon Abuse. Through the years, I earned a black belt fighting it.

John was weak and exhausted from the hemochromatosis. My strength was waning; caring for an invalid is a twin dilemma to anxiety over the alcoholic. Although we were no longer facing liver cancer and the prospect of imminent death, we still moved through grief, shock, and anger, to a point of bargaining with this new disease. Then depression descended. The ceilings got lower and lights grew dimmer as we adjusted to the unfamiliar presence of death in five to ten.

It wasn't just the prediction about his life expectancy. Hemochromatosis causes testicular atrophication. One day, when I saw how much his genitals had shrunk, I waited till I was alone in the house and screamed into a pillow in terror. Like the night Johnny ate his glasses and the huge spider appeared in Kathmandu, I felt like Job. Would we ever escape the genetic curses descending upon us? If it effected me that strongly, imagine how that devastated John's sense of manhood.

My ex-husband agreed to let the children live with him and his new wife, Jo. It broke my heart to see them go, but I hoped Michael and Megan would deepen their relationship with their father. Unfortunately, they had a rough time at Paul's. He was doing his usual emotional starvation routine with his wife. After his third marriage, he confided, "You know how I am. I'm great till I get married and then I withdraw."

Jo was already miserable. Just as with me, he spent all day and night at the car lot. She took her five-year-old daughter out for dinner most evenings, leaving Megan and Michael to fend for themselves, Cinderella-style. When they repeatedly complained that they were alone in the house with nothing to eat, we moved them back home. Forgetting that kids need food and attention, self-centered Paul felt abandoned. They changed their last names to Steinbeck later that year. They considered John to be their real father because he nurtured and loved them.

Johnny and I clung to each other in desperation, expressing our fears and sadness. *Why is our life filled with swells of pain and the undertow of sorrow? If I lay next to him or go everywhere with him, I can keep death away. If he dies, I'll be so bored. If he dies, I'll have lots of friends but no one so brilliant. I'll just muck around pretending I'm living. I'll do everything they tell you to do to carry on but it will be so bleak. I'll just be waiting for my own death.*

Weeks of tenderness would pass. Then John would go on a binge and turn monstrous. One night he reached in his pocket and pulled out a stiletto-thin Italian fruit knife we had bought in Rome. He pointed it at me and chuckled sadistically. I called the police and they charged him with felony menacing.

Boulder police are experts in domestic violence. If I didn't press charges, they would. When John drunkenly attacked me before we left for Nepal, a friend insisted my doctor record the assault, which involved a perfect set of teeth marks on my shoulder. Because of that evidence, John was put on probation. If he ever physically abused me again, the judge said he would send him to the federal penitentiary. That ended the violence between us.

We needed more support. Al-Anon friends recommended that I see a woman therapist, Tanya Zucker, at the county-funded Alcohol Recovery Center. John started seeing her partner, Don Roth, gifted in working with vets. Sometimes the four of us would meet together. Privately, Don and Tanya told me my recovery was extremely threatening to John. Because he could no longer control me, I was disturbing the family's unhealthy equilibrium. In Al-Anon terms, King Baby was feeling abandoned because I wouldn't be his caretaker anymore. He had been accusing me of trying to capture his elusive free spirit, and now my independence was frightening him.

Using the Al-Anon slogan *Don't accept unacceptable behavior,* Don and Tanya taught me to define abuse. While John was often infuriated that they were privy to the bizarre aspects of our relationship, I began to feel safe. His cover was blown, but I finally had a place to talk about my despair. The process exposed his monstrous excesses and screaming rages; things I'd kept secret from even my closest friends. At last, someone else knew of his drunken, late-night propensity to smash all the eggs on the refrigerator door, leaving them dripping until morning. Someone else knew he fired his gun into the rafters while I slept beside him. The fact that everything got reported to our therapists made him think twice. John could no longer criticize my Al-Anon meetings, massages, writing, cooking, not cooking, or spending time with the door closed.

"How can I work on people pleasing if you are constantly demanding I submit to your whims?" I asked. "From now on, I am focusing on my needs. You can take care of yours."

I wanted him to stop driving me crazy. Seeking instant gratification, I wasn't always rational. I often lacked the patience to practice communication skills. After the fear of death sobered John, he desperately wanted to change the qualities in him that created illness and insanity. The frozen feelings from our repressed childhoods were thawing. We made a pact to support the process.

Later that summer, they asked John to put on a fireworks display at Rocky Mountain Dharma Center for the yearly encampment, a gathering of Rinpoche's guards. People wore military uniforms and slept in tents, played mock war games. There was marching and whimsical calisthenics such as lying on your back and doing push-ups to the sky.

We arrived with a trunk full of fireworks at dusk. They ushered us to the front of the crowd Rinpoche was addressing. We had not seen him for almost a year. What we saw shocked us both. He was so drunk, two guards had to hold him up. His speech was unintelligible. *This man will drink himself to death and the community will be torn asunder.* Three years later, that's exactly what happened. When I went back to college for my degree in chemical dependency, I learned Rinpoche had passed over into chronic late-stage alcoholism during our year abroad. Soon after, he developed Korsakoff's syndrome, commonly known as "wet brain," and two years later he died of esophageal varicies.

The shock of his deterioration hit me hard that night. As John set off the fireworks, I sat alone on a hillside, watching the members interact. Coming from the warm, close-knit communal culture of Nepal, I saw white upper-middle-class adults behaving as if they were at a cocktail party. Little clusters would mingle and part, touching superficially, satiated bees on drained flowers. *I can't do this anymore. There's no spark, no depth of communion, just emotional distance. Are John and I the only ones who see through this charade? Isn't anyone else concerned about Rinpoche's drinking?*

We lingered till midnight, chatting in uneasy shallowness. I felt as if the skin were being peeled off my body. The shock of Rinpoche's deterioration had sent my grief process cascading. Raw and shaken, I was silent as we drove back to our hotel. Falling into a bewildered sleep, I awoke despondent and poured out my feelings to John. As he validated my horror, he lessened my feelings of alienation. When I studied the disease model, I realized I had seen five hundred people in denial about the drunken elephant in the living room. The brightness in their eyes, the glint of *Don't you dare mention it*, the brave attempt to carry on despite the guru's intoxication were poison to me. Like babies playing in a toxic waste dump, the community was oblivious to the time bomb's tick.

Back in Boulder, at my Al-Anon meeting, I developed a friendship with a fellow Buddhist. We dared to call Rinpoche "the A-word," like two naughty children who had been cast out from their garden of illusion. Slowly, we began to draw others into our fragile web through mutual education about the disease that was destroying our families, our church, and our spiritual leader. We learned how to give people the litmus test of nurturing. If you feel energized after an interaction, that is the sign of a healthy person. If you feel drained, run for your life, because that's the disease and it will kill you.

More Buddhist women started attending meetings. As we shared our insights, wisdom and strength began to dawn. Within the bonds of sisterhood, and as the men joined soon after, in fellowship, we formed a lifeline by sharing experience, strength, and hope from the perspective of our confused and denial-ridden spiritual community.

An article had appeared that summer in our Buddhist newspaper, the *Shambhala Sun*, about Dhyani Ywahoo, a female of Cherokee lineage who combined Native American teachings with Buddhism. Sensing an instant familiarity, I wrote her a letter about the need for female teachers to balance the steady stream of visiting male lamas. When she came to Boulder to address her Peacekeeper organization, I invited her to meet with our community, hoping to strengthen the link between the two traditions.

Dhyani's then-husband, Golden True, called a few days later and said she would be willing to give a short talk. I could tell from his deep voice, Texas accent, and kick-ass way of speaking that he and John would sniff each other out and find comfort in each other's maleness. "You know how to do that," John told me. "It's like walking behind a horse's rump. You make the clicking noise that tells a man he can relax."

We fell in love with Dhyani's beauty. As a Vietnam vet, Golden had Post

Traumatic Stress Disorder written all over him, so he and John clicked. Instantly, we became family. Their rowdy two-year-old adored Michael. Feeling a spark of recognition, like coming home, we swapped many war stories about our lives.

I discovered Golden had witnessed one of those incredible magic moments in my life. It happened the year we moved to Boulder. Paul was selling shoes at Kinney's. The kids and I had gone to the mall with our dear Tibetan lama friend, Karma Thinley Rinpoche, to pick Paul up from work. We found the salesmen struggling with the huge door that slides to lock up the store. It simply would not budge. Afraid Paul would have to guard the store all night, I looked helplessly at Karma Thinley. He made a pass with his hand and muttered a mantra under his breath. "Now try," he said. The door slid shut like butter.

Golden passed by the store just as that happened. He saw the family with two small children squirreling around the shoe displays and the red-robed monk murmuring incantations at the door. "It blew my mind! I wondered who the heck y'all were." When we went out for dinner that night, Paul took me for a spin on the dance floor. When I returned to the table, Karma Thinley announced very enthusiastically, "Oh, you have best-y body for dancing!" When I told Johnny that story, he nicknamed me "Best-y Body." He called me that a lot; it cracked him up.

The recovering members of the community attended Dhyani's talk. The next morning, over breakfast, she probed the issues of Rinpoche's health and the community's morale. John and I told her everything. Our loyalty was to the truth of the situation, not protecting the Emperor's New Clothes.

"Rinpoche has drunk so much that he has holes in his brain," she explained. "That is how the Native Americans describe the effects of alcohol destroying brain cells. He needs physical attention. You must gather people together and see if something can be done. It would be good if he would take a sweat with Wallace Black Elk, who knows how to cure those holes. Go to the nuns in your community. They are the most pure and they are concerned. Also, seek out the elders, who can see more in their maturity and wisdom."

"I don't want to be the target of criticism," I protested.

"In the entire community, you are the one who knows most about these things. You have no choice. Otherwise, he will die."

I called for a meeting with the nuns and elders. We asked Roger La Borde, a member of Wallace Black Elk's adopted family, to address the situation from his intuitive point of view. Roger was aware of the confusion and pain caused by Rinpoche's behavior. Although there was still clarity in Rinpoche's consciousness, Roger said damage to his brain cells had left him disoriented.

"Rinpoche cannot decide if he wants to stay alive. Those with clarity of heart and mind must learn to stand on their own two feet. If the conditions continue, Rinpoche will die. Your community is suffering from the same masculine imbalance as the rest of the planet, along with the suppression of the feminine. The women must unite in truth. You will not accomplish any healing by challenging the male-dominated hierarchy. You must all assume responsibility for having relinquished your hearts, your power, and your intuition." Roger went on to say that the Buddhist teachings could not flourish in a form that suppressed honesty. He accurately predicted that tension would be created by increased jockeying for influential positions in the hierarchy.

Roger had confirmed our deepest intuitions. We called another meeting for all the recovering women. Twenty of us gathered at our house in confidentiality. This was the first time students could ask questions without fear of rejection and scorn. Apart from Rinpoche's physical health, another concern was the fact that he was in the process of marrying six other women. They were to assume positions above the board of directors. While the party line claimed this was Rinpoche's way of empowering the feminine, we believed it was his way of getting his sex poodles to jump through their hoops. We viewed them as opportunistic airheads, simultaneously smug and confused about exactly what it was that made them so special. The weddings were secret; only inner sanctum-ites knew of them. The women were subjected to a rigorous examination about the Buddhist teachings. Rinpoche drunkenly nodded in and out of the ceremonies, and his wife never objected. If this were empowering the feminine, we'd eat our meditation cushions.

We discussed the arrogance and closed mindedness of the community, the blatant chauvinism that proclaimed *ours is the only way*. We met their doubts and concerns with kindness instead of censure. Emerging from denial about our own erratic behavior or a loved one's, it was time to acknowledge that we had more clarity than the flock of untreated codependents. Feeling tremendous sadness about the confusion, we also felt freedom as we moved from the role of victim to warrior, searching for clarity and truth.

I had rented a carriage house near the mountains to escape from John's illness and write. We gathered there every Tuesday at noon under the guise of a Women's Buddhist Al-Anon meeting. Wives of the community's most powerful men timidly discussed their domestic problems. When they started practicing the principles of Al-Anon, change invariably followed, and we celebrated each other's growth. As we revealed family secrets, from the microcosm of our homes to the cocaine debauchery at Rinpoche's court, we grew in mutual strength and support. This infuriated the hierarchy, who objected with derision and scorn. They said we were missing the point, that the crazy wisdom lineage gave Rinpoche license to do whatever was needed in the name of "teaching." As a result, we lost superficial friendships but gained a depth of intimacy we had never known. A large extended family formed, not to replicate the harmonics of our abusive childhoods, but one that was loving and full of joy. We learned how to play, to celebrate our success, share pain, become supportable, and speak from our hearts. These skills would save our lives, but not the life of our teacher.

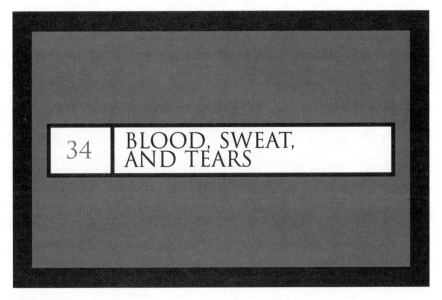

34 BLOOD, SWEAT, AND TEARS

NANCY

Immediately after returning from Nepal, I started to experience flashbacks of my father sexually abusing me as a young child. The woman he had planned to marry after my mother died left him when she realized how neurotic he was. During a visit to San Francisco, he vented his bitterness on Megan and Michael. He started by teasing them and it got out of hand. When confronted, he lashed out at me with all the pain of his loneliness and failure. The monster who had tortured me during my mother's death had returned. While my brother remained predictably mute, my father spoke to his lawyer about disowning me.

The first flashback hit me in the hotel bed, cuddling with John. I saw myself as a tiny baby. My mother was bathing me but something felt wrong. A man was looking at my body in a sexual manner. I realized it was my father. Frozen and confused, I knew that confronting him would be foolish. Anxious to escape his presence, we packed hastily and drove down to Carmel to visit Thom.

John, Michael, and Megan felt the turmoil as strongly as I did. Calling upon every ounce of dignity and skillful means that Rinpoche had taught me, I struggled to keep my balance. Determined that my father would never attack me again, I held my head high, but my heart was broken.

Thom had been living quietly for the past two years with a woman named Joanna off the coast road south of Carmel. The brothers met for the first time without fisticuffs or hysterical midnight harangues. It was touching to both Joanna and me to see John and Thom interact calmly and lovingly. We formed an instant support group, "Women Who Love Steinbecks." Comparing notes and finding out how much they were alike was great fun.

"When he can't find something, does he expect you to drop everything and look for it?"

"Do people always ask how you tamed the beast?"

Back in Boulder, our lives were a three-ring circus. The drama of John's health and our recovery was the focus of our daily existence. Now that John was ready to talk about his childhood, we faced our sexual abuse issues together. While mine was more blatant, John became aware of the degraded atmosphere in which he'd been raised, where Gwyn's friends had drunkenly fondled him as they removed their coats from the pile on his bed. Memories of finding his mother in various states of disarray brought up emotions ranging from embarrassment to shame.

Then we had the ongoing tragedy of Rinpoche's alcohol and drug addiction. Johnny and I had our own tightropes to walk, but we chose at times to make death-defying leaps into each other's arms. We were learning to create a support net for each other. A deeper tenderness grew as we recognized the similarity of our individual wounds. When John realized what my father had done to me, he stopped feeling so misunderstood about his own miserable childhood.

Tanya sent me to a therapist who specialized in sexual abuse. Under hypnosis, I saw my father molest me repeatedly as an infant. It continued up to age three. I had very few memories, but my therapist claimed that feelings were the evidence, not the concrete recollections. Surprisingly, my brother supplied the missing pieces. "When I was nine," he said, "you accused me of doing something sexually inappropriate and I got punished. I remember thinking you couldn't have made it up, because there was no way a three-year-old would imagine something that explicit." Blaming my brother had been safer than blaming my father.

Although it was excruciating, I went straight to the heart of the abuse. After a session with my therapist, I would cry into my pillow until the kids came home from school. Johnny was at his supportive best, fascinated by the process. He wanted to hear everything; he never judged me, and I was grateful for that, because sometimes I felt so dirty.

In the fall of 1984, John and I took Michael and Megan to Wallace Black Elk's sweat lodge, on a farm east of Denver. We arrived at the farmhouse at sunset and waited for the stones to heat. The house was one of those places where everything is functional. They devoted one table to cherries, pitted by a little hand-cranked machine. Another table held apples for pressing. The house was filled with old magazines, newspapers, rakes, hoes, brooms, shotguns. People who can live in clutter fascinate me. It seems to be a peculiarly American trait not to disguise domestic functions. Asian homes take pride in a tidiness that could welcome the Buddha. We had shrines in every room, even one by the kitchen sink where a Kachina doll named Soot Boy, given to us by a Hopi elder, guarded us from fire. I have always envied people who could live in such disarray. I have to tidy the house every morning, straighten pillows, wash dishes, and sweep the floors. It's like clearing the stage so more creativity can blossom.

At dusk, we wandered down to the tepees. A dozen young Sioux men, with their wives, babies, and some elders, watched rocks heating in a fire pit. We were the only white people on the land besides the farmer and his family. They told us that Michael might be uncomfortable with the intensity of the heat, but he was willing to risk it. Dhyani had warned that if a person left early, he might carry negativity with him. Grandfather Wallace said he'd keep an eye on the boy. When it came time, we were summoned to the door of the tent and smudged ourselves with sage to purify our bodies and minds. Cupping handfuls of smoke from smoldering sage twigs, I brought it toward my face and then the rest of my body, inhaling deeply. Then we entered the lodge, a structure made of bent tree limbs covered with blankets.

Wallace is renowned for the relentless heat of his sweats. That's why they work. Not for the squeamish, they were nothing like the mild sweats we did as hippies on the shores of Kootenay Lake in British Columbia. While I entered the tent with trepidation, John was totally game, intrigued by the energies of the other men. They told him to remove the small gold Buddha that hung from a chain around his neck because it would get too hot against his skin. We were packed in tight; there was barely room to sit cross-legged. Megan and I wore swimming suits under kimonos, which were quickly drenched with sweat and made gritty from sitting on the earth.

It was completely dark in the tent; you couldn't see anyone. They placed Michael close to the door, just in case he couldn't make it. He lasted about forty-five minutes and then asked if he could be excused. Wallace told him he'd be fine and he bolted through the flap. Several men outside tended the heating of the rocks that were added when the ones in the lodge cooled. As an attendant poured sizzling water over the hot rocks, the steam drove the temperature to 130 degrees. Wallace had people pray out loud, taking turns around the circle, supplicating the spirits for aid in all manner of tribulation. Everyone else spoke Sioux, pouring out their hearts. John asked for release from his addictions. I asked for deliverance from anger. Megan was the best. She sat in perfect meditation posture, as if there were no heat, no discomfort, a graceful princess perfectly at ease among the boiling stones.

Three hours later, when it was over, I crawled weakly through the tent flap on my belly like a snake. Wallace provided hoses to bathe away the sweat and then invited us to join in a feast. We ate the simple food, hot dogs, Kool-Aid, macaroni and cheese, under bright stars, as one being. There was only sharing and community, even though we were strangers, in that way that native people include you. Not with all the phoney smiles and missionary posturing at which our culture is so adept. People just looked at you, with no overlay of expression. Those are the times when John and I felt most at home.

Wallace spoke about the Star People coming down to aid the planet when they would be most needed. "It will blow the White Man's mind, but we will welcome them because we always knew they were coming. Then there will be great changes and the native people will finally reclaim what was stolen from them." Michael and Megan said it sounded like Bob Dylan's song about when the ship comes in.

We didn't get back to Boulder till dawn. Driving along the deserted farm roads, I wondered what effect the sweat would have on each of us. In the morning, John discovered he'd forgotten to put his gold Buddha back on, and when he went to look for it in his jeans pocket, it was gone. He called the farmer and asked them to look in the dirt around the lodge, but it didn't turn up. He'd worn that little Buddha since Vietnam as protection.

"The Vietnamese clamp those Buddhas between their teeth when they charge into battle. They believe it can save them from being struck by a bullet."

Maybe it's a sign John is shedding his PTSD. Perhaps now he can stop viewing life as a series of firefights, and be a little easier in his skin. This fight-or-flight stuff is getting old. I loved that Buddha too, especially the sexy way it would fall on my breasts when we made love.

35 | HELL BENT

NANCY

After meeting Dhyani and Wallace Black Elk, John and I continued to study with various Native American teachers, along with other members of our Tibetan Buddhist community. Both cultures had prophesied that modern technology would alienate people from the earth, resulting in its abuse and neglect. They foresaw a time when Native American and Tibetan Buddhist teachings would join in one voice to warn the people of perilous times ahead. The way to survive the predicted upheavals is by mindful action and right relationship with the earth and all beings. They place a strong emphasis on spiritual practices and rituals to give a depth of sacredness to life, which has been lost in the scramble of materialism.

As our friendship grew, Dhyani asked if I would write her biography. I stayed with her and Golden, and the boy, Tatanka, for ten days. We spent hours taping sessions about her childhood and her magical life. The energies were always wild around her, and she often asked if I could handle it, afraid I'd be blown away. I wasn't. It was a perfect segue, moving from John's intensity to the chaotic dance of a sky-traveling *dakini*. Although Dhyani eventually decided to write her own book, I treasured the hours we spent together exploring our inner and outer cosmos.

The following spring, Naropa's Anthropology Department asked me to help organize a Native American and Buddhist Women's Council. The Buddhist elders were represented by my mother's teacher, Dr. Rina Sircar, and a Polish nun. One of the Native representatives, Grandmother Carolyn, the elfin Hopi Corn Mother, who knows all the magic and natural fairy circles in the seen and unseen world, interrupted her planting season to attend. The Hopi warriors, as legend has it, gave up the lance for an ear of corn so that they could hold the law, the prophecy, and the records of all the creatures' journey from the stars through the swastika of the earth-walk migrations, back to the spiral of the stars again and again. The physical devastation of the Mother Earth compelled Carolyn to leave her little shack and corn rows so that she might plead with us two-leggeds to reconsider the way in which we are headed.

Johnny titled the Council "Nurturing in Times of Peril." He participated fully in the event. I was so grateful to have him there, clearly present and attentive to the elders, who stayed with us. It was a blessing to be around those people, and we felt a new dimension was added to the sacredness of our marriage. Because we agreed in our hearts with the basic family values they were laying out, we felt renewed appreciation for the spiritual path we were traveling together. It was a blessed time. I noticed the contrast between the Naropa Kerouac Festival, when all the flamboyant, male Beat heroes gathered at our house. Now we had a gathering of a different nature, a celebration of feminine wisdom and power, led by the strong grandmothers who held the fabric of hearth and home together with their matriarchal bonds. It was an affirmation that John and I were reaching the level of equanimity and balance we had long been seeking.

One night, Johnny told Dhyani he had been noticing his shadow did not move as fast as his body. A definite lag time was apparent. Without hesitation, she pierced the air. "It means you are deciding whether to live or die." When I heard these grave warnings from people who study signs, I was terrified. My fears proved to be well-founded when, a month later, in the summer of 1986, John ruptured a disc. Hemochromatosis had taken such a toll on his ravaged body that the doctors refused to operate. Afraid John's heart would not survive the anesthesia, they kept him in the hospital for weeks, drugged out of his mind on painkillers. He could barely hold his head up. No one felt sorry for him. Our recovering friends called it a junkie's wet dream.

The hospital's pain-control center diagnosed him as the type of addict who would always find a reason for using opiates. They did not recommend surgery because, even if it were successful, his body would invent another malaise. They suggested he manage his pain without an operation or the use of painkillers. Too far gone on the IV drugs the hospital had been giving him for weeks, they pronounced him ineligible for their pain-management program. Talk about a rock and a hard place.

Whether it was out of greed or compassion, John's doctors ignored the Pain Center's recommendation to take him off drugs. They released him from the hospital, with the assurance that they would monitor his heart to see when an operation might be possible. Incapacitated by Percodan, which the doctors continued to prescribe, John agreed to stay with a friend. If he needed anything from the house, he promised he would call first. Unfortunately, in his dementia, his first impulse upon being discharged from the hospital was to mark his territory at the house. I was still his touchstone; he came directly home.

When he walked in unannounced, I was standing in the kitchen. Marc, a friend whom he had asked for a ride, was right behind him. John's appearance was appalling. Barefoot, his clothes were filthy and he was staggering on a walker. He looked ancient, decrepit, like an animal on muscle relaxants. Fury erupted through my shock.

"We had an agreement that you would call first." It wasn't that I wanted a warning about him coming to the house as much as I wanted a warning about how horrible he looked. I ran to call one of my support-network friends. That wasn't enough; I called another. They came in seconds, just as Marc was screaming, "Quit being such a bitch. He has a right to be here. It's his house too."

My girlfriends never forgot Marc standing in my kitchen, yelling at me. Later, we awarded him the Primo Enabler Award for his knee-jerk, infantile rage at a woman refusing to shelter the beast. Mutt and Jeff left the house, misogynistic curses trailing behind them.

"I notice Marc's not taking him back to his house!" cracked one of my friends. I was in a rage because John had broken his promise to stay away. Behind the rage was horror.

Several nights later, I lay sleepless, overcome by unnameable terror. John called me early the next morning from the hospital. After wearing out his welcome at our friend's house, he had checked into the Boulderado the night before and fell asleep. Around midnight he woke up and could not move. He lay paralyzed for seven hours, screaming for help. Unable to reach the phone, he tried to send SOS signals with his bedside lamp, hoping someone across the street would see the light flashing on and off. The housekeepers discovered him in the morning and someone called an ambulance.

"I was terrified," he confessed. "I felt so alone. All I wanted was to come home to you. I'm really afraid for my life."

That same night, my father, recently diagnosed with liver cancer, was too weak to pull himself out of the bathtub. He lay there for forty-eight hours, screaming for help, just like John. Finally, a neighbor noticed he had not seen him for a couple of days and called the police.

The realization that both my husband and father had backed themselves into similar corners of isolation and despair was bone chilling. I felt no desire to help, only icy vindictiveness and very little compassion. I had recently found the courage to confront my father about the sexual abuse with a phone call.

"I want to say something without any feedback from you," I said with confidence. "I know what you did to me when I was a baby."

"What, you think I sexually abused you?" he yelled. His response said it all.

"I told you I am not going to discuss it." Quietly, I hung up and congratulated myself.

My father's reaction was to send a series of vicious letters condemning John and me. When he got no response, he tried to sell the house out from under us. When a real-estate agent called to schedule an inspection, I told her not to waste her time, that my father was delusional and my house was not for sale.

I cannot say that this was the worst part of my life. All those years were dreadful, but this was a new low. With my father dying, and my husband strung out on drugs, with both men enraged at me, I couldn't tell one from the other. Rinpoche was slowly dying as well. They hospitalized him the same week as my father and John. Father, guru, and husband, three separate basket cases, set to sail off on the ultimate abandonment trip. It was horrifying and it was fascinating, one-stop shopping for your grief. Freeway close, watch the three most important men in your life waste away simultaneously. You don't have to string this kind of torture out over years. They'll do it all in unison!

Thankfully, Johnny's miraculous sense of timing caused him to rally to my defense. Sensing I needed his support during my father's illness, he weaned himself off drugs. Suddenly, he was sober and eager to help, insisting that I let him stay with the children while I went to San Francisco. His stamina amazed me. In spite of all the confusion, the drugs, the pain, and his extreme denial, he was right there when I needed him. He took beautiful care of the children while I sat by my father's hospital bed for two

John at the Steinbeck Library's 1979 commemoration of the Steinbeck postage stamp *(Photo by Jenny Concepcion)*

Nancy and John—Chateau Lake Louise, 1979

John and Megan, our first Christmas in Boulder, 1979

Megan, Michael, and John in Boulder, 1980

Thom signing our marriage license, 1982

(Left to right) William Burroughs, Megan, Nancy, and John—Boulder, 1983

John and Nancy in our Boulder backyard, 1983 *(Photo by Barbara Gluck)*

(In back from left to right) Hetty MacLise, Nancy, Michael, and John, surrounded by our Tibetan friends at Rumtek, Sikkim, 1984

(Left to right) Michael, John, Elaine, Nancy, and Megan—Boulder, 1984

Nancy—Boulder, 1985

John—La Jolla, 1990 *(Photo by Megan Steinbeck)*

John and Michael in our hot tub—Encinitas, 1991

weeks. We talked on the phone several times a day. He'd call me at the hotel before I went to the hospital. Then he would set a time for us to chat later, in case things got too heavy. We talked every night before I fell asleep. It was like nothing bad had ever passed between us. Strong and funny, he was everything you'd want in a husband while watching your father die.

He offered to stay there with me, but I was content being in San Francisco on my own. The hospital was close to Japan town. For lunch, I walked down to the sushi bar where the boats go around a little moat and you lift the dishes off the decks as they sail by. Often, I'd drive to the Presidio cliffs overlooking the ocean where high school boys took me to "watch the submarine races." I sat by the stone buddhas in the Japanese Tea Garden. I felt my mother's presence, I felt my impending orphanhood, and I had no idea what turn my life would take with these unstable men. Strangely, I also felt a growing sense of serenity, that no matter what numbers they pulled, I was going to be fine.

In the evenings, I meditated at the San Francisco Dharmadhatu, our Buddhist center. I noticed while getting the latest update on Rinpoche's health that no one ever talked about his dying from alcoholism. We spoke freely now in Boulder, expressing our anger and frustration. The San Francisco members were guarded, whispering seriously about the latest report from the doctors. Watching it all go down, I only cared about John. I would not miss my father's abusive insanity and I no longer felt a connection with Rinpoche, who was gone, beyond wet brain. His time was up, and my father only had a few days left as well.

All my prayers were for Johnny's health. My rage had disappeared in the face of his noble efforts to sustain me and the children. Just a little while ago he'd been a derelict, straddling a walker with a demented smile on his face. Now he was the tender husband and father, happily nurturing and protecting his family. All my hopes and fears went into the repository of my prayers. *Please help him hold onto that strength upon which he is miraculously still able to draw.*

My father died and I flew home, immensely richer, both spiritually and financially, from the experience. I had conducted myself with a dignity that did not jeopardize my inheritance. Feeling no love while I sat with him, or pity for his suffering, or sadness when he died, I was learning there are some things you simply don't need to forgive. We had not talked about the sexual abuse. I was kind to him, filling his room with flowers, sitting quietly by his side.

During those two weeks, my brother came down once from Sacramento for several hours. As we went through the house, I took only some books and several pieces of art. My father had gotten rid of all the furniture when his college sweetheart had moved in with hers. She left him with an empty house, rooms that echoed in bleakness. As my brother hurried off, anxious to beat the freeway traffic, he admitted he couldn't stand being around death. I wondered why everyone just assumed I would be the one to sit by my parents' sides as they died. No one ever asked about how the kids were doing, if they missed me, if they were all right.

Rude and short-tempered with his nurses, my father died alone and bitter, and I let him. I was sick of propping up these guys. Learning to detach, to let them wallow in self-pity and dark moods, I stopped tap-dancing to change their reality. My father chose to die in the desolate reality he had created for himself. I did not want his blessing; I wanted his death to release me into my new way of being, the mirror opposite of my family's misery. I was learning to create intimacy with dignity. One-dimensional, egocentric, cardboard men would no longer manipulate me.

Before leaving San Francisco, I bought an elegant, new wardrobe. As I shopped at Saks and Magnin's, I sensed my financial independence would bring further autonomy. I had paid my dues. I was forty years old, feeling a new sense of freedom and pride. No living punitive parent could chastise me and the ones in my head were fading. My father's death was extraordinarily liberating. He remains frozen in my memory, with never a thought of warmth. It's not like I'm angry. If I feel anything, it's a peculiar sense of victory. My lesson in setting healthy boundaries was learned well. I may suffer fools for a time, but they will never take me hostage again.

Ten days later, the doctors decided John could survive the back operation. Within hours of being released, he was into his addiction to pain pills. After several weeks and another intervention, he checked into his second rehab at St. Luke's in Denver. I drove him to the hospital, flying on Percodan. Although he gave it his best shot, considering the mental and physical state he was in, after a month of in-patient treatment, John stayed sober for six days, and then resumed his hell-bent spiral toward destruction.

36 | LAST DITCH

NANCY

In the dead of winter, braving blizzards and black ice, I shuttled the children back and forth to Denver for their second round of family week, where the patient's family is educated about the disease. I resented the inconvenience of being left to care for children and pets while once again John played at rehab. During this round we began to understand exactly how dangerous we were for each other. When they sensed the rage I was feeling about John's inability to stay sober, the counselors talked to us about separating. If we wanted to heal, we could not continue to live in such agony. When the rage subsided, heartbroken and terrified, we clung to each other and prayed, but the red flags of doom were flying everywhere.

When John soon relapsed after his second round of thirty-day treatment, we began our decent into the tragic destruction of our marriage. I marvel at commitment that eventually finds resolution in resurrection and healing. It felt at the time like I was being burned alive, but that was an illusion. We were really on the verge of witnessing a miracle.

My therapist urged me to seek codependent treatment at Sharon Wegsheider-Cruz's facility in South Dakota. That ten-day program solidified my determination to beat the odds. When I returned home, we decided to fulfill Megan's dream of attending boarding school. We chose Verde

Valley School in Sedona, Arizona, for its curriculum in the arts. Michael and I flew down to register her and I fell in love with the breathtaking red-rock formations and the silent desert.

They say that Sedona intensifies whatever you bring to it. If you want to heal, Sedona will etch that possibility in its red rocks. If you want to abuse yourself, the land will provide carte blanche room for indulgence. Sensing Boulder had become a dead end for our growth, I didn't want to leave that enchanted land. Early one morning, sitting by the piñon fire in my hotel room, I called John.

"The scenery is spectacular. I want you to see it. Let's move here for a few months and then decide what we want to do."

The idea intrigued John. "You think we're ready to leave the strangle-hold of the Buddhist community? I could use a change. Besides, every cop in town knows my name. I can't walk down the street without one of them calling 'Hi, John!' over their loudspeaker."

He had been DUI'd twice more that winter. Desperately in need of a rest, I sighed. "I don't want to leave you, but I'm tired. There's no fight left in me. If you can't stay sober, I've got to figure out a way to live without you." It was my last-ditch effort at getting us out of the ditch.

When Michael and I returned home, there was another medical crisis to face. True to the Pain Center's diagnosis, John had developed excruci-ating gallstones, which demanded more drugs to kill the pain. The doctors were considering yet another operation. In February of 1987, they removed his gall bladder, which brought on another bout of Percodan addiction. We drove to Sedona ten days later with just enough luggage packed in our car to stay in a furnished condo. I begged John to throw away his stash before we left town, never really knowing how badly he was hooked. He complied and we drove off with John in heavy withdrawal and me in heavy denial, both hoping for the best.

We spent our wedding anniversary in a condo in Moab, Utah, where we stayed for several days. Discovering an alternate reality we never thought possible, we felt at peace there. The windows looked out on the simple streets where life felt so deliciously ordinary. We explored the land through bright blue-skied days, hypnotized by the fantastic red-rock formations and the willowy green trees. Fixing dinner at night, I would pretend that we lived there, that we had lost our shadow side, our diseases, any vestiges that set us apart from the unpretentious, wholesome life outside. Maybe we were schoolteachers, easily blending with the small-town simplicity. No one was famous, nor related to fame, nor going to be famous. Then we could have a life, instead of a myth, an opera, a Greek tragedy. If we could just quit being larger than life. Sick and tired of our terminal uniqueness, I prayed for humility.

The notion of an unencumbered life charmed Johnny, but an impetus was driving us like a hurricane. Although we didn't want to admit it, it was determined to drive us apart. I remember how the poplar trees waved outside the window when we had a clear view of the life we wanted. Perhaps we could cultivate the ability to experience a graceful flow instead of torturous rapids and labyrinthine roller coasters. As I daydreamed, watching the leaves shimmer in dappled sunlight, I had no idea Johnny's drowsiness was coming from a massive and dangerous withdrawal from Percodan. I thought he was just tired from his gall-bladder operation.

We settled into an easy rhythm in Sedona. Since Michael had stayed in Boulder with Paul to finish the semester, with Megan in boarding school down the street, we were without children. This was an important time for us, a chance to spend uninterrupted hours together for the first time in the eight years since we'd met. Our days consisted of long drives up to Flagstaff and on to the Grand Canyon, picnic lunches, lying in the sun, swimming at the condo, and working out at a marvelous spa down the street.

John was still weak from the operation. Since it was a fresh start, and he didn't know any doctors, he tried to get by without pain pills. He suffered from adhesions from the gall-bladder operation, and was often in agony. When the pain lessened, he swam dozens of laps every day, trying valiantly to create a health-oriented life.

I felt like a newborn baby, cut loose from all habitual patterns, trying to figure out what I wanted to do, instead of what I should be doing. Again, as in Kathmandu, I was freed from domesticity. We were in a comfortable condo, not a large house with lawns and gardens. I wanted desperately to do something creative, but I was too numb to come up with anything. The best times were late at night when we nestled in the hot tub and drank in the stars.

Two months later, Rinpoche finally died of acute late stage alcoholism. I saw a picture of him taken a few days before his death. He was bone-thin; his eyes had the haunted look of a madman. "I will never have another teacher in this lifetime," I swore to the silent red rocks at sunset. The ravens circled the valley, and I felt as though I had wasted every ounce of my practice and training with this maniacal Tibetan.

Anger erupted in both of us toward Rinpoche's henchmen, whom we felt had killed him. In their Emperor's-New-Clothes mentality, his guards had refused to face the reality of Rinpoche's addictions. It wasn't just alcohol. The truth leaked out about his $40,000-a-year coke habit and, the ultimate irony, an addiction to Seconal. Sleeping pills for the guru who advertised himself as a wake-up call to enlightenment. John and I felt duped, cheated, and outraged, especially toward the yes-men, who remained unaccountable for the deception inflicted upon our community. Rinpoche's enablers claimed that supplying him with drugs and alcohol was a measure of their devotion, while sneering at those of us who objected. In their sick denial, they couldn't see he was suiciding right before our eyes. John and I had fantasies about kidnaping Rinpoche and detoxing him ourselves, imagining what thirty days of sobriety would have done to his warped perceptions. In his last year, he'd become so deluded, he would summon his attendants and tell them he wanted to visit the Queen of Bhutan. They would put him in his Mercedes and drive around the block several times. As they led him back to the house, they laughingly asked how his visit went.

"Wonderful," he'd reply. "She was delightful."

And they called that magic. "He's so powerful," they'd whisper. It was pathetic.

Before Rinpoche's death, at a large community meeting, John asked the attendants why they hadn't refused to give him any more alcohol. They pompously claimed it was a mark of their devotion to give the guru what he asked for. "Whatever the teacher demands, all that I will give," was their vow. They believed that to break that vow, to refuse to administer the poison that was killing him, would literally send them to hell.

Johnny's question made everyone nervous. "Why do I have the feeling that we're pouring booze down his throat out of our own desire for comfort, which stems from greed? The guru's goose is being cooked, and we're all sitting by the oven, warming our hands, waiting for the feast." We shared common dreams about being ostracized by the community. If they knew how John and I were redefining our spirituality, they would have stoned us on the spot. Those nightmares were a reflection of the impending shunning, filled with hideous torture, staged in the sewers and cesspools of our incestuous community. Feeling uneasy about the vows we'd taken with Rinpoche, we didn't want our state of mind to be a reflection of his insanity. Dhyani suggested a releasing ceremony to give back his bad medicine. When John and I flew back to Boulder after Rinpoche's death, twelve of us gathered in a circle and proclaimed, "Rinpoche, we release any attachment to your behavior. We release our aversion to your self-destruction, for within that aversion is the seed of attraction. By returning your intoxication and arrogance, we affirm our relationship to enlightened mind and the development of compassion." A symbolic cup of *sake* was passed around but not imbibed. John then threw it out the window with a vow. "I will never again use Rinpoche's behavior to justify my own addictions."

Comments from other lamas about Rinpoche began to seep in. They finally admitted that for years they had feared for his sanity and thought he had been acting irresponsibly, but no one had spoken out. This news confirmed our discomfort, yet we still had no idea how much abuse was in store for the community in the coming years. As the true nature of corruption revealed itself, we were grateful that we'd participated in the ritual that severed us from the madness.

We attended Rinpoche's cremation ceremony in May of 1987 with Dhyani and her husband. I was glad to be there with them, safe in the VIP tent, away from the crowd of three thousand people in heavy denial. Sitting with visiting dignitaries from other religious traditions, John and I felt too raw to face the onslaught of frozen feelings. True to the community's stoic form, no emotions were shown. We might as well have been at a cocktail party. After the body was cremated, rainbows and traditional Tibetan symbols appeared as cloud formations in the sky, confirming Rinpoche's magical gifts. Why had he not used that magic on himself instead of drinking with such a vengeance? It is said that the guru manifests the most neurotic aspects of his students, so there was always the glib attitude that Rinpoche's addiction was a reflection of our proclivities. Did that mean it had to kill him? We were told he could vanquish any evil in the world. Did he just not want to fight anymore?

"He got caught in his own wringer," John said ironically.

The party line claimed Rinpoche's outrageous behavior was a powerful vehicle for awakening his students. If you viewed it as drunken unmanageabiiity, they said you were missing the point, throwing away a precious opportunity for spiritual growth. The people with the greatest awareness about addictions were shunned as being the most impossible to enlighten. We were told that we simply were not "man enough" to take the industrial strength of Rinpoche's selfless teachings. In the May 2000 issue of the *Shambhala Sun*, the organization's mouthpiece, Rinpoche's son stated: "My dad . . . was a drinking madman! How much of a madman are you? How brave are you to really do things? He was a warrior. A warrior with the pen. A warrior with the word. A warrior with the drinking. If you don't like his drinking, he was a fool, he's dead. If you don't mind the drinking thing and think he may have had incredible enlightened wisdom, then you are an eligible candidate for his teachings."

After his death, a Buddhist teenager asked me, "Did you know that some guys used to pimp for Rinpoche? They'd find him new women to sleep with." She was talking about the sharks that sought out eager new females, either at Rinpoche's request, or on their own recognizance, hoping to win favor with him. We discussed the obvious oxymoron to which everyone turned a blind eye, that an impeccable warrior's path cannot incorporate a voracious and sloppy appetite for drugs, alcohol, and hundreds of sexual encounters. While everyone was busy honoring Rinpoche's courage for being so blatant about his massive indulgences, his henchmen constantly skimmed the various centers for new blood. Women were trained as "consorts." That meant they knew what to do when he threw up, shit in the bed, snorted coke till dawn, turned his attention to other women, and maybe even got in the mood for a threesome.

Our little band of recovering Buddhists began to ask people if they thought this flagrant behavior constituted religious or sexual abuse. The standard answer you get from the male good old boys who buy into the system because it means their coffers will also be full to feed their own addictions, is that they never, in all their pimping, heard any woman complain about sleeping with Rinpoche. (I use that term loosely, because for years he was alcoholically impotent and would devise little sexual games such as using a dildo known as "Mr. Happy" or insisting women masturbate in front of him.)

You don't ask people in denial for reality checks. You ask those who have crawled though the trenches into the light, those who have dealt head-on with their own abuse issues. They are the ones who will proclaim the truth fearlessly in the face of mocking ostracism and threats of eternal damnation. Many women, who felt they were no more than chattel, silently left the scene. Sleeping with Rinpoche was like sleeping with a rock star. You got elevated for about an hour until he moved on to the next new face. There were always eager young initiates who mistakenly thought it was a way of gaining status in the community. Because of the spiritual trappings, women forgot that groupies are always relegated to the sloppy seconds category after they've been had. Like a bunch of high school jocks, the male-dominated administration smirked behind the backs of Rinpoche's conquests. A woman with low self-esteem and no education about abuse will acquiesce to such degradation out of ignorance.

Thankful to be removed from the scene, I found sanctuary in Sedona. Ironically, I realized I was getting all the help I needed to make the break from the battlefield. In Boulder, the typical recovering codependent attitude was if a guy won't quit drinking, you should kick him out and move on to a healthy relationship. Most of the Sedona Al-Anon women were grandmothers; they'd been married to their alcoholics for half a century. Accepting alcoholism as a disease, not an inconvenience, they mastered the art of detaching with love and humor. These grandmothers knew that you cannot take a disease personally. It's not out to get YOU, it's only out to get its host. They practiced the Al-Anon slogan—*Love the person, hate the disease*—with a sense of compassion that I wanted to emulate. Eager to transmit their wisdom, they shared their experience, strength, and hope with me.

These women loved their husbands. Whether for economic reasons or out of family loyalty, they did not see them as disposable. If, at times, their situation appeared hopeless, they closed ranks and nurtured each other. I marveled at their lack of vindictiveness, which often ate away at me. When they saw that my marriage was losing its lifeblood, their implanted vision of freedom from fear and anger carried me through the chaos. It has years of practice, but it was there that I learned to be gentle about dealing with addictions, because harshness just turns around and bites you back. My Al-Anon sages managed to impart the profound notion of powerlessness to me. I am grateful that they entered my life at a time when I desperately needed their wisdom and nurturing.

With the grandmothers' help, I faced a phone call from Thom that caused the bottom to drop out of our marriage. He had broken up with Joanna and was staying with friends on a farm in upstate New York. Footloose and free to party, he wanted Johnny to join him. We all knew half of John was suffocating, thirsting for a drink. In his perverse, Cain-slaying-Abel mode, Thom wanted to rescue him from the other half that was desperately trying to heal.

I was terrified that I would lose John. I knew if he continued to drink, he would die, and die soon. He'd been cirrhotic for five years; if he went to New York, he would ignore his biweekly phlebotomies. Thom was oblivious to the fact that alcohol increases the iron deposits that were strangling John's liver and heart.

I wasn't being perverse when I told John to go. As much as I dreaded it, I was ready to be on my own. I could no longer walk point around his slow suicide. I let go and faced my worst nightmare as John, following his brother's fatal cue, began to drink himself to death with a vengeance.

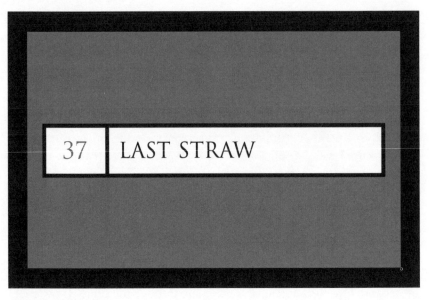

37 | LAST STRAW

NANCY

John missed his plane; he had stopped for a drink in the Phoenix airport bar. Frantic, Thom called from JFK. I had to laugh. After years of mocking my consternation, he was getting a bitter dose of John's irresponsibility.

Four blackout days late, Johnny fell off the plane into his brother's arms. I heard about fisticuffs in the taxi. Someone's glasses were broken again, as Cain and Abel set off for the farm in upstate New York. When things settled down a few days later, in their drunken grandiosity they created Steinbeck Films, a production company, to develop their father's works. When John called to crow, I greeted their little wet dream with barely veiled cynicism. A batch of linen letterhead was all that ever came out of that scheme. Up to their old tricks, they were making the rounds of producers, getting their feet in the door with their name, and then getting the boot when the straight guys figured out they were all hat and no cattle. I wondered how they would ever grow up if they made careers out of being their father's sons?

John called often, in non compos blackout, repeatedly telling me how they dazzled people with their magic and power. His subtext was imbedded with chastisement because I failed to be impressed with the cultivation of his celebrity image. I knew he couldn't even board a plane on time, and he resented that. In his convoluted mind, my mistrust was holding him back from soaring to the heights of his potential. When I wasn't bored by their tom-foolery, I felt anger and disgust. I struggled to focus on myself, trying not to drown in terror because John was drinking, learning not to react like a scalded cat. It wasn't easy work. *Who am I if I'm not focused on his high-wire act?*

The night before he was scheduled to fly home, John called at 4:00 A.M. from the Gramercy Park Hotel. "Four guys with knives just mugged me. They stole $500 and my driver's license. I need you to wire me some money in the morning."

Afraid he had been in mortal danger, my heart raced. However, intu-ition guided my response. "You probably spent it on drugs. I'm not sending a dime. Ask all those people who are so impressed with your power and magic for a loan."

Alcoholics have an uncanny way of knowing exactly when their enablers are about to detach. The next morning, John called with the proverbial "I've hit bottom in a New York hotel room, drunk and penni-less." Bewildered by my cool refusal to get hooked into the mugging drama, he was casting about for the habitual tension that strung my net under his balancing act. Expecting the usual pleas for vows of self-redemp-tion, he was ready to strike some phoney Ronald Colman pose, eyes fixed on the far horizon of movie deals. This time, he heard only silence as I let go. Shocked by my detachment, I could tell from the awkward stillness that he felt cornered and panicked. This was not the girl he had married.

When I met his plane, I saw a look in his eyes that said all the unspoken words it would take him another year to voice. *I don't know how you put up with me. I am sorry I put you through this misery. I am not the man I want to be, for myself, for you, for the children. You are the only person who really knows me. You are my only source of sanity. Please give me just a little more time to shed this burden. Thank you for meeting my plane. Thank you for loving me.*

My heart melted. In that look, he laid bare his struggle with the disease, with Thom's influence, with his unwillingness to practice the steps that could lead him out of the abyss. Sensing the end was near, I had to decide if I could witness it.

Upon his return to Sedona, John quickly established yet another sober honeymoon phase. He suggested we move to La Jolla. If any movie deals came through, we would be close to Hollywood. I could get the degree required for work in a treatment center at UCSD. We had been spending far too much time running interference between Megan and the deplorable drug scene at her boarding school, where the students got their dope UPS'd in from their dealers and were always dropping acid. She was uncomfortable in that environment and eager to leave. Michael's needs were simple. He just wanted to surf. We were all in accord, and I was delighted to be able to return to my native California.

We found a beautiful two-story ocean-view home on a cliff in La Jolla Farms. With four bedrooms and two offices, there was plenty of space to work on ourselves. The master bedroom had a secluded deck with a panoramic view of the coastline, surrounded by palms that seemed particularly auspicious. Nine years prior, I had a vision on the shores of Lake Louise. The frozen water and snowy banks melted into a turquoise ocean fringed with swaying palm trees. John and the children were joyously frolicking in the water. Perhaps the healing that I had been praying for would happen here. Sadly, thoughts like that never lasted more than a few, fleeting seconds. I was convinced the marriage was doomed.

I made it through the next six months with the help of kind friends and Al-Anon. Moving to a new city with two teenagers and a husband who soon relapsed again, while trying to establish a different direction for my own life, was torture. I was determined to save myself and any other family member who could join in my quest for serenity. When I talked to Johnny about my fears, he'd say, "I'm not afraid we won't make it. Love is never the problem. The fear is that I won't make it."

We traveled from Sedona to La Jolla in a caravan, across the smoldering desert, in three cars holding two teenagers, two cats, and two very confused adults. Somehow, we managed to stay cheerful against incredible obstacles, simultaneously filled with dread and prayers of hope. Megan's car blew a radiator in El Centro, but Johnny and I only saw it as one of those crazy signs that velcro'd our souls. As children, El Centro epitomized the armpit of hell, the worst part of every family vacation, propelled by eccentric mothers who found a deep resonance in the desert. It held memories of orange-painted motel rooms with creaking ceiling fans, the acrid taste of burlap water bags hanging from car emblems, miles of dead scenery, and boring silence. Johnny told us a terrifying childhood story of wandering into Death Valley with Grandmother and Gwyn. Tanked on gin fizzes, they ran out of gasoline on the blistering road.

We were at the mercy of a huge Mexican mechanic named Nacho who came to our hotel at sunset and swore on the Virgin that he'd have us back on the road by morning. While John helped him, I took the kids across the border to Calexico for a taste of street tacos and border-town charm. As John and I fell asleep, we giggled at the cosmic coincidence we shared

about the childhood trips to the desert. Those memories, intensely burnished in our psyches, were part of a twinspeak that never failed to amaze
us. Were we the only people on earth who tasted sadness in blueberries and
candied violets? The stiff little faces buried in our mothers' fur stoles, with
the glossy beaded eyes, made us both feel claustrophobic. Certain shades
of green were stifling, like a canvas awning baking in the sunlight. We
believed our childhoods were enchanted by the same fairy godmother.
Inextricably linked by a gossamer web, she was helping us valiantly master
the archetypal tests of spinning flax into gold or kissing frogs in order to
reveal our beloved.

We clung to each other that night in El Centro, praying our childhood
fairies would rescue us. Scared of the impending darkness, we knew we
were losing our way. Somewhere out there, a witch was warming her oven
for us. A giant was grinding his ax and striding toward us in seven-league
boots. I dreamed a leper was lying between us in our bed, his skull exposed
through rotting flesh. In that dream, and when I awoke, I saw disease dripping from the ceiling.

Once we were settled in La Jolla, I began to hunt for therapists. The
children would need help adjusting to their new schools, and John was
willing to go back to couples counseling. Although San Diego County has
enormous resources for recovery, back then the therapeutic community was
caught in black and white categorizations that did not fit us. Beyond the
obvious enmeshment, we were two highly creative, hot-blooded, strong-
willed individuals, desperately trying to sustain a family unit. The first
woman therapist claimed my childhood wounds caused me to confuse
John's bizarre behavior with love. Another woman told me I should dump
John because he'd never get sober and he was just wasting our time. I
sensed unresolved issues in each one, along with condescension toward me
and a groupie mentality about the Steinbeck name. The next one, who
wrote a popular recovery book and worked with Betty Ford, told me if John
ever got sober, I should stay away from him for two years, to see if he really
meant it. Who comes up with these theories? If I'd listened to her, I would
have missed the best years of my life and deprived the children of witnessing their father's recovery.

I wasn't looking for support to stay in my marriage. Nevertheless, I
needed to hear more than "My dear, you're so sick you wouldn't know a
healthy relationship if it came up and bit you." Wasn't it the sorry bite of
our disintegration that sent me to their doors? A doctor would never claim
that you are too sick to know you've got the flu. I decided these women

were driven by sadistic greed. By telling me how messed up I was, they could string me out for years and get paid for the abuse.

I was down to the wire. Desperately wanting to move past my rage at the disease that was killing my family, I didn't need any more opinions. I needed cheerleading from someone who would nurture me through the necessary and impending breakdown, someone who would work gently with my ambivalence instead of trying to convince me that I should leave my husband in the dust, with the veneer of anger and arrogance that belies the underlying heartbreak.

"Just get on with your life and find a healthy man," they'd trumpet, as if that were so bloody easy. Just say, *I'm so much better off after dumping that son of a bitch.* They ignored the torture of watching a husband caught in a self-imposed trap, chewing his leg off. Who could help me come to terms with the fact that John was choosing death over freedom? Harboring anger toward men and the disease, none of those women had sustained an intimate relationship. Blind leading blindness. Where was one who had heart?

Eventually I found one in Dr. Peter McDade, who became Michael's therapist. He listened to the grief and pain of all the family members, and when he met John, he understood the dilemma we were facing.

"When he's sober, John is one of the kindest, most sensitive, coolest guys I've ever seen. He adores you and the children. No wonder you all love him so much." He conveyed a genuine empathy for our predicament, without judgment. Instead of telling me how sick I was, he congratulated me on my clarity and perseverance. I've often wondered if Peter could afford such generosity simply because he was a man. Women can be so competitive and bitchy.

On one of our last nights together, John and I walked along the dusty, darkened freeway across the Tijuana border. As moonlight carved the outline of distant mountains, we were flooded with the familiar rush of entering a Third World country. It was like the first time I heard Janis Joplin sing "freedom's just another word for nothin' left to loose," or Dylan's "just to dance beneath the diamond sky with one hand waving free." Nothing ever compared to things like a simple border crossing with John. The earth's raw magnetism blended with his intoxicating magic. We didn't say a word. Holding hands, a moonlit glance said it all.

When we had to run across the freeway, I sensed danger. I didn't know dozens of people had been struck by oncoming cars on that stretch. John was exhilarated when we got to the other side, but I was still apprehensive.

"We made it, didn't we?" he laughed.

We're getting too old for the razor's edge. I don't want to live like this anymore. I love myself too much to endanger my life by flirting with death.

I listened with mixed emotions as John declared, "I'm so glad that after all these years, you haven't lost your spontaneity. You are still so exciting."

I remembered my guy friends in college voted me the Most Game Girl, the one you'd want to hop a freight train with. Twenty years later, I hadn't lost my spirit. Nevertheless, I was no longer attracted to licking honey from the razor's edge. My animus was changing. Whereas John's outrageous sense of adventure once mirrored mine, now I was more interested in creative and spiritual challenges. I wanted to accomplish something tangible. I sensed a seismic shift deep in my psyche as the bells of doom clanged wildly around us.

That night's border crossing severed my enmeshment. John's greatest fear had always been that I would outgrow him. I left him there, beside the freeway, emotionally and spiritually. The last fairy filament was cut. John was aligned with self-sabotage because feeling good about himself was so foreign. He was choosing defeat; I wanted victory.

A week later, after seeing Thom for "business" in LA, John returned home drunk. Wearily, I asked him to leave the house. When he refused, I went out to dinner with an Al-Anon friend. I returned to find him lying on the couch, the children tangled in his feet. I saw in their eyes. *Here comes Mom, uptight as usual. She just doesn't understand us. She spoils all the fun.* Later, I learned John had smoked marijuana with them. When I saw the look, I knew I had to cut his toxicity out of our lives or the kids would go down with him.

The next time John went to LA, I got a restraining order. When he called to tell me he was coming home, I said the words I had rehearsed for seven years. "You can't come within 100 yards of the house or I'll have you arrested. I'm filing for divorce. I will not watch you kill yourself. Your drinking has destroyed the sacredness of our marriage. I'm not playing anymore."

If I spoke to him on the phone after that, or let him enter the house, the restraining order would be invalidated, so I hung up quickly. No longer vacillating, I was not open to seductive reconciliations. I believed time would eventually bring me a better quality of life. Even if it felt like death, I was willing to do that time.

I enrolled in the rehab credential program at the University of California, which was conveniently close to the house. That simple act restored my self-confidence and esteem. I met other people who wanted to heal in those classes, and their support sustained me through the separation. Filing for divorce was the next step. My lawyers were concerned that I would be financially responsible for the consequences of John's drunk driving and his burgeoning debts.

Suddenly a single mother of two teenagers in a new town, with no close friends, I began to cultivate a support group of classmates and Al-Anon friends. Anytime I felt shaky, I'd pick up the phone. The long-distance bill to Boulder was enormous. Ignoring the restraining order, John called incessantly. My lawyer took him to court for harassment. Then he wrote daily, pleading for reconciliation. When that didn't succeed, he resorted to cruelty and rejection. "I'm tired of trying to be healthy. You're not going to tell me how to live."

I made a list of all the rotten things he'd ever done. Whenever I missed him, I read it. In my shock and grief, I went over the litany of events until I could absorb the reality. I kept a reminder taped to my desk and near the kitchen sink. "At times, John stayed sober and seemed to grow in health with us. Now he is powerless over alcohol and his life has become unmanageable. He seeks drunken camaraderie with Thom because *Sick Picks Sick*. Michael and Megan and I will continue to recover."

Grief was not the only texture. If the best revenge is living well, I accomplished that. I found solace in my beautiful home, walking my private trail down the cliffs to the secluded beach below. I especially enjoyed the psychiatric classes at UCSD. My teachers and peers were interested in what I had to contribute and I was maintaining an A average. The kids and I got along much better without John's triangulation. When I look back, it was John's attempt to label me as the mean mommy that broke me. It is so boring being seen as a punitive mother by a man with whom you have been passionately in love. *He hated his own mother. How can you expect him to support motherhood when he's drinking? The man would try to undermine a snake when he's in that state.*

Often I was seized by a debilitating fear that John was lying dead in some gutter. I had no idea how close it came to that. He was making rambling late-night calls to our friends, beseeching them to convince me to lift the restraining order. He mistakenly saw it as punitive, whereas to me it was a life raft.

The time of greatest stress is always in letting go. I felt as if my limbs had been amputated. My skeleton caved in to protect my broken heart. Nevertheless, a sense of timeless security came from the familiar sights and sounds of my childhood, the ocean's soothing pulse, the smell of eucalyptus, and crunch of ice plant. I loved La Jolla's spectacular beaches and elegant homes. My bed faced the curving northern coastline, toward Los Angeles. At night I would look at the twinkling lights, wondering if Johnny were even alive. I said the Serenity Prayer like a mantra, like counting sheep, to quell my nightmares. Maybe he'd been knifed in the back behind some liquor store. Robbed while sleeping in his car. After he got sober, John always prayed passionately during AA meetings when they take a minute of silence for those who are still "out there." Grateful for the grace that finally descended upon him, he knew of no lonelier spot on earth. It was to that spot that I sent my love and prayers every night before I fell asleep. *Why are you giving in to the disease? Where did all your goodness go? You always wanted me to think of you as a stand-up guy. You've become a coward. Why are you letting this tragic flaw conquer you? It breaks my heart that we can't be together.*

The words he'd whispered hundreds of times echoed in my heart. *If it weren't for you, I'd be dead from boredom. You are the only person I can really talk to.* Why were we losing each other? Who were we becoming?

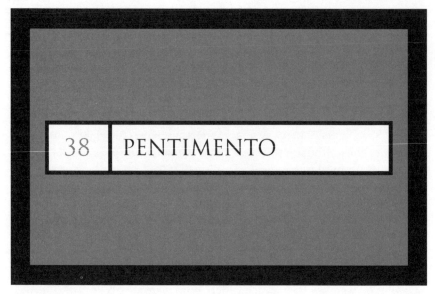

38 | PENTIMENTO

NANCY

When the dust settled, the simplicity of my life amazed me. I felt a sense of pride for the way I was handling our separation. I was now financially independent. For the first time since living with John's extravagant overspending, my budget was manageable and our life was peaceful. Megan and Michael were adjusting to their new schools. Our grades were excellent, we were making new friends, and we were all in therapy.

In October, the Boulder house sold and we flew back to supervise the movers. Hoping to exert a final measure of control over me, John had a lawyer draw up an order that I couldn't remove his things from the house. My lawyer responded by claiming I would throw the antiques in the street if the order were not withdrawn.

Although I burst into tears upon entering our soon-to-be-dismantled home, I ruthlessly went through the house as the movers marked HIS and HERS. My friends gathered at a half wake/half celebration as we watched all the Steinbeck memorabilia being carted away. When the house was emptied, I went back for the last time to say good-bye. Standing in the driveway, I faced all the years of cop cars, ambulances, Buddhist guards, parties, and overdoses. I swore that would be the last place John would ever turn into a charnel ground. He would never again make our home a scary place, where depression and thoughts of suicide sat like stains on a ceiling.

That night, one of the Buddhist children was killed in a car crash while driving drunk. The son of a New Age prophet, his family was devastated. It was a ghastly reminder for those of us who were struggling with alcohol and drug abuse in our families. As the community ridiculed us for being silly, uptight teetotalers, we were fighting for our children's lives. The amount of alcohol consumed at the funeral dismayed us, as did the fact that it was offered to the boy's teenage friends. Would these adults ever get the message, even when it screamed in their faces?

In the raw, traditional Tibetan style, community members sat in the shrine room with the bruised corpse. The death deeply effected Megan and Michael; they had grown up with the young man. This tragedy came hard on the heels of the discovery that Kier, another childhood friend, had gotten AIDS from sleeping with the Regent. Kier had passed the HIV virus on to his girlfriend, who was the dead boy's stepsister.

Later, I spoke with recovering Buddhist friends about the ignorance we displayed as young parents, taking drugs around our babies. We had thought hallucinogens would bring enlightenment to the planet, not death and dismemberment. When reality hit, we faced the shadow side of our idylls. We were flower children and then we had children. We marveled at their purity and suddenly we were killing them with our addictions as the whole world turned black and crazy. In recovery, we traced the steps that brought us to the brink of destruction, determined that history would not repeat itself with a genocide of the innocent. Weathering the community's scorn, we educated our children about addictions. Now we were grateful about the simple fact that they were still alive.

Just before he died, that young man had asked, "Mom, you're always doing all these Buddhist practices and they don't make you happy. Why do you bother?" His profound observation fueled our conclusion that Buddhism could never address addictions as efficiently as the Twelve-Step program. Buddhist teachings may enlighten brains that aren't hardwired in the same way as addicts, but we needed something more. A two-thousand-year-old monastic tradition could not totally solve twentieth-century Western dilemmas.

When I called Dhyani for support that night, she said, "I have been concerned about that family for the past several years. Why didn't the recovering community confront their permissiveness? You need to call a meeting to discuss the guilt about not coming forth with your observations."

For the first time since Rinpoche's funeral, we gathered once again to mourn another alcohol-related death. As we went around the circle sharing our sorrow, we agreed to forgive ourselves. "I can no longer confront people who aren't ready to hear the truth," I said. "All I get back is abuse and ridicule. I am as powerless over that family as I am over my own husband. This is another example of how the disease, if left untreated, ends in insanity or death. I hate it." It was a sobering closure to our life in Boulder, and a strong message that in spite of the pain and loneliness, I had to stay focused on our recovery.

When I got back to La Jolla, John's lawyer started making noises about alimony from me. That's when I knew he had lost it. His creditors were calling daily. Then I met a woman at school who had heard about John's antics in Vietnam where she had been a journalist. Awestruck, she exclaimed, "Did you know your husband was a cult hero over there?"

"Oh, yeah? Well, I'm going to become my own cult hero!" I laughed.

We met at a seminar on Post Traumatic Stress Disorder attended by Vietnam vets, rape survivors, and police officers. The vets dominated every discussion, adamant that we civilians had never experienced the suffering they felt in the war. Now, John's vet buddies often gathered at our house after their support-group meetings at the Vet Center. I had seen *Platoon* with twenty of them, and listened as their feelings spilled out from the catharsis. I knew vet's issues firsthand. They had my complete sympathy. Nevertheless, when I heard them telling rape and incest survivors and a twenty-year-veteran Chicago cop that they had the handle on stress, I figured enough was enough.

"People in this room have seen horrendous things, without being in Vietnam. I've nearly been killed by my alcoholic husband. I'm an incest survivor. I've witnessed psychotic drug withdrawals, woken up to my husband firing his gun into the ceiling, and been threatened at knifepoint by him. You guys say I haven't suffered enough to know the stress you've been through? Give me a break. You can't compare pain; it's a waste of time. Don't try to make me feel guilty by claiming to have suffered more. Your attitude creates divisions and you're forcing sides right here in this room. Why can't we agree that as survivors of trauma, we all have Post Traumatic Stress Disorders in varying degrees? My vet husband wrote an article about PTSD and, as far as he was concerned, anyone who survived the sixties was traumatized. Why does this have to be reduced to some macho competition?"

Several vets got up and walked out, but I didn't care. I couldn't imagine anything more egotistical than to compete about pain. It reeked of the alcoholic's litany of accusations to their spouses. *You don't understand me and what I've been through and if you did, you wouldn't give me such a hard time about my drinking.* I was sick to death of being told I didn't understand some dysfunctional man who felt he had the right to assassinate my character in order to establish a sense of himself. As in war, their hard-line posturing erected walls and we were there to heal. A couple of the cops thanked me as I was leaving. They'd felt the same way, but they didn't feel like calling it.

Later that semester, I had a strong confrontation with a psychiatrist who taught classes in group therapy. There was something about his behavior, condescension, and misogyny that alarmed me. Three months later, he was sued by six women clients for sexual harassment and lost his license. My assertiveness was being honed, as well as my instincts for sick behavior.

At night, in my dreams, I sensed tremendous anger coming from John. Beneath his rage was terror. Surrounded with darkness and confusion, his batteries couldn't get their psychic charge from me. He was running on empty. Abandoned by his friends, he slept in his car for weeks so the police couldn't pick him up for drunk driving. "Only the thought of your love inspired me to hang on. Without your motivating force, if only to rebel against, my juice was gone, " he told me later. Ironically, he never saw Thom, who disdained his brother's antics when I wasn't around.

In spite of the manageability of my life, most of the time I felt joyless. In withdrawal from abusive characters, I worked constantly at trying to love myself, nurture my inner child, and find out exactly what it was that I needed from moment to moment. It was rich and fascinating at times, and often just plain boring and lonely. That stage of recovery is manual labor.

Paul drove a truck filled with our things to La Jolla just before Thanksgiving. I spent a bizarre holiday unpacking the pieces of my marriage to John and placing them around the new house, while my ex-husband cooked the turkey. I felt so depressed, I wanted to die, remembering previous holidays, our house filled with twenty-five friends, Johnny's signature chestnut stuffing, and the lovely sense of celebration our family always managed to create.

It was no surprise when John's call woke me late that night. Compared to the travesty of his childhood holidays, the sanctity of our lighthearted festivities had been deeply healing for him. Risking a breach of the restraining order, I let him speak when I heard the despair in his voice.

"I didn't want to let the holiday pass without saying I love you. This is really hard," he said softly, with dignity.

"It's very hard. I know." That was all I'd allow. I didn't need to say more;

it had been said zillions of times. *If you quit drinking, with the way I've been working on myself, we could have a lifetime of fabulous holidays.* I hadn't heard his voice in two months. In those few seconds, I could tell charm and a famous name and even booze weren't working any more. I quietly put down the receiver and wept with relief. He was still alive. I was still his touchstone.

A turning point came on the day I decorated the Christmas tree. Unwrapping the ornaments that had belonged to my mother and Gwyn, I celebrated a new richness and flow in my life, humming my favorite carols. Free from the bondage of brutal relationships, I had confronted each one with courage. As I congratulated myself, the phone rang and my life took a miraculous turn.

It was John. He was sober. "I don't want to spend Christmas without you and the kids. I miss you so much, I am willing to do anything to have you back in my life. I want to quit drinking and I don't know how. I know I need help. Can I see you? Will you help me?"

I needed to buy time. "Let me think about it. Call me later this afternoon."

I phoned several of my recovering girlfriends for a reality check. I was sure they'd groan and ask me if I'd lost my mind, but they all said I should give him a shot. "What if he really means it? You don't want to pass that chance by. If he doesn't, you can continue to separate from him."

When John called back, I agreed to see him. He was gentle with me, letting several days pass as we talked often by phone. He poured out his pain about the sabotage of his life, his ambition, his marriage, the relationship with his children, his dreams. "I don't want to lose everything, but I don't know what to do. I've had a series of dreams and visions about our marriage. We truly belong together. I need your friendship. I love you."

Without attaching to the outcome, I just listened. Powerlessness had become my ally. By scraping the bottom layer of my pain and anger, I had learned to trust my instincts, to know the truth from his con. If he only had lies to offer, then I would go back to my life without him. It was no longer a matter of what he could do to me, only what I allowed in my denial. He never mentioned Thom or the film company. He didn't try to dazzle. No grandiosity, no bullshit. As I sensed that the fruition of our separation contained a miraculous seed of unconditional love, I opened to him. And so, one night, when the kids were staying with friends, I let him come home.

The house was filled with flowers, candles, and delightful Christmas scents. I made a luscious curry; the ambience was cozy and luminous. I knew when he walked through the door and immersed himself in the warmth that his heart would burst. I loved creating an environment for

John, like performance art, and he was the most appreciative audience. It made his lonely inner child feel safe, the way it longed to when his mother was breaking scotch bottles at his head. Never the saint, it was also a feisty way of saying *Eat your heart out. This is the way we've been living while you've been in the gutter.*

We sat together in front of the fire after dinner, more tender than that first night when the silver mermaid dress slid to the floor. I sensed the fear in him was gone, the underlying tendency toward fight or flight. There was nowhere to run, and it was no longer my mission in life to batter down his fortress walls.

"You know," he whispered as he took me in his arms, "we cannot escape our love for each other. We are joined at the hips, eyelashes, and fingernails."

That night, sitting by the fire, we sifted through the potsherds of our relationship to see what could be saved. For three months I had been forced to rely on myself, to trust my integrity. All that was left was reality, raw and lonely, yet filled with dignity.

"Johnny, the dream we share is still alive. I want to celebrate our love. It has withstood the test of my letting go. If I'm capable of that kind of love, then I'm ready to receive it in return. If you can't give it to me, I will find it elsewhere."

"Let me try," he begged. "I had a vision of a past life where I was a wild yogi and you were my spirit windhorse. During the day, you grazed outside my door. However, at night, we had fantastic adventures in other dimensions. You are the best Christmas present I could ever receive, through countless lifetimes."

When they returned the next afternoon, Michael and Megan were delighted to have their Poppy home for the holidays. Johnny was adorable; one of his favorite poses was papa lion. He'd lie on the couch and they'd sprawl around him, chatting about deep things and silly things, musing, giggling and clowning around. We'd make up words, or names for the cats. The littlest Abyssinian had one hundred nicknames. It would do something cute and one of us would come up with a new name, like Anapurrrna, Kitty Purrrn, Happy Talk, Speedbump, and Pumpkin Peanut Butter.

Johnny held it together admirably through New Year's. He had been reading AA's bible, *The Big Book.* Anxious to discuss the disease, he wanted to know what I was learning in school. Sometimes we went to meetings together. He liked the funky, blue-collar ones best; he identified with the down-and-out guys. I had a sense of him standing on the edge of a cliff, calmly looking over at the vast expanse below, poised between life and death. He knew it wasn't really in his hands. In some final grasp of reality, he had come to believe the disease was bigger than him.

After the holidays, John asked the abbot of the Vietnamese Buddhist Temple in Los Angeles if he could live there. I didn't question his decision; I didn't even give it much thought. He couldn't stay with us, and it was better than living in his car. The monastery is in Korea Town, surrounded by a ghetto mix of many cultures. The abbot, Tich Man Jack, nicknamed Tai, was very fond of John. He let him stay in a room right off the main shrine area. When John drank, he interrupted the services, so Tai moved him down to the basement. When I visited, Tai took me aside and complained, "He too noisy, and he stink. People ask me why I let him stay in monastery. I don't know, but I love him. You his wife. Why you no take him home?"

"Because he too noisy and he stink!" We laughed.

Johnny hung out with the monks, or else sealed himself in his room and drank, leaving only to buy more scotch at the corner liquor store. Whenever he tried to recreate the romance of life he'd found in Vietnam as a young man, the time warp would strangle him. Thankfully, he never bothered me with those delusions.

I loved to visit him there; it was a world completely removed from the surrounding environs of Korean grocers and Salvadoran restaurants. As the spiritual leader of many Vietnamese Buddhists, Tich Man Jack had created an island to maintain their culture. On Sundays, the children would gather after the services for their youth-group activities, while the grandmothers cooked lunch. Michael and Megan fit in with the ease of world travelers, delighted with the exotic yet familiar panoply of rituals. Entering the courtyard, we would light long, thick sticks of incense, wave them up and down three times in front of the huge Buddha statue, and bow, as we had done countless times with John, in Boulder, in Hong Kong, Thailand, and Kathmandu. After the congregation left, we loved to chat with Tai while eating oranges in the sun-filled shrine room. Death joined us then, watched patiently, and waited.

Johnny was always sober when we visited and in return, I was respectful. In Tai's world of Confucian order, I was supportive of John's attempts to join the monastic scene. I never told him what I really saw, the waste of a life, the inability to care for himself, to actualize the potential that began gathering twenty-five years ago on his Mekong fantasy island where he began his career of dying young with opium, heroin, and a vengeance. He felt safe enough in our détente to reveal his shame and embarrassment that it had all come down to this, from the flaming promise of a cult hero in Vietnam to a derelict living in an LA ghetto basement.

This was a man who was given the grace each day to stay alive. In the face of his ravaging disease, there was too much respect between us to play destructive games. He quietly allowed me to see the pain and confusion that fastened his self-imposed trap. No longer sealed in a veneer of bravado, he never hid his sorrow when I returned to my house on the cliff above the sea, a place full of light and sun and promise. His vulnerability touched me in places I'd never felt before. He wasn't asking for a handout or for me to clean up after him. He simply wanted my love. This was not *Leaving Las Vegas*; this was a man on the verge of death who wanted to live. He just couldn't figure out how.

When he was able to eat, the old nuns cooked for him. When they saw death around him, they watched his back. Without language, judgment, or curiosity, they were so gentle with us. We felt completely at home around them. Their minds were still and steady in the face of this bizarre scenario. Conversationally skilled at reflecting reality in silence, their presence was a thousand times more powerful than therapy. Everyone knew death was waiting. Sitting in that quiet hall of mirrors with those gentle people served to magnify the truth, whereas chatter would have created defenses and denial.

Surrounded by the many photographs placed lovingly on the ancestors' shrine, feeling John's tenderness and respect toward Tai and me, I was profoundly touched by each passing moment. John's picture is on that shrine now, amidst offerings of flowers, incense, and oranges, still life in filtered sunlight, as Tai watches over him from this earthly plane, completing the cosmic full circle.

John spent three sober weeks at my house after New Year's. Things were going too sweetly. In a grand finale, Thom was compelled to resurrect the Steinbeck curse. He landed on our doorstep with the usual hidden agenda. I objected, but John assured me no alcohol would be allowed in the house.

We spent a quiet evening. The next morning I came downstairs to find them both plastered. Heartbroken, but hardly surprised, I told Thom to leave immediately.

"We only drank in the garage," he said defiantly.

"You'll have to go, too," I announced to John. "You've broken our agreement."

I ran upstairs and called an Al-Anon friend, sobbing. *How could I have set myself up so naively? Why can't John resist Thom?*

"You know, if Johnny drinks anymore, he's going to be dead soon," I implored when Thom said good-bye.

"Well, we all have to go sometime!" he said gaily, in his mindless, pix-ilated insanity. He was not so philosophical after John's death. The loss of his brother nearly killed him.

Later, when we discussed the relapse, John pointed out the irony of the situation. "He wouldn't cross the street to see me when we were living a few miles apart in Los Angeles. He can't stand to see me sober and he feels threatened when I'm happy with you."

What Thom did not know was that whenever Johnny drank, sponta-neous bruises broke out all over his legs, emblems of late-stage alcoholism that signal the end. We were staying at the Bonaventure in LA the first time I saw them, earlier that month. John was toweling off from a shower when I noticed seven glowering, purple splotches scattered all over his legs, the size of tarantulas and just as menacing. John looked at them with an amused detachment.

"You know what causes them?" he asked quietly.

"I forget."

"Alcohol affects circulation. When the system becomes toxic, blood vessels break near the surface of the skin. It's a sign that the cirrhotic liver is about to shrink, which is lethal and irreversible."

"Are you scared?"

"Shit, yes! I'm terrified. It's breaking down my denial. I've got to quit."

"You're not doing anything about your hemochromatosis, are you?" I asked for the first time in a year. "That's probably progressing at a merry rate."

"It will kill me, even if I quit drinking, unless I get back on my schedule of phlebotomies. I'm not facing that reality any better than I am my alcoholism."

I wondered if Thom would have sabotaged John if he knew how close he was to death. As he sauntered off to his car, I felt his thoughts. *No wonder John can't live with her. She's such an uptight bitch, always spoiling our fun. She's not going to control us. We'll show her.* Little did he know how soon their games would end. And when it did, he forgot to blame the relentless pro-gression of their disease. In his mind, he held only me accountable for the ravages brought on by their madness.

After I purged the house of their toxicity, I settled on the window seat, staring at the ocean, filled with dread and despair. I was the only person in John's life, among friends or family, who knew exactly how little time was left. *The situation was bound to explode. I forgot how enabling it is to expect rational behavior from an alcoholic. Until John makes a commitment to absti-nence, this will keep happening. I have to clear the deck to do more work on myself.*

I did not know that John, angry and humiliated by the banishment, had stolen my bankcard just before he left the house. For the next month, he withdrew $400 from my checking account every day. My accountant never called it to my attention, thinking I knew. More than $10,000 later, I confronted John, who claimed to be broke.

"Where did the money go?"

"Hey, I've been in blackout for weeks. I bought some cheap furniture for my room and paid the phone bill."

"You're telling me you spent that amount of money in one month and you have nothing to show for it?"

Cocaine was the only explanation. This was the lowest he'd ever sunk. I kicked myself. *I've been an idiot, thinking I could play with John about sobriety. I was dead wrong to think if I kept my boundaries, I wouldn't get burned. You can't play with a drunk. It's like tickling a sleeping tiger.*

Johnny was chagrined. He apologized, concerned only that I still loved him. I noticed with amazement that my habitual level of fury and frustration had not been provoked. Poised on the razor's edge between death and recovery, we carefully measured each step in the grace period we'd extended to each other. I still loved him, but I knew what had to be done. *Sell the antiques and file for divorce. I can no longer call this man "my husband" with pride.*

Later, in his sobriety, we often shared the same unspoken train of thoughts, like a twin acid trip. A sense of synchronicity would cause us to marvel at the way our lives conjoined with the elegant precision of a well-crafted wristwatch. As we connected the dots that led us from confusion to wisdom, we understood the necessity of this last grisly pantomime. The pentimento of our mutual denial had to be scraped off by a lethal dose of reality.

I insisted that John pay me back the $10,000. "You stole that money from me, and I'm going to press charges if you don't."

I had often asked Thom and John what they wanted to do about the mounting bill for storing their antiques in Boulder. "Let them sell the whole lot," Thom declared. "I don't even want to think about it."

"I'll pay the storage bill and contact an auction house," I told John. "You take care of the authentication and sales. All I want is my money back."

I let him orchestrate the event. I did not want to be in the firing line if he or Thom ever sobered up enough to miss their beautiful possessions. I asked for a few of my favorite pieces to be shipped to me, making it clear that in doing so, I was rescuing them from the curious auction block. Since I was the only one who could afford the freight, John and Thom agreed they would be mine, no matter what happened between us. And so, the Chinese brush paintings, the Italian ceramic chandelier, the copper kettles, and Gwyn's Buddhas came to roost in my house. Johnny seemed relieved that a few of his favorite things would remain in the family.

The auction drew a flurry of media attention. Letters from Steinbeck to John and Thom were bought by collectors from all over the country, along with baby pictures, furniture, silver, and dishes. Thom never said a word. He knew it was either that or jail for John, which only served to solidify his resentment of me. I didn't try to spare them the pain of losing all that memorabilia. It made me sad, because they had so little of their birthright to begin with, but I couldn't rescue them anymore. It was a blood sacrifice for each of us. Unmanageability comes in many forms, and when it does, all you hear is *going, going, gone.*

"Looks like bottom to me," John said one night on the phone from the Temple. "Got any ideas where I should go for treatment this time?"

"What's different about your situation that makes treatment worth going to? You've already been twice."

"I was sitting here, wondering why I can't quit drinking. I picked up *The Big Book* and something hit me like a Zen koan. I can't stop because I'm an alcoholic! I can't quit on my own."

I had started working as an intake rehab counselor at Scripps Hospital's posh McDonald Center. John would not have fared well among the Yuppie, uppity patients and follow-the-yellow-line rules. A friend recommended Azure Acres, a small treatment center in Northern California. Unlike most facilities, she claimed they had a laissez-faire attitude that encouraged taking responsibility as opposed to being herded into strict compliance. I had a feeling John would respond differently to being treated as an adult.

And so, in April of 1988, John began the long, arduous process of getting himself into treatment. It took nearly four weeks. He couldn't have done it without a struggle because that's the way he did everything back then. He had to win the internal dialogue with his disease. He had to face his fear of the unknown as well as the known, the murky depths that lay beneath the leap. He called often for support. I just let him ramble on, mulling over the pros and the cons, until the former outweighed the latter. The noose was getting tighter; Tai was making noises about kicking him out of the temple. On his way back from the liquor store one night, he was mugged. A few days later, he was arrested for his third DUI. It was time for the stand-up guy to take a stand.

"You want the best Mother's Day present you could ever imagine?"

"Sure!"

"I'm signing into Azure Acres tomorrow. Will you fly up there with me?

I'm afraid I'll go into convulsions on the plane. It's down to the wire; if I don't drink a few ounces, I'll go into seizure. If I drink more than a few ounces, I'll go into congestive heart failure. That's how I spent last night, in the ER at Cedars Sinai. I nearly died. If I drink a few sips of beer every hour, it may be enough to keep me out of convulsions, but there's no guarantee."

I had to be strong. In the face of death, I could also afford to be generous. I wouldn't have missed that flight for the world.

"I'll take the train down to La Jolla and spend the night," he offered. "Get two tickets to San Francisco and we'll fly up in the morning."

I asked Thom to drive John down. "I'm afraid he'll go into convulsions on the train."

Thom refused. "Can't do it. I'm too busy. I'll drive him to the station and then he's all yours," he laughed, oblivious to the severity of the situation.

I shuddered. When Joanna, Thom's ex-girlfriend, was a teenager, she lost her mother in a similar attempt at sobriety. The mother had gone cold turkey, attended her first AA meeting, but went into convulsions and died as Joanna was knocking on a neighbor's door for help. I had witnessed several seizures at the hospital and knew exactly how deadly the situation could be.

There's a bar car on that train. I had no idea whether John would be alive when it pulled into the station. I took an AA friend along for support. We stood on the platform and watched the last passenger emerge. No sign of John. *Has he drunk his way into a coma? Is he alive? Asleep? Passed out?* I went home, curled up in a ball, and prayed. An hour later, Johnny called from the San Diego station. He'd fallen asleep. *One day at a time. One minute at a time. One second at a time. That's all I have to get through. Tomorrow he'll be at Azure Acres and I can relax. Please God, let it go easy for us. He needs a treatment center with a medically supervised detox, like Scripps. But he won't get well there, and this is his last chance. He's got to risk going into convulsions on this flight. He's got to court death one more time. I have to let him do it his way; I cannot fight him on this decision.*

Sober and jovial, John insisted we celebrate Mother's Day with a lovely dinner at our favorite Mexican restaurant in Old Town. Underneath his sweetness, as he turned all of his attention toward me, motherhood, and the children, I sensed his terror. It was much more about staying alive than staying sober.

In spite of the blade pressed against his jugular, we sailed through the flight to San Francisco and the drive to Sebastopol. Heartened by a feeling of optimism, the sparkling stream between us sang more sweetly than ever. As we approached Azure Acres, we were delighted to spy a gloriously auspicious rainbow floating above the redwood forest that surrounds it.

I stayed for lunch and could tell John felt immediately at home. The main building had been an old hunting lodge; the grounds were filled with nature spirits. The food was hearty and the patients looked surprisingly jovial. I was asked to attend their weekend family program in two weeks. As we hugged good-bye, I sensed John was entering the situation with a new meekness. I hoped that meant he would be receptive. Under the rainbow's end, we parted as the best of friends. We sensed the possibility that the depth of our love could still prove victorious. As I drove back to San Francisco, I felt the peculiar sense of detachment that comes from being forced to live fully in the present. *One day at a time, one moment at a time, one second at a time . . .*

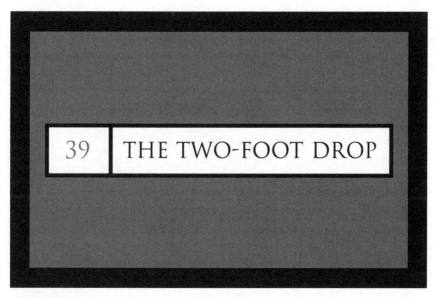

NANCY

T he treatment program at Azure Acres connects patients with their feelings in an honest, direct, and loving way. John settled in comfortably with the colorful mix of blue-collar types and professionals. His counselor, Kate, lived with an old Buddhist friend of ours, so she understood John's spiritual belief system. He couldn't hide behind the stumbling block of translating AA into Buddhism.

They call one of their basic educational tools the Two-Foot Drop. "I am learning to get out of my head and listen to my heart," John explained. "Another thing I really like is the way they describe the disease as a sleeping tiger. You can't mess with it. It will wake up and bite you every time."

After John died, one of his counselors told me, "For an intellectual like John, it's hard to turn off the mind and start following the intuitive process. Something profound happened to him while he was here. More than anything else, he came to believe in a higher power. Very few people have that kind of experience while they're in for their first twenty-eight days. It wasn't John's first shot at treatment, so maybe that is why he could hear it. He was in a place in his disease and his life where he was open.

"We work a lot on reprogramming a person's inner belief system. John was at wit's end with himself and wanted to get control of his life. He questioned everything presented. At the same time, he was open to listening to somebody else. He would ask, 'Why does it work that way?' as though he were genuinely curious. Most chemically dependent people are searching for something all their lives. When you get sincere in that search, whatever problems you may have, the power greater than yourself opens up and I believe that is what happened for John.

"He spent the rest of his life seeking and enlarging on his understanding of his higher power. I was sad to hear he died, but then after I thought about it, it felt okay, because he died sober. That's what all alcoholics and drug addicts strive for. That is the ultimate outcome of recovery, that we die sober."

During the first week in treatment, John had to write a wreckage list of everything that happened to him or others due to his addictions.

> There doesn't seem to be a way to fully answer this question. It would take as many years to complete as the years that I have been willful, believing that I had the power to manage my life. However, some things do stand out. I have wounded the people I love most both physically and emotionally. I have stolen money from my dear wife, arrogant with the knowledge that I could pay her back, but nevertheless not admitting the nature of the crime until I was caught. I wish I had been able to see my natural daughter, Blake, grow up; but I drank away the possibility of that situation happening by the time she was two. I have received three DUI's. I have introduced other people to chemicals that have served them no better than they served me. I have created blockages for myself and others by spreading cynicism as if it were THE intelligent approach to life. I have enabled fellow chemical dependents and codependents. In some sense, most of my wreckage has strewn a lovely garden with the nonbiodegradable manure of empty gestures. Many of my deeds have been socially inappropriate, and the wreckage has left a barren charnel ground, except for the love which is still in my life, from my wife, children, and friends.

While I was relieved to hear the depth of honesty in his amends, I didn't want John to rely on me for guidance through his recovery process. After a lifetime of living with alcoholics, studying the disease for a year, and now getting paid to work with them, I wanted him to find his own support system. "If we work our programs independently, then we can enjoy the serenity that will follow," I told him. Alcoholics are extraordinarily self-centered. There were times when he felt rejected because he was no longer the center of my universe. Although his counselors seemed hopeful, I wasn't totally convinced. I sensed he was still holding on to a corner of his disease.

My feelings were confirmed on the last weekend of the program. A friend of ours had come down from Los Angeles to teach a Buddhist seminar. We were having such fun, I decided to put off flying up north for another day.

"You said you'd be here the night before I get out," John pouted.

"Johnny, they won't allow us to see each other until tomorrow morning, anyway. What difference does it make?"

Like a child, he wanted to know that I was there for him, in that bleak motel room, with the sun beating down the windows. He panicked because he had lost his mommy; I was no longer waiting in the wings for his appearance in the spotlight of my codependence.

"My days of circumambulating the widow's walk are over. What are you going to do with all that frustration? Take a drink because I wouldn't obey your every whim? I'm having fun with Nina. Give me a break." By his reaction to that simple change of plans, I knew that John still had at least one more drink in him. Don't let any alcoholic tell you they're not controlling. They are freaks about it.

Rage hit me when I landed in San Francisco. Driving up to Azure Acres, I started boiling over. *Who the hell does he think he is? I've stood by him for nine years and it's still not enough. Oh sure, he can make the most beautiful amends. He's a sponge, soaking up every ounce of love from me and screaming for more, like an abandoned baby.* His disappointment that I favored the company of a friend to a night alone in a strange town caused me to suspect that once again, his participation in treatment was a farce.

He was leaning against a car, smoking, as I slid into the parking lot, spinning gravel. I saw the flicker of a sly little corner that held out for one more drink. *I'm not going to hold back this anger. If I do, we'll both be lost. He's got to adjust to the changes we're both going through.*

"How dare you treat me that way?" I hissed. "Are you jealous of our friends? If you think that's acceptable, you are no closer to sobriety today than when you came in here. You may have the counselors fooled, but I know you. You're a just few days away from your next drink.

"You tell everyone how sorry you are for how you've treated me. Yet you demand that I still play nursemaid. You've lost your option on manipulating and controlling me. I've been by your side, supporting your efforts during this month, not to mention the past nine years. You can't give me one lousy night of freedom. Your level of disappointment is way out of proportion to the reality of the situation and you can't even see it. I am not going to enable you by pretending this is rational behavior.

"I wanted you to say you don't ever want to see me stuck in a strange motel because of your disease. I wanted you to be glad that I was having fun with a girlfriend. Do you have any idea how lonely I've been for the past year? No, because it's always about you. I am sick of catering to your whims. If my focusing on my needs is so threatening to you, then I might as well just leave you here to figure out where you're going to live because I sure as hell won't wear your choke chain." I was so sick of his King Baby routine, I could have spit.

We found Mickey, a counselor, to mediate a sufficient détente so John could check out and get in the car. *I'd love to make one of these suckers a bet that John relapses within days.*

"This is a whole new ball game for both of us," I announced to Mickey. "He's lost the fawning wife who greets him with a brass band. We're done with the fanfare over John's attempts at sobriety. I have work to do, he has work to do, and the focus is off of him."

I turned to John. "If you can't live with that, I'm going home alone."

Noting his chagrin, and banking on the changes that had occurred during our separation, I took it to the limit. Now that I was a full-fledged therapist, John had developed a new respect for me. No longer the pitiful Al-Anon martyr who needed to get a life, I'd been accepted professionally into a world he was just beginning to master. Hired for my expertise on addictions, I worked with alcoholic patients, not their codependents. I had crossed the ubiquitous line of pride that many AA members draw between themselves and Al-Anons. Lately, I had heard him crow, "My wife is a counselor at Scripps McDonald Center." He was proud and a little in awe of my degree, of being hired by a top-notch treatment center, and for what he considered my Bodhisattva activity in trying to lessen the suffering of other sentient beings.

It was a crapshoot, but I played the hand well. Knowing I could see through him with X-ray vision, John rolled over like a puppy. In turn, I gave him one more shot. The victory of his sobriety may not have been won, but my personal goal had been realized. Working consistently to raise my self-esteem, both psychologically and professionally, I knew a time would come when I could hold my head high, turning my soap opera experience into on-the-job training about the disease. The pain I had suffered, combined with my education, had given me a special understanding about addictions that was met with respect and recognition. My job was a symbol of my inner work. It was an unyielding defense against John's abuse. Never again would this guy bite me like a rabid dog, pull a knife, lie, steal, or ridicule me. I had given up trying to change him. Instead, I changed myself. The payoff was golden.

John had signed a contract promising to attend at least one AA meeting a day and to find a male support system. That morning, I added another stipulation. "I'm not going to be your sponsor, your therapist, or your only sober friend. I don't want to work the steps with you. I started that process four years ago and I did it on my own."

I had seen many enmeshed couples continue to isolate themselves in early sobriety. The alcoholic claims to be working the program, but soon starts missing meetings. He forgets to call AA buddies and soon relapses into denial about his responsibility for working a program. Then the spouse is blamed for dragging them down. Another mistake newly sober addicts make is to seek understanding from the opposite sex at meetings. In this disease understanding kills. Men need other guys to kick their ass, not sympathetic women with soft shoulders.

"I really think you should go to a halfway house for at least six months," Mickey told John. "I'm not saying Nancy doesn't have a right to her feelings, but you need to be in a place of equanimity right now."

John insisted that he needed to come home. Given our style of leaning into adversity, we decided to give it a try. I went with my gut instinct, deciding I had nothing to lose. We spent several days in San Francisco enjoying quiet walks in Golden Gate Park, long exotic dinners, and AA meetings. Those days were filled with grace, celebration, and a burgeoning sense of gratitude that never left us.

Back in La Jolla, John attended one or two meetings every day for the first week. Then he decided to retrieve his car, which had died in the Temple parking lot. Thom picked him up at the train station in LA. I never bothered getting the story straight, something about a fight with the mechanic. I received the usual drunken phone call, in a tone of voice that told me it would take a miracle for him to escape their Cain and Abel labyrinth. *All that rage was simply my intuition screaming that he wasn't ready to quit.*

Realizing the need for a stronger support net, I consulted a psychiatrist named Gary Eaton.

"This is a matter of life and death," I told him. "I have a plan, but I need a professional reality check. If John should be in a halfway house, I would like to make arrangements for him to enter the best in the country. This is the last safety net I can provide him."

Gary did not waste time chastising me for what a lesser therapist could have considered enabling. He understood perfectly. "I can see how you would want help one more time, considering his health. You claim this will be the last thing you ever do for his sobriety. If you stick by that, I don't see it as enabling. If you don't, I'm going to call you on it."

I left his office knowing I had found a mature and responsible ally. Over the remaining years of John's life, Gary's expertise on the vicissitudes and joys of marriage greatly contributed to the pride with which we regarded our relationship.

When John called again, I gave him the names of several places that Gary had recommended. Once again, my task was to detach. The children and I struggled through Megan's high school graduation. We were tremendously disappointed that John couldn't be there for her. I held my head high during the dinner with Paul and his parents, but the psychic bond between John and me was sending out flares of desperation. I knew something was dreadfully wrong. Late that night, I called the Azure Acres hot line for solace.

"Nancy, have you tried to detach?" I was told.

"Only about seventy jillion times," I flung back at the woman on the other end of the line. I was sick of the glib slogans. Too drained to fight her simplistic condescension, I hung up the phone and cried myself to sleep. *One day at a time, one minute, one second . . .*

The next day was my birthday. I celebrated quietly, not knowing that John had spent the night back at Cedars Sinai, in congestive heart failure and acute alcohol poisoning, closer to death than he'd ever been. When he came to, he called.

"I guess whatever research I needed to do has been completed. I'm sorry I missed the graduation and your birthday." In his inimitable style he said, "If you give me another chance, I can promise you a lifetime of birthdays we can share, because now it's also my sobriety birth date."

I laughed. "The reason I'm giving you another chance is that I can finally hear truth in your voice. But no way will I share my birthday with you. Either drink today or change it in your head. You're not stealing my thunder any more."

He chuckled at the audacity. And so, Johnny came home for three miraculous years, for better and rarely for worse until the day he died.

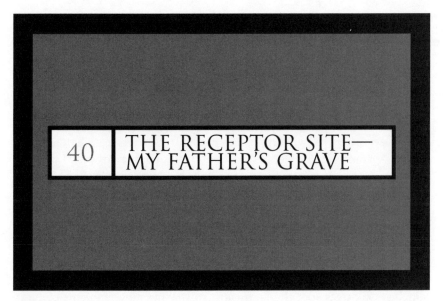

40 | THE RECEPTOR SITE—MY FATHER'S GRAVE

JOHN

So much time has since passed, but the sun shines even more brightly these days so I'm up early, outward at long last. After finally showing some kindness toward myself, my brain is beginning to heal. The wounds to the head and heart are reasonable and tolerable, though my mind has a stronger constitution than my body. Endorphines wave and drop by all the time now like old friends who have forgiven and put aside any estrangement that might have occurred due to an old quarrel over pain. Besides, the exact details have long been forgotten. Each new day has its own freshness, and its own solution. For no apparent reason at all, the stream of previously tangled thoughts present their own antidotes. Sometimes I even feel absolutely graceful treating my memories like fine Buddhist offerings of flowers and music. The goodness of equanimity sometimes now proceeds even wit, but still there seems to be the consistent invitation to try to understand what happened.

Churning through the past like a tramp freighter, I used to rummage around for insight, but the origin of my particular cargo remained a mystery to me. Fortunately, despite the enormous fear and the dreadful callousness that I had developed toward myself, I finally ran out of room and control. Grounding on bad chemistry and its diminishing returns when it came to manipulating my feelings, I suddenly experienced a genuine moment of clarity. Then I landed smack in the middle of my life and by God, it was OK. There was some spillage, but after flushing decades of analgesic support out of the system, when I could really taste the substance of me, I was surprised. I discovered that it was like molasses: rich, dark, and even sweet. Then I saw without any particular shame or embarrassment that it mingled with the deeper sap of my family. For the first time I was not so overcome by the kindred snake that kills by sight instead of bite. In fact it was never a snake at all; it was just a twig in the moonlight.

On October 5, 1989, I was driving as if floating through what my father used to call the pastures of Heaven. It is such a fine name for the rolling coastal land north of Santa Barbara through the Salinas Valley up to Santa Cruz. The ground is still and very dry now, compared to my father's time. In the fall, the lush green turns to ocher, but the easy, peaceful tone remains. Oak trees spot the landscape, soft insinuating emblems of tranquility. These lovely hills, so fixed in the memory of my people, swell and undulate like the waves of the Pacific Ocean that they border. Small ranches appear at the odd crest; naive impressions with simple fences running down like brooks. I think that this must have been a wonderful place to be a child, to have a pony, to love a dog, to skip stones with a frog in your pocket, and pull girls' pigtails.

That day was my daughter Blake's nineteenth birthday, and also the day when the Fourteenth Dalai Lama of Tibet finally won the Nobel Peace Prize. To me it was if he were given the keys to a kingdom that he already owned. I was filled with happiness.

Like a locust, I quite nonchalantly consume all events as being part of *my* story. So including my father's, I counted this reward as being the second Nobel Prize in my immediate family. And after all, Nancy and I were with His Holiness when he won it. The Dalai Lama is an example of much that I love, and my spiritual friend. I remain unfashionably Buddhist. I was a monk for a while myself before Blake was born in Vietnam, those long spiraling years ago.

As if pushed by a centripetal force, Nancy and I found ourselves driving north through Steinbeck Country on an otherwise leisurely mission to receive still more of the elevated teachings from the Dalai Lama in San Jose; hunting treasures, long buried and hidden in the mental continuum of the race. But this land, these pastures urged me to remember that despite my twenty-five years of acting out in an Asian kind of consciousness and devotion to an Indo-Tibetan lineage, *my* race, at least my event began with my parents.

As I got closer to the Monterey Peninsula and Santa Cruz, I began to feel somewhat teased. So many disparate spokes were converging at the hub of this wheel of time and family loyalties. Unlike Proust's cookie, this blitz of recollection seemed to be owing to Alfred Nobel's unique confection—dynamite. The earth actually quaked six days later, and a familiar mechanism began to purr creating a daisy chain of facts and memories.

At once I was on a ziggurat of association spooling up Ariadne's thread in search of a way in and out of what felt like a labyrinth laid out with real purpose by my forebears.

Like déjà vu, coincidence tickles the mind in a very special way. There is also a coy fallacy to coincidence, I think. When people like me feel a bit insecure, or they approach the death of cozy reference, or death itself for that matter, we need and take quick inspiration on the fly. Naturally anxious at such turns, we find cheap and vast resources of coincidence. It's always popular and mostly touted by people who always say with a sort of spiritual nudge and a wink, "I don't believe in coincidence," by way of implying divine intervention.

Since we are consistently getting mugged by the interconnected facts of life, coincidences measured by sheer amount are a dime a dozen. At random, order seems to abound. If you want something truly rare, find me something that isn't a coincidence. I'll sit up astounded.

Either way, it's a big thing for me, like a mental stutter. It makes me stop and take careful notice of the richness of projection. Also, there is comfort and something lyrically pleasing about the notion of coincidence. It soothes; it helps and reassures us that we are not disconnected from the world, even an awful world. They seem to rise and appear out of nowhere, though frankly I don't really believe in them. It's true that my mind lands like a drunken bug on these rosettes, but I also know that I am playing hopscotch on a rigged crossword puzzle. Most often, they are like good and sometimes expensive commercials in my handmade docudrama. But a big display, such as our ride through the Salinas Valley was turning out to be, is downright inspirational. It's as if these circuits were subcutaneously lodged in the tissue of the psyche. When the fuses are poked or prodded, a little army of coincidental lines radiates out like an immune system to ease or justify the pain of self-consciousness.

With little more than the touch of Narcissus, I catch myself jiggling the connections of my world. Interesting that my father had won the Nobel Prize in 1962 with Drs. Watson and Crick who had found and explained the structure of DNA; the mother code that carries her own hidden secrets; genetic secrets that wait like prophecy; garlands of emotion, genius, disease.

As I drive along in the car, I labor the point just a little bit more. It's a little like playing connect the dots. But of course it makes a very compelling picture. There is no special mystery here for me. After all, they're my dots. I put them there. Though like others, not letting the left hand know what the right hand creates, I sometimes may feign utter amazement at this harmonic convergence.

In its way, the whole thing could be a sad joke. But like acupuncture, this mosaic of pretense can sometimes bring relief from pain and disease without recourse to baroque denial.

Generally, my feeling has been that as long as you keep things in perspective and don't get airsick on "significance," one might as well get behind the little harmonies and take the raft merrily down a stream. Sure it's all empty stuff, but as the Chinese insist in referring to everything from Being to the hollow of a soup bowl, "Advantage may be had from whatever is there, but usefulness rises from whatever is not."

Since death and our ancestors tend to define some polarity, I have often noticed that sensations of coincidence are the psychic flotsam of charnel grounds. So at this point on the ride, more than just a little intrigued, yet not knowing whether or not the site was a common bead on a string of pearls or a jewel on a string of beads, I detoured for the second time since my daughter's birth to my father's grave in Salinas, California. Since by this time, I was already standing knee high in a field of home-grown free association, I felt a need and the freedom to communicate with my father about our life.

The last time I was here, I was frightened, or as I said to myself in those days, worried. In 1971 he had been dead for three years, and I had been drinking and drugging with a death-defying vengeance for at least six. Even by then at age twenty-five, I was already a really fine alcoholic and drug addict. I mean almost perfect, the best I could be. After all, I was in serious competition with my parents. Clean now, I wanted to receive some telegrams from home. I wanted to deliver some as well.

After exchanging a number of breaths with the space over the stones, I spoke to our memory. I had gone many places where my father had not. Independent of his rage or fears, I had cornered myself and was forced to face down many of my own. In this I had perhaps passed his mark. I needed to tell him that, here, where he couldn't bolt from me into his study, or die without saying good-bye.

I had always loved his light-handed way of delivering dramatic verse. I loved it that he could talk to us sometimes and be able to say at a picnic without so much as a blush, that he was "a rogue and peasant slave" and we should "sit upon the ground and tell sad stories of the deaths of kings." It was a great gift, and now I, too, can summon up this remembrance of things past. Now, for me it's time to sing those old Celtic blues again, those "sic transit" songs that make you feel clean, even haplessly wise.

Sometimes it's horrible and eerie, but sometimes it's quite wonderful when you feel your parents move inside of you. The smile, the grimace, the quick flicker of another's mind in yours. That sort of thread is so strong and irresistible, and in its queer pull, it is the tie that faithfully binds the molecules of lineage.

So now, at last I find myself trying to bridge heaven and earth with Welsh-Irish dots, with words. Alone, with all my ancestors gone, my history is all important. At my father's grave, a cascade of discursive thought and private myths course through my head to splash around with new authority, while coincidences twinkle and glow like the bright little motes of light that run up and down kindling paper in the hearth when the paper has been exhausted nearly to ash.

Since I always think I'm a tough guy when I'm not, at my father's grave I tried to make sure to carry some cynicism as Dramamine for the vertigo of significance, and to beware the rapture of the deep. It never works.

At my father's grave I remember something that I learned as incontrovertible truth at a mentor's knee. Beyond the realms of opinion, and beyond the customary requirements of memory or nostalgia, or even resentment, two things are known to be true. *Birds have nests, men have ancestors; and whatever thought rises from the heart will surely, safely, go to rest in the heart, forever.*

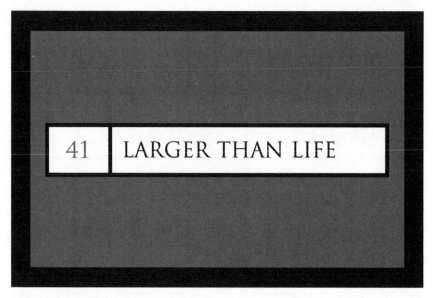

41 | LARGER THAN LIFE

NANCY AND JOHN

In most families, loyalty is defined as faithfulness to a person, an idea, a secret, a duty. In John's case, loyalty to his family of origin was perpetuating the myth that his father was the larger-than-life hero of his fans. In his proposal for his autobiography, John wrote for the first time about his lifelong struggle to individuate from his father's legendary persona. He felt more free to express himself fully because he knew his words would not be read by the public, and for that reason, I believe he spoke more intimately here than he did in his manuscript.

The reasons for attempting to write this book are not particularly noble or profane. The motivation could be summed up simply by my desire to live free from fear. However, the path leading to that sort of fruition has, along its border, a lot of fearful things that at first glance can cause panic, or resentment, or shame. There is also charity and sanity, which accompany this sort of voyage like good dolphins on a good quest. Frankly, I feel blessed that these guiding elements have never abandoned me and, as I and others continue to recover from the effects of my actions, I am encouraged that these qualities will endure, even shine.

I inherited two life-threatening diseases from my parents. Due to hemochromatosis, a genetic iron-retention disease, and alcoholism, I developed cirrhosis by the time I was thirty-four. It took me multiple slips as an extreme "low-bottom" addict and a lot of enlightened treatment to get me into a condition where I had the clarity of mind to be able to receive AA's help at all. Despite my lifelong dedication to spiritual pursuits, intellect blocked the road to surrender. Fortunately, when I truly accepted my powerlessness over my disease, the drama was over, and I could begin to understand the source of some of the behaviors that had taken over my life, apart from the fact that I am just a plain old alcoholic/addict.

Perhaps it is long past time when I should have expressed many of the feelings that tug at me due to the special circumstances of being my father's son. However, timing is not the forté of Adult Children of Alcoholics. Conflicting notions of propriety conspire to keep family secrets closeted in "borrowed shame" no matter how crippling or even lethal this toxic situation might be. Of course, this unconscious policy of Pavlovian loyalty (which seems to be universal) is accentuated when one of the parents is world famous. But further, when this wheel of shame and neglect and secrecy is perpetuated and actively enforced by a powerful, self-serving parent figure, such as my stepmother, Elaine, it becomes a devastatingly corrosive routine of abuse which then skewers love and memory. It would be more than misleading if I did not acknowledge the anger which I now have the ability to feel. Previous to working the first three steps in AA, I was drowning in perpetual resentments. On realizing my innate powerlessness over people and things, I experience a clean anger that doesn't fester with the need for resolution. This is great stuff, and it allows me to be more or less grateful in impossible situations. Naturally situations come down my chute all the time. An incident occurred just the other day which brought out this anger, as it was typical and clearly beyond the boundaries of acceptability or even common honesty.

It was around the fiftieth anniversary of the publication of *The Grapes of Wrath*. I had been asked to talk about my dad and that book at various functions in honor of the occasion, including an interview for CBS's *Sunday Morning* with Charles Kuralt, along with appearances at high schools and universities. Naturally I try to give readers insight into Steinbeck's works and some of the texture of his thinking. But, as you might imagine, due to some ancient paralysis, I keep running up against a dilemma. I find myself mostly talking in terms of what people seem to want to hear. In part due to my fear and family pressure, as well as wanting to choose the proper turf, I have remained circumspect about referring to the addicted side of my father's personality. This has been true despite the fact that several books currently in print about the disease of alcoholism and American writers named John Steinbeck as a case in point.

Anyway, a journalist who was recently interviewing me referred to my father as "arguably alcoholic." When Elaine Steinbeck got wind of this, she went to McIntosh and Otis, the literary agency which handles my father's estate, and attempted to rescind her approval for my brother, Thom, to develop Dad's short story "Flight" for a film adaptation. This was after he had already completed the script, and had nothing to do with the comment by the reporter in the paper to begin with. She went for Thom in order to get back at me. Her image, at least the image of the devoted acolyte behind the books, which she has assiduously cultivated since my father's death, is always at stake. And as will become painfully clear, her instincts are correct. Her dominance is probably nearing its end. She herself is very alcoholic, and her conduct as a stepparent to Thom and me has been outrageously sick.

It is unfortunate that this kind of thing creeps around the execution of this project but realistically it is just this sort of malaise that gives rise to the dysfunctionality that is at the core of what I need to express and go beyond. This book is not about grudges. Nor is it about being a hapless victim in an unfair world. It will be tougher and at the same time sweeter than that. As for Elaine, there is nothing I can do, unless perhaps she would like to go into family therapy with Thom and me. She would have to deal with the truth unprotected by the cunningness of this disease or her personal influence. Some day, she will have to face the truth, if only when she meets her Maker.

In short, the truth for me is that along with my father's destructive personality swings, which resulted from alcohol and amphetamine abuse, there remains Elaine's cavalier treatment of his children which has undermined almost all material, psychological, and spiritual connection that we have to the man himself, leaving us feeling isolated from ourselves and his basic decency; and perhaps even his true wish for us. He always told us that he wrote *East of Eden* for us. The messages about family and fathers and sons, as well as the poisonous principles in that triangle are hard to miss. These things are in fact part of our birthright as well as being part of the mythic archetype which I sometimes feel is implanted in the drama of sons and their need for resolution with the father.

In regards to the basic tension, the self-denial and self-destructive results of a potent regime of dysfunctionality is now well documented within the current understanding of family systems. In all cases, it leaves the survivors acting out messages and signals that can barely be recognized, and worse; it turns victims into offenders who go out and unknowingly recycle the whole vicious mess on a new generation. That is, if they live that long, or are not otherwise stunted by self-abuse of all kinds.

The only known fix for this kind of situation seems to be disclosure. Busting open family secrets without regard to reciprocity or reprisal can at least save what is left of our lives, and since no one else is going to do it, it's good that I begin. And since I'm a writer, I'm going to attempt it with art. Sometimes I feel hopelessly conflicted, and feel like I should understand or be beyond something. My feelings don't need to make sense on the hard turf of logic or be metered out with Republican prudence. I'm not looking for sympathy and we are not in court. As feelings, they are legitimate and stand on their own. Expressing them honestly is essential for the improved ecology of my mind.

I have this tough-guy stance which has often demanded that I take full responsibility for everything that ever happened, even as a child. But in truth, the damage incurred by being raised and role-modeled by untreated maniacs has been enormous. My mother looms violently in this three-ring circus. My father was a maintenance and binge alcoholic, though cross-addicted to speed and brooding rage. Mother, however, was always crazy drunk and deadly and sad. The abused little girl inside her acted out paroxysms of some devastating betrayal. She took no prisoners. Judging from her behavior with us when drunk, she was possibly an incest victim.

I love my father deeply. He had great kindness and humor. He taught my brother and me about so many magical things, and instilled in us the gift of curiosity. I have always been proud to be his son, and I am grateful to both him and my mother for giving me my life and the tools to interpret a wonderfully rich world. In spite of everything, I have been challenged to puzzle out my own fate with a large degree of poetic insight. They gave me this. It is not at all my intention now to break bubbles just for the sake of doing it, but rather to do myself a kindness, and in the long run, do my ancestors a favor and put them back in the realm of human process. As I try to do that with the gifts I have been given, the readers could share in that process.

To an undetermined extent, I think it is probably important for me to pass on a sober account of my experience for the benefit of others who face the same occupational hazards of being the children of the famous. In Thom's and my case, I believe that this was severely compounded by drugs and alcohol, and then open and flagrant threats of disownment, accompanied by Elaine's jealousy, manipulation, and greed. I certainly do not want to remain any longer as the apologist, despite my lifelong training for the roll.

These things are not questions, nor should they imply any request for restitution, or remorse, or even any response from the other side. Needless to say two of the principals are *way* on the other side in their graves. As for Elaine, the one who remains, with her stated intention to "leave nothing to the boys," I foresee a great shame and a crime of memory should the Nobel Prize sit on the mantel of an unrelated, illiterate Texan's ranch house, due to the fact that she feels free to continue to try to separate us from the nourishing aspects of our birth into a family that was never hers. A great deal of time has gone by where Thom and I endured the negative consequences of our connection with the "Conscience of America," only to be denied that positive connection to him, muzzled by Elaine's ego. Though it is clear that by now she thinks that she wrote the books, his name is mine, and that's all there is to it.

I wish I could say that this book was the story of my life, or the story of a life from the point of view of the son of a famous person. Or the story of the son of a famous person using the models available for understanding dysfunctional family systems due to chemical dependency or other addictions, a book about the symptoms such as sexual or verbal abuse. I don't want to write a book about that. Not exactly. The language of dependency and dysfunctionality as it pertains to family systems can be somewhat desiccating. It is a metalanguage. Used as a speculum in a therapeutic setting, it is extremely useful and timesaving. But, like Sanskrit, metalanguages can seem unbearably privileged. To the uninitiated they can be oppressive. I mean, who wants to read about Denial over and over again unless one understands that its main function is to relieve anxiety. Without that understanding, being "in denial" sounds scurrilous and a character defect of the worst sort. It would be fantastic if I could write this book without once using "recovery language" or Buddhist jargon, which is a second language to me due to a twenty-five-year immersion in the psychology of that tradition.

Putting this usage totally aside is a nice idea, but we also live in modern times, and readers are not so uninformed about things that this book should not be seasoned with some direct, if odd terminology; particularly if it is done poetically so that the words dance somewhat akimbo to expectation. Then it has this funny sort of strobe effect which can really grab at you. I think that if it is done lyrically, throwing it in could be like hearing a Japanese instrument rising out of a Western composition. It can stop your mind. This is how I want to use it here. Also, like the proverbial spade, sometimes a thing is just what it is, and there is no other word for it. *Grief* is one of those things.

The unveiling of my father's feet of clay is a one-shot deal. I don't plan to be the new maven of an endless string of talk shows. By offering some insight, the whole point of this is so that I can get free of it and get on with my life. I used to be stuck in my disease, and I don't want to be stuck in my recovery. I think that a vaster form of recovery is really what needs to happen in our society. The environmental issues such as rain forest and ozone depletion are examples of how we have grown to abuse all substances to include the planet. This is not a metaphor, but a fact. I don't want to sound grandiose, but it occurs to me that there are a vast number of people out there who may never read Alice Miller or Claudia Black, Pia Melody or Susan Forward. They just won't get hooked up with that kind of material regardless of the fact that they are suffering from a simple lack of information about the effects of being raised in a dysfunctional family. However, these same people may well be fans of John Steinbeck's novels, and out of curiosity, they may read this book and end up discovering that they have a common dis-ease, and that help is available through Twelve-Step programs and therapy.

I pray that this might be true and that I could have this unique opportunity to give away the tremendous blessing that I have received from the program and powers higher than mine. In this way, I will also be able to continue to fulfill my Buddhist vows, so that people may wash off a borrowed leprosy and be free.

42 GRACE NOTES

NANCY

It has taken me years to understand the correlation between traumatic relationships and spiritual evolution. Jack Kerouac's lover and Neal Cassady's widow, Carolyn, is one of the few women who can share this insight with me. Another is R. D. Laing's widow, Marguerite. Our marriages plumbed the extremes between abuse and ecstasy. The spiraling roller-coaster ride through deepening levels of pain and exultation required tremendous strength. Our brilliant, creative husbands didn't make it. As rage, indignity, and loneliness laid bare our shadow natures, we were simultaneously rewarded with passion, humor, and excitement. The centrifugal force of those dramas deflated our expectations and attachments. Swallowing intensity like a drowning man, our consciousness and capabilities expanded, and our faith was made deeper.

After Azure Acres, John and I noticed a marked difference in the quality of our recovery. Having lost the pink-cloud naiveté about living happily every after, we honored the fragile rituals that grant success. Gratitude replaced self-pity and depression. Quiet joy permeated our lives.

"You guys should bow to each other every morning in appreciation for the love you've found," Thom had once said in frustration when he heard us fighting. Johnny and I spent those final three years in obeisance to each other and our Higher Power. He went to daily AA meetings and formed a close-knit sober support group of men he could trust. I focused on my job at the rehab. Finally we were working our programs in sync, and there was no longer any need for a halfway house. We'd created our own.

Living in a state of grace, we began to travel and meet fascinating people again. That summer, Naropa Institute invited me to speak at a conference on recovery and Buddhism. John and I had a marvelous time visiting our old friends, and we made a new one. Terry Williams was the head of the family program at the country's foremost treatment center, Hazelden, in Minnesota. Allen Ginsberg had suggested we invite him to be part of the conference, as they were friends. The three of us spent long evenings together talking about recovery and the disease.

Terry's insight into the difficulties of loving an alcoholic helped me feel human again. He spoke of Al-Anon Abuse, the patronizing that occurs, as when someone asks, "Have you tried to detach?"

"Feeling the stress from loving a very sick person is not a character defect," Terry said. "Codependants are often castigated for their anxiety, which automatically lessens when the alcoholic quits drinking."

"Denial is a coping mechanism, isn't it?" I asked.

"It's a way of dealing with an untenable situation. The naked truth about loving a person with a terminal disease is often too painful to face head-on."

"I've always viewed denial as a way of cutting up reality into doable doses."

Terry's wisdom helped me shed volumes of guilt and self-criticism about the way I'd dealt with John's disease. Sure, you try to incorporate Al-Anon slogans such as *Live and Let Live* and *Detach with Love*, but to expect anyone to achieve the Al-Anon ideal without a deluge of tears and bloodshed is deluded and abusive. They would never offer the glib pieces of advice tossed at Al-Anons to the spouse of a terminal cancer patient. I had been railing against those insults for years and Terry's perspective confirmed my instincts. When you love a dying man, the grief process imprisons you. Thrashing like a hooked fish, your mind flops between shock, anger, depression, bargaining, and acceptance.

I told Terry about the insult I had received when a fellow therapist heard I accompanied John to Azure Acres. "I don't know how you Al-Anons do it," my coworker sneered. "Why didn't you let him go by himself? You're continuing to enable him by holding his hand." Terry's wince absolved my shame. The time we spent with him smoothed the ragged edges of our frayed dignity.

"An alcoholic is so much more than the sum of his problems," he said.

Our track record wasn't much better with our Buddhist friends, many of whom we lost in our recovery process. They were disturbed by our use of prayer and a Higher Power. We quit trying to figure out if we were *theists* or *nontheists*, as Buddhists like to call themselves. If our lives were miserable because we had failed to define a spiritual belief system that sustained us, then we were determined to find answers for ourselves, not in Buddhist textbooks. The program forced us to create a relationship with a power greater than ourselves. And professionally, I needed to be able to transmit my spiritual beliefs to my clients, who were lacking spirit. "You know how sometimes when you walk on the beach during a beautiful sunset, you feel touched by grace? Make that your Higher Power."

"My Higher Power is whatever makes the sky blue and the trees green," John decided.

In a spiritual freefall, trying to create a life without constant struggle and pain, we searched for new companions who would sustain and nurture us. One of the most painful breaks was the distance I saw John putting between himself and Thom. He did it kindly, so Thom didn't really notice much, but Johnny was definitely detaching from their mythic drama. Thom was involved with a bulimic woman named Esther, whom Johnny and I nicknamed "Fester" because she ran Thom through so many hoops. It troubled John that his brother was in another tortured relationship with no desire to stop drinking.

Finally, as Thom deteriorated, we did an intervention with the help of one of my coworkers, Mark Bornstein. Thom made an attempt to control his drinking during the last two years of Johnny's life. Ironically, Johnny never stopped worrying about the disease killing his brother.

In the summer of 1988, we joined Dhyani Ywahoo at a UN Peace Conference in Costa Rica, along with His Holiness, the Dalai Lama. John and the Dalai Lama had a special connection. Whenever he saw John, in a small gathering or a huge crowd, he would single him out and walk across the room to hug him, like a favorite child. It touched John deeply.

We spent marvelous hours with fascinating people like Father Thomas Berry and Robert Thurman, the Buddhist scholar. Our friendship with the Dalai Lama grew and we made plans to travel with him in California that fall, where he would receive the Nobel Peace Prize for his efforts to keep Tibet stable despite the Chinese invasion.

When the conference was over, the Costa Rican government provided us with a chauffeur and a translator so that John could gather material for some travel articles. We toured cloud forests; white, sandy Pacific beaches; the turbulent Atlantic coastline; and spent a day white-water rafting. It was an enchanting vacation.

That fall, a bombshell hit the Boulder Buddhist community when we discovered Rinpoche's spiritual successor, Tom Rich, had been diagnosed with AIDS. Although he had known of his condition for several years, he continued to have unprotected sex with scores of students as well as male prostitutes. He himself had been a Times Square prostitute as a teenager and had a penchant for seducing straight men like Kier Craig, the young son of a community member. Kier ended up infecting his girlfriend and died soon after. The group was instantly divided between moral outrage and staunch denial of any wrongdoing. While the adults fought amongst themselves, the children who had grown up with Kier could only ask "Why?"

The phone lines were burning up between Boulder and our house in La Jolla. We received daily reports about the political machinations as the organization sought to keep the matter secret, lest they lose favor with the general population of Boulder, as well as the world at large. When Rich came to La Jolla to do a retreat at a posh mansion by the seashore, we learned that he had been trying to seduce Megan's boyfriend, another straight young man whom we had known since his childhood. This hit too close to home for John, who was fiercely protective of Megan and Michael. A chilling story had recently been reported by one of Michael's teachers at the Buddhist private school. This straight, married male was pinned face-down across Rich's desk by the guards while Rich forcibly raped him. John feared Megan's boyfriend might suffer the same fate.

Infuriated by Rich's criminal behavior and the fact that once again, as with Rinpoche's drinking himself to death, no one was doing a thing to stop the madness, John decided to take matters into his own hands. Unbeknownst to anyone, even our closest friends, he picked up the phone and called the Boulder newspaper to break the story. Ironically, the reporter he spoke with immediately confessed that she had some very good friends in the community and she feared their wrath if her byline were on the story. John gave her a terse lesson on the responsibilities of a journalist and suggested that she find another occupation if she could not stomach dealing with the truth. Intimidated by his name, his reputation, and his razor-sharp insistence, she dutifully reported the facts as he fed them to her. Rich was out of control and needed to be stopped. If he couldn't stop himself, at least people would know not to have sex with him.

When the papers hit the street, and the story was picked up in syndication, the roof blew off the community. Twenty-year friendships were irrevo-cably shattered. Those who were outraged that Rich's attendants had stood by in silence for years while he had sex with hundreds of people were con-fronted by community members who vehemently objected to the accusa-tion that Rich was acting irresponsibly. Some even had the audacity to claim that if Kier had better karma, he wouldn't have been infected. These people were victims of their own magical thinking, as was Rich, who claimed Rin-poche had told him as long as he practiced meditation, his partners would be protected. "This isn't a matter of human foibles and a need for compas-sion for a sick man," John raged. "This is a matter for the police."

Just as when Rinpoche drank himself to death, when John and I ran out of the adrenaline necessary to metabolize the shock and anger, we were left with a terrible feeling of emptiness and heartbreak. How many friends would we have to lose? How much vilification could we take simply because we believed that a spiritual teacher has a responsibility to uphold moral and ethical principles? Yet, because of our own inner work and the distance we had put between us and the Boulder community, we were stronger this time. At the grocery store, tabloids were screaming the story of Jim and Tammy Faye Baker, which lent a humorous parallel to our Bud-dhist soap opera. We had a life; we had friends outside the vicious, closed circle of intrigue and deception. We had severed our affiliation to the cult of Vajradhatu.

Something about that phone call to the Boulder newspaper gave John a much-needed jolt of energy. He remembered parts of himself that had been long buried. The Saigon cowboy emerged from hibernation, stimu-lated by the thrill of breaking a story based on his commitment to telling the truth, no matter how sordid or tragic. He announced that he was ready to write his autobiography. Friends recommended a topnotch literary agent who was thrilled with the project. We flew to New York so John could inter-view a dozen publishers. Once again, we were ensconced at the Gramercy Park Hotel, with the usual veal marsala room service, but without the alco-holic haze. Johnny met with several publishers each day, and in the evenings we went out on the town.

"You're the most gorgeous woman in New York City," he announced one morning. "I see all these women looking so uptight and miserable. You have a freedom and a light in your eyes that make them all look blasé. You still have the eyes of a twelve-year-old."

Suddenly, everything fell into place. After a lifetime of procrastination, Johnny began to write daily. He was still attending AA meetings religiously.

The doctors at Scripps Clinic began a regime for his various physical ailments, including regular phlebotomies. They reduced his iron levels down to anemia as the hemochromatosis went into remission. Having lost the taste for La Jolla's pretentiousness, we found a house in rural Encinitas. On picturesque Crest Drive, which is lined with Monterey pines, the area reminded Johnny of Steinbeck Country in the early days, before the golf set moved in. Megan attended the Nova Scotia School of Art and Design in Halifax. With Michael in boarding school, although we missed both children, we appreciated the peace of our empty nest.

When I worked evenings at the McDonald Center, Johnny liked to attend their AA meetings. Mark Bornstein's office was next to mine, and when he was free, he and John would talk about painful childhood memories that had been unearthed by writing. Johnny found him very easy to talk to, and they taped hours of sessions. I had such a sense of peace and accomplishment during those times. When John died, Mark was my most supportive and understanding friend. He came over to the house the earliest and left the latest, content just to chat with everyone. He was there when the box of John's ashes arrived from the crematorium. I was so relieved that he wasn't squeamish. We looked at the coarse powder for a long time, sifting through the granules like kids playing in sand, silently remembering John's essence.

When he wasn't writing, Johnny lived in the hot tub. He'd be waiting there for me when I came home from work. This was our ritual; I'd sink into the water and snuggle in his arms. Then he'd debrief me until the rehab's relentless suffering sloughed off like dead skin. When he could tell I was coming back to life, we'd put on thirsty white terry-cloth robes and fix dinner.

On Friday nights, John always went with six of his friends to a men's AA meeting. Sometimes the women from work would gather at my house for potluck dinners. Before he left, John loved to put jasmine-scented turquoise dye in the hot tub. He'd pick gardenias and lovingly float them in the water, along with candles. It made him happy to create a beautiful atmosphere for my girlfriends and me. After he died, I noticed how some husbands don't like their wives to socialize on their own and it made me sad for the wonderful generosity I had lost.

John bought a creamy Le Baron convertible with a tan top, and we'd drive up and down the coast, with rock and roll blaring. He sang the most beautiful harmony. I used to treasure every note. *If he dies, I will miss his singing more than anything.* We'd invent riffs, like the Supremes, with hand jive and head tosses. We'd stop at our favorite seaside restaurants, where they knew to give us quiet, intimate tables. We lingered for hours, lost in the magic that had never left us.

That's when my fear started. I thought it was some vestigial paranoia seeping through the cracks of my recovery. I fought it and prayed about it, but it never went away. When we were driving with the convertible top down, especially at night, sometimes I was seized with a terror. *Something is going to take John away from me. I can feel it lurking in the shadows. This isn't rational. Am I going insane?*

Not knowing, only sensing, what lay ahead, I wondered if I would ever truly recover. Even Gary Eaton was mystified. Of course, when John died, we knew it had been a premonition of the tragedy. I wish I'd been more gentle with myself, for I was merely sensing death in the backseat. Johnny was very tender about my fears, perhaps because he'd caught a glimpse of the specter in the rearview mirror.

We took little trips to Sedona, Palm Springs, Lake Arrowhead. In Sedona, we offered prayers at all the places where we'd been torn apart by the disease. Johnny loved to show me the places in Palm Springs and Big Bear where he'd lived as a kid with Gwen and Gwyn. Closer and more comfortable than ever before, we sailed the highways. A cloud of serenity settled between us. There was always laughter, or delicious, easy silence.

Friends would comment that we seemed like newlyweds. "Especially when he gives you those puppy dog looks," they'd say. I believe John sensed then that he was going to die. He showered affection equally on me, the children, and the pets. Whenever we traveled, he liked to bring along one of the cats or our German shepherd, Sable. Sometimes he'd call and leave a message for the pets on the answering machine. He'd whistle for them, talking in the particular anthropomorphic style he'd inherited from his father. All three Steinbeck men were fond of long soul-searching dialogues with their animals. While riding in the car, when our standard poodle, George, would bark loudly, Johnny would threaten to silence him with a replica of his father's "Dogifier." Based on the one Steinbeck built for Charley, he described it as a series of harnesses, ropes, and pulleys attached to the backseat. Both George and Charley had the annoying habit of furiously barking at both two- and four-legged targets. They would wait until the culprit was safely past and then scream "I'll kill you! I'll kill you!" with nerve-wracking ferocity.

Johnny loved to play endless rounds of fetch with Sable while he sat in the hot tub. He taught her the names of all her squeaky toys. "Go get your taco toy," he'd command. "No, not the hamburger, the taco," and she'd remember that she spoke English. When she brought him the right one, he would throw it across the lawn. In response to his loud cheers whenever she caught one, she'd trot back proudly and drop it in the tub. Then he'd hold the toy just far enough under the water so she had to her put her face in, just up to her eyes, to retrieve it. Johnny had an adorable way of creating domestic bliss. I wish those lovely days could have gone on forever.

He always had time for us. Megan called him often from Halifax for advice on her art projects, or just to chat about life, the favorite Steinbeck family topic. When Michael was home, after a date, Johnny would be waiting to debrief him in the hot tub. They'd talk about everything silly and deep, about sex, drugs, music, morality. All the things a young man needs to hear from his father were covered in those conversations. They would cuddle and gaze at the stars, running the gamut from the big bang theory to blond jokes. Johnny was in *samhadi* then. A calmness had descended upon him that was palpable. It allowed him to be extremely generous with the ones he loved. As we look back, we often wonder how much he knew.

"Do you think he was even more far out than we thought?" Michael asked me the other day.

"We knew how far out he was. That's why we put up with him." I laughed.

John would proudly tell me about recurring dreams in which he died with the requisite mindfulness that comes from years of Buddhist practice. I never took them as signs, and if he did, he never spoke of it.

When our venerable fifteen-pound Abyssinian cat, Sluggo, tenderly brought John a wounded hummingbird, Johnny took it to the San Diego Zoo's hummingbird aviary.

When he came home, he announced cheerfully, "I'm going to Kitty Heaven when I die. Sluggo will be there waiting for me. Hummingbird Heaven is right next door and everyone there is so happy."

On our last Christmas together, John and I locked ourselves in the bedroom to wrap presents for the children. He had brought in a huge cardboard file box full of discarded pages from his manuscript.

"What's that for?" I asked.

He smiled cryptically. "If my father had saved a box like this for me, I'd be very rich today. I'm giving it to the kids."

Just before he shut the lid, he placed a piece of paper on top that said "CHRISTMAS IN HEAVEN." We were all a bit confused by that present, until the next Christmas, when he *was* in Kitty Heaven and we were still on earth, missing him desperately.

43 | ICARUS'S FLIGHT

FULL MOON IN GEMINI

Sidereal coincidences are conspiring now for sure
They begin to hammer sweetly at the harp on some Cosmic piano

The melody begins to roll over the home in the year of
Squares. You sort through the board games of Karma and dice.

Coincidence is your song and sword which nicks the
Cataracts from the eye of confusion. Linear insight turns
Sharp and defeats even its own foolishness.

Like sorting rubies, you process the touch of time and
Feeling, playing hopscotch on my soul. A tear twinkles in
The eyes of Compassion.

Full moon in Nancy, my mate and mirror friend,
While I was looking the other way, you snitched my mind,
And lifted my heart.

Love on your Birthday, John (1990)

LIONESS

The cubs are crying
They are after all
Still chewing on
Each other's ears

Papa smokes,
Takes a pee
And goes way back
To his spot to snore some more

She knows about hunger
Her nature is to hunt
Her nails are sharp
And she likes the exercise

A day without some blood
Is a day without texture
As she watches phenomenon
Chase its own tail,
She smiles the secret
That I
Love
Her

NONRETURNER

Please return or I will be lonely in this Beehive
Please return or I will be lonely in this Garden
Please return or I will be left lonely in the Pond
Please return or I will be lonely in the South Wing
Please return or I will be lonely in the Dresser Drawer
Please return or I will be lonely in my Bright Armor
Please return or I will sweat all alone in the Lodge
Please return or I will be lonely on the Battlefield
Please return or I will be all alone in Town
Please return or I will be lonely in the Asylum
Please return or I will be lonely in Paradise
Please return or I will be lonely in the Shoe Store
Please return or I will be lonely on TV
Please return or I will be in the Shrine Room
Please return or I will be lonely in the Amazon

Please return or I will be lonely on the Subway in the Bronx
Please return or I will be lonely on the Plane
Please return or I will be lonely on Christmas
Please return or I will be lonely in all Realms
Please return to me.

HEARTHHENGE

On the Crest Hill over the Sea
My Druid Priestess sings songs of
Love out of the deepest of Winter

Without her, this Taoist toad would
Never know the colors Blue, or Sable in
A wreath of wildflowers.

She is as faithful as her magic hound,
But most wondrous of all, we are still
Bound this Valentine's Day

(1990)

Besides poetry, Johnny also left little notes for us. He wrote this to Megan, based on a family joke. After returning from our year in Mexico, when she was three, we stayed with Paul's parents in California, waiting for the British Columbia snows to melt. Every morning, Megan would ask where he was going as he walked out the door.

"He's going to work so he can buy you some peaches," her grandmother would say.

From then on, Paul walked out the door as Megan called, "You going-to-work-buy-some-peaches, Dad?" Through the years, Paul and I had incorporated many of her cute sayings into our speech, and John followed suit. He presented this note to her with a copy of his autobiographical manuscript, along with a beautiful mohair sweater.

Dear Megan,

There is an old Egyptian legend that tells of a poor prune farmer who could not dig a living out of the rocky ground to feed his family. But he had a daughter who loved to follow the Angora and Kashmiri sheep herds and buy the expensive cloths made out of their fine fur.

One day she went to her father and said, "Why don't you get off your butt and grow something that has fur on it?"

The father thought carefully about this, and not knowing exactly what she meant, he decided to grow peaches. He became very rich doing this, and then later, his daughter married a prince. Which leads to the famous old Egyptian saying . . . "Behind every successful peach farmer is a princess who made it necessary."

So, my darling Daughter, this Peach is for you. I hope you can turn it into a ton of sweaters. I love you.

Here's an example of the silly little notes he'd leave me.

Dear Nancy

I was looking at a picture of you taken six years ago and it is true, I have to say you look just as pretty today as you did then. Honest . . . no change. I guess this is due in part to the Gemini thing, but mostly it is due to your basic cheerfulness. Maybe it is in part due to me, but logically, you should look like shit, if I was any influence at all, so it must be all you really. Anyway, I just wanted to say I love you, oh God how I love you, before I go off to my meeting.

After our meeting with the Dalai Lama in Costa Rica, John pondered the subject of his next book. Johnny Avedon, another son of a famous father, had written a book focusing more on the politics of Tibet. John wanted to write more about the Dalai Lama's personal life and planned for us to spend time at his home in Dharamsala, India. When the Dalai Lama received the Nobel Prize, we were with him just north of San Diego, in Newport Beach at a conference on psychology and spirituality. I accompanied John when he did an interview with him for *California* magazine. By that time, he was the only Tibetan lama whom we trusted. He seemed to throw himself totally into the benefit of all sentient beings, instead of advancing himself, politically, sexually, and chemically, like most of the others. I loved his deep voice and clarity of thought, his ability to listen and grasp the heart of the conversation, without an ounce of pretension.

However, there were disturbing notes in the interview which left us even more cynical about the politics of Tibetan Buddhism, which was just beginning to be recognized as the hottest religion, attracting such luminaries as Richard Gere, Oliver Stone, and the Beastie Boys. *New York* magazine called it "the decade's belief system for the cultural elite, which includes wealthy lawyers, Wall Street yuppies, and members of the Rockefeller and Luce families." Some Asian American Buddhists are complaining that traditional Buddhist teachings have become too Americanized by the white middle class. Helen Tworkov, editor of *Tricycle* magazine, wonders if American Buddhism is evolving into "simply another projection of the white majority." Having hung out among so many Asians, this was of concern to Johnny. We were developing a distaste for these chic conferences, filled with wealthy spiritual shoppers. John asked the Dalai Lama how he felt about the elitism.

"Sometimes people unfortunately treat these conferences like vacations and participate with beautiful speech and not much true commitment," he replied. "At the same time, such conferences raise the public conscience and awareness to peace, to the importance of love and compassion. In that way, there is some use for them."

When asked about the consciousness in China changing since Tienamen Square, the Dalai Lama misjudged the situation, considering the genocide and ecological disasters he is predicting now that the Chinese are flooding into Tibetan cities and Buddhists are still killed for possessing his photograph. "The freedom movement in China is very strong. Actually, the present Chinese government is excusing the event, saying that only a handful of people participated. I believe we will see a great change in the next five to ten years. I have met Chinese students and elders who escaped. Their attitude toward the Tibetan problem is much different from the government. After Tienamen, many Chinese attitudes toward Tibetan problems became more clear, and they are taking more interest. Now they start to doubt the government worship that's been going on."

We wondered if His Holiness was aware that many lamas were hoping he would accept a position as head of all the lineages, like a pope. This would create a system of checks and balances that was lacking when Trungpa Rinpoche and other lamas started abusing their power.

"I am a believer in nonsectarianism. I try to provide as much motivation as I can. I have no interest in promoting myself. There are no Dalai Lama centers, no Dalai Lama monastery. Wherever I can contribute, I am willing." To our dismay, he continued, "It is not the Tibetan way to confront errant behavior on the part of the lamas. We prefer to let them learn about their mistakes on their own."

Then Johnny asked him the big question. "You know about the situation within Trungpa Rinpoche's community. Our teacher died of alcoholism after abusing his power with female students. His Regent transmitted AIDS in a similar abuse of power to a young male student. Many of us have experienced extreme heartbreak and a weakening of faith and devotion. Can you address this problem so that other students may avoid these pitfalls?"

"I would say that if you are going to follow a teacher, you must examine his behavior very carefully. In your case, with Trungpa Rinpoche, you had a lama who was drinking alcohol. We say, in our tradition, that a lama is never supposed to drink. Now, occasionally there have been some teachers who drink alcohol and claim to turn it into elixir. If I were considering following a teacher who drinks alcohol and claims to turn it into elixir, or excrement to gold, I would insist on seeing this happen. If I saw it happen, I may follow this teacher. Unless I see that happen, I would never follow him. The student has to take the responsibility of examining the behavior of the teacher very carefully, over a long period. You cannot be hasty about these things."

While we agreed with him, as John and I left the lavish grounds of the Heinz ketchup heirs' estate in Newport where the Dalai Lama was ensconced, we admitted to each other that the only person in whom we'd hoped to find an ally had left us, and the Buddhist world at large, flapping in the wind. "No amount of Tibetan lawyer talk," John sighed, "is going to cover up the stench of underlying corruption. He can blame the student all he likes, but isn't that the same as blaming the victim in any abusive situation?"

"How is their cover-up any different from the decades of secrecy in the Catholic Church regarding their priests' sexual abuse of choirboys?" I countered.

John and I continued to be disappointed as the Dalai Lama and other lineage heads maintained their silence and offered no consequences to renegade lamas. By deliberately ignoring the situation, in what appears to be a fearful political ploy, these titular deities, these so-called God Kings are adding to the confusion instead of delineating clear moral guidelines. Their concern about the truth leaking out, which might drain their monastic coffers, flies in the face of all the teachings and vows they give concerning "right action." Will it be a matter of time before they follow suit with the Catholics in offering apologies?

As a distraction from the painful process of dredging up childhood memories, John wrote several articles about the Dalai Lama's visit to California. His creative process was tremendously healing. In a Steinbeck biography published after John's death, Jay Parini claimed that John never got over his anger at his father. Nothing could be further from the truth. When you read these excerpts from an interview that appeared in the *San Diego Reader*, you see how much Johnny had grown in forgiveness and fondness toward Steinbeck.

"Thom and I talked with Dad about many things, languages and history and cultures and customs. We traveled around the world with him. I had a great education. My father had a lot of eclectic interests, as do my brother and I. We inherited a love of words and communication from Dad. When I was not doing my homework in boarding school, I was reading encyclopedias. He made me think learning things was not a chore, not a duty, but a really exciting thing to do.

"I'm sure that there are all sorts of deep-seated psychological issues in my being a writer and comparing myself to Dad, being under the shadow. They aren't crippling at this point, but they're there. I am sure that for children of famous people, there's a certain amount of pathology that comes with the territory.

"Artists by nature are not particularly gifted as parents. They can be very self-centered, very abusive, and dysfunctional when it comes to raising children. So the kid has to raise himself. Dad never had to be a parent except on his time and on his terms, and then he was very good at that, very good. Very Huck Finny. Had he had to do it day in, day out, he would have failed miserably.

"Dad was a disciplined worker. He would get up at five in the morning, generally, and fiddle around with breakfast. Then he would sharpen pencils for a long time. He had one of the first electric pencil sharpeners ever made. He'd take a pencil, put it in the sharpener, and by the time he had them all sharpened, he had gotten over what all writers have, that morning inhibition about *Am I really going to put my mind on a piece of blank paper?* By the time his pencils were sharpened, he'd negotiated with all that. And then he would write, from six or seven in the morning until noon. Then he'd quit and go fishing or whittling or invent. I thought that was really enviable, that he only worked until noon. But he did it with a great deal of discipline. He didn't give himself vacations. He didn't gnash his teeth about stuff. He worked out a lot of his mechanical problems by writing letters to his close friends and editors.

"He had a very pixie sense of humor. He liked writing *for* things. So if he saw, say, an outboard motor that he wanted to have but didn't feel he should spend the money on it, he'd call the Evinrude company and say, 'I'd like to borrow one of your motors and use it fishing, and if I like it, I'll say I like it.' And then they'd give him the outboard motor. He thought that was one of the best parts of the job. Of course, he was well into the dollar-a-word category when this worked out for him, but he still liked being given things for free.

"He once wrote about racing oak trees. I was visiting him and saw, next to his writing desk, a baking dish filled with peat moss and rows of acorns, turned upside down. I didn't let him know I'd read the article, and I asked him, 'What are you doing here?' and he said, 'I'm racing oak trees. Well, it hasn't caught on yet, but if it does, I'll have one of the first stables.'

"It was so strange. He had a very funny private little thing going on, up in the attic where he kept his mousetraps. He'd have a plate of poisoned grain, with signs everywhere saying *Mouse Beware. Poison. Do not eat.* He was a very funny guy."

When asked about Steinbeck's response to the *New York Times* suggestion that the Nobel Prize award committee might have found a better recipient, John answered, "I'm sure his feelings were incredibly hurt, that he was pissed off. I think he had a certain amount of insecurity because he was a Western writer. He lived on the East Coast with the Ivy League literate crowd. He never pretended to be an intellectual. He was a shy man, and I think it made him insecure and then furious. They were such snobs.

"I do know that one person came up to him in Stockholm, when he went there for the prize. An East Coast-type lady said, 'I wonder how long it would take to earn $50,000 tax free.' He looked at her and said, 'Forty years, lady. I just did it.'

"He worked very hard at what he did. He was poor for a long time. His success of any remark was in his late thirties. He worked at a lot of things, manual labor, a night watchman. He helped pour cement for Madison Square Garden.

"Some odors remind me of him. A certain Florida toilet water. I noticed very pleasantly the other day when I walked into my office and it smelled like my father's office. Certain humor reminds me of Dad. My brother and I share a lot of his humor. Thom's quite like him. Walking down the street, without even thinking about it, my father would tip his hat to a dog. My brother does that, spontaneously and genuinely. When it's most touching is when you see your own hands picking up something in a way that your father or your mother did.

"I communicated better with him after he was dead then when he was alive. After he died, I got some writing lessons from him. I got some lessons about how to deal with people, sometimes by reading something he told to someone else. The most gratifying thing he gave me, both before and after he died, was to know that the most refined, highest wisdom and human knowledge is found in the everyday ordinary world. Not in a library of Sanskrit, not at Oxford, but from the guy down the street. That guy knows as much. The common wisdom is the most profound. Ordinary mind is enlightened mind. Fortunately, my Buddhist training reinforced that truth.

"Not that my father didn't believe scholarship was useful, but that it had its place. If he needed to learn something about the language of the

Middle Ages, he would go to the books or scholars who could teach him, but he did that only so he could learn what ordinary people said in the Middle Ages.

"The first time I saw *The Grapes of Wrath* was when Dad screened it for some guests. I was quite young. It was the most depressing thing I'd ever seen in my life. Later, when I was a teenager, I read it and was equally depressed. In the seventies, I was holed up during the monsoon in an old French hotel in Vientiane and I read it again. That's when I got the most out of the book as a writer. By that time, I was writing. So then I actually saw how deft he was. I saw the nuts and bolts of the writing. That was as impressive to me as the historical value of the book, making America aware of the Dust Bowl and Depression from the farmers' point of view. People think of Steinbeck as being 'oh-so-realistic' and really catching the sound of the way people talk. If you look at the book closely, nobody talks like that. It's a big kind of cartoon in the fresco sense of the word, an overdrawn image of the way people *might* talk.

"But by the time it filters down to you, it sounds real. Kind of like Chinese political theater, it's supposed to reach the guy in the last row. It resounds hugely."

When asked about his father's attitude toward the Monterey Peninsula, John said, "He wasn't the town's favorite son. They didn't like him. His works were not well received. People were outraged that his characters were loosely based on real people. He'd be confused and amused by the homage now being paid to him. There was a long time when he couldn't even get arrested in this town. Even after winning the Nobel and the Pulitzer, many local people refused to acknowledge him as an important writer. Now he's an institution.

"Back when he was writing about the Peninsula, he felt rejected. He was very discreet when he came back to visit relatives in the area. There were no bands waiting for him. Today, the hostility of the community has changed. I don't think those feelings exist anymore. Now he's a hero, but when the stories were written, residents were sensitive about what they saw as their portrayal in Steinbeck's combination of fiction and nonfiction.

"Every square inch of the county resounds deeply for me. It almost seems genetic, because of my father's books. Last time I was here, I was attending a ceremony for the issuance of the John Steinbeck commemorative postage stamp. In a strange confluence of history and coincidence, Cesar Chavez was also in town at the time and there was a lettuce strike going on.

"What was extraordinary was to be in front of the Steinbeck Library, where the podium was set up in sight of a strike demonstration just a block away. No one at the stamp ceremony seemed to make the connection between the strikers and Dad, who chronicled farm-labor struggles here in the thirties.

"I'm not criticizing, just pointing that out. I'm sure that in New York tonight, many people will see the current Steppenwolf production of *The Grapes of Wrath*. As they leave the theater, they'll step over some homeless person and not even make any connection to what they've seen, and probably been very moved by, on stage."

On the day that we got the word that he was getting a sizable advance from his publisher for his autobiography, Johnny wanted to visit the Paramahansa Yogananda Ashram near our house. We loved to sit in the lush gardens and stare out at the ocean. "I need to meditate about the future and what this book is going to bring us."

I have to admit, while I was sitting there, I mostly thought about the money. Johnny and I had a penchant for living well, and we had been planning to spend a year in Tuscany after the book tour. When we were driving home, he said quietly, "Writing this book is going to bring me to the Source. All I saw was God." That evening, he wrote this letter to his inner child.

Dear Boy,

I have wanted to tell you about myself and where we come from for a long time. I thought that I should wait for a sign that you were old enough to understand, but I have come to think that I am not the right judge of these matters. So believe me, the fact that it's your birthday is more poetic justice than some insipid bequeathal on my part. You are far more than just a clever boy and I am sure that you will be able to use whatever part of this is appropriate to you. The stories are free and clear, and I really don't have any fear for slippage in their application or interpretation. As your Tibetan and Indian ancestors say, "Even when the most beautiful bird flies in the sky, sometimes shit falls on a stone." I think they mean by this that understanding happens all by itself; independent of the intentions of the source, or the relative merits of the recipient.

Speaking of flying, I want to tell you about your secret name, Icarus. Some people will tell you that you are named after a hapless fool. Don't believe it. This is the propaganda of old men whose penises have shrunk like salted slugs out of fear. Some will tell you it is the story of recklessness and rebellion over common sense. They will tell you that disobeying his father, Daedalus, Icarus flew too near the sun and the wax on his wings melted and that he plunged to his death into the Aegean Sea. In truth, his body was never found, only the insufficiently functional wings that

Daedalus had fashioned for him. As you know, they were both trying to escape the Labyrinth and the monstrous Minotaur of Crete, both of which Daedalus also had a hand in creating it seems.

Anyway, the myth of Icarus is extremely colorful and full of symbolic meaning no matter what version one chooses to follow. Contained in it are the thoughts of imprisonment, and intellect and love, as well as grief and transcendent vision born of courage and genius. We all love wings because we know by instinct that, in the sphere of complete happiness, our hearts will enjoy the power to wheel through space as a bird flies through the air. Inasmuch as it's your name you might want to look into it. But since we have all had a hand in creating each other, let me give you my take on the story.

I don't think that Icarus's aspirations were too high. He knew enough about his homeland of Greece from his father who had been the most famous craftsman of his time and who had been hired by everybody to solve their problems mechanically. Most of the inventions worked fine, but like the wings (and the fake cow that the queen of Crete had him construct to attract the bull that resulted in the Minotaur) an awful lot of them seemed to have a skewered effect farther down the line. This was hardly his fault. Daedalus was a craftsman, and though he was extraordinarily gifted and sure of himself, he was not a seer.

But that part doesn't matter too much. Icarus did not just want to go home. I believe he yearned to go to the source of life, the blazing mystery. He wanted to live in the very life of life, and so he caught a thermal that matched his inspiration. The son set off to the Sun. True, there were some technical problems, but as I said, they never found the body, only the busted wings. I choose to believe he made it.

Like his father, Johnny kept a journal during the writing of his autobiography. Here are some excerpts:

10/14/89

So here I go with a journal of my autobiography. It's six in the morning. "Off to work early" as Dad would say. This is the way he started his workday, though with him it would start by sharpening pencils, writing letters, or crafting lies and emotions that would most certainly be read later and considered art, a treasure. That guy was smart, I'll tell you. It did so many things at once, this keeping a journal business did. Not the least of which was to establish a discipline that he could measure and fuss about.

So, I'm going to try it, Dad. This may be the only entry in the whole fucking thing, but I'm going to try it. I won't be able to go fishing later in the afternoon, like you, yet. But the rest, I will try. Your treasures and legacy obviously weren't in cash, so perhaps if I imitate you I will grow to be like you. You know, like Buddhism. So, like a monkey imitating a man imitating his father imitating his guru imitating the Buddha, maybe we can get somewhere with this and forge the outer container at least. My prayer this morning to all the higher powers that guide my life, including the ancestral powers that include, but are greater than even you, Dad, to all this I pray that I might have the willingness to stick to this form till I get this out of me. Grant your blessings. I supplicate my entire immense lineage, spiritual, corporeal, genetic, and sublime. Please grant your blessing.

10/15/89

This is so difficult. I just pray that I have the discipline to continue it. Our old Buddhist friend, Duncan Campbell, called this morning. Nancy and I talked for three hours with him about Vajradhatu dysfunction, group and individual denial, Rinpoche's sickness, the spread of it, and on and on. One thing becomes so clear to me and that is my instinctive resistance to breaking out of my abused child mold. More exactly, the will is there but the folds of the covers that I have grown to protect myself from a cold, naked view of the situation are incredibly thick. The body of this work so far is a perfect example. Yesterday's writing session is almost indecipherable. This journal is a great idea. I don't feel such a need to "write" here. I don't have the urge to encase my feelings in poetry and intellect as much. I know that Dad did it even in his journals. He lied like hell in them. He knew they would be read. I openly hope that this will be read, too, but I will try not to lie and aggrandize my motive as much as he did. This is in fact the only way that I can get through the business of writing my story.

If I think that my self-conscious writing style constitutes the truth of what I feel, then I am in worse shape than I think I am . . . and I think I'm in really bad shape as it is. My hope is that I am Gemini and schizophrenic enough to do both things without destroying the fruit of one or the other. So for now, today I will see if I can unravel yesterday's "written" page and move on a bit. As Dad would say, I got off to a slow start today, slept longer than I wanted to, and there was that call that went on for hours with lawyer Duncan filing his brief for the first time in a couple of months.

(Later) Well, I got through to a little "honesty" at the end of page 2 and have established that I am pissed off at least without wasting too much more time in the ozone. See what happens tomorrow, I think. I've had enough of me, but my office got a little cleaner and I got some more light in here, thanks to lamps from TARGET.

10/16/89

I spoke to Rick Fields this morning to try to find a chink in Duncan's grim view of My history. With all this adult child of an alcoholic stuff coming up, the stuff that is, in fact, the spine of this book, it was just too painful. I have a need to minimize the situation within the Vajradhatu community. Then I find myself around every turn in the river trying to sabotage myself. I don't want to see things clearly about my family either. The whole thing is so cunning. I could easily use even this journal to deflect myself from my own purpose, which is to write about the truth of what happened.

All right now, back to the writing. Time to describe some of the so-called coincidences that I then go on to spending so much time and effort to debunk. I have no sense of order. I'm just groping in the dark and one of the main reasons my agendas are hidden is that I don't have any light.

(Later) Well, I lost my cat twice today and roasted a chicken. Actually, I feel like I lost a chicken and roasted my cat twice. I seem to be very unsteady on my feet. I am stumbling around like in a silent film comedy, and it's hard to get the cobwebs out of my head. Not much work done except in my heart about me and the cat. I did get a little farther making sense out of the first three pages. See what happens tomorrow which will be:

10/17/89

Well, to start with, I hope there are no cat issues to deal with today. I can barely deal with the John issues. I'm appreciating the heirloom of this journal technique more and more. This is only the fourth day, but I can get my hands moving, and my brain into my ass and fingertips without just staring out the window.

10/18/89

I had a strange, perhaps healing dream about Dad last night. The details are fading fast, and really only two things were important enough to remain. We were preparing for some sort of gathering. He was trying to establish his moodiness and I wouldn't play, so he hit me over the head with a table. He was terribly tall, so I had to crane my neck to look up to him and speak. I started telling him he was full of shit, but I got tired of looking up. Almost casually, I forearmed him in the groin, and, as he buckled, I told him that the days of his domineering techniques were over. He was totally shocked by the blow, and further astounded that I was cogent enough to know where he'd been coming from. The worm had turned, and though I was sorry in the dream for having hit him, I was also pleased with myself for having interrupted the flow of his complacence about his own anger.

I have never kept a journal, with the exception of the one that Terrence McNally made us keep on the long trip with Dad. This is the first time I have tried to sustain this sort of discipline. There is something that feels a little forced, even phoney about it all. I mean, why bother to write this stuff when I can just think it. Perhaps I will return to imagining that this is the greatest thing in the world by tonight.

10/19/89

Before I get down to anything here, I have to write an antique store in Boulder to authenticate some of the last family heirlooms so they can be sold. It is very painful. Not the selling of it, but I have been so badly ripped off in the past, the whole business pricks memories of MY unmanageability to such an extent that I want to whistle or something . . . you know, like you do when a memory of what you did in a blackout drunk comes back to you. Jesus, I hate this shit.

On Saturday, I'm going up to LA, to Pacifica Radio to read the first chapter of *The Grapes of Wrath* for a group that is going to raise money for the homeless. I am looking forward to that, though it brings back many issues of Elaine's cachet with the name that I don't have. When I am through with that stuff, perhaps I will be able to get back to putting a few words down on the book, but there are no guarantees. Nancy is home today, and though she has PMS and behaves like a Bouncing Betty Mine, I love having her around nonetheless. Codependency? Who cares?!

It appears that I may have to be three not two people to accomplish this work: recovering alcoholic with adult child of an alcoholic issues, writer, and strategist in finding a publisher and an advance. Whatever it entails, I suppose that I should do it and not make my head spin about motive, sequence, or how many roles I play. This is not so horrendous a task for a Gemini so I don't know what I am complaining about really. Probably just to complain, as usual. Whatever is going on with me and this, there always seems to be someone deep down there who is minding the store, and knows just exactly what is going on. I hope it is God and not me because I will fuck it up for sure.

10/20/89

I went up to LA on Saturday and did the thing for interview for Charles Kuralt's *Sunday Morning* show and the reading for KPFK radio. I was not happy with the TV thing. The interviewer had no energy whatsoever, and I felt as if I had to do all the work, and I just couldn't. Perhaps they will save something from it, but I doubt that it will be scintillating.

This week, I must do the piece on His Holiness or I will feel bad.

Later, or in between times, I will look at the Dad thing here. I love it, "the Dad thing." Christ, what people we are here in this century. I can't even bother to put a whole sentence together to describe an activity of the mind. We's in BIG trouble. Like, you know, "the big trouble thing."

11/16/89

I have to go see the doctor today to find out just how lethal my various genetic diseases have become. I have only really addressed my alcoholism, but I know that the Hemochromatosis is slowly doing the job. It depresses me if I let it. Then I think of the Dalai Lama's advice and that helps. If you can do something to change depressing circumstances, do it. Otherwise, don't worry, because it never helps. I just called my lawyer. He'll call back. Then I called my agent. She'll write back. I also called the Mormons for family junk about Steinbeck genealogy. They'll pray back, I suppose.

They're talking about a sizeable advance, which I'm trying to think of as a present from God, because He loves me, and I hope I will use the money wisely, for the benefit of sentient beings. I know that I want to get Thom some health insurance, me a fax machine, Nancy a Movado watch, and that's about it. Most of all, I'll use the money for us to live on and for me to write on and produce a really fine and unique book.

I probably will need some sort of outline. It could start in the present and work backwards, as in the ". . . let me tell you how it all started" style. Or, ". . . when I was a child of three, I used to see what looked like a big monkey on my wall, which gave me my first taste of barbiturates to get me to sleep." I don't know. Perhaps that would be needed. Probably I will need to do some reading of others to get a handle of the possibilities.

I have a great fear of becoming paralyzed with acceptance. I mean, it's not exactly like I have had this happen all that much before. Part of it is mythical, and then I feel as if I am being romantic about levels of neurosis that I don't even have the track record to actually have. Then I think this is further negative programming that I somehow perversely do all to myself. What am I afraid of here? I am afraid of the money. I am afraid that I am no good. I am afraid that I will not be able to remember the things that are necessary to flesh out the story, and that I will not have the skill to do it properly.

Thanksgiving 11/23/89

This was our first Thanksgiving without the kids. Nancy and I decided to celebrate it together, without guests. I put together a little turkey with dressing and while it was roasting, we went for a drive up the coast. It's been light and peaceful. Nancy's in bed now. The stress is mounting, and it's not always coming out in pretty ways. Last night I dreamed that Dad and I were in Vietnam somewhere, and he was critiquing my writing. It was sort of fun, certainly entertaining and picturesque, though the colors were somber, and there was some heroin involved. That is, the desire to score again. Those dreams don't go away immediately.

When I awoke, I started thinking about Elaine and Thom's relationship. It began to dawn on me how fucked their collusion really was, and how my denial about it, or to be more precise, how my minimizing the events has been very responsible for screwing up the flow of goodness from my father to me, along with any number of other emotional complexes, due to Elaine's shamelessness and Thom consistently caving in to her.

Now I am really angry. For instance, how could she have been executor of the will, looking out for our best interest? There must be something that my lawyer can do about that. I am really pissed off. I blame Thom a little bit, too. The problem is, I don't know where to start or stop with this blame thing. The best thing would be if I didn't start, but that just isn't going to be true for me, and that sort of pious trip is the very thing that has kept me frozen for all these years. I feel that there is a therapeutic need to blame them.

That was the last entry in Johnny's attempt at a journal. He decided to turn his full attention to the autobiography. It took him a year to complete the first half. He polished his words with the care of a jeweler. Often he brought me his work, a page at a time. He called me his cheerleading muse. I wish mine were so loving; she tortures me mercilessly when I don't write.

When the end came, it was quick. Seven months before he died, Johnny started to notice that he couldn't read freeway signs. He complained they were blurry. We were shocked at the diagnosis. It was diabetes, often a side effect of hemochromatosis. Johnny was crushed. He'd worked so hard on his health since he'd finally gotten sober, and now it seemed all in vain. Sticking to a strict diet, he carefully monitored his blood sugars, and within a matter of weeks he was able to get off the medication. That did not stop the death knell from sounding.

We joined an exercise class in the fall of 1990. After a month, Johnny's back went out in the same place as before. He consulted with a doctor who prescribed physical therapy, but when that didn't help, we went for a lethal second opinion.

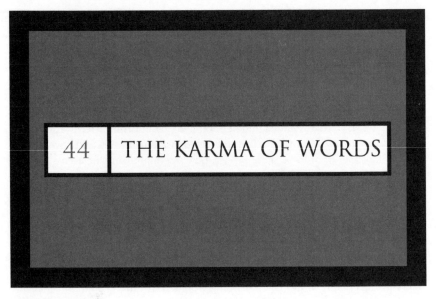

44 | THE KARMA OF WORDS

NANCY

Flash forward eighteen months after Johnny's death. I am sitting at a long conference table with the downtown skyline and San Diego Bay outside the window. Flanked by six lawyers who are deposing Megan, Michael, and me for the malpractice suit we have filed against four doctors and the hospital where John died. Dan Deuprey, the lawyer who represents John's orthopedic surgeon, has just succeeded in reducing me to tears with his sarcasm and innuendo. I ask to be excused from the room. Since he's there to defend the doctor we believe to be most responsible, he is merciless with me. After I leave, one of the other lawyers turns in anger to Deuprey. "Do you think you were mean enough to her?"

The sarcasm goes right over his head and he smirks. I'd been warned about lawyers like him who thrive on attempts to strip family members of their dignity in order to save money for the malpractice insurance company. I was warned that the defense lawyers would tear my life apart. Michael Kaplan, my lawyer, is there, holding my hand through all of it. We have become very good friends. Three days later, at the end of the twenty-seven-hour-long deposition, the court reporter tells me she has never seen a lawyer be so sensitive to his client's needs.

For four years following Johnny's death, the defense lawyers tried to level me. They pried into our lives, attempting to prove that Megan, Michael, and I didn't have a strong enough relationship with John to warrant any financial consideration. They demanded to see Megan's diary, and a list of each gift and every dollar Johnny had ever given us. Thinking this would force me to spend hours going over our bank statements, I frustrated their efforts by stating that Johnny gave me all his money to manage. They obtained confidential records from every therapist we'd seen, desperately trying to prove there was no love in our family.

"What right do they have to pry into our personal lives this way?" I asked Michael Kaplan. "The marriage isn't on trial here. We're talking about mistakes made by the doctors."

"If you deny them access to the records, they'll accuse you of hiding something," he explained.

That night, after two days of depositions, Deuprey took my lawyer aside. "Tell Mrs. Steinbeck she might want to leave the children at the hotel. I'm going to be attacking the marriage."

What those guys didn't know was that after we filed the lawsuit, an anonymous typewritten letter arrived at Kaplan's office.

To the attorney for the Steinbeck case:

Too many times hospitals cut corners and costs. It is only when someone dies that these areas of neglect are evident. _____ Hospital relies on it's "reputation" to get around many quality of care issues. What happened to Mr. Steinbeck was below the standard of care.

Here are some items that need closer inspection
1. Was there a crash cart in the OR? NO.
2. Was the OR staff familiar with it once it came into the room? NO.
3. Was a code called? NO. Why not?
4. Why is there no official code blue record as required? NO. Nothing was filled out.

There is a large liability all because the hospital did not want to spend dollars on lifesaving equipment. Ask the nurses.

When the doctors heard that Ralph Nader's group, Congress Watch, had asked if I would testify before Congress and Hillary Clinton about the rights of malpractice victims, their lawyers threatened me with slander suits. No matter how much they tried to torture me, nothing was going to stop me from seeing the lawsuit through.

Just before the operation, Megan had asked John if she could use his X rays and MRI film for an art project. A kind nurse provided them after his death. In the envelope, we discovered the written results of a chest X ray. "Abnormal finding in the patient's pulmonary vascularity. CAT scan recommended." That's when I called Michael Kaplan. For months, I spent a nightmare existence pouring over John's autopsy reports with my lawyer, learning the size and weight of his lungs and brain, the lengths of all fourteen scars, and the ways in which they had compromised his medical care.

Back in the conference room, I dried my eyes and was ready to resume the seventeenth hour of questioning. Deuprey leveled his guns at me again. He asked questions in a flat, needling voice, hoping that I would eventually wear down under his sneering. His nonverbal message was, "You're just a pathetic widow. What right to you have to question the authority of any doctor?" All the other lawyers had been extremely polite, but I could tell that their egos weren't involved the way his was.

Deuprey looked at the doctor's record of our first visit. "The next sentence I'd like to bring to your attention in this medical record dated January 17, 1991, is as follows—do you have that in front of you to read along with me—'I have advised Mr. Steinbeck that because of his medical problems, i.e., hemochromatosis, diabetes, and obesity, that we will need medical consultation preoperatively.' Does that appear to be an accurate account of the conversation you and your husband had with Dr. L.?"

"When we saw Dr. L., we told him about John's complex medical history, as well as his bouts with congestive heart failure, which aren't even listed here. Nor does the doctor say anything about our repeated requests for him to get all of John's medical records and to consult closely with an internist concerning the results of John's pre-op tests. We asked for all that to be done before Dr. L. decided to go ahead with the operation. None of that was done. L. might as well have put a gun to my husband's head." I knew Deuprey didn't like me talking like that, but it was interesting to bait him. He hated women and, sadistically, I wanted to remind him why. For the most part, I was imperious. Johnny taught me that one well.

"If he took my husband's medical condition and his life seriously, he should have ordered John's records from Scripps Clinic. We would never have consented to the operation had we known that they had not reviewed those records, let alone that they had ignored abnormal test results."

Over lunch, Kaplan said, "Deuprey never wants to face you in front of a jury. You're too good. You'd have their sympathy. You're the kind of witness he'd rather die than cross-examine." Since Johnny signed an arbitration agreement before the operation with Dr. L., this part of the lawsuit will never go to trial. A judge and two lawyers will try it in arbitration, which has the reputation in California for being a kangaroo court. Kaplan cracks, "You're being tried by three guys with a hundred-year cumulative history of thinking they're God."

Taunting, Deuprey attempted to undermine my anger. "What is your belief as to what any CAT scan would have shown, had it been done?"

He's not going to trap me on that one. "I'm not a medical expert," I snapped.

"Do you have a personal belief as to what it would have shown?" he tried again, flatly.

"I'll have an expert witness testify to that when the time comes."

"I don't want you to guess or speculate, but obviously you attach a great deal of importance to the failure to run a CAT scan. I would like to ask you why it is you feel that the CAT scan would have been important in your husband's case."

"Obviously the X-ray department felt it was important enough to rec-ommend, or they wouldn't have written the report. I believe that anything that cautioned the doctors into looking further into John's medical history was highly important. Perhaps if that CAT scan had been done, my hus-band would be alive today, and my children would have a father."

"All you can do is basically guess or speculate about that?"

This time it was my turn to sneer. "You just said you didn't want me to guess or speculate, and then you asked me why I thought the CAT scan was so important. That's what I told you I'd be doing in this answer, because I'm not a medical expert, so don't object to my response."

Wearily, he sighs, "That's fine. Thank you for answering the question."

The next day, I left Megan and Michael at the hotel. I wasn't trying to spare them Deuprey's attempts at airing dirty laundry, because they knew it all anyway. I wanted to give them a break.

For eight more hours, Deuprey asked me all kinds of questions about Johnny's drinking and the problems it had caused in the marriage. I had nothing to hide. His shameless questions about John's addictions weren't about me, or my marriage, or even the person who had died on the oper-ating table. They were about the disease. He acted as if I should be morti-fied to talk about the wreckage of John's life in front of strangers, but I wasn't. My pride in our relationship and Johnny's successes, my refusal to hang my head about the bad times, only caused consternation in him. I knew what he was doing. He hoped to portray John as a hopeless junkie loser, so they wouldn't have to compensate our loss. Deuprey looked par-ticularly ridiculous when he sanctimoniously asked, "Have you derived any comfort from the Buddhist belief that a person dies when his time is up?" As if that would let them off the hook.

Malpractice is hard to prove. We had such a clear case that local doctors appeared as our expert witnesses, which is highly unusual. Although we lost the arbitration, one of the doctors offered to settle out of court and, in the long run, John died a winner. The kids and I are winners because we loved him. He died at peace, having forgiven those who warranted his pardon, and eliminating people from his life who diminished him. You can't get more real or successful than that.

The night before John's operation, I had the dream that Sable, our German Shepherd puppy, had died. A voice told me, *I am taking my angel back today. You have spent as much time with him as can possibly be allowed. You must accept this, and never doubt that it was not meant to be. There is a greater plan here. Do not feel sorry for yourself. This is not an accident.*

I woke Johnny up with coffee and climbed back into bed, snuggling down with my cup, gingerly wrapping my ankle around his. He called that Chinese Love, where a couple feels so entwined, their feet naturally gravitate toward each other in a graceful knot of union. "When the marriage is that strong, you can run a village on the power."

I told him about the dream. He promised if anything happened, he would be our guardian angel and never leave our side. I promised I'd finish his book.

One of my girlfriends called to wish us luck. "I'm lying here with my beautiful wife, feeling so peaceful," he told her. "If I'd known life was going to be this good when I quit using, I would have stopped twenty years ago."

We finished our coffee and John took one last hot tub in the morning sun. I watched him through the bedroom window as I dressed. *What if he dies? What if something goes wrong?* I chose to ignore those thoughts. Later, friends would ask me why we failed to see the puppy dream as an omen.

I drove John to the hospital. An abandoned wheelchair sat near the entrance. Johnny waited in it while I parked the car. I carried his overnight bag and a cardboard Chinese Good Luck God that Megan and I had picked out the day before in Chinatown. He hadn't seen it before and he frowned at it through his pain, half kidding, "That isn't a funeral symbol, is it?"

After registering, they put us in a private room. It was brilliant with sunlight and in that light I felt waves of tenderness and hope for the return of John's health and mobility after the operation. I went to a nearby party store and bought crepe-paper garlands of vivid parrots and tropical fish and a massive bouquet of balloons. I wanted to fill that sterile anonymous cubicle with vibrant colors and life, to counter the antiseptic air and sterile gleaming instruments. I wanted to surround Johnny with colorful, exotic animals, symbols of my love for him and the realms in which we dwelt. As I transformed the room, I thought a hospital room had probably never looked like that, a tropical jungle paradise. Yet, in spite of the brilliant colors, I felt as though I were swimming through a murky dream, moving out of time. The day existed only to be gotten through.

Out in the hall I ran into the *Chicana* housekeeper who used to clean my office at the McDonald Center. I thought her familiar face was a good sign, and I brought her in to meet John. A doctor stopped by to ask routine questions. When he noticed John's abdominal gunshot wound from Vietnam, it suddenly hit me, after all those years of being with him, how lucky I was that it hadn't killed him. *He could have been struck in the heart and I would never have had the chance to know him. Why hasn't that occurred to me before? I have taken so much for granted with this man. Why does that bullet hole suddenly seem so meaningful? It's like watching a foreign movie, where you don't understand the symbolism.*

When the nurse came to fill the IV with pain meds, we agreed that I should go home and help Megan get ready for her trip to Costa Rica. She was leaving the next day to start her job as a photojournalist for the *gringo* newspaper in San Jose. John would be sleeping until the late afternoon, when they had scheduled the operation.

Four hours later, the kids and I returned to his room. They floated around his bed, playing with the electric controls and teasing him, giggling, and joking. Michael went out to smoke a cigarette on the stairs. Later, he said he had a strong feeling that something bad was going to happen, but he just ignored it. When he told me about it, he wondered if he had done something wrong by not speaking up.

"How can you follow up on every thought?" I asked. "You'd be paralyzed."

Later, Megan said she hated the way the orderly helped John up on the gurney. "He was so sloppy about it, like he didn't know how special Daddy was."

I did not kiss John good-bye. Whenever one of us was leaving, the other got kissed or it was "Where's my kiss? Come and kiss me! You want a kiss? Give me a kiss! Kissy-kiss!" We spent so much time kissing and saying I love you in those last years that I've never felt guilty. I know why I didn't kiss him good-bye. After all the drug crises and drunken ordeals, I still couldn't stand to see him drugged even on the painkillers he needed. I looked away. I'm not mad at myself about that. I understand why I couldn't. It's sad, but if you'd been through what I've been through with John's addictions, and kissed him as much as I had, you'd know it wasn't important.

As they wheeled him out, I never thought about going down to meet the anesthesiologist. I had fought so hard for his life in so many medical settings. Now that he was sober, I couldn't fight anymore. I had to let him handle the situation on his own. Perhaps if I had accompanied him, they might have asked more questions about his medical history. They might have noticed that his tests were abnormal and postponed the surgery.

Megan and I dropped Michael off at the house and went shopping for her trip. In the aisles of the grocery store I started feeling dread. I just wanted the hours to pass quickly. We mindlessly watched a rented video, *Daddy's Dying, Who's Got the Will?* while Michael took a nap. It was about a family squabbling over inherited money. Disgusted, we stopped the tape and never got the symbolism till the next day.

"Mom," Megan suggested, "why don't you call to see if John's out of the operating room?" As I put the phone to my ear and started to dial, I heard the doctor's voice. The phone never even rang.

"I want you to get in your car immediately and drive here very slowly."

"Is he all right?"

"There's a problem" was all he'd say.

I slipped into shock. Megan knew; she didn't ask for any explanation. We looked at each other in panic. I didn't want to wake Michael from his innocent sleep, so we left him, just in case. Within several minutes I had called every shaman, nun, psychic, and lama that we knew with the same short message: "I think John is dying, can you bring him back?" Megan grabbed John's *mala*, Tibetan rosary beads. We got in the car and tore down to the hospital.

They put us in a tiny room. It was airless and had no windows, designed by a heartless architect who thought it would be an efficient holding cell for the relatives of dying patients. Someone went to get the doctor.

"It will take about twenty more minutes for us to know what's wrong," he said breathlessly. He did not tell us they'd been pounding on John's chest for an hour trying desperately to bring back some brain-dead semblance of him so that they'd be absolved. I wasn't sure what he was going back to look for but I didn't want to waste time by asking.

Without a word, Megan and I began to pray. I remembered the dream,

I saw all the signs, I heard the voice saying this was no accident, not to feel sorry for myself, to accept the death.

If your time has come, I'm not going to hang on, I release you with all my heart and all my love. But if it's not time, and you can possibly come back to stay with us, please return because I'll die without you.

The doctor returned with four others. White coats all in a row. They said they were sorry in unison. He was gone. Do you want to request an autopsy? Please sign here. Do you want to go in to say good-bye? Is there anyone we can call?

Swimming in shock, without thinking I called a friend who had lost both her parents in a car crash. I knew she'd be smart about quick decisions. Buddhists don't believe in mutilating the body after death, but she urged me to have an autopsy in case the doctors had screwed up. Then she said very slowly and deliberately, as if she knew that's the way you cut through the cotton batting of trauma, "You need to go in there with the kids and say good-bye. You need to see him."

"I don't want that to be my last memory of him."

"Believe me, it won't," she said. "If you don't, you'll regret it later."

I called Ginny, a coworker from the McDonald Center, who'd been widowed the year before. I knew she'd understand the situation. I asked her to drive us home. And then I gently woke Michael.

"Something's happened with John. Come down here." I wondered how I would tell him. When he walked in, I could see he already knew.

We walked into the silent white room. I saw the body. I saw guilt on the faces of the OR staff. "I saw it too, Mom," Megan said later.

The kids took Johnny's hands and started to cry softly. I never touched him. In his life, John burned hot, like a meteor. His hands were always warm. I loved to squeeze them and play with his fingers. I didn't want to feel cold on his hands. Megan wasn't afraid; she just sat there braiding his fingers in hers. There was a tube in his mouth, so his lips were formed in a slack smile, cool as he was in life, like a musician in the middle of a riff. For a while it seemed like he was playing a trick on us, and we thought he could open his eyes anytime to see if we'd fallen for it. Megan burst out with a hysterical giggle. "It looks like he's faking, doesn't it?"

Then I knew it wasn't him anymore in that body. *This is your death, this is what you look like dead. This is the moment you have courted and flirted with all your life, Johnny.* His Bodhisattva sweetness was still palpable in the air.

I said good-bye to the flesh then and turned my attention to Megan and Michael while trying to savor the sacredness of that moment. They hadn't had my dream about taking back the angel. John hadn't just promised that morning that he would always be their guardian angel. I was more focused on comforting them than my pain. I knew that Johnny, the Night Tripper, was not clinging to his body. There would be no more sustenance from that body. I could feel him holding me up. That's when I saw all the bruises on his chest from the paddles, massive black and blue swirls. I wondered what in hell they thought they were bringing back. *How can I leave you here? I'll never play with that patch of hair on your chest. I'll never kiss the sweet place on your neck, behind your beard, or the Mick Jagger fullness of your lips. How can I say good-bye to those treasures? I thought I'd have their bliss for my whole lifetime.*

Then there was nothing left to do but gather his things. We went to his room and took down all the crepe-paper streamers. We released the balloons in the parking lot, giddy in our shock, laughing "Catch them, Johnny! These are for you!" as they floated above the hospital walls and faded into starlight.

All night, people gathered at the house. John's presence was so strong, the love was so palpable in every room, that most of us were months away from believing he was totally gone. There is a heightened sense when death is so near, and we stayed up till dawn, talking about him.

"He was a bearer of miracles."

"He was so utterly direct and clear and open-hearted."

"He was an incredible soul."

Three days later, one hundred people gathered in our house for the funeral service. Johnny's body had been autopsied and was awaiting cremation, but we went ahead because friends had flown in from all over the country. We held a Buddhist ceremony, burning his photograph and chanting him well wishes. Then, like an AA meeting, people spoke from the circle. It took two hours for everyone to empty out their feelings, and here are some of the sentiments which were expressed.

"I only knew John when he came to speak at my writing class," Karen Kenyon started. "I felt very touched by him and privileged to know him. The first time I ever heard him talk I thought that I'd never been around someone who was so completely honest, so completely down to earth, with such candor. One time he spoke about impermanence, and how that is a gift that is given when someone dies young. I think of that, and of his humor. I walked out to the parking lot with him and he pointed to his new car. He said it was financed by a Buddhist credit union, which meant you got to pay it back over your next lifetime."

An AA buddy remembered, "The first time I heard John share at a meeting, I said to myself, 'Holy tomoly, this guy is really something.' First I thought he might want to dominate the group, because his presence was so strong, but he was extremely genuine and caring. He had a lot of intuition and insight. He wanted to learn and contribute."

Paula, my receptionist, said, "I didn't know John very well. I met him through Nancy at work. The most vivid memory I have of him is that he called Nancy about five times a night. Instead of announcing him as John, I'd tell her 'The Hubala' was on the phone. He was like a teddy bear you could just hug. He was so gentle. The way he used to call her so many times, I thought he must really love her."

Allen, our elderly neighbor, added, "The thing that struck me most about John was the closeness we shared. We didn't get together very often, just for a minute here and there. I'll never forget the first time I met him out in front of our houses. He told me his name and I told him mine. As he walked away he said, 'Well, I'll see you, Allen.' It made me feel good that we were on a first-name basis right away. I appreciated that. Naturally, it was a shock to me when I heard his name was John Steinbeck. I had to think that over for about thirty seconds and I called him John from then on."

Then Thom spoke. "John and I came in like Twain and his comet. It never occurred to me that we wouldn't go out together. I think he'd be unhappy if we didn't get the joke. He's been practicing for this for as long as I remember. We'd better take up a collection for his parents the next time around because they're going to need all the help they can get.

"I don't remember a time in my life without having him. We've counted a lot of coup and we've never been done in, never lost a battle. I'm going to miss him. We used to have a lot of codes, shorthand for how things were going. When it was time to lick honey off the razor blade, one of the things he was perfect at, the codeword was, 'Say farewell to all my friends on shore.' For him, I say farewell. He loved you all, he needed you all, as much as we needed him. He loved the illusion. I'm proud of him. I'm prouder of him than any human being in the world. Hello John."

Megan was next. "The first time I saw John, it was instant recognition. I felt like I had seen him so many times before. I'll never forget every day I spent with him and every day I was apart from him. He'll remain forever in my heart. I can feel him walking behind me and protecting me and holding me and guiding me. I love him. I can feel his little hands in my hands and I don't have to say good-bye because he's always right here and he'll always be right here."

"Finding Johnny dead at the hospital was the worst thing that's ever happened to me," I said. "I've always expected it. He had nine lives and we were on his tenth. It's something we've all known, that he was too precious to be in our lives for a long time. I'm so grateful for every day I spent with him.

"When we got back to the house, Megan said, 'Mom, it seems so easy. It just happened so easily.' I feel like he's going to be with all of us forever in our hearts and in our wisdom. He loved and valued every person in this room. He knew there's a place where he could work on a higher, deeper level, where he could impart more truth, and I think that truth will come through us. It's not like we need to let go of John and forget him. We need to listen and carry him in our hearts. He was a truly holy being and this is a very dark time, with the Gulf War starting.

"I'm really scared and I want people to call me. Don't let me be alone. He filled our hearts with laughter and love, especially in the last three years when he was sober."

An old friend from Boulder said, "John and I shared something very precious. The number-one thing in his life is his beloved wife, Nancy. He shared her so beautifully. I never knew a man who loved his wife and told everybody and taught every man he came in touch with how to treat a woman like John did. He was such a good dad. He was the best husband and companion for his wife. I will miss him so much."

Another friend said, "John was one of the funniest people I've ever known. I loved him because his mind scared the shit out of me and I could count on him for that. Whatever exchange we had, I could count on that he would touch me deeply or terrify me. They were both really great feelings because they reflected his ability to eat life for breakfast. The thought of not having that piercing honesty around is hard to live with."

Then Michael spoke. "A lot of feelings are coming up for me. I've been thinking about all the good memories, all the stuff I ever did for him and all the stuff he ever did for me, all the things we did together. He was my best friend. I've never met anyone with such power and compassion. He could dazzle me with his wisdom. He used to brag to me, but I knew it was true, that he knew just about everything about anything. He'd tell me that in the hot tub. If anyone else ever told me that, I'd think, Man, that cat is full of shit. But I believed him.

"I'd look forward to the nights when I came home and he'd always have the hot tub ready for me. It was kind of like the guru sitting underneath a shady tree, and you go to mountaintop to meet him. I'd meet my guru in the hot tub, and his big fat guru belly would be there kickin' it and it was like instantly he'd know what was going on with me. I could tell him about my problems from girls to school to friends and he could always get me out on a good note. It was like he'd been there. He could relate ten times over and he'd share his solutions. I'd say, 'You are a fucking guru, man. You are God.'

"We've been looking at the photo albums and every part of his personality is there; no picture is the same because he had so many aspects about him. Actually, he gave me the runaround about everything. You couldn't slip much past him. His friends were my friends and he always told me how much he loved my friends."

One of the teenage boys laughed when he remembered, "John once called me a gratuitous motherfucker." His brother went on to say, "John turned our lives upside down. He was an example of tremendous will, of the fight to be free, to be outrageous just for the sake of being outrageous. He always threw himself out there and we stood around with our jaws on the floor. He had aggressive sides, scary sides, but his heart was so gentle. Sometimes he'd stay with us when I was little. He'd sleep outside on a lawn chair in the summer. I'd ask him why and he told me he just liked to be out there. He's out there now."

Another of Michael's friends said, "I remember the time I took Mike for a ride on my motorcycle. The next time I was at the house, John met me at the door. He put his hand on my shoulder and his face real close to mine and said, 'Say, Matt, the next time you take my son on your motorcycle without a helmet, you know what I'm going to do? I'm going to get a can of gasoline and pour it all over your bike and then I'm going to light a match and watch that sucker burn.' Then he grinned and said, 'You got it?' I got it."

A friend who'd lost a child said, "John listened in a special way that most people don't do. He talked in a special way that most people don't talk. He filled my heart with so much warmth, and so did his family. I know that he's here with all of us, but I hate death, and I hate that I'm not going to see him walk out of his office and feel the cuteness about him."

Another friend remembered the black powder bombs Johnny loved to explode in our backyard. "One time I was over visiting them and John set off several underground charges which left large holes in the lawn. The Boulder bomb squad showed up, complete with fire trucks. John was very polite with them. He took them around to the back and showed them the holes and asked if they'd seen the movie *Caddyshack*. He told them he had a gopher problem and had gotten the idea of blowing them up from the movie. The bomb squad guys were fascinated, though you couldn't tell if it was by the theory or by John's name. Anyway, they left without giving him a citation, so they must have bought his story. By the way, there are no gophers in Boulder!"

Gesar Mukpo, Rinpoche's teenage son, said, "My memories of John are as a young kid. There were never any problems when I came over to play with Michael. He never made it difficult for me. It was always fun to be around him. He always let us do pretty much whatever we wanted. He didn't give us a hard time about how crazy we were. He didn't need to take control because he had control. He died being who he was, fearless. He wasn't afraid at all. I want to say, 'Good job!'"

And Thom concluded, "I'd like to thank you all for coming, if only because I needed the healing. I couldn't do it by myself. I think we all need it, to the degree that we miss him. We want to keep intimately that part of him that affected each of us, affected by his recovery, by his humor. A lot has been lifted off me in the last two hours that I thought I was going to have to carry for a long time. I wasn't looking forward to it at all. Now that I know I can sucker you guys into the other half of the job, it makes it a lot easier."

Our old friend Denault Blouin wrote this poem the day after Johnny died. It is based on the Buddhist reminders we chant with each prostration:

This precious human body, free and well favored, is difficult to earn, easy to loose. Now I must do something meaningful. The world and its inhabitants are like a bubble. Death comes without warning. This body will be a corpse. At that time the Dharma will be my only help. I will practice it with exertion. Just like a feast before the executioner leads you to your death, I will cut desire and attachment and attain enlightenment through exertion.

GATÉ (which means "Gone" in Sanskrit)
In Memory of John Steinbeck IV

DEATH
8:30 A.M.: Standing in the unemployment line,
Thinking of you

COMES
And you're gone:
Rocket man
With your lazy rolling voice
Stupendous indulgences and generosities
Huge storehouse mind
And impossible neurotic upheavals

WITHOUT
Matt, 14, bursts into tears when he hears—
"This is the first person I've ever known who's died."

WARNING
But there are signs:
Famous alcoholic father,
Born-in-the-blood addictions
Magnified by late 20th-century maha-cravings

Liver literally rusting away
Chi splitting surgery
Back-breaking pain, walking with cane,
Not ever getting all better.

This pain never goes away
Can drive a man to drink and drugs,
Can wake him up, did.

You finally
Learned to let go
Embrace Big No
Every day

Not another drop
Self-intoxication stopped
Sober, boring path followed step by step
To cut root cause
And live with incurable loss.

In this raw war-fire wind
You were born and died in
Best medicine: compassion

Good-bye, John

Halifax
February 8, 1991

John Palmer, the director of the cult classic *Ciao, Manhattan,* starring Edie
Sedgwick, sent this from Maui after hearing about Johnny's passing. They

met in London during the early seventies. Palmer was so intrigued with John's stories about Vietnam that he promptly went over there in search of Sean Flynn—to no avail.

It's a funny thing about people. The effect they have on you. Who they are in the world. How they are in the world. Steinbeck was one of those people. One of those people who had an effect. We used to call him Steinbeck. And of course that had extra meaning beyond the obvious. I mean, in John's case, Steinbeck was not just the name. It was *the* name. A name much much more than the imputation that we do when we call people by their last names. He was . . . Steinbeck. Yet, no confusion with the father. No need for differentiation. It was all packed in. The father, the son, the war, the booze, the pot, the women. John was Steinbeck, pure and simple. On his own. In his own right. In spite of it all. Steinbeck.

And you loved him. Not adoration. But some kind of love he brought out. Love beyond the draw of the name. Beyond the absolutely soft, ordinary person beneath the persona. You just plain loved him because he had guts. Guts with a brain. Guts with words. Guts with heart. Guts that could get down.

John Steinbeck the Fourth was one complex cookie. You wanted him to like you because he was real and because he wouldn't put up with any bullshit and yet he understood your bullshit and accepted you for what was good in you. He knew what good was. Even when he couldn't do good and that further magnified his charm. Especially, because he was high grade, once removed. Closer than the real McCoy.

Of course, the fact that he was in binary orbit with a star, his silent star, made him all the more fascinating. And he knew it. He played with that in no-ego. Perfectly. As if the torment of all that was tedious. Like a cat playfully batting a mouse. Humor, the dance. You knew it. He knew it. Unspoken speech.

Now the fact that John had carried an M-16 and knew how to use it and did, the fact that he could describe the trip a grenade takes across a wide green valley high as a kite—slow-mo smoke on the other side. Stoned. Puff. Made him all the more fascinating. This was like getting high with Humphrey Bogart. Cigarette smoke, whiskey. And of course, the voice. The same kind of voice we all heard in the movies. Like when they first got those huge baritone speakers at the Strand in the fifties. John had the voice. Wraparound deep. Comforting and a little slowed down. Like the beginning of a hallucination. Totally clear. Enunciatively perfect. But still on the doorstep to oblivion. Just outside.

The fun of knowing him was what the magic was doing to you. Not just in the moment. That was the material. All the experiences needed material. But what was really going on had something to do with authenticity. The special truth that knows death at maximum risk. There's plenty of that around but very little that knows the lines and what they mean at the same time. John had all that going and knew it and wasn't particularly interested. This is one of the reasons he was a man's man.

Have you ever been in a tunnel on a train when another train was coming in the other direction? That's how John and I met. Imagine the noise and the excitement and then somehow it dissolves into a view from the side. His train is like a subway and everything is dark except his car. He's inside and walking around and then he comes to the window. That's kind of how we met and then it was gone. Then the noise comes back.

Several days after the ceremony, I was sitting in John's office pouring through the archives, starting to write this book. Feeling overwhelmed, I burst into tears. *Johnny, if you really are with me as you promised when I finish your work, show me a sign. I cannot do this alone.* There was only one window, and it faced the house next door. I figured all he had to work with was that and the telephone, but I was adamant. If I didn't get a sign, it was over between us.

Suddenly, in the patch of sky above the neighbor's house, a huge bouquet of balloons floated by. There must have been thirty of them, sailing way up high over the coastline. I was thrilled. I got up to watch them from the deck, closing the door to his office, on which Johnny had recently tacked a little poem by Po Chu-i.

THE KARMA OF WORDS

> *He gradually vanquished the demon of wine*
> *And does not get wildly drunk*
> *But the karma of words remains*
> *He has not abandoned verse.*

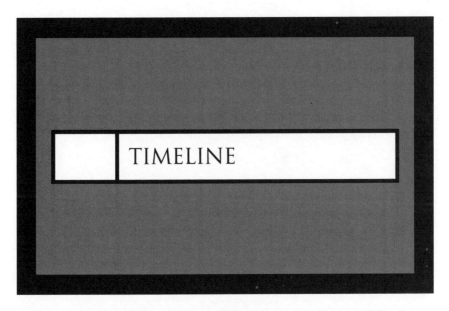

TIMELINE

1902 • John Ernst Steinbeck born February 27 in Salinas, California.

1939 • *Grapes of Wrath* published.

1943 • Steinbeck marries Gwyndolyn Conger.

1944 • Thom born August 2.

1945 • Nancy Lenn born June 18.

• *Cannery Row* published.

1946 • John born June 12.

1948 • Gwyn files for divorce which is final in 1949.

1950 • Steinbeck marries Elaine Scott.

1952 • *East of Eden* published.

1953 • John hospitalized for codeine addiction at age seven.

1954 • John sent to Eaglebrook boarding school.

1959 • Steinbeck spends nearly a year at Discove Cottage in England working on *Morte d'Arthur*.

1960 • Steinbeck returns to United States, embarks on cross-country journey for *Travels with Charley*.

1961 • Steinbeck travels to Europe with his sons.

• *Winter of Our Discontent* is published.

1962 • John returns to boarding school at Hebron Academy.

• Nancy attends San Francisco State College.

• Steinbeck awarded Nobel Prize for Literature.

• *Travels with Charley* published.

1963 • Gwyn moves to Palm Springs with John and Thom.

• John works as a disc jockey.

1964 • John is drafted.

• Nancy enters University of California at Berkeley.

1965 • Steinbeck takes John to meet LBJ at the White House.

1966 • John goes to Vietnam where he becomes a journalist for Armed Forces Radio and Television, and a war correspondent for the Department of Defense. Steinbeck visits him there.

• Nancy graduates UC Berkeley with a degree in philosophy. She becomes a counselor at the San Francisco Juvenile Hall where she meets her future husband, Paul Harper.

1967 • John returns to the United States. He is arrested for possession of marijuana; charges are dropped. He testifies in front of the Senate Armed Forces Subcommittee on Drug Abuse as an expert on marijuana. He writes "The Importance of Being Stoned in Vietnam" for the *Washingtonian*.

1968 • John returns to Vietnam to found Dispatch News Service.

• John wins an Emmy for his work on the CBS documentary *The World of Charlie Company*.

• Nancy and Paul leave San Francisco to live on a mining claim in northern California.

• Steinbeck dies December 20 in New York City.

1969 • John returns to California and writes *In Touch*, which is published later that year.

- Nancy and Paul immigrate to British Columbia, where daughter, Megan, is born June 17.

1970
- John returns to Vietnam. He lives on Phoenix Island with the Coconut Monk.

- Daughter Blake born October 5 in Saigon.

1971
- John returns to New York and meets Trungpa Rinpoche.

- Paul and Nancy move to Mexico.

1972
- Nancy's son, Michael, is born December 1 in Guanajuato, Mexico.

1973
- Nancy and Paul found a commune in British Columbia, Canada.

- John travels overland to India.

1975
- John and Nancy meet in Boulder, Colorado.

- Gwyn Steinbeck dies in Boulder.

1979
- John and Nancy fall in love at a Buddhist Seminary held at Chateau Lake Louise, Alberta, Canada.

- Nancy separates from Paul Harper, divorce final in 1980. John moves to Nancy's home in Boulder.

- Commemoration of Steinbeck postage stamp.

1980
- Nancy's parents buy them a home.

- Gwyn's mother dies.

1981
- John, Nancy, and Megan on the set of *Cannery Row* in Monterey and Los Angeles.

- Billy Burroughs Jr. dies of liver failure.

1982
- John and Nancy marry on March 6.

1983
- After the death of Nancy's mother, John, Nancy, Megan, and Michael embark on a round-the-world journey.

1984
- The Steinbecks return to Boulder.

- John diagnosed with hemochromatosis.

1986
- Nancy's father dies.

- John has back surgery for a ruptured disc.

1987
- The Steinbecks move to La Jolla, California.

- Trungpa Rinpoche dies.

1988
- John starts writing his autobiography.

1989
- John interviewed on Charles Kuralt's *Sunday Morning* show for the fiftieth anniversary of *Grapes of Wrath*.

- Abbie Hoffman dies.

1990
- John ruptures a disc in his spine. Diagnosed with diabetes.

1991
- John undergoes back surgery and dies in Encinitas, California, on February 7.

BIBLIOGRAPHY

Burroughs, William. *Naked Lunch*. New York: Grove Press, 1992.

Cassady, Carolyn. *Off the Road: My Years with Cassady, Kerouac and Ginsberg*. New York: Penguin, 1991.

Conrad, Joseph. *Lord Jim*. New York: Dover, 1991.

De Mott, Robert. "Legacies." *Steinbeck Quarterly* 2, no. 3–4 (1991).

Golding, William. *Lord of the Flies*. Perigee, 1959.

Huxley, Laura. *You Are Not the Target*. Metamorphous Press, 1995.

Harvey, Andrew. *The Direct Path*. New York: Broadway Books, 2000.

Kerouac, Jack. *Dharma Bums*. New York: Penguin, 1955.

———. *On the Road*. New York: Penguin, 1958.

Mann, Thomas. *Death in Venice*. New York: Dover, 1995.

Miller, Alice. *Thou Shalt Not Be Aware*. New York: Meridian, 1991.

Norwood, Robin. *Why? A Guide to Answering Life's Toughest Questions*. Deerfield Beach, Fla.: Health Communications, 1997.

———. *Women Who Love Too Much: When You Keep Wishing and Hoping He'll Change*. New York: Pocket Books, 1991.

Paul, Alexander. *Suicide Wall*. Tigard, Ore.: PakDonald Publishing, 1996.

Ram Das, Baba. *Be Here Now*. San Cristobal, N.Mex.: Lama Foundation, 1971.

Steinbeck, John. *East of Eden*. New York: Penguin, 1992.

———. *The Grapes of Wrath*. New York: Penguin, 1992.

———. *Once There Was a War*. New York: Penguin, 1994.

———. *The Red Pony*. New York: Penguin, 1993.

———. *Tortilla Flat*. New York: Penguin, 1995.

———. *Travels with Charley*. New York: Penguin, 1981.

Steinbeck, John IV. *In Touch*. New York: Knopf, 1969.

Trungpa, Chogyam. *Born in Tibet*. Boston: Shambhala, 2000.

———. *Meditation in Action*. Boston: Shambhala, 1996.

Yogananda, Paramahansa. *Autobiography of a Yogi*. Los Angeles: Self-Realization Fellowship, 1979.

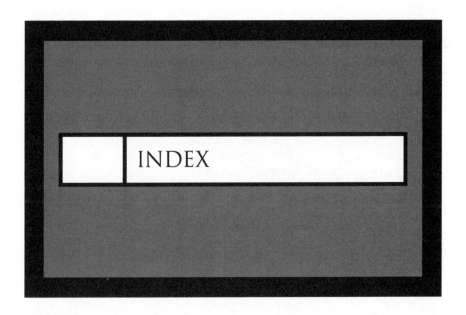

INDEX